From Judaism to Christianity:
Tradition and Transition

Supplements
to
Novum Testamentum

VOLUME 136

Thomas H. Tobin, S.J.

From Judaism to Christianity: Tradition and Transition

A *Festschrift* for Thomas H. Tobin, S.J.,
on the Occasion of His Sixty-fifth Birthday

Edited by
Patricia Walters

BRILL

LEIDEN • BOSTON
2010

This book is printed on acid-free paper.

Library of Congress Cataloging-in-Publication Data

From Judaism to Christianity : tradition and transition : a festschrift for Thomas H. Tobin, S.J., on the occasion of his sixty-fifth birthday / edited by Patricia Walters.
 p. cm. -- (Supplements to Novum testamentum, 0167-9732 ; v. 136)
 Includes bibliographical references and indexes.
 ISBN 978-90-04-18769-6 (hardback : alk. paper)
 1. Church history--Primitive and early church, ca. 30-600. 2. Religions--Relations. 3. Rome--Religion. I. Walters, Patricia, 1947- II. Tobin, Thomas H., 1945- III. Title. IV. Series.

BR166.F76 2010
270.1–dc22

BR
166
.F76
2010

2010024381

ISSN   0167-9732
ISBN   978 90 04 18769 6

PRINTED BY DRUKKERIJ WILCO B.V. - AMERSFOORT, THE NETHERLANDS

Tribute to a scholar of the highest caliber

Thomas H. Tobin, S.J., Ph.D.

*Scholar, Colleague, Mentor, and Friend
in the enduring tradition
of Ignatian Scholarship, Loyalty, and Service*

CONTENTS

A PARADIGM FOR BIBLICAL INTERPRETATION

PART ONE

TRADITION AND TRANSITION:
JEWISH RESPONSES TO A HELLENISTIC WORLD

PART TWO

FOUNDATIONS AMID FLUX:
CHRISTIAN RESPONSES TO A TRANSITORY WORLD

CONTRIBUTORS

HAROLD W. ATTRIDGE, Ph.D.
Dean of Yale Divinity School and the Lillian Claus Professor of New Testament
Yale Divinity School
Yale University
New Haven, Connecticut

DAVID E. AUNE, Ph.D.
Walter Professor of New Testament & Christian Origins
Department of Theology
University of Notre Dame
Notre Dame, Indiana

ELLEN BIRNBAUM, Ph.D.
Post-doctoral work at Brandeis University and Harvard University.
Research expertise in the Jews of ancient Alexandria
Cambridge, Massachusetts

ADELA YARBRO COLLINS, Ph.D.
Buckingham Professor of New Testament Criticism and Interpretation
Yale Divinity School
Yale University
New Haven, Connecticut

JOHN J. COLLINS, Ph.D.
Holmes Professor of Old Testament Criticism and Interpretation
Yale Divinity School
Yale University
New Haven, Connecticut

WENDY COTTER, C.S.J., Ph.D.
Associate Professor of New Testament and Early Christianity
Department of Theology
Loyola University Chicago
Chicago, Illinois

BRIAN E. DALEY, S.J., Ph.D.
Catherine F. Huisking Professor of Theology
Department of Theology
University of Notre Dame
Notre Dame, Indiana

LAWRENCE DiPAOLO, JR., Ph.D.
Associate Dean
University of St. Thomas School of Theology
St. Mary's Seminary
Houston, Texas

ROBERT A. DI VITO, Ph.D.
Associate Professor and Graduate Programs Director
Department of Theology
Loyola University Chicago
Chicago, Illinois

EDMONDO LUPIERI, Ph.D.
John Cardinal Cody Endowed Chair
Department of Theology
Loyola University Chicago
Chicago, Illinois
Appendix by Brian Dennert, Ph.D. candidate.

EILEEN SCHULLER, Ph.D.,
Professor of Early Palestinian Judaism and the Dead Sea Scrolls
McMaster University
Hamilton, Ontario
Canada

HANS SVEBAKKEN, Ph.D.
Department of Theology
Loyola University Chicago
Chicago, Illinois

PAULINE VIVIANO, Ph.D.
Associate Professor of Hebrew Scriptures
Department of Theology
Loyola University Chicago
Chicago, Illinois

Urban C. von Wahlde, Ph.D.
Professor of New Testament and Early Christianity
Department of Theology
Loyola University Chicago
Chicago, Illinois

ABBREVIATIONS

AB	Anchor Bible
ABD	*Anchor Bible Dictionary*
ABRL	Anchor Bible Reference Library
Abr.	Philo *De Abrahamo*
ACCS	Ancient Christian Commentary on Scripture
Adv. haer.	Irenaeus *Adversus haereses*
alt.	Translation of the ancient text is slightly altered
ANF	*Ante-Nicene Fathers*
Ant.	Josephus *Antiquitates Iudaicae*
ANTC	Abingdon New Testament Commentary
ANRW	*Aufstieg und Niedergang der römischen Welt: Geschichte und Kultur Roms im Spiegel der neueren Forschung.*
Apoc. Jn.	*Apocryphon of John*
ASE	*Annali di storia dell'esegesi*
ASNSP	*Annali della Scuola Normale Superiore di Pisa*
BDB	Brown-Driver-Briggs Hebrew and English Lexicon
BECNT	Baker Exegetical Commentary on the New Testament
BEHE	Bibliotheque de l'Ecole des Hautes Etudes
Bell.	Josephus *De bello Iudaico*
BETL	Bibliotheca ephemeridum theologicarum lovaniensium
Bib	*Biblica*
BTB	*Biblical Theology Bulletin*
CBNTS	Coniectanea Biblica New Testament Series
CBQ	*Catholic Biblical Quarterly*
CBQMS	Catholic Biblical Quarterly Monograph Series
CChrSA	Corpus Christianorum, Series Apocryphorum
CCL	Corpus Christianorum, series latina (Turnhout: Brepols, 1953–)
Cher.	Philo *De cherubim*
Comm. Matt.	Origen *Commentariorum series in evangelium Mattaei*
Conf.	Philo *De confusione linguarum*
Congr.	Philo *De congressu quaerendae eruditionis gratia*
CSEL	Corpus scriptorum ecclesiasticorum latinorum
CTM	*Concordia Theological Monthly*

Det.	Philo *Quod deterius potiori insidiari soleat*
DJD	Discoveries in the Judean Desert series
Ebr.	Philo *De ebrietate*
Ep. Aeg. Lib.	Athanasius *Epistula ad episcopos Aegypti et Libyae*
Epist.	Jerome *Epistulae*
ETL	*Ephemerides theologicae Lovanienses*
Eth. eud.	Aristotle *Ethica Eudemia*
Eth. nic.	Aristotle *Ethica Nicomachea*
Exp. Luc.	Ambrose *Expositio evangelii secumdum Lucum*
ExpTim	*Expository Times*
Fug.	Philo *De fuga et inventione*
Fug.	Tertullian *De fuga in persecutione*
Her.	Philo *Quis rerum divinarum heres sit*
Hom. Gen.	Origen *Homiliae in Genesim*
Hom. Jer.	Origen *Homiliae in Ieremiam*
Hom. Matt.	Chrysostom *Homiliae in evangelium Matthaei*
Hom. Rom.	Chrysostom *Homiliae in epistulam ad Romanos*
HSCP	*Harvard Studies in Classical Philology*
HTR	*Harvard Theological Review*
Ios.	Philo *De Iosepho*
JBL	*Journal of Biblical Literature*
JETS	*Journal of the Evangelical Theological Society*
JJS	*Journal of Jewish Studies*
JQR	*Jewish Quarterly Review*
JSNT	*Journal for the Study of the New Testament*
JSNTSup	*Journal for the Study of the New Testament* Supplement
JSOT	*Journal for the Study of the Old Testament*
JTS	*Journal of Theological Studies*
LCL	Loeb Classical Library
Leg. (all.)	Philo *Legum allegoriae*
LXX	The Septuagint
Marc.	Tertullian *Adversus Marcionem*
Migr.	Philo *De migratione Abrahami*
Mos.	Philo *De vita Mosis*
Neot.	*Neotestamentica*
NHC	Nag Hammadi Codex
NHMS	Nag Hammadi and Manichaean Studies
NHS	Nag Hammadi Studies
NICNT	New International Commentary on the New Testament
NIGTC	New International Greek Text Commentary

NovT	*Novum Testamentum*
NovTSup	*Novum Testamentum* Supplements
NPNF¹	*Nicene and Post-Nicene Fathers 1*
NPNF²	*Nicene and Post-Nicene Fathers 2*
NRSV	New Revised Standard Version
NTS	*New Testament Studies*
Opif.	Philo *De opificio mundi*
OT	Old Testament
PA	Philosophia Antiqua
PAPM	*Les œuvres de Philon D'Alexandrie*. Edited by R. Arnaldez, J. Pouilloux, C. Mondésert. Paris, 1961–1992.
Pat.	Tertullian *De patientia*
PE or P.E.	Eusebius *Praeparatio evangelica*
PG	Patrologia graeca (ed. J. Migne)
Ph&PhenR	*Philosophy and Phenomenological Research*
Plant.	Philo *De plantatione*
Post.	Philo *De posteritate Caini*
Praem.	Philo *De praemiis et poenis*
Prob.	Philo *Quod omnis probus liber site*
QD	*Quaestiones disputatae*
QE	Philo *Quaestiones et solutiones in Exodum*
QG	Philo *Quaestiones et solutiones in Genesin*
QGE	Questions and Answers on Genesis and Exodus
Quis div.	Clement of Alexandria *Quis dives salvetur*
RB	*Revue biblique*
RevQ	*Revue de Qumrân*
RSV	Revised Standard Version
Ruf.	Jerome *Apologeticum adversus Rufinum*
SBL	Society of Biblical Literature
SBLDS	Society of Biblical Literature Dissertation Series
SBLMS	Society of Biblical Literature Monograph Series
SC	*Sources chrétiennes*
Serm.	Augustine *Sermones*
SIDIC	*Service International de Documentation Judéo-Chrétienne (International Service of Jewish-Christian Documentation)*
Sobr.	Philo *De sobrietate*
Somn.	Philo *De somniis*
SPh	*Studia Philonica*

Spec. (Leg.)	Philo *De specialibus legibus*
s.v.	*sub verbum*
TCH	Transformation of the Classical Heritage
TDOT	*Theological Dictionary of the Old Testament*
Trim. prot.	*Trimorphic protennoia*
TS	*Theological Studies*
VC	*Vigiliae Christianae*
VTSup	Supplements to *Vetus Testamentum*
WMANT	Wissenschaftliche Monographien zum Alten und Neuen Testament
WJT	*Westminster Journal of Theology*
WUNT	Wissenschaftliche Untersuchungen zum Neuen Testament
ZNW	*Zeitschrift für die neutestamentliche Wissenschaft*

HONORING THOMAS H. TOBIN, S.J., PH.D.

PATRICIA WALTERS

Impossible as it is to capture in words the life of any human being, it seems particularly daunting to try to set down the significant events in the life of Thomas H. Tobin, S.J., Ph.D., whose sixty-fifth birthday is on November 8, 2010. In tribute to his erudite and enduring contributions to the study of ancient religious texts and their contexts, twelve long-time colleagues and two former graduate students of Fr. Tobin offer new research to celebrate the occasion.

Fresh perspectives into the ancient eastern Mediterranean religious milieu hallmark this volume's contributions. Challenged by Hellenistic and Greco-Roman domination in the political and cultural spheres, the religious approaches of Jewish and, later, Christian groups sought to both maintain *tradition* and mediate *transition*. As the dual foci of Fr. Tobin's scholarship, the strivings of Jewish communities to give voice to their own age as well as the struggle of Christian communities to ground their nascent beliefs in that same world represent the governing themes of this volume. Thus, it is with great pleasure that these essays are offered to Fr. Tobin as a sign of deep regard for his own contributions as scholar, colleague, mentor, and friend.

The Life and Work of Fr. Thomas H. Tobin, S.J.

Born on November 8, 1945, Fr. Tobin was raised in Chicago, a city in which he takes great pride and about which, to the delight of those around him, he never lacks tales of intrigue and politics, both religious and political. Graduating *summa cum laude* from Xavier University in Cincinnati, Ohio, in 1967, Fr. Tobin was awarded a Bachelor of Letters in the classical languages, Greek and Latin. A student of philosophy at Loyola University Chicago from 1967 to 1969, he received a Master of Arts in Theology from the Jesuit School of Theology in Chicago in 1973, and he was ordained a Jesuit priest on June 7, 1973. After studying Rabbinic literature at the Hebrew University of Jerusalem from 1976 to 1977, Fr. Tobin attended Harvard University where he was awarded a Ph.D. with distinction in 1980, under the Committee on the Study of Religion, Department of New Testament and Christian Origins. His dissertation, entitled *The Creation of Man: Philo and the History of Interpretation*, was directed by Professor John Strugnell with readers Professors Dieter Georgi, George MacRae, and Zeph Stewart.

In his professional life, Fr. Tobin began teaching Philosophical Theology, New Testament, and the Synoptic Gospels at Xavier University from 1969 to 1970; then he taught Pauline literature and the Gospel of John at the Institute of Pastoral Studies at Loyola University Chicago in the summers of 1972, 1973, and 1975. During his graduate studies at Harvard, he taught elementary and intermediate Coptic, also taking on a tutorial position on the Committee on the Study of Religion, in New Testament and Intertestamental Literature. In 1980, Fr. Tobin joined the faculty of the Theology Department at Loyola University Chicago as Assistant Professor; there, in 1985, he was promoted to Associate Professor, and in 2004, to Full Professor.

Fr. Tobin is the author of three books: *The Creation of Man: Philo and the History of Interpretation* (1983); *Paul's Rhetoric in Its Contexts: The Argument of Romans* (2004), and *The Spirituality of Paul* (1987; reprint 2008). In addition, he has edited, with Harold W. Attridge and John J. Collins, *Of Scribes and Scrolls: Essays in Honor of the Sixtieth Birthday of John Strugnell* as well as edited and translated Timaios of Locri in *On the Nature of the World and the Soul* (1985). At this time, Fr. Tobin is preparing a two-volume commentary on Philo of Alexandria's *Legum Allegoriae I–III*, a significant contribution to the new commentary series on the treatises of Philo of Alexandria, to be published by E.J. Brill in Leiden, The Netherlands. Fr. Tobin is also writing an essay, "How and Why Philo Matters," for a Centenary volume, edited by David E. Aune and Frederick Brenk, which celebrates the Pontifical Biblical Institute.

A long-time member of the Studiorum Novi Testamenti Societas, the Catholic Biblical Association of America, the Society of Biblical Literature, the Chicago Society of Biblical Research, the North American Patristic Society, and the American Theological Society, Fr. Tobin has also assumed editorial duties as associate editor of *New Testament Studies* (2000–2003), associate editor of the *Catholic Biblical Quarterly* (1989–1996), associate editor of the *Journal of Biblical Literature* (1994–1999), member of the editorial board of *The Studia Philonica Monograph Series* (1990–), chair and member of the editorial board of *The Studia Philonica Annual* (2006–), and member of the editorial board of the Commentary Series on Philo of Alexandria (1995–).

Although by no means exhaustive, these few paragraphs illustrate the extent of Fr. Tobin's impressive achievements in scholarship. It has been observed many times that despite his brilliance and astounding breadth of learning, he is never one to put on airs. Joining intellectual acumen with great kindness, humility, and wit, Fr. Tom Tobin represents the best of Jesuit scholars and dedicated university professors.

Festschrift *Synopsis*

The volume begins with a provocative and programmatic essay on biblical hermeneutics. In "Interpretive Disagreements and the Ontology of a Text: Scandal or Possibility?" Robert A. Di Vito applies speech-act theory to the nature of biblical interpretation and, in doing so, challenges current hermeneutical trends. He argues that an utterance, or, in this case, a text, is properly determined by the speaker or writer, *not* the hearer or reader. Without a focus on (authorial) intentionalist interpretations, "meaning" allows for an indeterminate number of interpretations, all of which, in fact, "re-author" the text. Moreover, ethical questions arise: who actually determines "meaning" and what is the "right" of authors to fair representation? Di Vito maintains that every serious effort to interpret a text will, *of necessity*, involve the effort to grasp the author's intended meaning.

The thirteen essays that follow are partitioned into two groups: (1) the five contributions in Part One engage the dynamics of tradition and transition in Jewish contexts and (2) the eight in Part Two apply these two themes to the multiple religious streams of early Christianity. During the Hellenistic and imperial periods, momentous religious and political changes were underway in Judaea and nearby regions. Under Hellenistic influence, many Jewish writers in the Diaspora strove to present their heritage and legacy as not only familiar to Gentiles steeped in philosophy and science but also superior to the Gentile texts. Further, at the turn of the Common Era, Roman hegemony dealt a swift response to Jewish rebellion as the second temple period met its fiery end in 70 CE, although it will be seen that not all Jewish groups considered the temple's destruction catastrophic. What is more, within Judaism, the founding of a pivotal religious movement was taking shape. Notwithstanding its emergence from a Jewish context, the fledgling Jesus movement soon developed conspicuous Gentile characteristics, and, to be sure, the climate of political unrest and religious fervor colored the outlook of these burgeoning communities as well.

Leading the five essays in Part One, "Tradition and Transition: Jewish Responses in a Hellenistic World," is Pauline Viviano's "*Qārā'* and *'ānâ* in the Hebrew Scriptures." By analyzing the Hebrew words for "call" (*qārā'*) and "answer" (*'ānâ*) attested in the same verse or close proximity and intended as an appeal to or from God, Viviano not only probes the formidable intimacy of the human-divine relationship, which, in some cases, even suggests sexual overtones, but also addresses the question of its immediacy. Relying on the reality of this communication, the biblical writers reveal in perpetuity that they long for and indeed expect the certainty of response.

In "The Dead Sea Scrolls and Jewish-Christian Dialogue," Eileen Schuller, a Scrolls specialist, moves the subject to the significance of the Dead Sea Scrolls and asks a thought-provoking question. Has the discovery of the Scrolls had an impact on how Jews and Christians understand themselves and relate to each other? Ironically, to a great extent, Scrolls scholarship and Jewish-Christian dialogue have functioned in completely separate spheres. Despite the Scrolls' controversial publication chronology and its effect on scholarship, the Scrolls have served as a catalyst for a major revolution in the study of Second Temple Judaism as well as in the relationship of Christianity and Judaism in the century so formative for both. Levels of trust and commitment have now increased after decades of isolation, intense emotion, and mutual suspicion in the late 1980s around the issues of closed access and slow release. Furthermore, public exhibitions and education events are ways to tap the interest generated by the Dead Sea Scrolls, making them another entry point for bringing Jewish-Christian relations more broadly to the public venue.

The next three essays address more direct encounters between Judaism and Hellenism. In "Artapanus Revisited," John J. Collins responds to recent Artapanus research and advances his own thinking about this Hellenistic Jewish writer who colors his accounts with drama, mischief, humor, and fantasy. The argument by Howard Jacobson that, because of his deviation from the biblical account and claims that Moses instituted Egyptian animal cults, Artapanus was probably not "Jewish" Collins finds unpersuasive. Ethnic pride for those in the Diaspora derived from ancestral heritage and customs; Artapanus therefore should be understood rather as "Judean." Indeed, no other "Gentile" account so fully extolling the legacy of ancient Judaism has yet been found. Next, examining the research of Holger Zollentin who proposes 118–116 BCE as the date of Artapanus' composition, Collins concurs with narrowing the date to the second half of the second century BCE but cautions against a date tied so specifically to the Ptolemaic amnesty decree in 118 BCE. Lastly, with characteristic insight, Collins considers with the often over-looked, but undisguised, *tension* in Artapanus' work. To wit, on the one hand, Artapanus depicts Moses as a benevolent and euergetistic leader who, having established Egyptian animal cults, evokes the Ptolemaic culture of tolerance for diverse religious traditions and practices. On the other hand, during his Exodus exposition, Artapanus dramatically recounts the divinely orchestrated drowning of all Egyptian sacred animals in the Red Sea. Collins suggests the tension may be designed to *elevate* the Judeans. Thus, although tolerance of Egyptian gods may have had legitimacy in Jewish communities, Judeans in Egypt could be reassured their God had the superior power. The God of Moses is none other than the master of the universe, signifying that Jewish Egypt could prevail in the face of any difficulty.

The next two essays explore the work of Philo of Alexandria, philosopher and exegete, arguably the most famous of all Hellenistic Jewish men of letters. In "Exegetical Building Blocks in Philo's Interpretation of the Patriarchs," Ellen Birnbaum draws attention to Philo's reinterpretation of the Abraham, Isaac, and Jacob sagas, which he identifies as models for acquiring Hellenistic virtues via "learning," "nature," and "practice," respectively. Birnbaum intriguingly maintains that, although literary sources for such virtue acquisition were not unknown, no other Jewish documents *link* the patriarchs and these three paths. When Philo remarks that some give the name "Graces" to these paths or virtues (*Abr.* 54), is he revealing the influence of a prior allegorization of these Greek mythological figures?

Continuing the allegorical study of Philo, Hans Svebakken explores Philo's interpretive lens in "Exegetical Traditions in Alexandria: Philo's Reworking of the *Letter of Aristeas* 145–149 as a Case Study." Here, Philo proves his acquaintance with the symbolic interpretation of the Torah reputedly taught by the High Priest Eleazar in the *Letter of Aristeas*. Svebakken argues that, in the case of Eleazar's interpretation of winged creatures, Philo not only respects but also reworks the earlier exegetical tradition to fit his own much broader claim: Mosaic dietary laws promote observance of the Tenth Commandment's prohibition of desire (*epithymia*).

The eight essays in Part Two, "Foundations amid Flux: Christian Responses to a Transitory World," address early Christianity's adaptability to a world increasingly viewed as ephemeral. Before the fall of the second temple, apocalyptic expectation gave rise to increasing social unrest. In "The Second Temple and the Arts of Resistance," Adela Yarbro Collins calls on research in James C. Scott's *Domination and the Arts of Resistance: Hidden Transcripts* to argue that resistance to the temple elites by the power-poor is manifest in seditious "hidden transcripts" whose meaning may be obscure or confusing to the dominant group but is unquestionably clear to the powerless. Repressive social conditions gave rise to disguised but intense criticism in 1 Enoch's "Animal Apocalypse," the book of Daniel, the Dead Sea Scrolls (*Damascus Rule, Community Rule, Temple Scroll*, and *4QFlorilegium*), and Josephus' works (*Jewish War, Antiquities of the Jews*). These forces also influenced the production of Christian texts such as the Gospel of Mark and 2 Thessalonians, as both allude to the book of Daniel and the "abomination of desolation." The point is that the presence of "hidden transcripts" discloses greater complexity in attitudes toward the second temple than commonly thought; not all social groups appeared to be distressed about the temple's destruction in 70 CE.

Parables, similarly, contain hidden metaphors, the meaning of which has spawned a complicated interpretive history. Edmundo Lupieri in "*Mamona iniquitatis*: Can We Make Sense of the Parable of the Dishonest Steward?" unravels the context of the enigmatic parable in Luke 16:1–9. It is a case in which the evangelist describes a carefully nuanced transition from the old "economy" (16:2) to the new one, the one we now call Christian. The real meaning of the Law is no longer the one offered by the Pharisees but rather the one attributed to Jesus. The Parable of the Dishonest Steward in the Lukan discussion wants to bring the faithful to the realization that radical inclusion of the outcast, whether religious or social, although a hard pill to swallow, *is* the will of God. In an extensive appendix, Brian Dennert, Ph.D. candidate at Loyola, meticulously surveys the interpretive history of this parable.

Moving the conversation to the Pauline letters, David E. Aune in "Galatians 3:28 and the Problem of Equality in the Church and Society" focuses on evidence for the theoretical and practical conceptions of *equality* in early Christianity, with emphasis on ethnicity, social status, and gender. For Paul, human equality is limited to the church of God in that anyone who believes and is baptized may be a member. It is also clear Paul did not consider equal as a reality only *coram deo* ("before God"), since he was convinced all believers, regardless of ethnicity and social standing, were obligated to share table fellowship as part of their collective life "in Christ Jesus." Of special interest to the history of Pauline interpretation is the "ideology of gender hierarchy" that has, for example, obscured and downplayed the roles of Phoebe, deacon and patron of Paul (Rm 16:1–2), and Junia, the apostle (16:7).

Wendy Cotter, C.S.J., reopens the question of Paul's expectation of Philemon in "'Welcome Him as You Would Welcome Me' (Philemon 17): Does Paul Call for Virtue or the Actualization of a Vision?" She challenges the usual reliance on the Letter to the Colossians, namely, that Paul asks only kindness of Philemon as Philemon receives his slave, Onesimus, once more. Cotter calls for Paul's expectation of an imminent end-time as the backdrop for Philemon, just as it is for 1 Corinthians 7:21–22 and Galatians 3:28. Evidence in Paul's letters that he sought the dissolution of social distinctions leads Cotter to conclude that Philemon 17 is Paul's test to see whether Philemon is ready to relinquish the master-slave relationship.

In "'In the Form of Man'—The New Testament and the Language of Transformation," Lawrence DiPaolo, Jr. moves the focus to the question of how language and, in particular, titles address early Christian under-standings of Jesus. DiPaolo demonstrates that Philippians 2:7, John 1:14 and 1 Timothy 3:16 have centuries-old literary antecedents, which he recovers in numerous pagan religious and philosophical writings of the archaic, classical, Hellenistic, and Roman imperial periods and which range from Homer, Hesiod, and Herodotus to Euripides to Suetonius, Virgil, and Ovid. The hymnic fragments now embedded in the New Testament, DiPaolo argues, most closely resemble the Hymns of Isidorus and the writings of Apollodorus, Plutarch, and Lucian of Samosata. Yet for all the literary correspondences, the parallels are not wholly aligned with the particular, and perhaps confusing, image in the Christian canon of Jesus Christ as flesh (*sarx*).

Urban C. von Wahlde re-opens a discussion about the presence of Gnostic influence in the Gospel of John in "The Johannine Literature and Gnosticism: New Light on Their Relationship?" Building on his forth-coming Johannine commentary, von Wahlde analyzes the evidence for the striking resemblance to "Gnostic" features seen in the Gospel's sec-ond compositional stage or "edition." Signs of this influence are seen in major themes such as "knowing" and "knowledge," Jesus as revealer and heavenly redeemer, attitudes toward the material world, and the "I am" statements. When the second and third editions are viewed in combina-tion, the confusion is understandable, but this composite material actu-ally attests the worldview of apocalyptic dualism found in the Dead Sea Scrolls. The Fourth Gospel's alleged parallels to "Gnosticism," although remarkable at times, remain accidental and indicate the Gospel's thoroughly Jewish background.

Harold W. Attridge also examines the influence of the Fourth Gospel on diverse early Christian traditions in "The Gospel of John in the Second Century: The Case of the Acts of John." Analyzing a work of second century Christian fiction entitled the *Acts of John*, Attridge finds evidence of both dependence on the Fourth Gospel (and others) as well as striking distinctiveness. Johannine influence is clearly seen in motifs such as the Cross and the one lifted up or exalted on it, the intimacy between beholder and the Beheld, and Jesus' "departure" as a prerequisite to the attainment of understanding. At the same time, highly distinctive motifs are visible such as those in the Passion when the apostle is shown to flee to the Mount of Olives where he encounters a "vision" of the Divine Word and "Voice," teaching him enigmatically that those who respond to him (Jesus) are in truth *spiritual only*, that the true nature of suffering is its irrelevance, its meaninglessness. In dialogue with *The Johannine Corpus in the Early Church* by Charles Hill, Attridge understands the second-century Christians who produced the Acts as not so much "anti-Johannine" (Hill's proposal), but rather "alternatively Johannine" or "symbolically Johannine." That is to say, appreciation of the Gospel traditions co-existed with that of "Gnostic" teachings.

In the second to fifth century, the early Church Fathers sought biblical guidance for their Christological interpretations, as Brian E. Daley shows in "Christ, the Church, and the Shape of Scripture: What We can Learn from Patristic Exegesis." When heresies, among them "Gnosticism," appeared to threaten the articulation of "proto-orthodox" views, the Fathers of the Church such as Irenaeus, Origen, Athanasius, and Augustine set down principles for biblical interpretation for orthodox teaching. Although their conception and application of the Christological hermeneutic vary considerably, they all agree on Scripture as a *single unified narrative*, extending to all people, through Christ and his Church, the call and the promise originally made to Abraham and his children. Their exegesis is marked, therefore, not so much by a distinctive "method" but rather by their distinctive theological assumptions.

ACKNOWLEDGEMENTS

In view of all that precedes, heartfelt thanks go to those who assisted in the development of this volume, especially Dr. Wendy Cotter, C.S.J., Dr. David E. Aune, and Dr. Sarah Tanzer. I am also grateful to Dr. Susan Ross, chair of the Theology Department at Loyola University Chicago, and Dr. Robert Di Vito for their helpful suggestions, to the professors of the Theology Department who so warmly supported the endeavor, and to Ms. Catherine Wolf, Administrative Assistant to the Department, for her many kindnesses. I offer warm regards to those unable to contribute because of other scholarly commitments as well as sincere apologies to any who would have wished to participate. Special thanks go to the Editors-in-Chief of *Novum Testamentum* Supplements, Dr. Margaret M. Mitchell and Dr. David P. Moessner, for their generous guidance, and to Ms. Mattie Kuiper of Brill Publishers for her helpful counsel. Most especially, I thank the fourteen contributors for the gift of their essays, so rich in depth and diversity, and for their collaboration, which made this project such an honor and privilege.

With highest esteem,
Patricia Walters
March 17, 2010
Feast Day of St. Patrick

BIBLIOGRAPHY

Books

Attridge, Harold W., John J. Collins, and Thomas H. Tobin, eds. *Of Scribes and Scrolls: Essays in Honor of the Sixtieth Birthday of John Strugnell*. Washington, D.C.: University Press of America, College Theology Society, 1990.

Timaios of Locri. *On the Nature of the World and the Soul*. Translated and edited by Thomas H. Tobin. Texts and Translations 26. Graeco-Roman Religion Series 8. Chico, Calif.: Scholars Press, 1985.

Tobin, Thomas H. *The Creation of Man: Philo and the History of Interpretation*. Catholic Biblical Quarterly Monograph Series 14. Washington, D.C.: Catholic Biblical Association of America, 1983.

———, *Paul's Rhetoric in Its Contexts: The Argument of Romans*. Peabody, Mass.: Hendrickson, 2004.

———, *The Spirituality of Paul*. Message of Biblical Spirituality 12. Wilmington, Del.: Michael Glazier, 1987. Reprint, Eugene, Oreg.: Wipf & Stock, 2008.

Essays

"Tradition and Interpretation in Philo's Portrait of the Patriarch Joseph." In *SBL Seminar Papers*. Atlanta, Ga.: Scholars Press, 1986.

"The Prologue of John and Hellenistic Jewish Speculation." *Catholic Biblical Quarterly* 52 (1990): 252–269.

"4Q185 and Jewish Wisdom Literature." In *Of Scribes and Scrolls: Essays in Honor of the Sixtieth Birthday of John Strugnell*. Edited by Harold W. Attridge, John J. Collins, and Thomas H. Tobin. Washington, D.C.: University Press of America, College Theology Society, 1990.

"Romans 10:4: Christ the Goal of the Law." In *Heirs of the Septuagint: Philo, Hellenistic Judaism and Early Christianity*. Edited by D.T. Runia, et al. *The Studia Philonica Annual* 3. Atlanta, Ga.: Scholars Press, 1991.

"Logos." In *The Anchor Bible Dictionary*. Edited by David Noel Freedman, et al. 6 vols. New York: Doubleday, 1992.

"Interpretations of the Creation of the World in Philo of Alexandria." In *Creation in the Biblical Traditions*. Edited by Richard J. Clifford and John J. Collins. Catholic Biblical Quarterly Monograph Series 24. Washington, D.C.: Catholic Biblical Association of America, 1992.

"Miracles, Magic and Modernity: Comments on the Paper of Marilyn McCord Adams." In *Hermes and Athena: Biblical Exegesis and Philosophical Theology*. Edited by Eleonore Stump and Thomas P. Flint. University of Notre Dame

Studies in the Philosophy of Religion 7. Notre Dame, Ind.: University of Notre Dame Press, 1993.

"Controversy and Continuity in Rom 1:18–3:20." *Catholic Biblical Quarterly* 55 (1993): 298–318.

"Was Philo a Middle Platonist? Some Suggestions." *The Studia Philonica Annual* 5 (1993): 147–150.

"4 Maccabees." In *The Harper Collins Study Bible*. London and New York: Harper Collins, 1993.

"Justification." In *The Modern Catholic Encyclopedia*. Edited by Michael Glazier and Monika K. Hellwig. Collegeville, Minn.: Liturgical Press, Michael Glazier, 1994.

"Apostle" and "Apostolic Age" and "Catholic Letters" and "Ephesus" and "Epistle" and "Pastoral Letters" and "St. Paul" and "Philemon" and "St. Timothy" and "St. Titus." In *The HarperCollins Encyclopedia of Catholicism*. Edited by Richard P. McBrien. San Francisco: Harper, 1995.

"What Shall We Say That Abraham Found? The Controversy behind Romans 4." *Harvard Theological Review* 88:4 (1995): 437–452.

"Philosophy" and "Providence." In *Dictionary of Judaism in the Biblical Period*. Edited by Jacob Neusner and William Scott Green. New York: Simon & Schuster Macmillan, 1996.

"Philo and the Sibyl: Interpreting Philo's Eschatology." *The Studia Philonica Annual* 9 (1997): 84–103.

"The Beginning of Philo's *Legum Allegoriae* 1." *The Studia Philonica Annual* 12 (2000): 29–43.

"The Jewish Context of Rom 5:12–14." *The Studia Philonica Annual* 13 (2001): 159–175.

"Response to John L. White's *The Apostle of God: Paul and the Promise of Abraham*." *Biblical Research* 48 (2003): 21–26.

"The World of Thought in the Philippians Hymn (Philippians 2:6–11)." In *The New Testament and Early Christian Literature in Greco-Roman Context: Studies in Honor of David E. Aune*. Edited by John Fotopoulos. Supplements to *Novum Testamentum* 122. Leiden: Brill, 2006.

"Wisdom of Solomon" and "4 Maccabees." In *The HarperCollins Study Bible*. Rev. ed. San Francisco: HarperSanFrancisco, 2006.

"Romans." In *Blackwell Companion to the New Testament*. Edited by David E. Aune. West Sussex, U.K.: Wiley-Blackwell, 2010.

"Logos." *Encyclopedia of Early Judaism*. Edited by John J. Collins. Forthcoming.

"The Importance of Hellenistic Judaism for Studying Paul's Ethics." In *Early Christian Ethics in Jewish and Hellenistic Contexts*. Edited by Joseph Verheyden and Jan Willem van Henten. Studies in Theology and Religion. Leiden: Brill, forthcoming.

Papers

"The State of New Testament Scholarship Today." Response to Nils Dahl. Presented at Harvard University, May 1980.

"Système implicite dans l'exégèse de Philon. Un exemple: le *De Praemiis*." Response to Jacques Cazeaux. Presented at the annual meeting of the Society of Biblical Literature, November 1980.

"Philo and the Fall." Presented at the North American Patristics Conference, May 1981.

"Allegory in Hellenistic Philosophy and Religion." Presented for the Philosophy Department, Loyola University of Chicago, February 1982.

"The Creation of Man: Philo and Tradition." Presented at the Midwest Patristics Seminar, March 1982.

"The Creation of Man in Hellenistic Judaism." Presented at the annual meeting of the Catholic Biblical Association of America, August 1982.

"Gnilka and Pesch: Two Recent Commentaries on the Gospel of Mark." Presented for the Theology Department, Loyola University of Chicago, October 1982.

"Levels of Interpretation in Philo's *De Sacrificiis*." Presented at the annual meeting of the Society of Biblical Literature, December 1984.

"Tradition and Interpretation in Philo's Portrait of the Patriarch Joseph." Presented at the annual meeting of the Society of Biblical Literature, November 1986; the Midwest Patristic Seminar, December 1986.

"The Prologue of John and Hellenistic Jewish Speculation." Presented at the annual meeting of the Catholic Biblical Association of America, August 1988; Midwest Patristics Seminar, October 1988.

"Gnosticism and Platonism: Major Points of Contact." Presented as part of a panel at the annual meeting of the Society of Biblical Literature, November 1989.

"The Role of Miracles in Luke—Acts." Response to a paper by Marilyn Adams. Presented at Philosophical Theology and Biblical Exegesis Conference at the University of Notre Dame, March 1990.

"The Fate of Plato's *Timaeus* in Middle Platonism." Presented at the annual meeting of the Society of Biblical Literature, November 1990.

"Controversy and Continuity in Rom 1:18–3:20." Presented at the Chicago Society of Biblical Research, February 1991.

"Interpretations of the Creation of the World in Philo of Alexandria." Presented at the annual meeting of the Catholic Biblical Association, August 1991.

"Was Philo of Alexandria a Middle Platonist?" Presented at the annual meeting of the Society of Biblical Literature, November 1992.

"What Shall We Say That Abraham Found? The Controversy behind Romans 4." Presented at the annual meeting of the Catholic Biblical Association, August 1993; Midwest Patristics Seminar, November 1994.

"Paul's Place in the Roman Diaspora: New Assumptions." Response to A.T. Kraabel. Presented at the annual meeting of the Studiorum Novi Testamenti Societas, Birmhingham, England, August 1997.

"Rethinking Romans: The Case of Romans 8–11." Presented at the Midwest Patristics Seminar, November 1997; University of Chicago, February 1998.

"Was Eupolemus an Old Boy?" Response to Robert Doran. "The Cost of a Good Education: Reflections on the Gymnasium in 2 Maccabees." Presented at the conference on Hellenism in the Land of Israel, University of Chicago, April 1999.

"Structure and Argument in Philo's *Legum Allegoriae* I–III." Presented at the annual meeting of the Society of Biblical Literature, November 1999.

"Rethinking Romans: Literary Cues and the Legacy of Controversy." Main paper, presented at the annual meeting of the Catholic Biblical Association, August 2001.

"Universality and Particularity in Philo of Alexandria Reconsidered." Presented at the conference on Natural Law: Ancient Origins and Contemporary Debates, University of Notre Dame, September 2001.

Response to Gregory Sterling's Commentary on Philo's *Hypothetica*. Presented at the annual meeting of the Society of Biblical Literature, November 2001.

"Issues of Eschatology in Paul." Presented at the Chicago Society of Biblical Research, April 2003.

"The Structure, Genre, and Purposes of Romans." Presented at the annual meeting of the Studiorum Novi Testamenti Societas, Bonn, Germany, July 2003.

"Philo and the Transformation of Tradition." Presented at the annual meeting of the Society of Biblical Literature, November 2003.

"Jesus Christ and the End of the World in Saint Paul." Yves Simon Lecture, presented at the University of Chicago, November 2004.

"The World of Thought in the Philippians Hymn (Phil 2:6–11)." Presented at the annual meeting of the Society of Biblical Literature, November 2004.

"The Importance of Hellenistic Judaism for Studying Early Christianity." Presented at a conference sponsored by the Netherlands School for Advanced Studies in Theology and Religion at the Catholic University of Leuven, October 2006.

"Philo's *Legum Allegoriae*: The Thread of the Argument." Presented in the Philo of Alexandria Group at the annual meeting of the Society of Biblical Literature, November 2006.

"Issues of His Own Making: The Relation between Paul's Letter to the Romans and to the Galatians." Presented at the annual meeting of the Studiorum Novi Testamenti Societas, Lund, Sweden, August 2008.

"The Importance of Hellenistic Judaism for Studying Paul's Ethics." Presented at the Chicago Society for Biblical Research, February 2009.

Book Reviews

The Rich Christian in the Church of the Early Empire: Contradictions and Accommodations, by L. William Countryman. *Religious Studies Review* 7 (1981): 259.

The Knowledge of the Truth—Two Doctrines: The Book of Thomas the Contender (CG II,7) and the False Teachers in the Pastoral Epistles, by Jesse Sell. *Catholic Biblical Quarterly* 46 (1984): 590–591.

Gerechtigkeit und Christusgegenwart: Vorpaulinische und paulinische Tauftheologie, by U. Schnelle. *Catholic Biblical Quarterly* 46 (1984): 799–800.

Die hellenistische Gestalt des Judentums bei Philon von Alexandrien, by Yehoshua Amir. *Catholic Biblical Quarterly* 47 (1985): 571–572.

Two Treatises of Philo of Alexandria: A Commentary on De Gigantibus and Quod Deus Sit Immutabilis, by David Winston and John Dillon. *Journal of Biblical Literature* 105 (1986): 352–354.

Paul, Apostle of Weakness: Astheneia and Its Cognates in Pauline Literature, by David Alan Black. *Catholic Biblical Quarterly* 48 (1986): 130–132.

The Concept of Purity at Qumran and the Letters of Paul, by Michael Newton. *Catholic Biblical Quarterly* 49 (1987): 347–349.

The Opponents of Paul in Second Corinthians, by Dieter Georgi. *Catholic Biblical Quarterly* 50 (1988): 317–319.

From the Maccabees to the Mishnah, by Shaye J.D. Cohen. *Journal of Religion* 69 (1989): 284–285.

Philo of Alexandria and the Timaeus of Plato, by David T. Runia. in *Critical Review of Books in Religion* (1989): 378–381.

Text und Textwert der griechischen Handschriften des Neuen Testaments. I, edited by Kurt Aland. Die Katholischen Briefe. 4 vols. *Bulletin of the American Society of Papyrologists* 25 (1988): 179–180.

Letters That Paul Did Not Write: The Epistle to the Hebrews and the Pauline Pseudepigrapha, by Raymond F. Collins. *Catholic Biblical Quarterly* 52 (1990): 551–552.

Fourth Ezra: A Commentary on the Book of Fourth Ezra, by Michael Edward Stone. *Catholic Biblical Quarterly* 55 (1993): 777–779.

On Aristotle's Categories, by Porphyry, translated by Steven K. Strange. *Religious Studies Review* 20.1 (1994): 55.

Text und Textwert der griechischen Handschriften des Neuen Testaments; Part III: Die Apostelgeschichte, edited by Kurt Aland. *Bulletin of the American Society of Papyrologists* 30.3–4 (1993): 179–180.

Das Selbstverständnis der jüdischen Diaspora in der hellenistisch-römischen Zeit, by Willem Cornelis van Unnik. *Catholic Biblical Quarterly* 57 (1995): 197–198.

The Apocryphon of Jannes and Jambres the Magicians, by Albert Pietersma. *Journal of Biblical Literature* 114 (1995): 548–550.

The Corinthian Body, by Dale B. Martin. *Theological Studies* 57 (1996) 740–741.

Romans and the Apologetic Tradition, Genre and Audience of Paul's Letter, by Anthony J. Guerra. *Anglican Theological Review* 78 (1996): 503–504.

Wrestling with Rationality in Paul: Romans 1–8 in a New Perspective, by John D. Moores. *Anglican Theological Review* 78 (1996): 664–665.

An Introduction to the New Testament, by Raymond E. Brown. *Commonweal* 125, no. 22 (December 18, 1998): 17–18.

The Theology of Paul the Apostle, by James D.G. Dunn. *Theological Studies* 60 (1999): 350–352.

Understanding Josephus: Seven Perspectives, edited by Steve Mason. *Catholic Biblical Quarterly* 62 (2000): 184–185.

Un playdoyer en faveur de l'unité: la lettre aux Romains, by Odette Mainville. *Review of Biblical Literature* (2000): 446–448.

Antike und Christentum: Gesammelte Aufsätze IV, by Hans Dieter Betz. *The Journal of Religion* 80 (2000): 667–668.

Texts in Transition: The Greek Life of Adam and Eve, by John R. Levison. *The Catholic Biblical Quarterly* 64 (2002): 381–382.

The Irony of Galatians: Paul's Letter in First-Century Context, by Mark Nanos. *Theological Studies* 64 (2003): 839–840.

Heroikos, by Flavius Philostratus, translated by Jennifer K. Berenson Maclean and Ellen Bradshaw Aitken. *The Catholic Biblical Quarterly* 66 (2004): 161–162.

Japheth in the Tents of Shem, by Pieter W. van der Horst. *The Catholic Biblical Quarterly* 66 (2004): 348–350.

A PARADIGM FOR BIBLICAL INTERPRETATION

INTERPRETIVE DISAGREEMENTS
AND THE ONTOLOGY OF A TEXT:
SCANDAL OR POSSIBILITY?*

Robert A. Di Vito

Introduction

Among the many complaints lodged against historical-criticism in recent years, a recurrent charge has been the failure of its practitioners to deliver on its promise of providing an objective, if not scientific, means of ascertaining *the* meaning of the biblical text. This would be a (single) determinate meaning universally available and typically identified with the intention of the author. Yet the promise has gone unfulfilled and the incredible array of interpretations proposed in the name of historical criticism as the best, if not only, way to arrive at textual meaning underscores the pretentiousness of its claim and heralds its ultimate demise. Luke Timothy Johnson, in a work devoted to the future of Catholic biblical scholarship and speaking for a "third generation" of Catholic scholars disillusioned with historical criticism's claims to exclusive interpretive legitimacy, puts the issue faced by scholars focused on historically-fixed, publicly determined, textual meanings as well as any. The historical-critical paradigm, he says:

> ... has promised more than it can deliver, and is, in Walter Wink's prescient characterization, "bankrupt." ... The more obvious [aspect to this bankruptcy] is that the use of this approach has not in fact led to an agreed-upon historical reconstruction of ancient Israel, of the human mission of Jesus, or of the development of early Christianity. In fact, the opposite is true: the more scholars have pursued these questions, the more allusive

---

* I have known Thomas Tobin since I was seventeen years old—a long time, to say the least! And, not surprisingly, in those years I have met many a distinguished scholar. Thomas Tobin is that, to be sure, but also something rarer still: an intellectual whose depth and breadth of learning has been a constant source of stimulation to students and colleagues alike. To a loyal friend, a superb colleague, an inspiration to his many students over the years—I offer this essay in humble tribute.

such agreement appears. There are on offer today more versions of "the historical Jesus" and of "early Christianity" than are compatible with the perception of history as a scientific discipline.[1]

Leaving aside the question of historical criticism's status as a "science" and a now largely discredited historical positivism, there is no gainsaying *prima facie* how embarrassing the multiplicity of contradictory interpretations has been to a methodology dominant for the last two centuries and now subject to constant criticism. This is all the more the case in the face of newer interpretive approaches that, for their part, are skeptical of the idea that texts can have only one "fixed" meaning, identified or not with the intention of an author. In fact, they relish the interpretive freedom that comes with the suggestion of textual plurivocity and boundless depths of meaning surpassing what any original author could intend. For these approaches, every encounter with a text is nothing less than an "event" of new meaning, one wherein the reading represents fundamentally a reconfiguration of the text whose very mode of production as a writing has once and for all severed the claims a (dead) author has on it. Yet the author's loss is the reader's gain, for in the act of writing the author has opened her text now to subsequent semantic enrichment by generations of countless readers.[2] So no scandal here—only the promise in the play of multiple interpretations of interpretation without end.

So how should the multiplicity and conflict of interpretations be viewed? Is it a bad thing, something that shows the futility of trying to fix textual meaning? Or might it show just the opposite? In fact, if we leave aside again pretensions to scientific exactitude and examine the issues involved with a certain amount of pragmatism, it is not at all clear that the sometimes bewildering multiplicity of interpretations comprising a text's effective history undermines the claims of historically-minded critics that their texts have determinate meaning, indeed, a meaning that can be identified with an original author's intention. This is my argument: not only is the historical-critic's assumption of textual determinacy a well-grounded belief but the play of interpretation in the history of a text's reception is not an occasion of embarrassment so much as a reasonably expected outcome. Even more, a genuine appreciation of the origins of

---

[1] Luke Timothy Johnson and William S. Kurz, *The Future of Catholic Biblical Scholarship: A Constructive Conversation* (Grand Rapids, Mich.: William B. Eerdmans, 2002), 14–15.

[2] A position famously identified with Paul Ricoeur. See, for example, his preface (with André LaCocque) in *Thinking Biblically: Exegetical and Hermeneutical Studies*, trans. David Pellauer (Chicago: University of Chicago Press, 1998), xi.

such critical beliefs would see this expected outcome as a sign of interpretive health, a sign of this approach's fecundity and continuing success. And it is that—to put it succinctly for now—only because a text whose identity is determined by the author's intention gives interpreters some "thing" about which they can argue with civility. So, far from putting an end to interpretation as critics contend,[3] and even proponents[4] have been wont to sometimes argue, these beliefs generally associated with historical criticism in fact undergird the possibility of on-going interpretive activity, precisely because textual determinacy makes any and all argument even possible.

Of course, this begs a host of questions starting with the most basic, What is a text? Or, if we may put it this way, what is the metaphysic or ontology of a text? Is it simply the words on the page or is it perhaps something more? So what constitutes the identity of a text and allows it to perdure through time? How does an author and author's intention relate to this? Can a text bear both the meaning of its original author and the meanings subsequent readers gives to it and still be the same text? What would allow a text to do this? And is it true that authors, in writing, relinquish all claims to the texts they compose? By endeavoring to address these and other such questions, my hope is to cast in a new light the multiplicity of interpretations we see in our application of an historical-critical approach, taken by its critics as the scandalous outcome of an approach past its prime.

To start, I will turn to the philosophy of language and speech-act theory,[5] in particular, for the help it provides in making important common-sense distinctions about language and the way it works. Focusing on what is entailed in an utterance by a speaker will enable us to articulate how a (written) text is related to live speech and what constitutes the identity of a text. It is here also we will need to address the whole knotty issue of the author and authorial intent, which plays an important part in my understanding of how to address the major questions before us. To be sure, intentionalist proposals inevitably face an "uphill battle" these days, since the "Intentionalist Fallacy" more often than not is taken as a given of any literarily sophisticated study. Yet intentionalist interpretation is not

---

[3] Stephen E. Fowl, *Engaging Scripture: A Model for Theological Interpretation*, Challenges in Contemporary Theology (Malden, Mass. and Oxford, U.K.: Blackwell Publishers, 1998), 54, with reference to his views on Gary Phillips.

[4] *Ibid.*, 32, with reference to Benjamin Jowett.

[5] Hugh C. White, ed., *Speech Act Theory and Biblical Criticism*, Semeia: An Experimental Journal for Biblical Criticism (Decatur, Ga.: Scholars Press, 1988).

all of the same stripe and is far from dead, especially among philosophers of art.[6] It will prove central to the discussion of the ontology of the text, that is, the question of what constitutes the identity of the text and gives it its determination. As will be seen, that in turn has a real bearing on the ethics of interpretation and the issue regarding the significance of multiple interpretations of the same text. It also raises the issue of the status of historical criticism within an intentionalist theory. Although in the context of a historical-critical approach the role of the canon is significantly muted, I will nevertheless finish with some provisional observations on the differences a "scriptural" understanding of the biblical texts would entail for our conclusions.

The Ontology of a Text

Let us begin with a preliminary observation from speech-act theory about language generally: namely, to *say* something is always to *do* something. In other words, the conceptual shift speech-act theory calls for is to move from viewing utterances simply as descriptive of actions or as expressive of inner movements and states to seeing them as actions in themselves.[7] An utterance entails, at least typically, that one moves one's lips, utters certain noises, produces certain words in a certain order or construction, intones the words in a particular way, and perhaps accompanies them with certain facial or bodily gestures. Again typically, one also utters them with a "meaning," by which, for the moment, we mean only that the speaker says *something* and in saying something also does such things, as to assert, or promise, or command, or make a request.[8] Some utterances J.L. Austin called "performatives" are especially explicit kinds of such acts, as when one says "I promise" in making a promise or "I do" in a marriage ceremony. Interestingly, according to the rules of evidence in U.S. courts, someone else's report of these utterances is admissible as evidence precisely because they count as something *done*

---

[6] Noël Carroll, "Interpretation and Intention: The Debate Between Hypothetical and Actual Intentionalism," in *The Philosophy of Interpretation*, ed. Joseph Margolis and Tom Rockmore (Oxford, U.K.: Blackwell, 1999), 75.

[7] See, for example, Daniel Patte, "Speech Act Theory and Biblical Exegesis," *Semeia* 41 (1988), 88–89, with approval by Charles E. Jarrett, "Philosophy of Language in the Service of Religious Studies," *Semeia* 41 (1988), 152.

[8] J.L. Austin, *How to Do Things with Words*, 2nd ed., ed. J.O. Urmson and Marina Sbisa (Cambridge, MA: Harvard University Press, 1962), 94.

rather than *said* (which would be inadmissible as "hear-say").[9] In any case, the list of things one can do in making an utterance goes on and on to encompass utterances of every type, of which explicit performatives are but one example. Clearly, preoccupation with words or sentences, as if they alone are involved in linguistic communication, represents a misstep in understanding what is involved in even the simplest utterance.

Recasting our view of language in this way pays large dividends analytically by putting language into the larger category of human action and behavior, subject to the same sorts of conditions and constraints for success or failure as acts more generally,[10] and including acts beyond the agent's control. Instead of hanging suspended "in the air," words and sentences become part of intentional acts by speakers who typically employ all manner of conventional devices in rule-governed ways to achieve their ends. So in a real sense the issue of meaning now includes the concern for *how* language is being used.[11]

At the same time, the analytical interest with regard to speech acts is not only in their characterization as action but their characterization as *intentional* action, that is, instances of acts performed by humans, more or less voluntarily, with certain aims in view. How one interprets, for example, a dream or a sneeze or perhaps even a footprint is altogether different from how one deals with *intentional* acts such as speaking. While natural phenomena might "mean" something and might even stand in need of interpretation, typically one endeavors to make sense of natural phenomena by having recourse to various kinds of causal explanations.[12] Causal explanations will play a considerably smaller role in the interpretation of human cultural artifacts, including human utterances, even as the meaning or meanings associated with them also differs.

Taking a noise, or marks on a piece of pottery, as an example of language implies an understanding of these as the product of an intention, that is, of an intentional being, more or less like oneself; they are, in other words, the product of a speech act.[13] In fact, if one concludes that marks on a piece of pottery were produced naturally, by the forces of time and

---

[9] Ibid., 13.

[10] Ibid., 21.

[11] J.R. Searle, "What is a Speech Act?" in *The Philosophy of Language*, ed. J.R. Searle (Oxford, U.K.: Oxford University Press, 1971), 6–7.

[12] Peter Lamarque, "Objects of Interpretation," in *The Philosophy of Interpretation*, ed. Joseph Margolis and Tom Rockmore (Oxford, U.K.: Blackwell, 1999), 96–97.

[13] Searle, "What is a Speech Act?" 40.

nature—which is to say, *un*intentionally—typically the epigraphist would
not give them a second thought. She would not spend time trying to
determine their "meaning" as signs ("What do these marks mean?") but
at best only *what* produced them. Yet should she subsequently be per-
suaded that they were produced intentionally by humans (for example,
they belonged to other "marks" on the sherd she recognized as language),
there is no telling to what lengths she might go to make some sense of
them, even though initially they represent unknown forms of the characters of the language in question. It is not simply that the marks were
produced or sounds made intentionally, with any purpose in mind at all,
which triggers whether or not one endeavors to interpret them; rather, it
is essential that the marks, for example, be understood as "clues" intended
to *mean* something, that is, not only to produce a representation in writing of the elements of a language such as words and sentences (a *phatic*
act, in Austin's terminology), but to do so with *a certain sense and typically with a certain reference in mind* (a *rhetic* act).[14] So, the marks must be
both *intended* and intended to convey *a certain meaning*—not, of course,
distinct but as part of a single intention to mean something in producing
an utterance. Only then is there a genuine utterance.

To characterize more precisely the nature of "a certain meaning" is no
simple matter, nor will things be helped in the long run by avoiding the
term "meaning" and substituting talk only of aims and purposes.[15] As
Austin himself observed long ago, "'use' is a hopelessly ambiguous or
wide word, just as is the word 'meaning', which it has become customary
to deride."[16] If we remain on the side of the speaker for a moment,
substituting the word "use" for "meaning" can obscure its proper domain
in the analysis of the utterance: namely, in addition to what may be
called the "locutionary act" in Austin's terminology—the intention to
"mean" something or to communicate some propositional content[17]—
any complete speech act also includes "illocutionary" force. What the
latter underlines is that an utterance by a speaker not only entails saying
something but also *how* it is intended by the speaker: "*by* saying or *in*

---

[14] Austin, *How to Do Things with Words*, 94–96. In Searle's terminology ("What is a
Speech Act?" 2–3), "sense" is the descriptive content or meaning of an object's name; the
"reference," the object referred to.

[15] Fowl, *Engaging Scripture*, 56.

[16] Austin, *How to Do Things with Words*, 100.

[17] On the notion of the propositional content, see Searle, "What is a Speech Act?" 42–
43.

saying something we are doing something."[18] In other words, what is said is said to achieve a certain aim or effect: to ask a question, give an order, assure, warn, make a criticism, give a description, and so forth. That is what the "illocutionary force," or "illocutionary meaning," specifies in the utterance of any locution. If in the abstract a simple locution such as "He's coming" could be a question, a threat, an assertion (the possibilities are quite numerous), it is in the concrete utterance of "He's coming" that the precise *force*, or illocutionary intent, of what is being said gets determined. So a concrete utterance involves both a locutionary act and always some illocutionary force. An actual utterance is always an illocutionary act.[19]

Since what speech-act theorists refer to as the "force" of an illocutionary act is typically designated "meaning," it often happens that utterances by speakers will "mean" something different from the literal meaning of the sentences used, that is, the meaning ascertainable from the formal meanings of sentence elements and the various rules of syntax and grammar. A person asks, "Is there more coffee?" but "means" "Can you please pour me a cup?" What the sentence means *formally* in the abstract is quite different from what the speaker *intends* concretely in the utterance of the sentence: that is, the speaker is not checking the supply of coffee on hand, but indirectly asking for a refill. This results in what linguists call "an indirect speech act" where what the words mean and what the speaker actually means split in ways that are systematically related to each other. Other examples occur in utterances involving the use of metaphor or irony. In both cases a literalist understanding based on the conventional meaning of a sentence produces an obvious misunderstanding of the speaker's (intended) meaning. That is why, when the psalmist declares "The Lord is my shepherd," no one takes the point to be that the Lord is tending one's sheep.

This split between the dictionary meaning of words and what a speaker means in using them occasions the well-known distinction in speech-act theory between "sentence meaning" and "speaker meaning."[20] Where sentence meaning is purely formal, constituted by the conventional meaning of the sentence's elements and dependent upon rules of

---

[18] Austin, *How to Do Things with Words*, 12.

[19] Austin, *How to Do Things with Words*, 147: "... in general the locutionary act as much as the illocutionary is an abstraction only: every genuine speech act is both."

[20] John R. Searle, "Literary Theory and Its Discontents," *New Literary History* 25 (1994): 643–648. I am dependent throughout this section on Searle's treatment of the distinction.

syntax and grammar, speaker meaning is identified with the meaning of a specific utterance *in the actual context of its production.* For that reason, the number of ways in which the latter can be something different from the sentence meaning, or even be inconsistent with it, is potentially quite large, as numerous indirect speech acts, metaphorical meanings, and cases of irony illustrate. What someone's words mean and what he or she *means* are not necessarily the same thing, and this underlines why, as we shall see, a text (even one securely established from a text-critical viewpoint) can never be identified simply with the words on the page.

Evidently, then, meaning conventions do not alone finally determine the meaning of speech acts; the speaker's intention does, making them basically what they are and giving the acts their concrete *identity,* by specifying the intentional act being performed. As John R. Searle puts it, the identity of an intentional act, like a speech act, follows necessarily, if not trivially, from the (illocutionary) intention of the agent performing the act.[21] So what an utterance (or text) means and what its speaker (or author) intends it to mean are simply identical.[22] To be sure, for really successful communication, typically what the speaker intends in the utterance of a sentence is simply a purely conventional meaning; where the speaker departs from conventional meaning, the departure will be in ways that conform to certain rules. Meaning conventions are plainly crucial for signaling to any would-be interlocutor what you intend. That said, under optimal sorts of conditions, they are not essential. You can succeed as a speaker as long as you produce a meaningful sign by *intentionally* using some noise, even one not heard before, to signify your intentions.[23]

At this point, a clarification is needed of special relevance to the historical thrust of biblical scholarship as it has now been practiced for over two centuries. With philosophers of language, generally, if the weight in determining or identifying a speech act is put on the intention of the speaker, it does not necessarily mean that the act in question is *entirely* determined by the agent. No speech act takes place in isolation. It is always in the context of a particular time and place, not only as

---

[21] Searle, "Literary Theory and Its Discontents," 655.

[22] Steven Knapp and Walter Benn Michaels, "Against Theory 2: Hermeneutics and Deconstruction," *Critical Inquiry* 14 (Autumn 1987), 49. To readers familiar with the controversy inaugurated by the original publication of "Against Theory" (*Critical Inquiry* 8 [1982] pp. 723–742) my debt to the authors extends to my entire argument.

[23] Knapp and Michaels, "Against Theory 2," 65–66. Knapp and Michaels give an example of a passenger uttering a non-conventional noise to the driver at railroad crossing with a train's approach to say "Stop!"

it is in turn informed by intricate webs of knowledge, belief, opinion, and desire, but also as the speech act comes under the influence of various cultural, social, biological, and environmental factors. So Searle, for one, speaks of speech acts as always taking place within a "network of intentionality" and against a "background" of various capacities, abilities, and presuppositions that are not themselves part of the explicit semantic content of a particular speech act or of the speaker's intentions yet make the speech act possible. These provide the cues for correctly inferring a speaker's or author's meaning as well as furnish the basis for assumptions needed to understand it. Along with socio-cultural and socio-linguistic norms that are shared by both the speaker and the auditor, all these make communication possible without typically being brought to verbal expression. In fact, communication would actually come to a standstill if speakers / authors could not assume their hearers / readers shared with them a vast pool of presuppositions that includes essential knowledge about the world in which they live as well as the specific context in which they are communicating.[24] To use one of Searle's examples, consider the meaning of the verb "cut" and all that is involved in a simple utterance such as "Cut the grass" versus "Cut the cake" or "Cut the hair."[25] The meaning of an utterance is a function of the context in which it is produced and within which a complex system of rules about social and cultural behavior and language creates the possibility of shared meaning. Meaning is not, as Susan Lanser puts it, simply co-extensive with the words a speaker utters or "the words-on-a-page" but is "constituted by the performance of the text [or a living speech act] in a context which teems with culture-specific linguistic rules that are almost never articulated."[26] So rather than think of intentions as entirely sufficient unto themselves, it is better to think of the speaker's intentions as always doing their work within and against a certain background that is also necessary to determine more or less completely the meaning of a speech act.

Where, however, the determination of the act clearly lies beyond the scope of the speaker's intention are in the *effects* of the act, both those that are intentional and those that are not. This is of some relevance to the issue of multiple, if not contradictory, interpretations being proffered

---

[24] Max Turner, "Historical Criticism and Theological Hermeneutics of the New Testament," in *Between Two Horizons: Spanning New Testament and Systematic Theology*, ed. Joel B. Green and Max Turner (Grand Rapids, Mich.: William B. Eerdmans, 2000), 48–49.

[25] Searle, "Literary Theory and Its Discontents," 640–642.

[26] Susan S. Lanser, "(Feminist) Criticism in the Garden: Inferring Genesis 2–3," *Semeia* 41 (1988), 70–71.

of one and the same speech act (or text), although in a secondary sort of way. Speakers (and authors) can be misunderstood in the best of times as they may do a poor job of communicating their meaning; and similarly what the hearer of a speech act regards as the meaning of an utterance may not bear much relationship to the speaker's intentions for all kinds of reasons. Both speakers and their audiences vary in their knowledge of language conventions, just as they vary in their physical and intellectual gifts or in their grasp of a culture and its norms.[27] So, if the ugly truth be told, the *success* of any speech act can be an elusive thing; as in the rest of life, there are no guarantees, and speech acts are just as susceptible to failure as other kinds of intentional acts we perform.

For that reason, in addition to the locutionary and illocutionary acts that comprise an utterance in the concrete, Austin identifies a *perlocutionary* act: one that has an effect upon the thoughts, feelings, or actions of the hearer, for example, it is convincing, intimidating, encouraging, surprising.[28] What the perlocutionary effect of an utterance will be is not something determined by the illocutionary intention of the speaker; it lies beyond her scope to control and represents a sense of the term "meaning" upon which the author's claim, for good or ill, is indeed weak. That is why there is always a need in these discussions for clarity about the sense of the term "meaning" with which we are actually dealing.

If, with these qualifications, we can say that in any actual speech situation what really matters for the identity of the speech act is the speaker's meaning (ambiguous in itself or not) and that it is this that gives the speech act its determination,[29] this bears directly on the ontology of texts. In this view,[30] they may be considered speech acts, even if complex in ways different than the speech acts found in everyday conversation.[31] Or, perhaps it would be better not to refer to the text itself as a speech act but rather the "record," or "transcription," of such an act or even of an extended "speech event," in which, as Max Turner suggests, cotextual

---

[27] As Wayne Booth, *The Company We Keep: An Ethics of Fiction* (Berkeley: University of California Press, 1988), 88, says, how much we *get out* of a text will depend upon the interpreter and her abilities. This is one way in which to understand the significance of interpretive habits and practices within a community for interpretation (cf. Fowl, *Engaging Scripture*).

[28] Austin, *How to Do Things with Words*, 109–120.

[29] Searle, "Literary Theory and Its Discontents," 646–647.

[30] An alternative theory of writing will take issue with speech act theory precisely on this point, with major consequences of course for its understanding of the scope of authorial intent.

[31] On the issue of texts as speech acts, see, for example, Lanser, "(Feminist) Criticism,"

(the text before and after the utterance) and contextual (the real or imagined world of the utterance) factors furnish determinate meaning (sense,
reference, illocutionary force).[32] It would be, in Kevin J. Vanhoozer's language, the "medium of illocutionary acts," a "work of discourse," where
someone has either made or discovered the attempt to say something
about something by putting into motion the language system at home in
a particular place and time. The text thereby becomes the locus or "the
site for a work of meaning" between persons.[33]

On these terms, it becomes difficult to see how the author of a text can
get left behind since inanimate objects cannot mean. Even the words in
a language system with their dictionary meanings only bear meanings
they have had in concrete circumstances by actual speakers at a given
time and place.[34] I say "It's hot in here" and mean "Please open the
door!" To imagine a live speech act changes its identity as a speech
act in being televised, recorded for subsequent replaying, or printed
in a newspaper simply because it is further removed from the direct
"control" of the speaker, confuses intentionality (an intentional act gets
its identity from the intention of the agent performing it) with the issue
of "control." It would have us believe that live speech is more likely
to "succeed" than writing because the speaker is able to "control" the
reception of her communication immediately by her presence. How
might she do that if the auditor is either unwilling or uninterested? The
idea that the interpreter of a written text need no longer concern herself
with the *author's* discourse just confounds the real scope of the agent's
intentionality or ability to specify the meaning of an utterance with
the issue of communicative success. The act may no longer be "bound"
in precisely the same way to the original communicative situation, but
unclear is how a change in the identity of this speech act (what it "means")
occurs with the publication or reproduction of the author's text and even
the multiplication of its copies (tokens).

72; or, Patte, "Speech Act Theory and Biblical Exegesis," 89. What kind of speech act the
production of a literary text is, continues to be the subject of debate, i.e., whether this
constitutes a particular kind of speech act or is simply a member of a broader class of
acts. See here Hugh C. White, "Introduction: Speech Act Theory and Literary Criticism,"
Semeia 41 (1988), esp. 4–16.

[32] Turner, "Historical Criticism," 46.

[33] Kevin J. Vanhoozer, "Discourse on Matter: Hermeneutics and the 'Miracle' of
Understanding," in *Hermeneutics at the Crossroads*, ed. Kevin J. Vanhoozer, James K.A.
Smith, and Bruce Ellis Benson (Bloomington and Indianapolis: Indiana University Press,
2006), 20–21.

[34] Ibid., 20.

Alternatively, one might also ask why one would even wish to claim that the text in question is still the same text over time if it no longer means the same thing. The words themselves as marks on a page (even if we could be certain of them over time) in this example clearly do not constitute the "text." Authorless "texts" don't perform speech acts, such as to promise, request, warn, or admonish; only people do.[35] And it is the author's intention in that sense—and not the manner of reproduction—that gives a text its autonomy as a work and allows it to perdure as itself over time, in such a way that it does not cease to mean at all.[36] As most would acknowledge, if the aim of interpretation is to understand the discourse, it is always *someone's* discourse with which we are dealing; and that is as essential to the notion of discourse as the fact that a text is *about something*.[37] That is why, especially when we are talking about biblical texts, they can genuinely be a locus for "otherness," one wherein the relation between the text and the reader is always an asymmetrical one.

In stark contrast to this understanding, in various hermeneutical projects, it seems the status of a text *does* change insofar as the criterion for what constitutes textual identity is not the illocutionary act(s) of the author producing the text but rather "sentence meaning." What really constitutes the identity of the text over time—its remaining the same work—is simply the formal meaning of the sentences it contains.[38] Authorial intention, rather than being identified with the meaning of the text as we shall maintain, is conceived as something altogether "outside" the text, a kind of psychological reality, "often unknown to us, sometimes redundant, sometimes useless, and sometimes even harmful as regards the interpretation of the verbal meaning of his work."[39] In living speech the speaker's intention and the meaning of the discourse overlap such that to understand one is to grasp the other, whereas in writing (for some reason) "the author's intention and the meaning of the text cease to coincide," the gain being that the text can go on independently of the

---

[35] Turner, "Historical Criticism," 47.

[36] To be sure, other factors enter into the preservation of a text (physical preservation of the manuscript, knowledge of the language in question, etc.) but these factors do not bear on the metaphysics of the text itself.

[37] Vanhoozer, "Discourse on Matter," 19–20.

[38] Searle, "Literary Theory and Its Discontents," 655.

[39] Paul Ricoeur, *Interpretation Theory: Discourse and the Surplus of Meaning* (Fort Worth: Texas Christian University Press, 1976), 76.

author and free to enter into new relationships. It can even mean *more* over time than its author ever intended.[40] Gadamer puts it this way:

> The real meaning of a text, as it speaks to the interpreter, does not depend on the contingencies of the author and whom he originally wrote for. It certainly is not identical with them, for it is always partly determined also by the historical situation of the interpreter and hence by the totality of the objective course of history. … Not occasionally only, but always, the meaning of a text goes beyond its author.[41]

So a text necessarily will be understood differently every time, not just because understanding is always contextual, but in the deeper sense that the interpretation of a text belongs in fact to the meaning of the text.[42]

As Michael Knapp and Walter Benn Michaels point out, the idea that the text becomes detached from the intentions of the author recalls the argument of W.K. Wimsatt and Monroe C. Beardsley in their enormously influential essay "The Intentional Fallacy."[43] In its wake, most sophisticated interpreters of texts simply take for granted the uselessness of seeking to ground readings on what authors intend their texts to mean, even with access to their intentions or motives. But unlike many who follow them, for Wimsatt and Beardsley, the meaning of the text had itself become *permanently* fixed, apart from authorial intention, by the public nature of language and its conventions. In stark contrast, for Gadamer, each new interpretation and with it each application to a situation produces a new understanding of the text that is itself a part of the text's potential for meaning, so that it remains in his view "the same work" over the course of time.[44] But how is it really the same work? Can it, as Knapp and Michaels ask, remain the same while its meaning changes, simply on the basis of the so-called verbal meaning (formal, "dictionary" meaning) of the text and without regard to the author's intention?[45]

To some extent, we have already addressed this question with our example of a speech act such as "It's hot in here!" Take again the example of the verb "cut" in the sentence "Cut the grass!" If, as our point was, its

---

[40] Ibid., 29–30.

[41] Hans-Georg Gadamer, *Truth and Method*, ed. Garrett Barden and John Cumming (New York: Seabury Press, 1975), 63–64.

[42] Knapp and Michaels, "Against Theory 2," 51–52.

[43] W.K. Wimsatt and Monroe C. Beardsley, "The Intentional Fallacy," in W.K. Wimsatt, *The Verbal Icon: Studies in the Meaning of Poetry* (Lexington, KY: University of Kentucky Press, 1954), 3–18.

[44] Gadamer, *Truth and Method*, 336.

[45] Knapp and Michaels, "Against Theory 2," 51–54.

meaning depended upon a host of assumptions being shared by speaker and hearer, it would seem that the verbal meaning of a text is a sufficiently elastic criterion for textual identity and for a text to both remain the same and yet change as various readers actualized different possibilities latent in the word. The work of interpretation would lie in selecting a meaning or nuance the language itself makes possible ("dictionary" meaning), whether or not this agrees with anything the author intended. The choice is guided only by the interpreter's own preferences. This is what the verbal criterion for textual identity permits: for a text to mean what its author means and also something beyond that. The problem, as Knapp and Michaels point out, is that if this is what is needed, why choose this criterion when other criteria are equally serviceable?[46] One could choose, for example, to fix the text's identity by reference to just the letters or characters printed on the page so that the text means whatever the letters suggest in any language, living or dead, or any language we invent. More (if not an infinite number of) valid meanings would then be possible, and presumably we could come up with other criteria of "validity" as well.

One can only suspect that interest in this kind of "game" is bound to wane. Although the verbal criterion had the advantage of *limiting* the number of valid readings and allowing one to go beyond what the author intended, the problem is that other criteria could do the same thing. For example, Knapp and Michaels suggest, one could have stipulated that a text means what its author meant plus whatever else it can mean in a particular language except for the verbs, as they can mean what the author intended *and* their opposite. There seems to be no way to justify limiting our rule for textual identity to the verbal meaning of the text—except, that is, by claiming it is a more *appropriate* criterion than the kind of examples proposed by Knapp and Michaels. What seems to make it more "appropriate" is simply its relationship to an author's intention in producing the text in the first place. The verbal meaning criterion alone, however, cannot guarantee that kind of relationship since the meanings of words can be completely upended over the course of time as my daughter reminds me, what was once "hot" can now be "cool" and what is "good," "wicked." Knapp and Michaels conclude:

---

[46] Knapp and Michaels, "Against Theory 2," 55–59. For the argument in full, see the authors at the pages cited.

> What such examples show is that there is no necessary relation between the meaning the author intends and any one of the meanings the author's words can have in the language—except for the one the author intends. And the relation there is not one of relative proximity but of identity.[47]

In the end the verbal meaning "rule" runs the risk of being arbitrary if it does not invoke its relevance to authorial intent, since its value lies only in the clues it provides to the author's meaning. It does not provide a criterion for the identity of the text that is actually independent of some notion of authorial intention to mean; and without an identity the "text" quite literally disappears. This is what authorial intention secures, regardless of how firm or how weak one's grasp of that intention may be for any specific text. Whether or not typos, smudges, coffee stains, and even the white spaces in an author's manuscript belong to the work and ought to be reproduced in its publication along with the "letters" all depends for the publisher upon the author's intention in producing the text at hand.[48] The reason it can provide an effective criterion is not because there is always agreement about an author's intended meaning, but because prime evidence, if not the primary evidence, of authorial intention is precisely what the text offers.

It is within this context of speech-act theory and inquiry into the intentional acts that have been performed by authors in and through what has been written by them (and not some psychological models) that we need to understand what authorial intention is and how it relates to textual meaning. In this view, what the text means and what its author intends are one and the same. That is why arguments about authorial intention are often so sharp. It is always only an "embodied" or "objectified" intention that is the object of interpretation, "intention" being, as Meir Sternberg puts it, a kind of:

> shorthand for the structure of meaning and effect supported by the conventions that the text appeals to or devises: for the sense that the language makes in terms of the communicative context as a whole.[49]

In fact, other evidence of authorial intention beyond the text (authors' diaries, biographical details, even face-to-face interviews) is still only

---

[47] Knapp and Michaels, "Against Theory 2," 57.

[48] See here the provocative discussion by Walter Been Michaels, *The Shape of the Signifier: 1967 to the End of History* (Princeton: Princeton University Press, 2006), 1–18, of the eight-six blank pages in the manuscript of Thomas Shepard's *Autobiography*, as interpreted by Susan Hope.

[49] Meir Sternberg, *The Poetics of Biblical Narrative: Ideological Literature and the Drama of Reading* (Bloomington, Ind.: Indiana University Press, 1987), 9.

that—*other* evidence that is in no case a substitute for the evidence the text itself provides. From this perspective, the anonymity of the biblical authors presents no decisive obstacle to their interpretation, simply because one always has evidence of the author's intention just by having the text in hand. To have one is already to have the other; likewise, if you don't have one, you don't have the other. For that reason, the author's intention can never function as a basis outside the text for grasping the meaning of the text or furnish grounds beyond the text for the choice of one method over another.[50] What the author's intention does is provide a criterion for textual identity, equating a text with an illocutionary act of an author at a particular time and in a particular place. It is the act of *someone*—someone whose communicative intentions will be discerned by others with more or less success, with more or less openness. With its meaning determined by an agent's intention, what the act loses in potentially inexhaustible depths, it nevertheless gains in the possibility of definition that allows the intended work to come into focus and to perdure through time as itself rather than another. That definition is *always* open to argument, but there is *something* here at least actually to argue about—and equally something often to be understood.

This takes us to the heart of the argument about the significance to be attached to interpretive disagreement and textual plurivocity. Even if appeals to authorial intention are largely useless methodologically, what locating the criterion of textual identity in authorial intention does is to make interpretation "contestable," if not agonistic, as opposed to the play of a "game." If a text means only what its author intended in the production of an illocutionay act—and whatever she intended, including to be ambiguous or to be elusive—and not something else, the possibility arises of genuine argument about what the text means. (The one true interpretation of Joseph Jastrow's duck-rabbit is that it is ambiguous and

---

[50] Steven Knapp and Walter Benn Michaels, "Against Theory," in *Against Theory: Literary Studies and the New Pragmatism*, ed. W.J.T. Mitchell (Chicago: The University of Chicago Press, 1985), 12. For the authors, since there is no limit to what someone can mean and anyone can use most anything to mean anything, there is no point in attempting "to devise a general interpretive procedure, an interpretive *method*, that will … help resolve interpretive controversies. The object of every interpretive controversy … is always and only a particular historical fact, and there is no general way to determine what any particular historical fact might be" in their "Reply to George Wilson," *Critical Inquiry* 19 (Autumn 1992), 187.

can be seen as either, though not both at the same time.[51]) Rather than stifling argument or calling an end to interpretation, textual determinacy with its denial of a potentially unlimited number of valid or legitimate readings and interpretations actually opens it up. One may prefer not to argue about texts or what the intended meaning might be, in which case an alternative would seem to be to reject textual determinacy, to "argue" about the interpretive aims and interests of readers[52] and, more broadly, of their experience of texts. If the "argument" turns about *your* aims and desires or what *your* experience is as opposed to *mine*, genuine argument, at least, soon becomes quite pointless. When what you see in the text looks like you and what I see looks like me, there may be no harm in the expression of viewpoints—and they may even be interesting. Even differences in this case do not constitute disagreement: we are merely "apples" and "oranges;" and there is no way to resolve the difference short of the elimination of one of us. Indeed, if every encounter with a text is "an event of new meaning" born at the intersection of certain textual "constraints" and the expectations and aims of readers subsequent to authors,[53] is there anything possibly to argue about? Your reading is *yours*; my reading, *mine*, and we are quite literally not on the same page. In fact, interpretive exercises that make genuine disagreement about texts impossible or arguments about *their* meaning otiose run the risk of becoming a lot like games, where of course it never *really* matters who wins and who loses. As Knapp and Michaels say with characteristic pithiness, "no one cares what you *meant* [italics mine] by immobilizing your opponent's king, they just care that you did it."[54] It makes sense to embark upon the interpretation of a text only if there is something at stake, if there is some *thing* to argue about, which there only can be if the interpretive possibilities are not endless.

One need not be a professional to engage in interpretation anymore than one *has to* interpret a text, in our sense, at all. The fact is that texts, including biblical texts, may be engaged in any number of ways, including serious ways, without involving one in their interpretation. A "book" like the Bible may, for example, take on the status of a kind of religious icon, becoming an object of intense religious devotion and a vehicle of religious

---

[51] David Novitz, "Interpretation and Justification," in *The Philosophy of Interpretation*, ed. Joseph Margolis and Tom Rockmore (Oxford, U.K.: Blackwell, 1999), 16.

[52] See, for example, the argument of Fowl, *Engaging Scripture*, 56–61.

[53] LaCocque and Ricoeur, *Thinking Biblically*, xi.

[54] Walter Benn Michaels, "The Shape of the Signifier," *Critical Inquiry* 27 (Winter 2001): 278.

experience, without becoming the object of serious interpretation; rather, the reader uses the text prayerfully to suggest images or thoughts which further communion with God. Interpretation focused on an author's communicative intent, in our view, does not diminish the possibilities for this kind of actualization of the text and may even deepen it; it would be idle, however, to think that this kind of actualization of the text depends upon it. To the extent that we can speak of the Bible as a text, it can, like any classic text, be read on different "levels" with benefit. On the one hand, there is the author's meaning (speaker's meaning) and, on the other hand, the significance(s) of the text for the reader. While the former, particularly in the case of an ancient text, necessarily looks "backward" imaginatively to the occasion of the text's production as a speech act, a text's significance for the reader—indeed what some call its "meaning"— always depends upon the *present*. This is the import or value of the text to the reader in his or her own socio-cultural situation and experience, based on his or her more or less complete reading of the text (or part of the text) or "use" of the text as an occasion for another kind of experience. Since this "value" is always relative to the social and historical location of the reader, the (historical) meaning of the text, even a sacred text, really never controls the text's present value or significance.

It also happens, either because of new circumstances, viewpoints, and insights, or simply the passage of time, that the original text becomes the occasion for its own "re-writing," which is to say, the occasion or model on which one grapples anew with the question or subject matter to which the original author's discourse gives witness. One's interlocutor in a conversation, as Gadamer would have it, the original text now is superseded, becoming an occasion in which one produces a new or further "application" of the text that actually goes beyond its original (authorially intended) meaning and may even contradict it. Let us be clear: regardless of the precise wording, this would not be the *same* text; nor ought it be called even a "bad" interpretation. It is *a new text*, related more or less obviously to the text rewritten, not any less "valuable" simply for being so; its relation to some previous act of authorship is not what gives it significance now. A "re-authoring," while not an interpretation engaged in the effort to discover the text's authorially intended meaning, is the way tradition develops and moves forward in "the *construction* of meaning for the present" (italics mine).[55]

---

[55] See on this last point, Jarrett, "Philosophy of Language," 155.

The possibilities for such re-authoring of texts are quite numerous and there is no intention on my part to be exhaustive here. Instead of taking up anew the questions or subject matter that gave rise to the original text, one may, for example, focus instead simply on one or two of its aspects—for example, a character or a particular scene—as in the case of a detail in a landscape painting to which one is ineluctably drawn because of its resonance with past experience. By reading the work exclusively through the prism of these details magnified by their resonance with one's experience, a kind of re-authoring can take place that may have little relationship to the author's intended meaning. The value of this "reading" as an interpretation is one thing; its present value or significance for the reader as an occasion for retrieving one's past, another.

The Ethical Dimension

To recapitulate the argument thus far on the basis of speech-act theory, a speech act, and, by extension, a written text, attains its identity, precisely as an *intentional* act, from the intention of the one who performs it, which is to say, the speaker's, or author's, intention. While we may distinguish different aspects within this unitary intention of the agent (for example, locutionary and illocutionary force), the point to which we want to draw attention is that what the act *means* and the intention of the author are one and the same. As embodied, authorial intention is of no use methodologically to the interpreter: that is, it cannot dictate a choice of the methods the interpreter should use in a particular case of textual interpretation. Nevertheless, by securing the identity of the text (the text means *this* and not just anything at all), the author's intention grounds the possibility of serious argument precisely over what the identity of the act is. Far from calling a halt to on-going interpretive activity, it secures for it a future.

This conclusion suggests an ethical dimension to the commitment or preference by the historical critic in focusing her interpretation on the discovery of an author's meaning, what Turner, with Anthony Thiselton, would even call an "ethics of reading."[56] It is not a question of making a choice among various meanings according to certain ethical criteria. On the contrary, the whole point of this line of argument, with its

---

[56] Turner, "Historical Criticism," 60–61.

insistence on the role of authorial intention, is to make conversation, and, ultimately, choice, possible by making genuine disagreement possible. When historical-critical scholarship has been censured for seeking to cut off argument and preclude debate by insisting on a determinate meaning—a meaning intended by its author—to the exclusion of multiple and even contradictory meanings that extend beyond what authors intended, the charge is wholly misguided. It is not the insistence on a determinate meaning that has squashed argument so much as an exclusive focus on historical kinds of readings (that is, a kind of relational meaning or significance) instead of attention to the (intended) meaning of the text, *whatever* that may be. As we have argued, insistence on a determinate meaning for the text actually encourages argument and debate by grounding its possibility in an argument about the interpretation of the text. Why? Because if a text can mean anything its readers or various communities of readers want (meaning not being a property of the text itself but simply a function of various aims and purposes), debate about the text as such becomes impossible. What counts is what the text looks like to an interpreter as a function of his aims, purposes, and desires, rather than the meaning intended by the author.[57] Genuine argument is also impossible, at least to the extent that these same aims and purposes are taken to be constitutive of a reader's identity (viz., the reader's or reading community's race, gender, religion, class, and culture)—a matter of what you are rather than what you believe, which is to say, difference without disagreement. In valorizing the position of the "subject" of the interpretation, or the reader's "vantage point" over against the text's, inevitably the identity of the interpreter controls textual meaning and effectively precludes the possibility of genuine debate. A space for the *play* of multiple readings and meanings that go beyond or stand in contradiction to what is intended by the author is opened up; it comes, however, at the price of robust argument and the possibility of healthy criticism. For if what determines the text's meaning and identity comes from its readers, so that there are as many texts as there are readers or reading communities, what is controversial about *different* texts having *different* meanings? In the words of Knapp and Michaels, there is

---

[57] Barbara Herrnstein Smith, *Contingencies of Value: Alternative Perspectives for Critical Theory* (Cambridge, Mass.: Harvard University Press, 1988), 30–53. Though her perspective results in a view quite different from my own, her remarks on the constitution of the subject position as this relates to the evaluation of literary works are suggestive. I owe this reference to Dr. Pamela Caughie.

only controversy "when there is a disagreement about what some particular author meant on some particular occasion, the occasion on which the author produced the text in question."[58]

In principle, the insistence on a determinant meaning for religious texts and complex works like the Bible should result precisely in the kind of vigorous debate and argument about their interpretation that we have seen take place—the kind of debate some see apparently as a sign of failure and scandal. Instead of proving that insistence on a determinant meaning is a wrong-headed mistake, it is precisely "the persistence of hermeneutical conflict," resulting as it does in a multiplicity of interpretations, which provides "an empirical sign"[59]—in a way mere agreement could not—that interpretation is always about something other than your aims and purposes in reading a text. When debate ceases to be personal, in the sense of being about "who you are," and is focused instead on texts, the result will not be less interpretation but more. In our view, the real threat to (multiple) interpretations comes precisely from those circles or communities of readers who seek to make themselves immune from critique, either from within or from without, by valorizing the aims and intentions of their identity and viewpoint over argument on the basis of the *text's* (authorially intended) meaning.[60] "Communities of interpretation," to the extent that they do exist as distinct communities, ought not to try to insulate themselves from criticism or stand aloof from the struggle to justify their readings of texts. To the extent they do, it is at an awful price.

In an age of growing religious fundamentalism and violence against the "other," the roots of biblical scholarship's insistence on the text and authorially sanctioned meaning should not be forgotten. For contrary to what its own proponents have said often enough, under the allure of the sciences, the historical-critical approach never really was a neutral, disinterested, and value-free encounter with the biblical text but one that operates out of an anti-authoritarian ideal in the determination of the

---

[58] Steven Knapp and Walter Benn Michaels, "A Reply to Richard Rorty: What is Pragmatism?" *Critical Inquiry* 11 (1985): 467.

[59] The wording in quotes is from A.K.M. Adam, "Twisting to Destruction: A Memorandum on the Ethics of Interpretation," *Perspectives in Religious Studies* 23 (2002): 220, whose own position regarding these issue of textual determinacy is opposed to view endorsed here.

[60] As a result, "ostracization" seems to be the only way A.K.M. Adam envisions resolutions to interpretive disagreement taking place within interpretive communities (Adam, "Twisting to Destruction," 218–219).

truth and a conviction about how that contributes to a civil society. So in
the aftermath of the so-called "Wars of Religion" (1562–1648) and their
horrific bloodshed, Spinoza's great treatise on the Bible and its interpretation carries appropriately enough the title *Tractatus Theologico-Politicus*
(1670) out of the conviction that the interpretive practices advocated
therein were essential to a "civil society." They were essential to a civil
society because they *methodologically* refused to accept assertions of privileged knowledge that could not be publicly adjudicated, especially when
those claims were made by those in positions of power or authority and
often enough simply served as a mask for their own ambition or greed.
The insistence of Spinoza (whom many regard as the "father" of modern
biblical criticism) can be disarmingly simple when it comes to the Bible's
interpretation:

> ... so scriptural interpretation proceeds by the examination of Scripture,
> and inferring the intentions of its authors as a legitimate conclusion from
> its fundamental principles. ... [F]or as we have shown, we cannot wrest
> the meaning of texts to suit the dictates of our reason, or our preconceived
> opinions. The whole knowledge of the Bible must be sought solely from
> itself.[61]

If the commitment to interpret by focusing on the discovery of an author's
meaning be in the interest of the good of civil argument, there is another
aspect to its ethical significance that ought be mentioned. This has to
do with the "right" of authors to the fair representation of their intentions. It is a moral right that Robert Morgan (with John Barton), for
example, alludes to and affirms in live conversation: in a conversation,
one is bound to the speaker's meaning quite simply because he is still
alive and has "some moral right to be understood as intended." But this
is not the case for most written texts like the Bible, and that means for
Morgan the "balance of power" shifts to interpreters who become the
"masters of meaning now" and agents with their own aims and interests.

> Texts, like dead men and women, have no rights, no aims, no interests.
> They can be used in whatever way readers or interpreters choose. If inter-
> preters choose to respect an author's intentions, that is because it is in their
> interest to do so. They want to know what the author meant.[62]

---

[61] Benedict de Spinoza, *A Theologico-Political Treatise*, trans. R.H.M. Elwes (New York:
Dover Publications, Inc., 1951), 99, 103.

[62] Robert Morgan and John Barton, *Biblical Interpretation*, Oxford Bible Series (Oxford, U.K.: Oxford University Press, 1988), 2–7, 7.

The idea that the loss authors sustain upon "death" extends even to the fair representation of (what we understand to be) their works *as their own* seems, at the very least, questionable. If to disregard for whatever motive the author's intention implicates one in the production of a new text rather than in an act of interpretation as we understand it,[63] then the representation of the newly authored work as the original—or one's own "work" as really another's—is surely a kind of misrepresentation by today's standards (regardless of how the ancients viewed pseudepigraphy). It is not altogether unlike passing off a painting that is a forgery as an original, understandably offensive both to the creator of the original and those in receipt of the "copy."[64] This is true whether the supplementation of the text or the effort to go beyond what the author intended results in a better or more satisfying text. It is not that such "changes" to the text are illegitimate activities in themselves, acts of betrayal by the interpreter, or an infringement of a speaker's/author's right. Perhaps they even ought to be encouraged. The only issue is how the changes to or augmentation of a text are represented—that is, whether they are represented by the serious interpreter as "changes" productive of a new and necessarily different text or as the original text whose identity is determined by its author. Particularly when one is dealing with texts where the stakes in a reading can be relatively high as is the case with certain religious texts, the representation of textual re-authorings or creative augmentations as *simply* interpretation would seem to compromise interpreters morally and ethically, every bit as much as the representation of a probable reading as an unquestionably certain one.

To put it simply, interpretation is not authorship and the two activities, even if overlapping at times, can and ought to be distinguished. Where the logic of interpretation is the retrieval of an author's intended meaning in a new time and place, authorship is burdened with no such self-limitation or constraint. For her part, the interpreter, laboring under the constraint to articulate what the author intended, is to that extent dependent upon the author's work even as another *qua* author is simply not dependent upon the original in a corresponding way.[65]

---

[63] Knapp and Michaels, "Against Theory 2," 53.

[64] Alternatively, would there not be revulsion instinctively to the desecration of the work of a master painter, even by its so-called owner? Or to the willful distortion of the words of Jesus by one seeking to wrap his ambitions in the mantle of authority?

[65] All literature depends in an obvious way upon a shared cultural knowledge, so that texts can only be actualized by readers belonging to communities sharing certain practices and traditions of reading. On the idea of literature as "constitutive context," see

Implications and Conclusion

If recent discussions of the ethics of biblical scholarship have focused on historical-criticism's insistence on a kind of textual determinacy as the key to its practical failure, looking at interpretation within the framework of speech-act theory and the philosophy of language allows for a more nuanced description of interpretive practice and what is at stake ethically in interpretation. Doing so reinstates the value of an intentional theory of textual identity where the latter is the product of an illocutionary act performed by an individual author. Moreover, such a theory also highlights how every serious effort to interpret a text will necessarily involve the effort to grasp the author's intended meaning. To be sure, in this understanding of what an ethics of reading entails, interpretation does not itself constitute an ethical or moral act in the sense of involving one in choosing among various meanings according to certain ethical criteria; nonetheless, the determination of the text by an author's intention actually provides the groundwork for an ethics of reading by making disagreement on the basis of the text possible. Where theories of textual indeterminacy attribute differences in interpretation largely to the differences between readers' identities, a robust intentional theory promotes debate about interpretations.

It remains for us only to draw out the implications or potential consequences of our view, two of which seem especially important in this context: (1) whether this view of authorial intention entails the practice of historical criticism as currently conceived; and (2) how what we have said here bears on the interpretation of a biblical text, not within the context of a historical-critical study, but of the canon of Scripture where the latter has an explicit religious understanding.

With regard to the first, that is, the implications of this view for the current practice of historical criticism, we need to recall what has been said already about the notion of "significance" insofar as what makes the Old Testament, for example, potentially of significance to a reader today has to do with the present, that is, the contemporary social, historical, and political context within which the interpretation is taking place. It

---

Lanser, "(Feminist) Criticism," 72. While there is no gain saying the fact that interpreters play a major role in the development of this cultural knowledge, the author's work, however, does not depend in a strong sense upon its being interpreted, rightly or wrongly, anymore than the existence of its author depended on it for her existence. On this point, see Searle, "Literary Theory and Its Discontents," 656.

is this relationship that can well be elucidated by the interpreter and ought to be. Although this relationship is not a part of a text's meaning in the sense spoken of before, as a speech act produced by an author at a particular time, such "commentary" articulates the text's relation to us, that is, what Jorge J.E. Gracia refers to as its "relational meaning."[66] This may even make from the textual object an icon "parasitic" on the original that invites in turn its own interpretation.[67]

In fact, an *historical* treatment of a text like the Bible typically pursued under the rubric of historical-criticism might well be viewed as engaged with this kind of relational meaning of the text rather than with what we call the author's meaning. The reason is that many so-called historical interpretations are directed above all to fitting the text or work into a historical context rather than to its meaning per se. As such, the effort is directed to relating the text to other historical phenomena, the social conditions pertaining at the time of the text's production, other contemporaneous works in its cultural horizon, leading figures and institutions of the time, or influences on it and deriving from it.[68] That this kind of knowledge of the historical context and the social location of a work's production frequently provides information necessary to understanding the meaning of the text is not in question. What is in question is how much of what goes by an interpretation of the text under the guise of an *historical* approach really bears on the meaning intended by the author or authors. So the foregoing analysis cannot be taken as a blanket endorsement of the historical-critical approach in biblical studies.

The importance given to the ethical dimension of our commitment to authorial intention also highlights the fact that while interpretation is focused on the meaning of the text intended by an author, the significance of texts for readers need not be confined to this. Texts have relational meanings too and it is in this context that historical readings of texts are perhaps best seen. It would suggest that, while an emphasis on specifically historical readings of the biblical text may not be any more illegitimate in

---

[66] Jorge J.E. Gracia, "Relativism and the Interpretation of Texts," in *The Philosophy of Interpretation*, ed. Joseph Margolis and Tom Rockmore (Oxford, U.K.: Blackwell Publishers, 1999), 47–50.

[67] This moves in the direction of, even if it is not identical to, a distinction between the "work," or cultural artifact, and the "object-of-interpretation" (e.g., *Hamlet* versus Olivier's *Hamlet*), as articulated by Peter Lamarque (Lamarque, "Objects of Interpretation," 109–111).

[68] Gracia, "Relativism," 49–50.

a specific case than other types of relational approaches to its meaning, the interpretation of the biblical text, insofar as it focuses seriously on the meaning intended by the author(s), cannot be limited a priori to any one method but must be open to a full array of possible approaches.

With regard to the second issue, the implications of our view for the reading specifically of canonical Scripture, it should be obvious that with respect to a textual object as complex as the Bible, issues of meaning and value / significance will play out in some complex ways. For example, when one is talking about historical books (for example, Joshua, Judges, Samuel, and Kings) as opposed to wisdom books such as Job, the "intended meaning" of a particular text might well look like a "dead history," a situation in the past irrelevant to contemporary concerns. This is where the recontextualization that the Bible's books have undergone as a result of a process of canonization needs to be examined. To be sure, recontextualization does not establish exactly a *literary* unity for the Bible; yet it does bring these books into a new (intentional) relationship with each other where in essence they become "sources" for what are really new "works"—indeed, even a new work—within a canonical unity that creates a new (hermeneutical) genre. The implications of this reworking of the original biblical texts in an obviously largely anonymous "re-authoring" process are enormous and need to be spelled out more fully elsewhere. Clearly, "dead histories" may again become "our history" to lend a sense of direction and depth to life, just as texts hoary with antiquity find their "wisdom" modulated by—perhaps even contradicted by—newer canonical texts, creating in the process occasions for further thought and reflection. Perhaps in the manner of Proverbs where it is the thought occasioned by the interaction of individual proverbs that seems key to meaning, individual biblical books (if not individual pericopes, as we have seen throughout the history of the Bible's reception) have been brought into a potential dialogue to be realized by the reader / interpreter. There is no question of the canonization process having harmonized these individual biblical books and smoothed the differences between them. The resolution of tensions—whether through harmony, selection, complementarity, supplementarity, or synthesis—remains to be done at a non-literary, interpretive level as part of the process of *scripturing*, to use the language of Wilfred Cantwell Smith, by which people engage their world. In other words, "scripture" does not denote a noun but rather something more like a verb or even an adverb. That is not to say it names a relationship between certain texts and a community of persons, a mode of how we humans relate to the world. As people *scripture* their texts, the

effort involved is less to "understand" the texts in question than to understand and interpret the universe through their mediation, opening up a
"window" to a transcendent reality.[69]

If Turner is right to suggest that within the biblical corpus (as outside
it) different types of texts (letters, narrative works like the gospels, the
Apocalypse of John) should be distinguished and the question of "meaning" distinguished accordingly,[70] authorial meaning will function differently across the various genera. Following Umberto Eco, some texts are
more "open" to their interpreters, others more "closed." Of all writings,
letters typically are the most "closed" insofar as they intentionally function in such a way as to project the presence of their authors, address their
readers most immediately, and universally are read precisely for their
authors' intentions.[71] Beyond the speech acts they intentionally autho-
rize (the determinant meaning of the letter), there may be little "left over,"
as it were, underdetermined and of potential significance for the reader
herself to make determined. What of large narratives, rich in metaphor,
imagery, and symbolism? Beyond having authorized these aspects of the
discourse, it would seem the potential for various relational meanings
by readers, beyond the illocutionary acts performed by the writer and
any assumed pool of presuppositions, is magnified and, what's more, not
unwelcome.[72]

If we can speak of scripture as a kind of hermeneutical genre,[73] the
openness of scripture, understood in the sense above, to potential interpreters intent on understanding through scripture the world in which
they live, would be enormously large and far more "open" than these texts
would be when taken on their own outside of a canonical framework.
From a literary point of view, since there is little evidence of any biblical

---

[69] Wilfred Cantwell Smith, *What is Scripture? A Comparative Approach* (Minneapolis:
Fortress Press, 1993), 223.

[70] Turner, "Historical Criticism," 45.

[71] Ibid., 47.

[72] Ibid., 65–66. Turner refers in this context to the sorts of plot features, parallels, and
thematic "connections" almost inevitably the author would not have been conscious of
as type of *sensus plenior* and / or as perhaps "the subconscious workings of the writer's
major conscious intentions (p. 66)." His major concern is to underline that this sort of
"meaning" is not problematic for a "high view of authorial intention." I agree but I also
think this is where the notion of a "relational meaning" is helpful. Obviously, this is an
area where more work needs to be done.

[73] I owe this designation to my colleague Dr. John McCarthy, a constant dialogue
partner in reflecting upon these issues and who patiently read through this manuscript
even though he does not share my own viewpoint on authorial intention and textual
determinacy.

effort specifically to harmonize the individual biblical books (even in the Pentateuch a dominant priestly text and a dominant non-priestly text—D and J—have been combined but in such a way that they can be distinguished even today), the intent seems to be that these books may be read in their integrity but also are to be read in relation to each other. It seems clear that the intent behind the canon was to leave largely undetermined, as we said above, matters such as the weight to be given to each text, the selection(s) to be made among them, and any work of synthesis—what we might call the "canonical meaning" of a passage. That canonical meaning is the achievement of a "higher level" interpretive activity, as an aspect of people's *scripturing* the Bible and living according to it. Consequently, only in an impoverished sense, I think, ought the Bible, as Scripture, be regarded simply as an anthology of ancient Near Eastern and Hellenistic literature.

PART ONE

TRADITION AND TRANSITION:
JEWISH RESPONSES TO A HELLENISTIC WORLD

QĀRĀ' AND *ʿĀNÂ* IN THE HEBREW SCRIPTURES

Pauline A. Viviano

Richard Nelson Boyce begins his book, *The Cry to God in the Old Testament*, by stating:

> In a fundamental sense, the Old Testament is a story of a relationship—a relationship rooted in the crying out of God's people on the one hand and God's hearing of these cries on the other.[1]

The Hebrew terms underlying "cry out" to refer to Israel's appeal to God are *zāʿaq* and *ṣāʿaq*,[2] and Boyce's book is a study of how these terms are used in the Old Testament. Although I realize Boyce's intent is to introduce his own study of *zāʿaq* and *ṣāʿaq*, the statement is somewhat misleading, for "to cry out" happens *not* to be the most commonly used term to refer to one's appeal to God. Instances of *qārā'* (to call) exceed those of *zāʿaq/ṣāʿaq* (to cry out), *šiwwaʿ* (to cry for help), or any other related term studied by Boyce.[3] Indeed, *qārā'* (to call) is the more general term, the more inclusive term. If the Hebrew Scriptures can be considered a story of a relationship, it is a relationship between YHWH and Israel in which Israel feels it is quite appropriate simply to "call" upon YHWH and expect an "answer." "Calling upon" can become "crying out" or "crying out for help" in situations of extreme distress or desperation, but "calling" upon the Deity is more common and will be the subject of this study.

The frequent occurrences of the verb *qārā'* make it necessary to narrow the scope of this study, and thus we will study *qārā'* ("call") in its association with *ʿānâ* ("answer") in the context of an appeal made to or from God.[4] Although this makes the task more manageable, certain problems

---

[1] Richard Nelson Boyce, *The Cry to God in the Old Testament* (Atlanta, Ga.: Scholars Press, 1988), 1.

[2] According to G. Hasel, the "difference between *zāʿaq* and *ṣāʿaq* appears to be purely orthographic," *TDOT*, s.v. "*zāʿaq*." Boyce, *Cry to God*, 8, also considers the difference inconsequential.

[3] For statistical data, see note 5.

[4] Cf. Patrick Miller, *They Cried to the Lord: The Form and Theology of Biblical Prayer* (Minneapolis, Minn.: Fortress Press, 1994). Miller treats *qārā'* as a general term that has become a virtual technical term for prayer. He states that *qārā'* is "essentially a cry for help of some sort and thus a prayer" (44). My concern is with every appeal to God using *qārā'*

still need to be addressed when analyzing any word or combination of words found in the Bible. Critical study of the Bible results in the recognition that, in the Bible, we find a plurality of perspectives that derive from the involvement of different authors or editors working over centuries, writing and rewriting, interpreting and reinterpreting, earlier oral and written material. This, of course, makes tracing the use of any theme or word problematic. "Who wrote what" and "when was it written" become exceedingly difficult questions to answer. Should we consider how a word is used in the Pentateuch as a whole or must we separate the Yahwist work from that of the Elohist and Priestly author? How many editions of the Deuteronomistic History do we posit? How do we divide which verses go to which editions? Must we consider Isaiah as the separate First, Second, and Third Isaiah, not to mention trying to date the oracles within each section of Isaiah or, for that matter, in the book of any other prophet? If we analyze a word in the Psalms, need we date each Psalm? It is clear how complicated matters can become.

Complexity matters, however, are not the only problem and certainly not the major one. When all is said and done, little certainty exists about the date of most biblical material, even less so today than a couple of decades ago. At one time, it may have been appropriate to trace the meaning of a word from the Yahwist work to that of the Elohist and finally to that of the Priestly material in some presumed progression from primitive to developed theological reflection; today, we ask, whether the Yahwist is really post-exilic, or whether the material used by the Priestly author really is quite ancient, or whether the Elohist really is a viable source after all? Is there any indisputable evidence upon which we can secure a date for a particular edition of the Deuteronomistic History, the prophetic books, or an individual psalm? We could multiply the examples, but enough has been said to show that dating biblical material, once taken as certain, or nearly so, may no longer be assumed. In view of the lack of dating consensus, the task of chronologically tracing the development in the meaning of a word in the Bible is a more highly tendentious task at the present time than it used to be. In reality, it may have become an impossible task. Hence, let me say at the outset that this study of "call and answer" is not going to be developed chronologically. The fact that dating biblical material is difficult and uncertain, however, should not preclude the attempt; a chronological study of the use of the

---

followed by ʿānâ whether or not such an appeal, strictly speaking, may be considered a prayer.

terms, *qārāʾ* and *ʿānâ* is not absolutely necessary, for there appears to be no development or change in the way these words are used throughout the Hebrew Bible.

Another difficulty to be addressed before analyzing the use of *qārāʾ* and *ʿānâ* is the commonality of the terms under consideration. "Calling" and "answering" go on all the time in the Hebrew Scriptures. By focusing on these terms we risk belaboring the obvious or we go to the other extreme and find a concealed meaning so esoteric as to be incomprehensible. I hope to avoid both the mundane and the obscure, but if I err, it will be on the side of the mundane.

The verb, *qārāʾ*, is found 738 times in the Hebrew Bible. Of the 738 times, it frequently means "to name" someone or some place, "to summon or invite," "to proclaim," "to read," and, of course, "to call." In relation to God, "to call" is used 129 times. Other terms of address to God are *zāʿaq/ṣāʿaq* ("to cry out") which is found seventy-seven times, and the root, *šwʾ* ("to cry for help") thirty-six times.[5] *Zāʿaq/ṣāʿaq* and *šiwwaʾ* are found in parallel with *qārāʾ*, but they suggest greater emotional intensity on the part of the suppliant and perhaps indicate greater volume in one's address to God.[6] Even though *qārāʾ* may be modified by "in distress" or "in a loud voice" suggesting emotional intensity or increased volume, most frequently the suppliant simply "calls" upon God. In response to "calling" upon God, God "saves," "delivers," "heals," "rescues," or "answers." Of these terms, my concern is "answer." The root *ʿānâ* ("to answer") is found 316 times[7] and means "to reply, respond or answer," yet only a small percentage of these follow "call," "cry out," or "cry out for help."

Although "call" is found in virtually every book of the Hebrew Scriptures, "call" in conjunction with "answer" in the same verse or in close proximity and in relationship to an appeal to God or from God is found most frequently in 1 Kings 18, the Psalms, the prophetic literature, and the book of Job. Therefore, these passages will be the focus of this essay. Before considering them, let us, however, note for the sake of completeness that the terms are also found in 1 Sm 28:15, 1 Chr 21:26, 28; Prv 1:28,

---

[5] That the verb, *qārāʾ*, occurs 738 times in the Old Testament is based on F.L. Hossfeld and E.-M. Kindl in *TDOT*, s.v. "*qārāʾ*." Of these times, by my count, "*qārāʾ*" specifically addressed to God is found 129 times. According to Hasel in *TDOT*, s.v. "*zāʿaq*," *zāʿaq* and *ṣāʿaq* are used 77 times as an invocation to God/gods; the root *swʿ* is found only thirty-six times (Cf. J. Hausmann in *TDOT*, s.v. "*swʿ*."

[6] Boyce, *Cry to God*, 21.

[7] See F.J. Stendebach in *TDOT*, s.v. "*ʿānâ*."

and 21:13. In the Samuel text, Saul calls to Samuel because YHWH has
not answered him. In 1 Chr 21:26, 28, David calls and YHWH answers.
In Prv 1:28, Wisdom will not answer those who call upon her in times
of distress if they had previously refused the call of Wisdom (1:24), and
in 21:13 God will not answer those who call upon him if they have not
responded to the cry of the poor.

I Kings 18

The significance of "call and answer" in the story of the contest between
Elijah and the prophets of Baal on Mount Carmel is seen not only in
the frequency of the terms[8] but also in that these terms give expression
to the underlying theme of the passage.[9] Elijah, the prophets of Baal
and Asherah, and the people of Israel assemble on Mount Carmel where
Elijah sets before the people the following challenge: "If YHWH is God,
follow him; but if Baal, then follow him" (18:21). The people do not
answer, but Elijah proceeds to set out the terms of a contest to determine
whether Baal or YHWH is God. God will be the one who answers the call
of the prophet(s): "... you call upon the name of your god, and I will call
upon the name of YHWH; the god who answers by fire is indeed God"
(18:23). The prophets of Baal spend considerable time calling upon their
god, but there is no answer. Elijah mocks them with "Call louder!" which
they do, accompanied by other actions to contact the deity. This shouting
and increased activity of the prophets of Baal only serve to underscore
dramatically the lack of an answer from their god. In sharp contrast to the
extended hours of calling on the part of the prophets of Baal, when Elijah's
turn comes, he utters but a short prayer and immediately "the fire of
YHWH fell" (18:30–38). The prophet's call upon YHWH is answered at
once and dramatically. YHWH shows himself to be a God who answers.
The people, silent at the beginning of the story, (18:21) are answered, and
they now affirm that "YHWH is indeed God" (18:29). This text shows
clearly what is needed to make contact with Israel's God. It is not frenetic
activity accompanying hours of intense prayer. An appeal to God is all
that is needed. If YHWH is "called" upon, he will "answer."

---

[8] In 1 Kings 18 *qārā'* is found six times (vv. 24 [2], 25, 26, 27, 28) and *'ānâ* seven times
(vv. 21, 24 [2], 26, 29, 37 [2]).

[9] Cf. Jerome T. Walsh, *1 Kings*, Berit Olam: Studies in Hebrew Narrative and Poetry
(Collegeville, Minn.: Liturgical Press, 1996), 254.

Psalms

The psalms are the most obvious place for "call" and "answer," and the two terms are found sixteen times in the same verse or close proximity (Pss 3:5; 4:2; 17:6; 20:10; 22:3; 27:7; 81:8; 86:7; 91:15; 99:6; 102:3; 118:5; 119:145; 120:1; 138:3; Jon 2:3).[10] In these psalms, the Psalmist testifies that his "call" has been "answered" (81:8; 99:6;[11] 118:5; 138:3; Jon 2:3) or expresses confidence that God will "answer" his "call" (3:5; 17:6; 91:5); most often the Psalmist turns to God hoping that God will "answer" his "call" (4:2; 17:6; 20:10; 27:7; 86:7; 102:3; 119:145; 120:1). The Psalmist also prays from the certainty that if "called" upon, YHWH will "answer." For example, "I call upon you for (*kî*) you will answer me, O God" (Ps 17:6). Or again, "In the day of my trouble I call on you, for (*kî*) you will answer me" (Ps 86:7). The use of *kî* testifies to the causal relationship between "call" and "answer." The assurance of an "answer" is given by YHWH himself in Ps 91. "When they [that is, those who 'love God' and 'know his name'] call to me, I will answer them" (v. 15). The repeated use of "call" and "answer" in the Psalms indicates it was understood that YHWH was a God his people could "call" upon with the realistic expectation that YHWH would hear and "answer" them.

Prophetic Literature

In the prophetic material, the combination of "call and answer" is found one time in Second Isaiah (50:2) and four times in Third Isaiah (58:9; 65:12, 24; 66:4). In Jeremiah, "call and answer" pairs are found four times, twice in the Temple Sermon (7:13, 27), a prose text; the other two times are also in prose texts (33:3; 35:17). The only other instance of "call and answer" in a prophetic text is Zechariah 13:9. There are, thus, ten instances in total. Interestingly, in six instances, the call receives no answer; of these, in five, it is YHWH who calls and the people who do not answer (Is 50:2; 65:12; 66:4; Jer 7:13; 35:17; the exception is Jer 7:27[12])! This suggests that "call" is not the exclusive act of the people, nor

---

[10] All verse numbers are from the Hebrew Bible, not from an English translation. Jon 2:3 in included because the terms, *qārāʾ* and *ʿānâ*, are found in the psalm recited by Jonah.

[11] In Ps 91:5, however, it is not the psalmist, but Moses, Aaron, and Samuel who are said to have called upon God and he answered them.

[12] In Jer 7:27, it is Jeremiah who is to "call," but the people will not "answer" him. As the prophet speaks on behalf of God Jeremiah's "calling" to them should be considered

is "answer" the exclusive act of God. The people can also be called by God, and they are expected to "answer" the "call" of God.

The other four instances of "call and answer" are in passages dominated by hope (Jer 33:3; Zec 13:9; Is 58:9; 65:24). The people will "call" upon YHWH and YHWH will readily "answer" them. Indeed, in Is 65:24, YHWH will "answer" even before they "call!" Overall, the people will be punished for their failure to respond to YHWH's call, but, after the time of punishment, the relationship between YHWH and Israel will be restored: Israel will call upon YHWH, and YHWH will answer. It is of interest to mention that in the Zechariah text (13:9), the very next sentence (after "they will call on my name and I will answer them") reads "I will say, 'They are my people'; and they will say 'YHWH is our God.'" This is of significance in one more passage we shall consider, Hos 2:16–25 [NRSV: Hos 2:14–23].

Before leaving the prophetic material, it is important to mention a text in Hosea, in which the term "answer" without "call" figures prominently and significantly. Hosea 2, commonly understood to be patterned on formal divorce proceedings, turns from indictment and sentence to hope in 2:16–17, "Therefore I will now allure her, and bring her into the wilderness, and speak tenderly to her ... There she shall answer me as in the days of her youth ..." Further, in 2:23–24, "On that day I will answer, says YHWH, I will answer the heavens and they shall answer the earth; and the earth shall answer the grain, the wine, and the oil, and they shall answer Jezreel; and I will sow him for myself in the land." Even though the Hosea text does not use "call," there is justification for considering the text. In both Hos 2:16 and Is 40:2, the expression "speak tenderly" (lit. "speak upon the heart") is used; in the Isaian text, it is used in synonymous parallelism with the word "call" ("Speak tenderly to Jerusalem and call to her ..."). In addition, the passage ends with the same line as the passage from Zechariah, "and I will say ... you are my people, and he shall say, you are my God" (Zec 13:9; Hos 2:25).

The sexual overtones of "answer"[13] in the text from Hosea are hard to ignore. YHWH "will allure" Israel, and Israel will "answer." The people

---

God's "calling" to them; their refusal to "answer" the prophet can be seen as a refusal to "answer" God.

[13] Although both its root and meaning are disputed (cf. F.J. Stendebach in *TDOT*, s.v. "'ānâ'"), the root of 'ōnâ is given as 'nh (see *BDB*, s.v. "'nh"), the same root as "answer" and its meaning is given as "cohabitation, that is, marriage rights" (see Ex 21:10). In the Song of Songs 5:6 "call and not answer" are in parallel to "seek and not find" after a rather passionate "dream" of the lover longing for intimate union with her beloved.

will return to that moment in the wilderness before sin entered the picture; they will return to that "honeymoon" period in the wilderness following the Exodus, the time before Israel was unfaithful to its God. The sexual innuendo is even more obvious in the remainder of the passage. The answering of God to the heavens and the heavens answering the earth results in the fertility of the land (Hos 2:23–24). Certainly, I do not want to generalize that sexual overtones are present whenever "answer" is used, but I do want to underscore that "call and answer" suggest a relationship of closeness between YHWH and Israel, a kind of familiarity in which an answer from the one called upon is expected. Israel need only call and YHWH will answer; and conversely Israel is expected to answer when YHWH calls. Calling and answering between the divine and the human is possible because there exists a relationship, "I have called you by name, you are mine" (Is 43:1).

The most intriguing use of "call and answer" is found in the book of Job. The combination is found six times (5:1; 9:16; 12:4; 13:22; 14:15; 19:16), but we will not consider 19:16 for here Job is calling to his servant, not to God. Of the remaining five verses, the pair occurs four times in Job's speeches. The one exception, Jb 5:1, is a speech of Eliphaz, in which he challenges Job, "Call now; is there anyone who will answer you? To which of the holy ones will you turn?" Presumably there is no one to answer. Except for Eliphaz' rhetorical question to Job in 5:1, Job's friends never speak of calling upon God; only Job does. Job's friends do not even speak of crying out (ṣāʿaq) or crying for help (šiwwaʿ) to God, but Job speaks of both (ṣāʿaq 19:7; šiwwa 30:20). It is important to reiterate that only Job speaks of "calling" upon God from whom he expects an "answer."

In 9:16 Job is overwhelmed by the thought of confronting God, afraid he will be speechless in the face of the Almighty: "How can I answer him" (9:14) and again "... though innocent I cannot answer him" (9:15). He hopes God will answer his call, but even so he is not convinced God will listen to him, "If I called him and he answered me, I do not believe he would listen to my voice" (9:16). In earlier times, Job had called upon God and God had answered (12:4); if only the hand of God would be removed, then God would call and Job would answer (13:22). The "hand of God" is parallel with "dread" (13:21) suggesting the oppressive nature of God's hand upon him. Job wants the oppression to stop so that the relationship can return to the give and take of "call and answer" that once character-ized it. Later in the same speech Job longs for God to hide him until a better time then, "You would call and I would answer you" (14:15). Job wants the return of a relationship in which call and answer are a reality.

As noted above, Job's three friends never use "call" or "cry out." They hold fast to retributive justice and insist that Job must be at fault or he would not be suffering at the hand of God. In a world ruled by retributive justice, what need is there to call upon God? Reward and punishment function automatically: the good are rewarded, the wicked punished; and appeals to the deity are unnecessary. Elihu never uses the term, "*qārā*," but in his speeches we find the use of *zāʾaq* and *šiwwaʿ*. Elihu says that the wicked who cry out are not heard (*šāʾaq* 35:9; *šiwwaʿ* 35:12); Job's cry (*šûaʿ*) alone will not save him (36:19), he must also stay away from iniquity. For Elihu, God turns away from the cries of the wicked. If Job's cries are not heard, it must be because he is one of the wicked.

Apart from these instances of "crying out" in the Elihu speeches, only Job speaks in terms of a relationship wherein communication with the divine can have meaning. Only Job conceives of a relationship in which "call" and "answer" are possibilities. Echoing through Job's speeches is the longing for a response from God and in his final speech he challenges God to "answer" him (31:35). YHWH "answers" Job from the whirlwind, but how is what YHWH says an answer? The problems of interpretation of the book of Job, especially the interpretation of the YHWH speeches, are numerous and I do not want to descend into that maelstrom of debate. An intriguing interpretation, however, was set forth by John Curtis in "On Job's Response to YHWH."[14] Curtis argues the YHWH speeches are an ironic caricature of the God who is too big to care about the petty affairs of humanity. The gauntlet that God throws before Job is not a response, but an evasion of Job's concerns. With all the great works of creation to occupy his thoughts, what time does God have for the complaints of a mere human being? It is significant that YHWH comes to Job, but the terms of the answer are no answer. Note the contrast: YHWH does not say, "I have heard your call and now I answer;" rather he says, "I will question (*šʾl*) you, you declare (*ydʿ*) to me." Job speaks from a position consistent with the psalms, 1 Kings 18, and the prophetic texts, namely, that YHWH is a God who when called upon will answer, but this is precisely what Job is denied when YHWH answers. YHWH's so-called answer contains questions about creation, all irrelevant to Job's dilemma,

---

[14] John Curtis, "On Job's Response to YHWH," *JBL* 98, 4 (1979): 497–511. For some recent studies that take a different approach, see William P. Brown, *Character in Crisis: A Fresh Approach to the Wisdom Literature of the Old Testament* (Grand Rapids: Mich.: Eerdmans, 1996), 89–111; and Kathryn Schifferdecker, *Out of the Whirlwood: Creation Theology in the Book of Job*, Harvard Theological Studies 61 (Cambridge, Mass.: Harvard University Press, 2008).

and a description of Behemoth and Leviathan, the purpose of which has yet to be shown convincingly. One sees behind these speeches a God closer to the friend's description of God than to the God who will answer the call of his creature. In effect, the point of the book would be that this God, exalted and supreme, who is removed from intimate involvement with his people, a God who is remote, unfeeling, and unjust, is not Israel's God. Rather Israel's God enters into relationship with his people; they can call upon him and he will answer. The use of "call and answer" in the book of Job would support Curtis' view.

To "call and answer" are terms that give expression to the reality of communication, not only between humans, but between humans and the divine. The author of 1 Kings 18, the psalmists, the prophets, and the author of Job accept the possibility of communication with the divine; they not only long for it to become a reality, but also expect it to become so. The frequency and commonality of these words should not obscure the wonder to which they give expression. To paraphrase Boyce's statement with which I opened this essay:

> In a fundamental sense, the Old Testament is a story of a relationship—
> a relationship rooted in the recognition that God's people need only call
> upon God and God will answer.

THE DEAD SEA SCROLLS AND
JEWISH-CHRISTIAN DIALOGUE

EILEEN SCHULLER

It is now over sixty years since those early months of 1947 when a Bedouin boy threw a stone into a cave on the northwest shore of the Dead Sea and struck clay jars stuffed with dirty, smelly rolled up scrolls and decaying bits of ancient leather.[1] Given the political realities of life in Jerusalem and Bethlehem in wartime conditions, coupled with a long-standing skepticism about whether any written materials on leather or papyrus could really survive from Greco-Roman era, conditions were such that even those most closely involved did not quickly grasp the real significance of the find. But already by March 1948, William F. Albright, the world-renowned biblical scholar and epigraphist at John Hopkins University had seen some of the first photographs and was ready to pronounce these seven scrolls "the greatest manuscript discovery of modern times! ... an absolutely incredible find!"[2] The publication of a scholarly edition of all of these materials, the remains of approximately nine hundred manuscripts recovered from eleven caves, proved to be a long and complicated process; the first editions began to appear in the mid 1950s,[3] and the last volume of the *Discoveries in the Judaean Desert* series was not completed until early in 2009.[4]

---

[1] For the earliest accounts of the discoveries and an analysis of some of the problems and discrepancies in the oral stories, see the discussion of Weston W. Fields, *The Dead Sea Scrolls: A Full History* (Leiden-Boston: Brill, 2009), 24–25, 520–521.

[2] Letter of W.F. Albright, received by John Trever in Jerusalem on March 15, 1948; quoted in Fields, *The Dead Sea Scrolls*, 76.

[3] Eleazar L. Sukenik, *The Dead Sea Scrolls of the Hebrew University* (Jerusalem: Magnes Press, 1955 [Hebrew edition, 1954]); D. Barthélemy and J.T. Milik, *Qumran Cave I* (Discoveries in the Judaean Desert I; Oxford: Clarendon Press, 1955).

[4] Émile Puech, *Qumrân Grotte 4: XXVII, Textes Araméens Deuxième Partie 4Q550–4Q575a, 4Q580–4Q587* (Discoveries in the Judaean Desert XXXVII; Oxford: Clarendon Press, 2009). Another volume of DJD appearing in 2009 presented a new reconstruction of the physical shape of a manuscript first published by Sukenik in 1954 (see note 3): Hartmut Stegemann with Eileen Schuller, *Qumran Cave I.III: 1QHodayot^a with Incorporation of 1QHodayot^b and 4QHodayot^{a-f}* (Discoveries in the Judaean Desert XL; Oxford: Clarendon Press, 2009).

The occasion of the fiftieth (1997) and sixtieth (2007) anniversaries of
the discovery of the scrolls called forth numerous academic conferences
and survey volumes that attempted to articulate and synthesize the wide
ranging importance and influence of this discovery for the study of the
Hebrew Bible, Second Temple Judaism, New Testament, Apocrypha and
Pseudepigrapha, Septuagint, Hebrew and Aramaic linguistics, and still
more related fields of scholarship.[5] But it seems to me that the discovery
of the Dead Sea Scrolls has also played a role, both directly and indirectly,
in the Jewish-Christian dialogue as it has developed in the post-World
War II era. Influences and relationships of this type are less easy to isolate
and to document, and surprisingly little has been written assessing the
influence of the scrolls from this perspective.[6] The question that I want
to take up is quite specific: has the discovery of the Dead Sea Scrolls been
important for how Jews and Christians understand themselves and relate
to each other? If so, how, and to what extent?

When we turn to a standard reference work like the *Lexikon der
jüdisch-christlichen Begegnung*, we find only a rather brief entry on the
scrolls, their content and history, and the author, Clemens Thoma, concludes with the evaluation: "für den Dialog zwischen Christen und Juden
ist Qumran von untergeordneter Bedeutung."[7] The more recent *A Dictionary of Jewish-Christian Relations* from the Cambridge Centre for the
Study of Jewish-Christian Relations likewise commissioned only a very
short article on the Dead Sea Scrolls and did not think it necessary to
turn to a scholar who had worked directly and primarily on the Qum-

---

[5] Some of the major anniversary and conference volumes would include: Peter F. Flint
and James C. VanderKam, eds., *The Dead Sea Scrolls after Fifty Years: A Comprehensive Assessment*, 2 Vols. (Leiden: Brill, 1998); Lawrence H. Schiffman, Emanuel Tov,
James C. VanderKam, eds., *The Dead Sea Scrolls: Fifty Years After their Discovery: Proceedings of the Jerusalem Congress, July 20–25, 1997* (Jerusalem: Israel Exploration Society and
the Shrine of the Book, Israel Museum, 2000); Robert A. Kugler and Eileen M. Schuller,
eds., *The Dead Sea Scrolls at Fifty: Proceedings of the 1997 Society of Biblical Literature
Qumran Section Meetings* (Atlanta: Scholars Press, 1999); Adolfo Roitman, Lawrence
H. Schiffman, Shani Tzoref, eds., *The Dead Sea Scrolls and Contemporary Culture: Proceedings of the International Conference held at the Israel Museum (July 6–8, 2008)*, (Leiden: Brill, forthcoming).

[6] The stimulus for my thinking about the question in these terms came from a
conference held at the Pontifical Gregorian University, Rome, 2005, to celebrate the
40th anniversary of the promulgation of *Nostrae Aetate*, the document from the Second
Vatican Council that treated, albeit very briefly, relations with the Jews and laid the
foundation for subsequent theological reflection for both Roman Catholics and many
other Christian churches.

[7] Clemens Thoma, *Lexikon der Jüdisch-Christlichen Begegnung* (Freiburg: Herder,
1989), 322–323.

ran materials.[8] On the basis of a random survey (not complete of course, but fairly extensive) of books and collections of essays about Jewish-Christian relations, I think it is certainly fair to say that a treatment of the scrolls and their importance is not a standard or anticipated topic in such volumes; the essay by Lawrence Schiffman, "Judaism and Early Christianity in Light of the Dead Sea Scrolls," in a 1994 collection stands out precisely because it is the exception.[9] Occasionally I found the testimony of an individual scholar or an account of a personal experience that speaks explicitly about what the Dead Sea Scrolls have meant for that person's involvement in dialogue. For instance, one of the great leaders in the Jewish-Christian dialogue, the Swedish bishop Krister Stendhal, credits "my life-long quest for a better way to understand Jewish-Christian interplay" to a seminar that he took on the scrolls with André Dupont-Sommer in 1951.[10] But for the most part, it is my impression that scholarship on the Dead Sea Scrolls, on the one hand, and the Jewish-Christian dialogue, on the other, have functioned as quite separate "worlds," and although I am proposing that there are significant points of contact, the dynamics of the relationship are not simple nor easy to trace.

Nevertheless, there is often an overall, though unspecified, assumption that the discovery of the scrolls was somehow important and "good for" Jewish-Christian relations. William F. Albright has been credited with having made the statement: "had the Dead Sea Scrolls been found but a few years earlier the Holocaust could have been averted." Like any apocryphal statement, this one is virtually impossible to trace (Lawrence Schiffman says that he heard it from Samuel Iwry, a Holocaust survivor and student of Albright[11]). Schiffman, who frequently quotes this statement in newspaper articles, goes on to say:

> Behind this exaggeration, however, was a prescient observation. By showing us the extent to which Christianity is based on Jewish roots, the scrolls call for greater understanding between Jews and Christians in the modern world ... We do have a wonderful new treasure, one which can illuminate

---

[8] Edward Kessler and Neil Wenborn, eds., *A Dictionary of Jewish-Christian Relations* (Cambridge: Cambridge University Press, 2005), 122.

[9] Lawrence H. Schiffman, "Judaism and Early Christianity in Light of the Dead Sea Scrolls," in *Jewish-Christian Encounters over the Centuries: Symbiosis, Prejudice, Holocaust, Dialogue*, ed. M. Perry and F.M. Schweitzer (New York: Peter Lang, 1994), 27–44.

[10] Krister Stendahl, "Qumran and Supersessionism—And the Road Not Taken," *Princeton Seminary Bulletin* 19 (1998): 134–142.

[11] Personal note from Lawrence Schiffman, August 2005.

the history of Judaism and the background of Christianity, and one which, when studied properly, has the power to help us to heal the wounds of two millennia.[12]

But not everything has been positive; much has happened with the scrolls that has reflected and at times intensified tension between Jews and Christians on both the individual and the collective level. We need only recall the long span of twenty-years (1948–1967) when Jewish and Christian scholars worked in isolation from each other on different sides of the Mandelbaum Gate in Jerusalem. Israeli scholars, such as Eliezer Sukenik, Yigael Yadin and Sh. Talmon had access only to the scrolls owned by Hebrew University and the State of Israel (those from Cave one purchased in November–December 1947: *The War Scroll, Hodayot,* Isaiah[b], and those purchased from Archbishop Anathasius Samuel in the summer of 1954, *Rule of the Community, Pesher Habakkuk,* Isaiah[a], and *Genesis Apocryphon*); the International Team formed by the Jordanian Department of Antiquities and the Palestine Archaeological Museum of young scholars from England, France, Germany, Poland, United States—all Christians—had access at the École Biblique and the Rockefeller/Palestine Archaeological Museum to the material that poured in from Caves four to eleven.[13]

The situation changed—though very slowly—after the 1967 war, when the Palestine Archaeological Museum and the scrolls that were physically housed there came directly under the Israel Antiquities Authority. Jewish scholars became actively and officially involved in the work of publication, beginning with Emanuel Tov, Elisha Qimron, and Devorah Dimant in the early 1980s. But then came the traumatic days in the fall of 1990 when charges of anti-semitism played a significant part in the ter-

---

[12] Lawrence H. Schiffman "The Scrolls and the Search for the Secret Gospel," *Jewish World* (April 16–23, 1993), 18–19.

[13] To get some feeling for the realities and complexities of this situation, the personal and autobiographical reflections of some of the key players from this era remain a fascinating source of information; e.g., John Trever, *The Untold Story of Qumran* (Westwood, N.J.: F.H. Revell, 1965), reprinted as *The Dead Sea Scrolls: A Personal Account,* (Grand Rapids, MI: Eerdmans, 1977); Yigael Yadin, *The Message of the Scrolls* (New York: Simon and Shuster, 1957); Mar Athanasius Y. Samuel, *The Treasure of Qumran, My Story of the Dead Sea Scrolls* (Philadelphia: Westminster Press, 1966). Other non-autobiographical works indicate how individual scrolls scholars were involved in and identified with the religious and political divisions, e.g., Millar Burrows, *Palestine is Our Business* (Philadelphia: Westminster Press, 1949). Also the biography of John Allegro by his daughter, Judith Anne Brown, *John Marco Allegro: The Maverick of the Dead Sea Scrolls* (Grand Rapids, MI: Eerdmans, 2005).

mination of John Strugnell as the editor-in-chief of the DJD publication project. Though serious mental and physical illness was involved, and a public letter of clarification and support was signed by over a dozen Jewish students and scholars who had worked and studied with John Strugnell over the years,[14] the tensions and suspicions were real, traumatic, and lingering, on both the personal and academic level for anyone involved in any way. Since that time, the "hard questions" have come to be formulated in different ways. The provocative title that Lawrence Schiffman gave to his 1994 book, *Reclaiming the Scrolls*, expresses concisely and explicitly the claim that there had been "a Christianized interpretation of the scrolls" by "the first generation of scrolls scholars, primarily Christians interested in either the Hebrew Bible or the New Testament, [who] did not understand the scrolls for what they really were;" only now, as Jewish scholars became actively involved on every level, could the scrolls be "reclaimed" to show their "Jewish character."[15] Most recently, some of the current controversy in the public milieu has shifted to the question of "who owns the scrolls?", that is, to the claims of both the Palestinian Authority and the government of Jordan for legal ownership of the actual materials.[16] Over the years, the "touch points" surrounding the scrolls often have seemed to encapsulate, in microcosm, both the very positive advances and the underlying, even unstated, tensions in Jewish-Christian relations both theologically and politically.

For the purposes of this paper, I will look at three areas that are distinct, though often overlapping. I want to suggest that in each we can see different ways in which the scrolls have had an impact on Jewish-Christian relations: (1) on the academic study of early Judaism and early Christianity; (2) on statements from Jewish-Christian dialogue, and (3) on personal relationships.

---

[14] The letter, entitled "No Evidence of Anti-Judaism in Strugnell's Work," was published in the March / April 1991 issue of *Biblical Archaeological Review* 17 / 2 (1991): 15.

[15] Lawrence H. Schiffman, *Reclaiming the Dead Sea Scrolls: The History of Judaism, the Background of Christianity, the Lost Library of Qumran* (New York: Doubleday, 1994), xxiii. Also his article, "Confessionalism and the Study of the Dead Sea Scrolls," *Forum of the World Union of Jewish Studies* 31 (1991) 3–14.

[16] On January 11, 2009, Jordan filed a complaint with UNESCO after Canada refused to seize the Dead Sea Scrolls that were on display at the Royal Ontario Museum in Toronto and hand them over to the Jordanians who are claiming ownership. Earlier in the year that Palestinian Prime Minster Salam Fayyad had likewise made an official request to the Canadian government to seize the scrolls and hand them over to the Palestinian Authority.

1. *The Academic Study of Early Judaism and Early Christianity*

It is in the academic study of both early Judaism and early Christianity that the impact of that the discovery of the scrolls is most clearly and explicitly recognized. I could pick quotations from numerous scholars who would attest to how the scrolls have been a catalyst for a major revolution in the study of Second Temple Judaism and in the study of the interrelationship of Christianity and Judaism in the century which was so formative for both. In this example from the introduction to a collection of essays that issued from a joint conference between Princeton and Oxford Universities, the editors wrote in the Preface:

> Postwar developments paved the way for the new rapproachment between Christian scholars and Jewish scholars in recent years. In this a contributing factor was the publication of the Dead Sea Scrolls which helped to open a space in which much needed interdisciplinary dialogue could flourish. In the library of the Qumran community experts in Second Temple Judaism, early Christianity and Rabbinics alike have found sources that shed new light on key issues and debates in their respective fields. Furthermore, these newly unearthed sources have exposed the dazzling diversity of Second Temple Judaism and the profound continuities that connect it with *both* rabbinic Judaism *and* early Christianity ... both Jewish and Christian scholars now speak of "Judaisms" or a "multiform Judaism" of which the Jesus movement was a part and from which Christianity only gradually took form.[17]

All of the elements of this statement (1) that Judaism in the Second Temple period was a vital, rich, diverse and complex reality, (2) that Jesus and the early Christian community are to be situated firmly within the Judaism of the time and cannot be understood apart from that environment, (3) that the Dead Sea Scrolls have played a singular and unique role in bringing about this way of thinking both by new information that they supplied and, more indirectly, because they "helped to open up a space" to rethink much of what we once thought about Judaism and the beginnings of Christianity—all these ideas are very much accepted today, and this paper is not the place to rehearse the detailed argumentation, nor hopefully is it necessary in 2010 to continue to make the case.

---

[17] Annette Yoshiko Reed and Adam H. Becker, eds., "Introduction: Traditional Models and new Directions," in *The Ways that Never Parted: Jews and Christians in Late Antiquity and the Early Middle Ages* (Tübingen: Mohr Siebeck, 2003), 14–15.

There is, of course, always the danger of falling into a simplistic pan-Qumranica.[18] I do not want to claim it was *only* the Dead Sea Scrolls that brought about the revolution in how we think about Second Temple Judaism and the beginnings of Christianity. In the last half century, there has been renewed interest and major advances in the study of all of the Apocrypha and Pseudepigrapha, resulting in a rash of new textual editions and commentaries,[19] as well as a revival of Septuagint and Targum studies—though I think it could be shown that much of the impetus for these developments was, in fact, triggered by the discovery of the scrolls. Furthermore, I do not mean to downplay in any way the impact that the Shoah has had on the reading and study of the Bible, both in the church and in the academic world. As Cardinal Ratzinger, now Pope Benedict XVI, wrote in his Forward to the 2002 document of the Pontifical Biblical Commission, *The Jewish People and Their Sacred Scriptures in the Christian Bible*, "the shock of the Shoah has put the whole question [of the Scriptures] under a new light."[20]

As we attempt to think more carefully about *how* the scrolls have exercised their influence, the chronology of their publication is relevant. It is certainly true that a major portion of the material from the Qumran caves has been published only relatively recently (after the appointment of Emanuel Tov as editor-in-chief in 1990), more than thirty volumes of *Discoveries in the Judaean Desert* in the past twenty years, versus only eight volumes in the span from 1955–1990. Even specialists in the scrolls (much less scholars in New Testament studies, textual criticism and other related areas) are still trying to learn and absorb all these new texts (many of them extremely fragmentary and difficult to interpret) and integrate them into an overall interpretative framework. Yet it is important to remind ourselves that, in a certain sense, the scrolls made their

---

[18] For cautionary warnings, from a somewhat different perspective, about the real limitations on what we can expect that the Dead Sea Scrolls can contribute, see Robert Alter, "How Important are the Dead Sea Scrolls?" *Commentary* 93 (1992), 34–41; James Kugel, "What the Dead Sea Scrolls Do Not Tell." *Commentary*, 99 (1998) 49–52.

[19] For example, the new commentary series initiated in 2002 of a projected fifty-eight volumes, *Commentaries on Early Jewish Literature*, ed. L. Stuckenbruck, P.W. van der Horst, H. Lichtenberger, D. Mendels, J. Mueller (Walter de Gruyter Press); also the inclusion of books of the Pseudepigrapha in the prestigious Hermeneia Series: *Fourth Ezra* by Michael Stone (1990), *I Enoch* by George W. Nickelsburg (2001).

[20] The Pontifical Biblical Commission, *The Jewish People and Their Sacred Scriptures in the Christian Bible* (2002). For a recent discussion from an academic perspective, see Marvin Sweeney, *Reading the Hebrew Bible After the Shoah: Engaging Holocaust Theology* (Minneapolis: Fortress Press, 2008) and the bibliography included there.

real impact already in the late 1950s and 1960s. Cave 1 contained the best preserved of the scrolls (with linen wrappings and in clay jars) and included the major sectarian works (*The Rule of the Community, the War Scroll, Pesher Habakkuk, The Thanksgiving Scroll*) and the most complete biblical manuscript (1QIsaᵃ). All these were available (photos and transcription) by 1956; the major outline of a framework for interpretation was worked out and published in readily accessible handbooks in the late 1950s and early 1960s;[21] collections of specialized studies, especially on the scrolls and the New Testament, were compiled.[22] Thus, for example, when Marcel Simon undertook to revise his influential 1948 book *Versus Israel* about the relationship between the two religions, he was asked to comment on what had happened in the past fifteen years that would require him to modify or rethink his work; in 1963 he could already say: "the discovery of the Dead Sea Scrolls has been of prime importance."[23] That is, although it is entirely correct to emphasis the importance of the "release" of the scrolls in 1990 and the availability only quite recently of the full corpus, the fundamental impact of the core of the discovery was made almost half a century ago.

For a period of time it seemed, both in academic circles and on a popular level, that the scrolls were of more importance for the study of early Christianity than for the study of early Judaism. It was not until 1975 that the *Journal of Jewish Studies*, for instance, published the first survey article on "The Impact of the Dead Sea Scrolls on Jewish Studies."[24] This slant-toward-Christianity was the case at some levels, ironically, even in Israel where much of the on-the-street-familiarity with the scrolls in the early years came via both the writings of David Flusser and his popular talks on Israel Army Radio in the 1960s and 1970s—and Flusser presented the scrolls largely as pre-Christian documents.[25]

---

[21] For example, in English, Géza Vermes, *Discovery in the Judaean Desert* (New York: Desclee Co., 1956); Frank Moore Cross, *The Ancient Library of Qumran and Modern Biblical Studies* (Garden City, NY: Doubleday, 1958); Josef T. Milik, *Ten Years of Discovery in the Wilderness of Judea*, trans. J. Strugnell (London: SCM Press, 1959).

[22] Krister Stendal, ed., *The Scrolls and the New Testament* (New York: Harper, 1957); Pierre Benoit and Jerome Murphy O'Connor, eds., *Paul and Qumran: Studies in New Testament Exegesis* (London: G. Chapman, 1968).

[23] Marcel Simon, *Versus Israel: A Study of the Relationship between Jews and Christians in the Roman Empire, 135–425*, Littman Library of Jewish Civilization (Oxford: Oxford University Press, 1986), 386–387.

[24] Geza Vermes, "The "The Impact of the Dead Sea Scrolls on Jewish Studies in the Last Twenty-Five Years,"" *Journal of Jewish Studies* 26 (1975): 1–14.

[25] For a description of the particular shape of Israeli scholarship and popular percep-

Thus in the 1950s and 1960s the agenda was set by Christian scholars who focused attention on passages that discussed themes formulated in the theological language of messianism, eschatology, grace, salvation, justification; documents in which legal regulations predominated were set aside as either less interesting or too difficult. On the Jewish side, in some circles any works outside of the rabbinic corpus were considered as *sefarim chitzonim*, and the Judaism they represented evaluated as "some digression which turned into a cul-de-sac" and ultimately a "dead end."[26] It was only post-1990 when 4QMMT, the multiple copies of the Damascus Document, and the mass of very damaged legal fragments were published that the importance of the scrolls for Jewish Studies could be fully recognized and explored.

2. *Statements from the Jewish-Christian Dialogue*

Now let us turn from the study of early Judaism and early Christianity in the academy to look at documents that arose specifically within the framework of Jewish-Christian dialogue. Chronologically, the scrolls were discovered just at the time that the post-war Jewish-Christian dialogue was taking its first and tentative steps, including the formulation of public statements (e.g., the "Ten Points" from the Seelisburg Conference in 1947). But considerable time passes until we find much explicit reference in the various dialogue statements to the scrolls or their significance.[27] The document of the Second Vatican Council in 1965,

---

tions, see Emanuel Tov, "Israeli Scholarship on the Texts from the Judaean Desert," in *The Dead Sea Scrolls at Fifty: Proceedings of the 1997 Society of Biblical Literature Qumran Section Meetings*, ed. Robert A. Kugler and Eileen M. Schuller, Early Judaism and Its Literature (Atlanta, Ga.: Scholars Press, 1999), 123–127. There have been surprisingly few resources on the Dead Sea Scrolls geared to the general public available in Modern Hebrew. In 2009, the Yad Ben-Zvi Institute in Jerusalem published a two-volume collection of essays in Hebrew, *The Qumran Scrolls and their World*, edited by M. Kister, but this also is more scholarly than popular in approach.

[26] For this language, see Samuel Sandmel, *The First Christian Century in Judaism and Christianity: Certainties and Uncertainties* (New York: Oxford University Press, 1969), 85. For comments on the more traditional Jewish reaction to the scrolls, see Joseph Baumgarten's review of *Reclaiming the Dead Sea Scrolls: The History of Judaism, the Background of Christianity, the Lost Library of Qumran*, by Lawrence Schiffman, in *Jewish Action* (Fall 5756 / 1995): 92–93, 96.

[27] I have chosen examples primarily from Roman Catholic documents. I have not examined all of the statements from Protestant Churches and confessional bodies, although a preliminary survey leads me to suspect that the overall trajectory is much the

Nostra Aetate, Declaration on the Relation of the Church to Non-Christian Religions, spoke only in very general terms of "the spiritual patrimony common to Christians and Jews" (Section 4.12).[28] In the 1974 *Guidelines and Suggestions for Implementing the Conciliar Declaration Nostra Aetate,* prepared by the Vatican Commission for Religious Relations with the Jews, there is a slightly more expansive statement, "Judaism in the time of Christ and Apostles was a complex reality, embracing many different trends, many spiritual, religious, social and cultural values" (Section III). I assume that the authors of this document had in mind the apocalyptic piety of the community at Qumran as one of these different trends and values, but this is not named explicitly. Frequently in documents such as that prepared by the United States Bishop's Committee on the Liturgy in 1988, *God's Mercy Endures Forever: Guidelines on the Presentation of Jews and Judaism in Catholic Preaching,* there is encouragement for Christians "to draw on Jewish sources (rabbinic, medieval and modern) in expounding the meaning of the Hebrew Scriptures and apostolic writings" (Section 30 i).[29] But in this important study text, there is no explicit mention of how both sectarian texts found in the Dead Sea Scrolls such as *pesharim* and works of biblical interpretation as the *Genesis Apocryphon* that were shared more broadly within Second Temple Judaism might contribute to our understanding of Jewish bible interpretation at the time of the Gospels. It is in documents prepared by the Pontifical Biblical Commission that the scrolls are mentioned explicitly.[30] In 1984, in *Instruction on Scripture and Christology,* the need to study the "literature from Qumran" along with the Palestinian targum is acknowledged in a single brief sentence (Section 1.1.5.1). In the 1993 document, *The Interpretation of the Bible in the Church,* note is made of "the man-

---

same, namely, that only in more recent documents are the scrolls named or discussed explicitly. For example, in *The Church and Israel: A Contribution from the Reformation Churches in Europe to the Relationship between Christians and Jews,* 2001, 3.4.2, we find some mention of the scrolls and a brief comparison of the early Christians to the Qumran community: "The Jews who believed God had raised Jesus naturally saw themselves as part of the people of Israel. But at the same time, like, for example, the Jewish community living at that time at Qumran by the Dead Sea, they also felt they were a special community within Israel."

[28] This and other Vatican documents are readily accessible on the Vatican website: http://www.vatican.va/archive/hist_councils/ii_vatican_council/index.htm.

[29] Available on the website of the United States Conference of Catholic Bishops: http://www.usccb.org/liturgy/godsmercy.shtml.

[30] Documents from the Pontifical Biblical Commission can be found at: http://www.vatican.va/roman_curia/congregations/cfaith/pcb_index.htm.

ifold research stimulated by the discoveries at Qumran" specifically, the *Genesis Apocryphon* from Cave 1 at Qumran is mentioned by name as an example of "the abundance and variety of interpretations of the Scriptures themselves" that emerged in extracanonical Jewish literature, and the importance of studying the quotations of the Old Testament in Qumran literature is acknowledged "since the New Testament often quoted the Old Testament in a similar fashion" (Section I.C.2). The most recent document from the Commission, *The Jewish People and Their Sacred Scriptures in the Christian Bible* (2002), deals explicitly with Jewish exegetical methods; Section 2.13 is devoted to "Exegesis at Qumran and in the New Testament," acknowledging that "with regard to form and method, the New Testament, especially the Gospels, presents striking resemblances to Qumran in its use of Scripture."

Perhaps the scant attention paid to the scrolls in many of these documents should not be too surprising. There are definite reasons that are intrinsic to the very nature and genre of dialogue documents: these were usually short statements, written in non-academic language, to be accessible for the general public; the primary focus was often on presenting to Christians a revised understanding of the Pharisees whom they encounter regularly in the gospel readings (while the Essenes are not mentioned). Furthermore, I suspect that many of those involved in authoring these statements (or the Jewish colleagues whom they consulted) were more at home in traditional rabbinic studies than in what is still perceived as the more peripheral and specialized field of Dead Sea Scrolls research.[31]

When there has been explicit mention of Qumran and the Essenes in these dialogue documents, this has evoked various reactions. On the one hand, such passages have been highlighted and praised because they give a much richer and more nuanced presentation of Second Temple Judaism. Yet, in examining the 2002 Pontifical Biblical Commission document, Amy-Jill Levine draws attention to the lack of "sustained engagement with ancient Jewish sources, especially those preserved by

---

[31] See, for example, the exchange between Dr. Joseph Sievers, Director of the Cardinal Bea Centre for Judaic Studies, Gregorian University, and Dr. Edward Kessler, Director of the Cambridge University Centre for the Study of Jewish-Christian Relations, during the Bea Lecture (London, May 18, 2000). Dr. Kessler called for the study of rabbinic interpretation in Christian seminaries; in a written comment, Sievers called attention to the richness of biblical interpretation found in some of the Dead Sea Scrolls and their potential as an indispensable resource for "appreciating the context in which both rabbinic Judaism and early Christianity were rooted," *SIDIC* 34 (2001).

the Synagogue," given that "the Dead Sea Scrolls and Philo receive as much if not more attention than the Rabbinic texts."[32] The question has been voiced whether it is possible that undue attention is being given to establishing a relationship between Qumran and Christianity as a subtle way of avoiding links between Christian origins and "real" (rabbinic) Judaism or the Judaism of today.[33] Or, as David Satran asks: can focusing on the Dead Sea Scrolls be a convenient way for Christian scholars to avoid having to know and to deal with the abundance and complexity of rabbinic / Talmudic literature?[34] Obviously the precise way in which the scrolls can and should be used in such statements is still being explored.

3. Personal Level

In addition to their contribution in the academic world and to Jewish-Christian dialogue, the Dead Sea Scrolls have made and continue to make a distinctive contribution to Jewish-Christian relations in a less tangible way, in the realm of personal and lived experience. *Nostra Aetate* spoke in general terms of the importance of encouraging "that mutual under-standing and respect which is the fruit, above all, of biblical and theolog-ical studies as well as of fraternal dialogues" (Section 4). The 1974 *Guide-lines and Suggestions for Implementing the Conciliar Declaration "Nos-tra Aetate"* called more explicitly for "collaboration with Jewish schol-ars" (Section III), and this plea for personal contact has been reiterated and intensified in many subsequent documents. Yet both for "ordinary people" and even for those teaching and writing in academia, situations that bring together Jews and Christian can be still few and far between. I would like to suggest that the scrolls have provided some unique, and often unrecognized, opportunities, and these should not be forgotten.

---

[32] Amy-Jill Levine, "Roland Murphy, The Pontifical Biblical Commission, Jews and the Bible," *Biblical Theology Bulletin* 33 (2003):105; idem, "A Jewish Reading of the Document," *The Bible Today* (May / June 2003).

[33] In a conference shortly after the publication of the Commission's statement, in December 2002, at the Pro Unione Centre in Rome, Rabbi Jack Bemporad, Director of the Centre for Interreligious Understanding of Englewood, New Jersey, observed: "to use these Dead Sea texts, of which I am personally skeptic and to reject the rabbinical interpretation endorsed by Judaism is like approaching Christianity while forgetting the Gospels and using instead apocryphal texts like the Gospel of Thomas."

[34] David Satran, "Qumran and Christian Origins," [in Hebrew] in *The Scrolls of the Judaean Desert, Forty Years of Research*, ed. M. Broshi, S. Japhet, D. Schwartz and Sh. Talmon (Jerusalem: Bialik Institute and The Israel Exploration Society, 1992), 152–159.

Already in the 1950s Cardinal Tisserant, the Dean of the College of Cardinals in Rome, wrote a letter to Msgr. John M. Oesterreicher, one of the pioneers in Jewish-Christian work at Seton Hall University in New Jersey, in which the Cardinal expressed his hope that "the findings of Qumran will open a new field of studies where Christians and Jews will be able to collaborate."[35] Collaboration, of course, has not always been the norm or even possible. I have already referred to the physical separation for over twenty years (1948–1967) between Jewish scholars and the International Team of Christians scholars.[36] The barriers have not only been political, but also linguistic. In the early years, much important Israeli scholarship (for example, the rich commentaries of Jacob Licht on the *Hodayot* and the *Rule of Community*[37]) was in Modern Hebrew and thus often inaccessible and ignored; even Yigael Yadin's edition of the *Temple Scroll* (1977) had very little impact until the English edition appeared in 1983.[38] Fortunately, this is slowly changing as more scholars become fluent in Modern Hebrew.[39] In addition, the separation of Christian and Jewish scholars in the early years must be situated within the norms and practices of the times with regard to interrreligious relations on any level. In the 1950s, the International Team was considered radical, and even suspect, because Protestant and Catholic scholars were sitting at the same table to work on biblical texts—few people even imagined that Jews might join the table.

In contrast, since the middle 1980s, work on the scrolls has brought together Jewish and Christian scholars in shared scholarly endeavors at a level and with an intensity that has few parallels. This cooperation has been real and practical, and the results concrete: for example, the

---

[35] The letter is quoted in "A Word of Thanks," in *The Bridge: A Yearbook of Judaeo-Christian Studies*, ed. J.M. Oesterreicher, Vol. 2 (New York: Pantheon Books, 1955), 9.

[36] Yet, even though these years, there seems to have been some limited correspondence between Père Benoit and Yigael Yadin via a European postal-box (in a personal note to me in August 2005, Weston Fields confirmed that he had recovered copies of some of this correspondence).

[37] Jacob Licht, *Megilat ha-hahodayot mimegilot midbar yehuda* (Jerusalem: Mosad Bialik, 1957); idem, *Megilat ha-serakhim: mimegilot midbar yehuda* (Jerusalem: Mosad Bialik, 1965).

[38] Yigael Yadin, *The Temple Scroll* (Jerusalem: Israel Exploration Society, 1983).

[39] As Carol Newsom pointed out some years ago in "Response to George Nickelsburg 'Currents in Qumran Scholarship,'" in *Dead Sea Scrolls at Fifty*, ed. Robert A. Kugel and Eileen M. Schuller (Atlanta, Ga.: Scholars Press, 1999), 115–122, in the early years in both North American and Europe, scrolls scholarship was often situated academically within the domain of New Testament studies, and many New Testament scholars had very limited Hebrew, whether biblical or modern.

publication of the *Encyclopedia of Dead Sea Scrolls* with James VanderKam and Lawrence Schiffman as co-editors.[40] The level of trust and
commitment that allows and calls forth such endeavors did not come
about by chance. I would suggest that the decades of isolation and the
intense emotion and mutual suspicion that was generated in the late
1980s around the issue of closed access and slow publication could not
have been overcome without intensive experiences of personal contact.
This took place above all in a remarkable series of international conferences that were held almost every year, literally around the world
(Oxford, New York, Haifa, Groningen, Mogilany to name just a few
places) under various auspices, in the decade between 1987 and 1997.[41]
Of particular import was the Congress held at El Escorial palace in
Madrid and at the University of Salamanca in 1991, at the invitation of the
King and Queen of Spain, where for five intense days Jewish and Christian scrolls scholars, most of whom had not met personally before, shared
not only formal academic meetings but lived together (even as the palace
staff tried to figure out how to handle kosher!) and traveled together (to
sessions at other Spanish universities).[42] As always in dialogue, ideas and
persons cannot be separated.

In addition to this scholarly level of interaction and collaboration,
on another level, it has often been the case that it is the remarkably
persistent and virtually unprecedented popular interest in the Dead Sea
scrolls that provides unique opportunities for Jewish-Christian contact.[43]
Much happens locally (and for this type of thing it is almost impossible

---

[40] Lawrence H. Schiffman and James C. VanderKam, *Encyclopedia of the Dead Sea
Scrolls* (London: Oxford University Press, 2000). A few manuscripts were assigned for
joint publication to a Jew and Christian; for example, 4Q371–373 (Narrative and Poetic
Composition) was assigned jointly to Moshe Bernstein and myself, in *Qumran Cave
4.XXVIII, Miscellanea, Part 2* (DJD XXVIII; Oxford: Clarendon Press, 2001), 151–204.

[41] The papers from most of these conferences were published quickly in conference
volumes, many of them by E.J. Brill in the series Studies on the Texts of the Desert of
Judah. Often these were preliminary editions of previously unpublished texts, so that in
these years much material was actually circulated and shared among a small group of
"Qumran specialists" before it was published more formally in *Discoveries in the Judaean
Desert*.

[42] Published by Julio Trebolle Barrera and Luis Vegas Montaner, eds., *The Madrid
Qumran Congress: Proceedings of the International Congress on the Dead Sea Scrolls,
Madrid 18–21 March 1991*, 2 vols. (Leiden: E.J. Brill, 1992).

[43] The popular interest in the scrolls has itself become an object of study! The Society of
Biblical Literature devoted a special session to the topic at its 2004 meetings, and some of
these papers were gathered together for a thematic issue of *Dead Sea Discoveries* 12/1
(2005), "The Dead Sea Scrolls in the Popular Imagination," ed. M.L. Grossmann and
C.M. Murphy.

to provide comprehensive documentation), but I have talked to so many people who can immediately recall examples from their local situation where a lecture on the scrolls was the first occasion for a Christian congregation to invite a rabbi or a Jewish speaker—or for a synagogue to invite a Christian scholar with specialized expertise in the scrolls to speak at a study session or during a service.

In this context, the public exhibitions of Dead Sea Scrolls, which have been held from the 1950s up until the present, perhaps merit more explicit attention and documentation than they have been accorded.[44] Virtually every exhibit has reported high attendance figures, often much beyond what was anticipated, and including public education events such as a lecture series that are often held in conjunction with an exhibit.[45] While many of the visitors certainly belong to local churches and synagogues, many of them are almost certainly not "religious" in any formal or institutional sense. A museum exhibition is probably the only place in today's society where the general public would be exposed to, and invited to think about, such detailed information concerning fundamental questions of the origins of Judaism and Christianity and how the two religions are related. Although there is much to be critical about in terms of how the media has sensationalized and exploited the worst of bizarre theories and esoteric speculations about anything related to Qumran, the persistent popular interest in the scrolls is not to be scorned; perhaps there are ways to tap into this interest as a entry point to bringing Jewish-Christian relations more broadly to the public venue.

Let me close, not with a summary of this short paper, but by offering a very practical and concrete suggestion. Could the Dead Sea Scrolls be studied by "ordinary" Jews and Christians in the type of joint synagogue-church study groups that have proven very attractive and successful in various programs in North America? The translations and study-helps are now available to make the texts accessible. In such a context, I suspect that some interesting discussions could ensue precisely because these are

---

[44] For a short consideration, see Aldofo Roitman, "Exhibiting the Dead Sea Scrolls: Some Historical and Theoretical Considerations," in *Archaeology and Society in the 21st Century: The Dead Sea Scrolls and Other Case Studies*, ed. N.A. Silberman and E.S. Frerichs (Jerusalem: Israel Exploration Society, the Dorot Foundation, 2001), 46–66. On their website, the Israel Antiquities Authority lists twenty-two exhibits around the world that they were involved with between 1993–2010; other exhibits have been arranged in conjunction with different sponsoring groups, including the Dead Sea Scrolls Foundation.

[45] The most recent exhibit, at the Royal Ontario Museum in Toronto, held from June 2009–January 2010, reported an overall attendance of 350,000 people.

not the "canonical texts" of either group. Reading selected passages from
the scrolls would raise fundamental questions on the level of ideas: What
were the expectations about the coming of the messiah in first century
Jerusalem? What kind of biblical interpretation was going on that people
could read the prophet Habakkuk and think that he was talking about
the Teacher of Righteousness? How do we read the ancient prophets
so that they are relevant for us? What do we do with these strident
statements about hating the enemy? Such reading together would also
raise questions on the level of identity and practice: how strong do the
lines have to be between "insiders" and "outsiders"? What determines
group identity? How does any community deal with competing claims to
authenticity? Is the most stringent legal interpretation the most effective
means of ensuring survival—or is this why this particular Jewish group
did not survive? In such a shared reading, it would be important to move
beyond the level of ideas and concepts to explore what the discovery of
these ancient texts have meant on an emotional and religious level: for the
Christian members of the group to hear Yigael Yadin talking the impact
of the fact that his father purchased the first scrolls on November 29,
1947, the day of the United Nations vote for the establishment of the
state of Israel, so that "there is something symbolic in the discovery of the
scrolls and their acquisition at the moment of the creation of the state of
Israel;"[46] and for Jews to try to understand why Christians are so moved
by the simple fact of being able to see and touch physical materials from
the time and place of Jesus. Joint reading and shared study might be yet
another way for both Christians and Jews, on a personal and local level,
to experience for themselves that the discovery of the Dead Sea Scrolls
has been "an absolutely incredible find."[47]

---

[46] Yigael Yadin, *The Message of the Scrolls* (New York: Simon and Schuster, 1957), 14.
[47] Letter of William F. Alight; see n. 2.

ARTAPANUS REVISITED

JOHN J. COLLINS

The fragments of Artapanus are surely among the most colorful of all the writings from antiquity relating to Judaism. In the words of Howard Jacobson, "his narrative is dramatic, somewhat frenetic, full of conflict and intrigue, and one might say, not rarely bizarre."[1] For all that, they have received only intermittent scholarly attention. Two recent contributions, however, by Howard Jacobson and Holger Zellentin, are worthy of comment. Jacobson's article is provocative, but in my judgment mistaken. Zellentin's treatment is not persuasive in every respect, but he has advanced our understanding of Artapanus considerably by clarifying the date of composition.

Jacobson

The recent article of Howard Jacobson, "Artapanus Judaeus," provides a welcome stimulus to reconsider Artapanus, by suggesting that he is "likely not Jewish."[2] I have not seen much scholarly reaction to Jacobson's piece, but Brent Nongbri in his article on "Greek Authors on Jews and Judaism" for the *Dictionary of Early Judaism* comments that "neither the titles of the works attributed to Artapanus nor the apparent contents of these works seem out of place in the non-Jewish Greek ethnographic tradition."[3] While it is difficult to say that anything is absolutely impossible, I do not find Jacobson's arguments very persuasive, and I do not know of any analogous treatment of Moses or the patriarchs by non-Jewish authors. Admittedly, Artapanus stands out among Jewish treatments too, but I do not think there is much reason to doubt his Judean identity.

---

[1] Howard Jacobson, "Artapanus Judaeus," *JJS* 57 (2006) 210–221 (quotation 210).

[2] Ibid., 210.

[3] Brent Nongbri, "Greek Authors on Jews and Judaism," in *The Dictionary of Early Judaism*, ed. John J. Collins and Daniel C. Harlow (Grand Rapids, Mich.: Eerdmans, 2010).

The questions raised by Jacobson may be reduced to two:

1. Is it conceivable that a Jew could have written an account that deviated so radically from the biblical record, and that claimed for Moses the invention of the Egyptian animal cults?
2. Is there any reason to think that a non-Jewish author could not have composed this narrative?

The first of these questions needs to be reformulated. Much ink has been spilled in recent years on the translation of the word *Ioudaios* and the question of whether it is appropriate to speak at all of "Jews" rather than "Judeans" in pre-rabbinic times.[4] Various ethnic groups retained ancestral customs even in exile. Judeans in Hellenistic Egypt were similar to Idumeans in this respect, even if they were more numerous and are better documented. Or we might think of the earlier case of the Judeans at Elephantine, who were attached to their temple and religious observances but seem to have revered a number of deities, including some goddesses. Without entering into all the ramifications of that debate, it may be more helpful to ask whether Artapanus was Judean rather than whether he was Jewish. Ethnic pride may be a bigger consideration than religious orthodoxy. It is striking, and significant, that Artapanus does not mention the law in his account of Moses.

Also, it is misleading to speak of the Bible in this context. Even texts that are greatly concerned with orthodoxy and orthopraxy, such as Jubilees, treat the text we call biblical with great freedom. Most scholars since Freudenthal have accepted that Artapanus knew the Septuagint account of the Exodus, because of corresponding terminology, especially in the story of the plagues. This point may not be entirely beyond dispute. He could conceivably have known it from an oral tradition that was influenced by the LXX translation. But he does seem to know what we call the biblical story. It is not clear, however, whether he regarded that story as revealed, inspired, or in any way sacred. The books of Genesis and Exodus, in some form, were widely regarded as authoritative in the second century BCE, but there was not necessarily a standard view of the nature of scriptural authority, shared by all Judeans. It is misleading to

---

[4] Shaye Cohen, *The Beginnings of Jewishness: Boundaries, Varieties, Uncertainties* (Berkeley, Calif.: University of California Press, 1999) 3; Steve Mason, "Jews, Judaeans, Judaizing, Judaism: Problems of Categorization in Ancient History," *JJS* 38 (2007): 457–512.

speak of the Bible in this context, as if any deviation from the received stories was heretical.

Jacobson recognizes that not all deviations from the supposed "biblical" text are problematic. Many can be categorized as embellishments, and in these matters Artapanus "is no more extreme than many midrashim, pseudepigraphic and other Greek Hellenistic texts."[5] But items that contradict the biblical text are more difficult. In particular, Jacobson finds "the notion that Moses of all people instituted animal worship in Egypt … hard to stomach. What could be more contrary to the letter and the spirit of the Pentateuch?"[6] But as many scholars have noted, Moses does not himself worship the sacred animals, nor does he prescribe their worship for Judeans, only for Egyptians. And in the end, these sacred animals are destroyed in the Red Sea. What is crucial here is the intention of the story, to which we will return below. While the animal cults are said to be beneficial for the Egyptians, there is considerable condescension, and even satire, in the story. Jacobson's blanket assertion that "no Jew could have used the tale of Moses as institutor of Egyptian animal worship"[7] is too dogmatic in any case, but it also fails to notice *how* Artapanus used this tale.

With regard to the second question, most scholars have found it incredible that a pagan author would have written an account that glorifies Moses and the patriarchs without any hint of criticism. Even Hecataeus, whose account of Moses is sympathetic, says that he introduced "an unsocial and intolerant mode of life."[8] Some 300 years after Artapanus, the Pythagorean philosopher Numenius affirmed the spiritual truths of oriental peoples, "the Brahmans, and Jews, and Magi and Egyptians," and said that Plato was Moses speaking Attic,[9] but he did not, as far as we know, devote a whole work to the praise of Jewish heroes. Authors can write idealizing accounts of nations to which they do not belong, but we have no example of such a Gentile account of ancient Judaism.[10] Again, the Septuagint may have been readily available in Alexandria, but what

---

[5] Jacobson, "Artapanus Judaeus," 213.

[6] Ibid.

[7] Ibid., 219–220.

[8] Hecataeus in Diodorus Siculus *Bibliotheca Historica* 40.3.4, in *Greek and Latin Authors on Jews and Judaism*, trans. and ed. Menahem Stern, Vol. I: From Herodotus to Plutarch (Jerusalem: Publications of the Israel Academy of Sciences and Humanities, 1976), 1.28.

[9] Stern, *Greek and Latin Authors*, 2.209–216.

[10] The account of Pompeius Trogus, mentioned by Jacobson, 216, is not hostile to Judaism, but it is by no means idealizing.

is the evidence that Gentiles availed of it? The only example of which I am aware is the treatise on "The Sublime" attributed to Longinus, which Stern dates to the first half of the first century BCE, and it only cites the first chapter of Genesis.[11] So, while it may not be theoretically impossible that a Gentile composed the narrative of Artapanus, the balance of probability is heavily against that possibility.

Whether Artapanus was a pseudonym, intended to hide the author's Jewish identity, as Freudenthal thought, is more difficult to say. We have many Jewish writings from the Hellenistic Diaspora that are written under Gentile pseudonyms. Most of these are better known, and more prestigious, than Artapanus (e.g., the Sibyl, Phocylides) or are given a context that lends them importance, in the case of Aristeas. It is not apparent why a Jewish author would choose an obscure name like Artapanus. But the possibility cannot be excluded.

In all, then, I do not find Jacobson's article persuasive. He does succeed, however, in highlighting the exceptional character of Artapanus and making the point that he deserves attention.

Zellentin

Holger Zellentin has offered a much longer and more substantial analysis of Artapanus.[12] Instead of attempting to address the question of Jewish or Gentile authorship directly, he engages in a detailed analysis of the text with a view to determining the nature and purpose of the work. In the process, he leaves little doubt, to my mind at least, that the author is in fact Judean. He also sheds new light on the date of the book. The statement in Eusebius *P.E.* 9.27.5 that the Egyptians would sometimes reinstate leaders whom they had earlier deposed, points to a date in the second half of the second century BCE, as the only Ptolemies who were so reinstated were Ptolemy VI Philometor and Ptolemy VIII Euergetes II (that is, Physcon, who was recalled twice, in 145 and 126 BCE). Zellentin argues for a much more specific date than this, between 118 and 116 BCE. His argument depends on alleged reflections of the Ptolemaic decree of amnesty in 118 BCE. The issues in question include land reform, but the achieve-

---

[11] Stern, *Greek and Latin Authors*, 1.361.
[12] Holger Zellentin, "The End of Jewish Egypt: Artapanus and the Second Exodus," in *Antiquity in Antiquity*, ed. Kevin Osterloh and Greg Gardner (Tübingen: Mohr Siebeck, 2008), 27–73.

ments attributed to Joseph are more likely to reflect the fundamental measures taken to organize agriculture in the time of Ptolemy II, in the early third century BCE.[13] More intriguing is the fact that the Ptolemies assumed the burial costs for the Apis bull and other sacred animals in the decree. Artapanus accuses Chenephres of burying the sacred animals to hide the inventions of Moses. But there had always been elaborate ceremonial burials of the Apis bull, so it is not necessary to see an allusion to the decree of 118 CE here either. It seems to me unwise, then, to tie Artapanus too specifically to the events in specific years, but I accept Zellentin's argument that Artapanus is likely to have written in the second half of the second century BCE, probably in the reign of Physcon.

A major part of Zellentin's argument concerns Artapanus' use of sources. He argues that Artapanus is in direct dialogue with Genesis and Exodus, on the one hand, and with sources that are also reflected in Diodorus Siculus, on the other. Diodorus is taken as representative of commonly accepted stories about Sesostris, Dionysus / Osiris, and Hermes. The parallels with the material known from Diodorus have long been noted, but seldom if ever set out so fully. In essence, Artapanus claims that the ancestral heroes of the Judeans surpass the other legendary heroes. For example, Dionysus had not been able to subdue Ethiopia; Sesostris had succeeded; Moses succeeds with an amateur army. Moreover, his motives are more noble than those of Sesostris and are purely concerned with euergetism. This is the phenomenon that I have called "competitive historiography," which is well attested in the Hellenistic period, also in other Hellenistic Jewish writers.[14] It strongly suggests that Artapanus wrote, at least in part, to glorify Judean history, as a matter of ethnic pride.

Many scholars, including myself, have also argued that Artapanus was in part refuting Manetho.[15] Manetho had alleged that Moses forbade the people to worship the gods or abstain from the flesh of the sacred animals. Artapanus claimed that it was Moses who established these cults. Manetho alleged that Moses had invaded Egypt. Artapanus says that Moses restrained Raguel and the Arabs from invading: "But

---

[13] Günther Hölbl, *A History of the Ptolemaic Empire* (London: Routledge, 2001), 62. J.G. Manning, *The Last Pharaohs: Egypt under the Ptolemies, 305–30 BC* (Princeton: Princeton University Press, 2009), 157.

[14] John J. Collins, *Between Athens and Jerusalem*, 2nd ed. (Grand Rapids, Mich.: Eerdmans, 2000), 39–40.

[15] Ibid., 40–41.

Moses restrained him, taking thought of his compatriots."[16] According
to Manetho, the pharaoh had to protect the sacred animals from Moses.
Artapanus claims that the pharaoh buried the animals, which Moses had
made sacred, since he wished to conceal Moses' inventions. In Manetho,
the pharaoh sought refuge in Ethiopia when Moses invaded. In Artapanus, Moses conducted a campaign against Ethiopia on behalf of the
pharaoh. In light of these contrasts, it is difficult to avoid the conclusion
that Artapanus is, *inter alia*, responding to Manetho, or at least to the kind
of derogatory account of Judean origins that Manetho represents. The
fact that Artapanus gives a euhemeristic explanation of the animal cults
that is paralleled in Diodorus does not lessen the contrast with Manetho.
Neither does the fact that Ethiopia also figures prominently in the stories
preserved by Diodorus. The essential point here is that Artapanus is not
only affirming the *philanthropia* of Moses, and implicitly of the Judeans,
but he is also refuting the charge of *misanthropia*, which was widely made
against the Judeans in the Hellenistic world and was implicit in the work
of Manetho.

Zellentin rejects this conclusion, largely because of Artapanus' dramatic exaggerations of the Exodus's carnage.[17] After he has restrained
Raguel, Moses is told by a divine voice to wage war against Egypt. He
resolves to lead a fighting force against the Egyptians, but it is not clear
that he does so, because of a gap in the excerpts preserved in Eusebius.
He is instrumental, however, in afflicting the Egyptians with the plague.
All the sacred animals are drowned in the end, and Zellentin argues that
the scene at the Red Sea was unlikely to gain sympathy for Jewish concerns in Egypt. Nonetheless, in his own summary of Artapanus, Zellentin
says that Artapanus recasts Abraham, Joseph and Moses as the most
benevolent and egalitarian leaders.[18] But is the benevolence of Moses not
also put in question by the carnage of the Exodus? There is indeed tension between the account of the Exodus and Moses' earlier euergetism
towards the Egyptians, and how we explain this tension is crucial for
our understanding of Artapanus. In brief, an interpretation of Artapanus
must reckon both with the euergetism of Moses towards the Egyptians
and with the carnage of the Exodus.

---

[16] Eusebius *Praeparatio Evangelica* 9.27.19, trans. John J. Collins, "Artapanus," in *The Old Testament Pseudepigrapha*, ed. James H. Charlesworth, Vol. 2 (New York: Doubleday, 1985), 900.
[17] Zellentin, "The End of Jewish Egypt," 46–47.
[18] Ibid., 48.

The theology of Artapanus

Scholars have tried to balance these conflicting themes in various ways. Erich Gruen captures well the element of mischief and humor in Artapanus: "this was no somber contest for supremacy between Jewish and pagan intellectuals."[19] He adds that "Jews would certainly not take it seriously." But did Jews not take it seriously when other authors claimed that Abraham taught astrology to the Egyptians, or that Plato was influenced by Moses? One does not have to be somber to be serious. Gruen leans heavily on the positive side of Artapanus's attitude: "this is no mere syncretism; it is appropriation ... His Moses, having absorbed Hermes and Mousaios, emerged as cultural progenitor of Hellas itself."[20] But Gruen does not deal at all with the carnage of the Exodus. His Artapanus has a light touch: "The humor is mischievous rather than malicious. It sets the author in a superior posture of detachment, disengaged from ideological battle, and thereby augments the authority of his judgment. What stands out is not so much polemics as inventive imagination."[21]

John Barclay also sees Artapanus as an example of "cultural convergence."[22] He is an example of "Jewish syncretism," who "effected an important measure of synthesis with Egyptian culture; even Egyptian religion."[23] Barclay even claims that "while he held that 'the master of the universe' required Egypt to release the Jews, this does not elevate 'monotheism' over 'polytheism,' or 'the God of the Jews' over the Gods of Egypt. Like many of his contemporaries, Artapanus can refer interchangeably to God (singular) and Gods (plural): even as a Jew he is both a monotheist and a polytheist."[24] Barclay does not explain how Artapanus is a monotheist, if 'the master of the universe' is not elevated over the gods of the Egyptians. But, again, he blithely ignores the carnage of the Exodus, which indisputably *does* elevate the God of the Jews over the gods of the Egyptians.

---

[19] Erich Gruen, *Heritage and Hellenism* (Berkeley: University of California Press, 1998), 158.

[20] Ibid., 159.

[21] Ibid., 160.

[22] John M.G. Barclay, *Jews in the Mediterranean Diaspora: From Alexander to Trajan (323 BCE – 117 CE)* (Edinburgh: T & T Clark, 1996), 127–132.

[23] Ibid., 132.

[24] Ibid., 132.

Rob Kugler makes an innovative effort to illuminate the context of Artapanus by use of the Heracleopolis papyri.[25] For Kugler, Artapanus reflects the Ptolemaic culture of tolerance for different religious beliefs. Readers would infer that they should imitate Moses, the hero of the tradition. "And what would one do to emulate Moses? Seek the stability and well-being of one's Egyptian neighbors and respect and appreciate their religious practices. After all, acting on the authority of their sovereign God, Moses, a founder of their tradition established those religious realities for Egypt." The Septuagint famously translated Exodus 22:28 as "thou shalt not revile the gods," and Philo expounded this as meaning that one should not revile the gods of other peoples lest they revile the Most High.[26] Whether this is exactly the nuance of Artapanus, I am not sure. On the surface, at least, Moses is more than respectful to the Egyptian gods; he is the one who establishes the animal cults. But the very fact that the Judean ancestor Moses prescribes these cults for the Egyptians is in itself something of a put-down.

Unlike Gruen and Barclay, however, Kugler gives due weight to the end of the story: "But with this Moses narrative Artapanus would have also reminded recipients that in spite of the legitimacy of their neighbors' religious choices and traditions, their God was still sovereign ... The latter half of the fragment shows that not only did the God of Israel sponsor the religions of Egypt; when the practitioners of those religions were hostile to the people of Israel, this God did not hesitate to take action against the perpetrators ... The God of Israel remained master of the universe."[27]

Among recent authors, Zellentin goes furthest in ascribing to Artapanus a negative attitude towards Egypt. Pursuant to his highly specific dating of Artapanus to the years 118–116, he reads Artapanus as a political satire, bordering on allegory. The benevolent king of Joseph's time is meant to remind Jewish readers of Ptolemy VI Philometor, who allowed Onias IV and his followers to settle in Leontopolis. The evil

---

[25] Rob Kugler, "Hearing the Story of Moses in Ptolemaic Egypt: Artapanus Accommodates the Tradition," in *The Wisdom of Egypt. Jewish, Early Christian, and Gnostic Essays in Honour of Gerard P. Luttikhuizen*, ed. Anthony Hilhorst and George H. van Kooten (Leiden: Brill, 2005), 67–80.

[26] Philo, *Spec. Leg.* 1.53. See P.W. van der Horst, "'Thou Shalt Not Revile the Gods:' The LXX Translation of Ex 22:28 (27), its background and influence," in *Hellenism, Judaism, Christianity: Essays on their Interaction*, ed. idem. (Kampen: Kok Pharos, 1994), 112–121.

[27] Kugler, "Hearing the Story of Moses," 77.

Chenephres is a stand-in for Ptolemy Physcon. Accepting the report in Josephus that Physcon persecuted Jews after regaining power in 145 BCE (the report, a variant of the story in 3 Maccabees, is dubious historical evidence), he infers that this Ptolemy again posed a threat to the Jews when he was restored in 126 BCE. The Oniads and their followers, according to Zellentin, "would easily have compared Onias IV with Joseph and themselves with Moses and Aaron ... Artapanus's amplification of the Exodus narrative and his insistence on treachery and conspiracy would have made his message clear to Jewish military leaders: leave the country, an assassination attempt is imminent; there is no shame in fleeing. The patriarchs had likewise all fled—and were justified in doing so."[28]

If Artapanus wrote in the time of Euergetes II Physcon, it is not unreasonable to suspect that Chenephres would bring this Ptolemy to mind. But the idea that Artapanus is urging people to flee the country seems to me an over-reading, and counter-intuitive. Should we make the same inference from other re-tellings of the Exodus story, such as the Wisdom of Solomon? Surely not. Of the readings summarized here, I find myself closest to Kugler. Artapanus affirms a form of Judaism that is quite different from the philosophical religion of Philo or the Wisdom of Solomon. It is a more popular form of religion, interested in the magical power of the divine name, and willing to acknowledge the legitimacy, and value, of Egyptian cults—for Egyptians. The respect for Egyptian religion, however, is undercut by the author's mischievous humor. In the end, the God of the Judeans is the "master of the universe," and can dump all the gods of Egypt into the Red Sea. This is not, I think, a complete repudiation of Egypt and its religion, which was, after all, supposedly established by Moses. But it most certainly elevates the Judeans and their God over the Egyptians and their gods, and it is not polytheistic in any serious way. The gods of the Egyptians are fine, for the Egyptians, but Jews know that they were invented by Moses. This narrative could, I think, provide reassurance to Judeans who felt somewhat imperiled in a hostile environment, rather like the fantastic tale of deliverance in 3 Maccabees, which is also not without its humorous elements. But fundamentally the story affirms that Judeans can thrive and excel in Egypt. I doubt that any Judeans reading it would draw the lesson that Jewish Egypt was at an end or that they should flee to Syria. Artapanus was not announcing the end

---

[28] Zellentin, 39.

of Jewish Egypt, but using humor and fantasy to affirm the superiority of the God of Moses, and to assure his compatriots that any difficulties they encountered from a hostile ruler could be overcome.[29]

---

[29] It is a pleasure to offer this article to Tom Tobin in appreciation of his many contributions to the study of Hellenistic Judaism and of his friendship over several decades.

EXEGETICAL BUILDING BLOCKS
IN PHILO'S INTERPRETATION OF THE PATRIARCHS

ELLEN BIRNBAUM

One of the more fascinating and ingenious tropes in Philo's grand exegetical corpus is the interpretation of the patriarchs Abraham, Isaac, and Jacob, as symbols of the acquisition of virtue through learning (or teaching), nature, and practice, respectively. Indeed, in Philo's brilliant employment of this trope to illuminate the narratives of Genesis, Yehoshua Amir sees the Alexandrian interpreter "at the peak of his achievement."[1] The motif is so developed and sophisticated that it seems improbable that Philo alone could have created it in all its details. Whether the interpretations are original with Philo, however, or whether they belong to an exegetical tradition that evolved over time, they clearly rely on several discrete elements that join together impressively in different configurations. In this essay, I will identify or suggest what some of these elements—or exegetical building blocks—may be and try to illuminate the origins of and/or influences behind these elements. Such an exercise will, I hope, be a fitting tribute to this volume's honoree, whose monograph on Philo's interpretation of the creation of man is a model study of how interpretive currents related to this creation may have evolved and developed to reach their final expression in Philo's writings.[2]

---

[1] Yehoshua Amir, "The Transference of Greek Allegories to Biblical Motifs in Philo," in *Nourished with Peace: Studies in Hellenistic Judaism in Memory of Samuel Sandmel*, ed. Frederick E. Greenspahn, Earle Hilgert, and Burton L. Mack (Chico, Calif.: Scholars Press, 1984), 20.

[2] Thomas H. Tobin, S.J., *The Creation of Man: Philo and the History of Interpretation* (Washington, D.C.: The Catholic Biblical Association of America, 1984). It is a pleasure to submit this article in honor of Professor Tobin, whom I met years ago when he was spending a year's leave in Cambridge, Mass., and I was struggling to define my approach to Philo. At the encouragement of Professor John Strugnell, mentor to each of us, I contacted Tom, and he graciously agreed to meet with me periodically. Since then, I have benefited from his insight, advice, and clarity of thought and expression. With much gratitude for his friendship, on this special occasion I wish him good health, happiness, and continued productivity for many years to come.

General Observations

The motif of Abraham, Isaac, and Jacob as exemplars of learning, nature, and practice appears in all three of Philo's exegetical series—the Allegorical Commentary, the Exposition of the Law, and Questions and Answers on Genesis and Exodus (QGE).[3] In the Exposition treatise *De Abrahamo*, Philo clearly sets forth the basis of this motif. Although Scripture appears to speak about "men of holy life," he observes, the sacred writings

> are also statements about an order of things which is not so apparent but is far superior to the order which is perceived by the senses. For the holy word seems to be searching into types of soul, all of them of high worth, one which pursues the good through teaching, one through nature and one through practice. The first called Abraham, the second Isaac and the third Jacob, are symbols of virtue acquired respectively by teaching, nature and practice (*Abr.* 52).[4]

Philo also explains that each patriarch "possesses the three qualities, but gets his name from that which chiefly predominates in him; for teaching cannot be consummated without nature or practice, nor is nature capable of reaching its zenith without learning and practicing, nor practice either unless the foundation of nature and teaching has first been laid" (*Abr.* 53).

Although Philo helpfully provides the key here to the symbolism of the patriarchs, elsewhere in the extant treatises of the Exposition his explicit references to this motif are rather sparse.[5] By contrast, in the Allegorical Commentary and QGE, Philo frequently alludes to this motif and often takes for granted his readers' familiarity with it. He refers to the motif fleetingly, for example, by speaking of Jacob as the "practicer" (*ho askētēs*), with or without mention of his name, and by using similar shorthand descriptions for Abraham and Isaac.[6] Occasionally in these

---

[3] On these series and their possibly different audiences, see Ellen Birnbaum, *The Place of Judaism in Philo's Thought: Israel, Jews, and Proselytes* (Atlanta: Scholars Press, 1996), esp. xvii–xviii and 17–20.

[4] Unless otherwise noted, all translations of Philo (and Greek biblical verses cited by Philo) are from *Philo in Ten Volumes (and Two Supplementary Volumes)*, trans. F.H. Colson, G.H. Whitaker, and Ralph Marcus, LCL (Cambridge, Mass.: Harvard University Press, 1929–1962). For another explanation of the motif, see *Somn.* 1.167–168, in which Philo ascribes the allegorical meaning to Moses. Following Philo's usage, I refer to learning and teaching interchangeably.

[5] E.g., *Ios.* 1, *Praem.* 24–51; see also *Mos.* 1.76 (the relationship between *Mos.* 1–2 and the Exposition is debated). Philo's lost treatises on Isaac and Jacob probably contained additional references, especially in the titles (see *Ios.* 1 and below, n. 20). On the relevance of the full Greek title of *De Abrahamo*, see below.

[6] Abraham is often "the sage" and Isaac, "the self-learnt kind"; see below. While the

shorthand references, the patriarchs' roles serve as mere epithets without directly contributing to the sense of the interpretation. Often, however, Philo integrates these roles meaningfully into his exegesis. Indeed, the splendid intricacy of the motif is most apparent and Philo's application of it, most impressive when he draws upon the respective roles of each patriarch to explain puzzling Scriptural differences among all three of them.

A fine example of this sophisticated application may be found in *Mut.* 83–88, in which Philo addresses three perplexing questions based on Scripture. First, he asks why Abraham, whose name was changed from Abram (Gn 17:5), is no longer called by his earlier name, whereas Jacob, whose name was changed to Israel (Gn 32:28, LXX), continues on several occasions to be called Jacob. The answer, according to Philo, is that

> these are signs differing according as virtue acquired by teaching differs from virtue acquired by practice. He who is improved through teaching, being endowed with a happy nature, which with the co-operation of memory assures his retentiveness, gets a tight grip and a firm armhold of what he has learned and thus remains constant. The Practiser on the other hand, after strenuous exercise, takes a breathing-space and a relaxation while he collects and recovers the force which has been enfeebled by his labours. In this he resembles the athletes who anoint their bodies. When they are weary with exercise they pour oil upon their limbs to prevent their forces being utterly shattered by the intensity and severity of the contest (*Mut.* 83–84).

In the same way, then, that one who acquires virtue through teaching permanently retains what he has learned with the help of natural gifts and memory, so too does Abraham permanently retain his new name. One who acquires virtue through practice, however, must keep up the effort required for the achievement, which remains unsteady, a circumstance reflected in the vacillating references to Jacob and Israel even after this patriarch's name is changed.

Philo provides yet another explanation for why Abraham's name is used consistently while Jacob's fluctuates between Jacob and Israel. This additional explanation also illuminates a second issue, that is, why each

---

association of the patriarchs with their respective roles can itself be understood as allegorization, Philo sometimes interprets the patriarchs on an even more abstract level. Thus he understands Jacob, for example, as the practicing (*askētikos*) powers (*dynameis*, *Fug.* 15), soul (*psychē*; *Mut.* 82, *Somn.* 1.182), reason (*logos*, *Deus* 120) or understanding (*dianoia*, *Somn.* 1.115; see also *Leg.* 3.18). For similarly abstract interpretations of Abraham and Isaac, see, e.g., *Leg.* 3.83–84, *Congr.* 63, and below, n. 36.

patriarch receives his new name from a different agent—Abraham, from
God (Gn 17:5), and Jacob, from his wrestling adversary at the Jabbok ford
(Gn 32:28, LXX).[7] According to this second explanation, the one who is
taught (i.e., Abraham)

> has to aid him the voice of his monitor ringing in his ears, deathless as that
> monitor himself, and thus never swerves: the Man of Practice has only his
> own will which he exercises and drills to aid him to overthrow the passion
> natural to created being, and, even if he reaches the consummation, yet
> through weariness he returns to his old kind. He is more patient of toil,
> the other more blessed by fortune. This last has another for his teacher,
> while the toiler, self-helped only, is busied in searching and inquiring and
> zealously exploring the secrets of nature, engaged in labour ceaseless and
> unremitting (*Mut.* 85–86).

In line with the observation that one who is taught "has another for his
teacher," Abraham receives "his new name from God, the unchangeable,
that the stability of his future might be set on a firm foundation by
Him Who stands and is ever the same in nature and condition." Jacob,
however, who must continually struggle by dint of his own will, "was
re-named by an angel, God's minister, ... in acknowledgement that
what is below the Existent cannot produce permanence unswerving and
unwavering ...." (*Mut.* 87).[8]

Continuing with the interpretation of the three patriarchs as different
paths to virtue, Philo now applies the trope to Isaac to explain why he,
unlike Abraham and Jacob, does not receive a change of name but instead
has the same name throughout. The reason is that

> both the scholar's form of virtue and the practiser's are open to improving
> influences, since the former desires to know what he is ignorant of, the
> latter desires crowns of victory and the prizes offered to a soul which
> rejoices to toil and seek the vision of the truth. On the other hand the kind
> which has no teacher or pupil but itself, being made what it is by nature
> rather than by diligence, goes on its way from the first equal and perfect
> like an even number with no other needed as complement (*Mut.* 88).

Thus, because Isaac is naturally virtuous and perfect, he needs no further
adjustments or improvements, and this situation is symbolized by his

---

[7] Although Philo frequently alludes to this episode at the Jabbok ford, he does not
mention this location explicitly. Philo ignores Gn 35:10, in which God Himself changes
Jacob's name.

[8] On the interpretation of Jacob's adversary as an angel, see James L. Kugel, *Traditions
of the Bible: A Guide to the Bible As It Was at the Start of the Common Era* (Cambridge,
Mass. and London: Harvard University Press, 1998), 384–386.

name remaining unchanged, unlike the names of Abraham, the learner, and Jacob, the practicer.

In this extended interpretation, then, Philo employs the motif of the three patriarchs as exemplars of learning, nature, and practice to account for 1) why Abraham's name change persists while Jacob's does not, 2) why Abraham's name is changed by God but Jacob's is changed by a different agent, and 3) why Isaac's name is not changed at all. Philo's application of the motif here is particularly effective because it builds upon differences between the learner and the practicer and between both of these strivers after virtue and the one who is virtuous by nature. Similarly, Philo elsewhere employs differences among the three paths to virtue to explain other discrepancies about the patriarchs.[9]

Each of these explanations is remarkable for its careful attention to Scriptural detail and the imaginative and penetrating use of the learning-nature-practice motif. To my knowledge, this motif is not found in any other Jewish sources—whether from Judea/Palestine or other diaspora communities. It may therefore be a precious example of uniquely Alexandrian exegesis. Without evidence of this trope in earlier Alexandrian Jewish literature, however, we cannot determine when and how it originated. Nonetheless, we can break down this complex motif into several smaller and simpler elements, or building blocks, and try to account for their origins and related factors.[10] At the most obvious level, the motif is based upon the assumption that virtue can be acquired through learning, nature, and/or practice. In addition, this motif depends upon the association of Abraham with learning, Isaac with nature, and Jacob with practice. Let us examine each of these exegetical building blocks more closely.

---

[9] For some of these interpretations, see the section on Isaac, below.

[10] Although I am sympathetic to the attempt to identify earlier traditions in Philo's exegesis, in this essay I restrict myself to identifying components in the motif about the patriarchs. Some of these components seem logically prior to others, but I deal only tangentially with the question of which are Philonic and which, pre-Philonic. For different approaches to this intriguing issue, see Tobin, *The Creation of Man*; Burton L. Mack, "Exegetical Traditions in Alexandrian Judaism: A Program for the Analysis of the Philonic Corpus," *Studia Philonica* 3 (1974–1975): 71–112 (see also below, n. 25); Richard Goulet, *La philosophie de Moïse: Essai de reconstitution d'un commentaire philosophique préphilonien du Pentateuque* (Paris: Librairie Philosophique J. Vrin, 1987).

Learning, Nature, and Practice

The notion that improvement of the self relies on learning (or teaching), nature, and/or practice is widely attested in Greek philosophical and other literature. This triple formulation may have arisen out of a larger discussion—traces of which are found already in sixth- and fifth-century BCE writers—of the relative importance of nature (*physis*) and convention (*nomos*).[11] In the various debates, writers consider the factors necessary both for skills—such as oratory, poetry, and medicine—and for moral qualities like happiness and virtue. Philo himself mentions learning, nature, and practice in connection with the attainment, for example, of virtue (*Abr.* 52), the good (*kalos, Abr.* 52), the summit of excellence (*Ios.* 1), and wisdom (*Mos.* 1.76).

Concern about the prerequisites for improvement became especially relevant because of important political and social changes in fifth-century Athens. There, the shift from aristocratic rule to democracy gave rise to a class of sophists who, for a fee, trained and educated potential leaders for their political roles. The rise of new kinds of leaders and educators brought to the fore the question whether or not virtue can be taught. An early grouping of teaching, nature, and practice as essential elements appears in a fragment from the sophist Protagoras, who declares that "[t]eaching needs endowment and practice. Learning must begin in youth."[12]

In his dialogue named after Protagoras, Plato has Socrates conversing with this sophist about whether virtue can in fact be taught.[13] At the start of a subsequent dialogue, *Meno*, the question is again taken up, with Meno—a young aristocrat from Thessaly—inquiring, "Can you tell me, Socrates, whether virtue can be taught, or is acquired by practice, not teaching? Or if neither by practice nor by learning, whether it comes

---

[11] Paul Shorey, "*Physis, Meletē, Epistēmē,*" *Transactions and Proceedings of the American Philological Association* 40 (1909): 185–201; W.K.C. Guthrie, *The Sophists* (Cambridge, U.K.: Cambridge University Press, 1971), esp. 55–134; G.B. Kerferd, *The Sophistic Movement* (Cambridge, U.K.: Cambridge University Press, 1981), esp. 111–130.

[12] Translated by Kathleen Freeman, *Ancilla to the Pre-Socratic Philosophers: A Complete Translation of the Fragments in Diels*, Fragmente der Vorsokratiker (Cambridge, Mass.: Harvard University Press, 1978), 126; quoted also in Greek by Shorey, "*Physis, Meletē, Epistēmē,*" 189.

[13] See, e.g., 318a, 320b, 323de.

to mankind by nature or in some other way?"[14] After Socrates and others address a range of issues, Socrates declares at the end of the dialogue that virtue comes through a divine dispensation (*theia moira*, 100b).

Pythagoras and Plato were not the only thinkers to consider the significance of teaching, nature, and practice. The sophist Isocrates, for example, alludes to these factors in a discussion of oratorical, practical, and other skills (e.g., *Antidosis* 186–188). In a possible—though indirect—reference to the opening question in Plato's *Meno*, Aristotle inquires "whether happiness is a thing that can be learnt, or acquired by training, or cultivated in some other manner, or whether it is bestowed by some divine dispensation or even by fortune."[15] He also mentions nature, habit, and teaching in connection with virtue and goodness (*Eth. nic.* 2.1.1103a and 10.9.1179b).

Debate about the relative importance of nature and nurture—with the latter encompassing education and practice—persists for centuries and also occurs in Latin literature. Thus in the first century BCE, Horace, writing about poetic skill, mentions nature, teaching, and practice, and Cicero refers to these factors in relation to himself when he addresses a jury on behalf of the poet Archias (1.1).[16] Significant for our purposes, however, is that for philosophers and others in antiquity, the question of how virtue can be acquired was a live issue, and key to the debate were the three factors of teaching, nature, and practice. This triple formulation, then, could have found its way into Philo's thought along any number of avenues.

---

[14] *Meno* 70a; in *Plato in Twelve Volumes*, vol. 2, trans. W.R.M. Lamb (London: William Heinemann and Cambridge, Mass.: Harvard University Press, 1967). On the sophistic background, see Guthrie, *Sophists*, 250–260; Kerferd, *Sophistic Movement*, esp. 131–138. One important manuscript of *Meno* omits the reference to practice in the opening question, and scholars debate whether this was a later addition; see Dominic Scott, *Plato's Meno* (Cambridge, U.K.: Cambridge University Press, 2006), 14–18.

[15] *Eth. nic.* 1.9.1099b; *The Nicomachean Ethics*, in *Aristotle in Twenty-three Volumes*, vol. 9, trans. H. Rackham (Cambridge, Mass.: Harvard University Press and London: William Heinemann, 1982). See also *Eth. eud.* 1.1.1214a and the saying attributed to Aristotle in Diogenes Laertius, *Vitae Philosophorum* 5.18. Xenophon considers the three factors in relation to courage (*Memorabilia* 3.9.1–3).

[16] Horace *Ars Poetica* 408; Cicero, *Pro Archia* 1.1; see also Quintilian, *Institutio Oratoria* 1.26–27; all cited by Shorey, "*Physis, Meletē, Epistēmē*," 185. The nature-nurture debate continues in our own times of course, particularly in the spheres of natural and social science.

Abraham, Isaac, and Jacob as Exemplars
of Learning, Nature, and Practice

Introducing the Loeb Classical Library volume that contains his translation of Philo's *De Abrahamo*, F.H. Colson rightly remarks that although the learning-nature-practice motif is "one of [Philo's] leading ideas, he takes little pains to show how it fits the three great Patriarchs." Colson understands how the "checquered career" of Jacob, "long trained in the athletics of adversity" (*Ios.* 26), might earn him the title of "practicer," but he (Colson) finds it harder to grasp why Abraham is associated with teaching and Isaac with nature.[17] Indeed, while Philo explains *that* the patriarchs represent different ways of acquiring virtue, he does not tell us as directly *why* each one symbolizes each different path. He does, however provide enough clues—and the rare explicit statement—to allow us to hypothesize about how these associations came about.

Abraham, "The Sage Made Perfect through Teaching"

The link between Abraham and learning or teaching is perhaps the most complex of the three associations. As we shall see, this link seems to rely on more than one interpretation and each interpretation is itself an intricate combination of discrete elements and / or influences.

In the Exposition, Philo devotes an entire treatise to Abraham entitled "The Life of the Sage Made Perfect through Teaching or [the First Book] of Unwritten Laws, Which Is about Abraham." More frequently referred to as *On Abraham* (*Abr.*),[18] the treatise is one of several in which Philo presents themes and people from the Mosaic books. In a treatise on Abraham with this title—especially if the title is Philo's own—one might certainly expect that Philo would explicitly address the role that teaching had in Abraham's life. It is therefore rather ironic that although Philo does include material relevant to Abraham's role as a learner, he does not discuss this role directly at all.[19]

---

[17] F.H. Colson, "General Introduction," in Colson, Whitaker, and Marcus, *Philo*, 6:x–xi.

[18] I have translated the Greek title, in which an equivalent for "the First Book" is missing but usually inserted. By convention, abbreviations depend on the Latin titles of Philo's treatises.

[19] Adding to the mystery of Philo's neglect of this issue in *Abr.* is that presumably this is the treatise that he mentions in *Somn.* 1.168, in which he writes that he will show else-

A clue about the reason for this curious oversight, however, may be found in the remaining part of the title. For not only is Abraham the sage made perfect by teaching but he also represents one of the unwritten laws and thereby exemplifies obedience to the Mosaic laws even before they were written. As Philo explains it, following the account of creation and before the presentation of the specific, written laws—including the Ten Commandments and the many individual laws recorded in parts of Exodus through Deuteronomy—the Book of Genesis presents the lives of six figures, who symbolize general, unwritten laws (*Abr.* 3). These figures are grouped in two triads: Enosh, Enoch, and Noah; and Abraham, Isaac, and Jacob, with the second triad surpassing the first (*Abr.* 48).[20]

According to Philo, as unwritten laws, Abraham and the other five men show by their example that

> those who wish to live in accordance with the laws as they stand have no difficult task, seeing that the first generations before any at all of the particular statutes was set in writing followed the unwritten law with perfect ease, so that one might properly say that the enacted laws are nothing else than memorials of the life of the ancients, preserving to a later generation their actual words and deeds (*Abr.* 5).

A complication, however, may arise when Philo declares that

> they were not scholars or pupils of others, nor did they learn under teachers what was right to say or do: they listened to no voice or instruction but their own: they gladly accepted conformity with nature, holding that nature itself was, as indeed it is, the most venerable of statutes, and thus their whole life was one of happy obedience to law (*Abr.* 6).

Because Philo presents Abraham and the other figures from Genesis as naturally following the law without anyone to guide them, it may have been difficult for him then to depict Abraham as the model of a learner

---

where how Abraham was guided by teaching. In *Abr.* he also omits an interpretation very pertinent to Abraham's link with teaching, namely, the allegorization of Abraham's mating with Hagar prior to his conception of Isaac with Sarah. This omission is particularly striking since Philo recounts the episode on the literal level (*Abr.* 247–254), although here the focus is on Sarah.

[20] In addition to his treatise on Abraham, Philo probably also wrote works on Isaac and Jacob, which have regrettably not survived. Because the latter three patriarchs surpass the first three, it is sometimes overlooked that all six personages are considered unwritten laws (see, e.g., *Abr.* 16). For background, see, e.g., John W. Martens, *One God, One Law: Philo of Alexandria on the Mosaic and Greco-Roman Law* (Boston-Leiden: Brill Academic Publishers, Inc., 2003); Hindy Najman, "The Law of Nature and the Authority of Mosaic Law," *The Studia Philonica Annual* 11 (1999): 55–73; eadem, "A Written Copy of the Law of Nature: An Unthinkable Paradox?" *The Studia Philonica Annual* 15 (2003): 54–63.

who "has another for his teacher."[21] Nonetheless in other writings, Philo provides ample indications of the ways in which he viewed Abraham in the role of a learner. Most of these indications cluster around complex interpretations of three incidents in Abraham's life: 1) his mating with Hagar, in accordance with Sarah's instructions, prior to his conception of Isaac with Sarah (Gn 16:1–6); 2) his departure from Chaldea to Haran and then to Canaan, where God appeared to him (Gn 11:31, 12:1–7); and 3) the change of his name from Abram to Abraham (Gn 17:5), an interpretation that depends on the second one listed here.

Of these three interpretations, the one that places Abraham most obviously in the role of a learner is Philo's construal of Abraham's mating with Hagar. Philo develops this exegesis most extensively in the treatise *De Congressu* (*Congr.*), which focuses on Gn 16:1–6. Here Philo explains that Abraham symbolizes the mind; Sarah, virtue; and Hagar, the handmaid, the so-called "encyclical studies," a school curriculum of such subjects as grammar, geometry, astronomy, rhetoric, music, and others (*Congr.* 11).[22] As narrated in Gn 16:1–2, Sarah was not bearing Abraham children, so she told him to mate with Hagar. According to the allegorical meaning, these details signify that "[m]ind desires to have children by virtue, and, if it cannot do so at once, is instructed to espouse virtue's handmaid, the lower instruction" (*Congr.* 12).

Abraham's mating with Hagar before he conceives a child with Sarah thus represents his education in preparation for the acquisition of virtue. By engaging with the school studies to ready him for a successful union with virtue, Abraham becomes a symbol of one who acquires virtue through learning. Throughout the treatise, in fact, Philo refers in various ways to Abraham as a learner: e.g., "one that strives after speculation and knowledge" (*Congr.* 23, my translation), "he who gains wisdom by instruction" (24), "the learner" (*ho manthanōn*, 63, 69, 70, 122), "the lover of learning" (*philomathēs*, 68, 111), and "the recipient of teaching" (*didaskomenos*, 70).

This allegorical interpretation of Abraham's union with Hagar is thus one of the exegetical building blocks that contribute to the motif of the three patriarchs as symbols of different paths to virtue. This interpreta-

---

[21] *Mut.* 86. Indeed in *Abr.* 61 and 75 Philo emphasizes that anyone can learn what Abraham did; see below.

[22] On the encyclical studies—also called school studies and lower instruction—see Alan Mendelson, *Secular Education in Philo of Alexandria* (Cincinnati: Hebrew Union College Press, 1982); Monique Alexandre, *De congressu eruditionis gratia, Les oeuvres de Philon d'Alexandrie*, vol. 16 (Paris: Éditions du Cerf, 1967), 29–48.

tion itself, however, is composed of several discrete building blocks. As John Dillon and Yehoshua Amir have pointed out, some ancient Greek writers had likened students who did not move on from the school studies to philosophy to those suitors of Penelope in Homer's *Odyssey* who, unable to win Penelope, consorted with her handmaids.[23] In this analogy, Penelope represents philosophy, and her handmaids, the school studies. Amir further points out how Philo, drawing upon etymologies for Sarah and Hagar as "mistress" and "sojourner," respectively, applies this analogy to the biblical women—even if somewhat imperfectly, because Penelope's handmaids are many, while Hagar is but one person.[24] Philo's symbolization of Abraham as a learner, then, may depend on associations that were first developed in Greek thought in connection with Homer's *Odyssey* and then transferred to Jewish interpretation of Sarah and Hagar. Contributing to this interpretation, moreover, are etymologies, based on the Hebrew, of Sarah and Hagar.[25]

Regardless of how this complex allegorization took its final shape in Philo's works, it is not the only possible source behind his portrayal of Abraham as a learner. Less obvious, but no less pertinent, is Philo's understanding, discussed in *Abr.* 60–80, of Abraham's migration from Chaldea to Haran and beyond. After narrating the story on the literal level (60–67), Philo explains Abraham's journey as that of "a virtue-loving soul in its search for the true God" (68). In leaving Chaldea, this soul abandons the Chaldean way of thinking, here understood to be astrology and the glorification of creation rather than the Creator. This migration also signifies Abraham's recognition that beyond creation is a Creator, "a charioteer and pilot presiding over the world and directing in safety his own work ...." (70). As proof of Abraham's advancement to awareness of God, Philo cites Gn 12:7, "God was seen by Abraham" (77).[26]

---

[23] John Dillon, "Ganymede as the Logos: Traces of a Forgotten Allegorization in Philo," *Studia Philonica* 6 (1979–1980): 37–40; Amir, "Transference," 15–18; see also Alexandre, *De congressu*, 62–63.

[24] Amir, "Transference," 16. Amir distinguishes between reference to Penelope and her handmaids in an analogy and an allegorization; the latter appears to be later than Philo (Ibid., 17, n. 11). In *Congr.* 145, besides virtue, Philo also alludes to Sarah as a symbol of philosophy.

[25] In this intricate interpretation, it is difficult to distinguish Philo's own contributions from what may be pre-Philonic; see Amir, "Transference," 17–18; see also *Abr.* 99. For a detailed analysis of *Congr.*, see Burton L. Mack, "Weisheit und Allegorie bei Philo von Alexandrien: Untersuchungen zum Traktat *De Congressu eruditionis*," *Studia Philonica* 5 (1978): 57–105. Philo probably drew most, if not all, of his etymologies from traditional lists; for discussion and further references, see Birnbaum, *Place*, 67–70.

[26] Where the Hebrew intends, "God appeared to Abram," Philo emphasizes the passive

Abraham's next stop is Haran, a symbol of the senses and, correspond-
ingly, of self-knowledge.[27] The understanding of Haran as senses is based
on its etymology as "holes," "the seats of our senses" (*Abr.* 72). Just as the
universe has its charioteer and pilot, so too do the senses rely on "the
invisible mind," which serves as a "ruler which all the community of the
body obeys and each of the senses follows" (73–74). When considered
altogether, then, Abraham's journey signifies a progression from contem-
plation of the universe and of the self toward the realization that beyond
creation exists God the Creator who watches providentially over all that
He has made.

Like the allegorization of Abraham, Sarah, and Hagar, this interpretation of Abraham's journey is also constructed from several building
blocks. Among these are the understanding of Chaldea as symbolic of
a certain way of thinking, the etymological meaning of Haran as "holes,"
and the consequent link between Haran and the senses and thus self-
knowledge. Most important, however, is the perception that Abraham's
migrations from Chaldea and Haran are part of his journey toward the
discovery of the invisible Creator God. This perception is somewhat at
odds with Scripture: although Abraham first migrated from Chaldea with
his family (Gn 11:31), he was then commanded to go forth by the Lord
Himself (Gn 12:1).[28]

It is striking that for both stages of Abraham's advancement, in Chaldea
and Haran, Philo makes a point of saying that *anyone* (*tis*) who reflects
on the universe or on his own senses will discover the controlling presence of the Creator and the mind, respectively (*Abr.* 61, 75). Thus, in
accordance with Philo's earlier statement (*Abr.* 6) that the representatives
of the unwritten law are self-taught, it would seem as though Abraham
progresses without a teacher. Elsewhere, however, Philo does refer to this
journey as Abraham's education. In *Praem.* 58, for example, he describes

---

sense of the Greek verb *ōphthē*, was seen. Philo quotes this verse out of order, as God
appeared to Abraham in Canaan after Haran, not before. Although the patriarch is called
Abram at this point in the narrative, Philo calls him Abraham, and I follow his usage in
my discussion.

[27] Philo does not call this stage self-knowledge in *Abr.*, but see *Somn.* 1.52–60.

[28] Cf. *QG* 3.1, based on Gn 15:7, in which God is said to lead Abraham out of the land of
the Chaldeans. Philo's understanding is but one of a range of ancient interpretations about
Abraham's journey; see Kugel, *Traditions*, 243–254, 258–262. See also Burton L. Mack,
Logos und Sophia: Untersuchungen zur Weisheitstheologie im hellenistischen Judentum
(Göttingen: Vandenhoeck & Ruprecht, 1973), 122–130.

Abraham as one "who spurned the impostures of Chaldean astrology for the sake of the fuller spectacle which he beheld and followed the vision …, *thus changed by instruction from sophist to sage* …." (*anti sophistou genomenos ek didaskalias sophos*; my emphasis).[29]

In Abram's name change to Abraham, Philo finds further affirmation that the patriarch evolved from following Chaldean tenets to becoming a sage. Philo explains that Abram's original name, which means "uplifted father," signifies an "astrologer and meteorologist, one who takes care of the Chaldean tenets as a father would of his children" (*Abr.* 82). Abraham's new name, however, which means "elect father of sound" signifies the sage, because "father" represents the ruling mind, which is father to what is uttered (i.e., sound), and "'elect' signifies the man of worth" (83). This interpretation, then, with its etymologies for Abram and Abraham is dependent upon Philo's earlier understanding of the patriarch's migration from Chaldea, as described above.

In *Abr.*, perhaps for reasons that we have discussed, Philo again does not call attention to Abraham's change of name as a process of education. In *Mut.* 70, however, Philo speaks of Abraham's change of name as his transformation from being "the lover of learning" (*philomathēs*) to his becoming "the philosopher, or rather, the sage" (*ho philosophos, mallon d'ho sophos*, my translation). This depiction of Abraham as becoming a philosopher further calls to mind the Greek educational context, discussed above, whereby one advances from school studies to philosophy. His becoming a sage similarly represents the culmination of his educational achievement. Indeed, Philo describes Abraham as a sage (or as wise) more than he does any other patriarch, and this epithet seems intended to both affirm and evoke Abraham's role as a learner.[30]

---

[29] In relation to this journey, Philo also speaks of Abraham elsewhere as a mind that has an inexpressible love of knowledge (*Leg.* 3.84) and of Haran as a stage in his learning (*Somn.* 1.59–60); see also *Migr.* 192, 216–223 for general references to education in context of this journey. It is interesting, however, that while Philo portrays Abraham as a learner, he does not always focus on the teacher; see below, n. 36.

[30] For a similar interpretation of Abraham's name change, see also *QG* 3.43, in which God is said to be Abraham's teacher. For other references to Abraham as [a] *sophos*, see J.W. Earp, "Indices to Volumes I–X," in Colson, Whitaker, and Marcus, *Philo*, 10:278, note c. The description of Abraham as wise or a sage seems to belong to the tradition associated with his change of name but not to the allegorization of his mating with Hagar; see, e.g., *Congr.* 48, 92, 109, and 119, in which the description of Abraham as wise or a sage is independent of this latter allegorization.

Isaac, "The Self-Learnt Kind"

In all Philo's interpretations that use the learning-nature-practice motif to explain puzzling differences among Abraham, Isaac, and Jacob, Isaac—symbol of the acquisition of virtue through nature—stands apart from and appears superior to his father and son. We saw this above in the discussion about why Abraham and Jacob each receive a change of name, but Isaac maintains the same name throughout (*Mut.* 83–88). As one who is naturally and thus effortlessly virtuous, Isaac surpasses the other two patriarchs in other ways too. Thus, while Abraham and Jacob are gathered at their deaths to a people (*laos*), a collectivity of many, Isaac is gathered to a race or genus (*genos*), an integral unit, which in Philo's thought is imperishable and perfect.[31]

Similarly, Philo addresses why Abraham and Jacob have several wives and concubines but Isaac has only one wife. Just as a learner requires several kinds of studies, and a practicer, several trials and experiences, Abraham and Jacob require several partners. Isaac, naturally gifted, has no need of this plurality of studies and experiences and therefore has only one wife (*Congr.* 34–38).

In another example, Philo comments on Gn 28:13, in which God says to Jacob, "I am the Lord God of Abraham thy father and God of Isaac." Philo notices that Abraham is called the father—not the grandfather—of Jacob, and Isaac is not referred to as his parent at all. In addition, the Deity is spoken of as "Lord God of Abraham" and "God of Isaac" (*Somn.* 1.159–170). According to Philo the different appellations for the Deity show that, as one who gains knowledge through teaching, Abraham requires both of God's powers—the ruling and the kindly. The naturally gifted Isaac, however, requires the power of kindness alone without need of admonitions from the ruling power. Perceiving the significance of the different divine names linked to Abraham and Isaac, Jacob, the practicer, prays for the Lord to become God to him (Gn 28:21) "for he wished no longer to be in dread of Him as ruler, but lovingly to honour Him as bestower of kindness" (*Mut.* 163). In addition, Abraham is spoken of as Jacob's father because learning and practice are closely akin. Once Jacob the practicer "run[s] to the end of the course," however, and receives his new name Israel, which means "one that sees God," he can now claim

---

[31] *Sacr.* 6–7; this interpretation depends on different wording in the Greek Bible between the verses about Abraham and Jacob, on one hand, and about Isaac, on the other; see Birnbaum, *Place*, 56–58.

Isaac as his rightful parent and address God's kindly power alone, for it says that "Israel ... offered a sacrifice to the God of his father Isaac" (Gn 46:1) (*Mut.* 171–172).

Finally, of the three patriarchs, only Isaac is told by God not to go down to Egypt (Gn 26:2), whereas both Abraham and Jacob each sojourn there for a while. As a symbol of perfection and virtue acquired naturally, Isaac can completely avoid involvement with the passions, symbolized by the land of Egypt. Unlike the impassive Isaac, as strivers toward virtue, Abraham and Jacob represent moderation in passion and therefore follow the "middle way" by having at least some experience in Egypt.[32]

Anyone familiar with the patriarchal narratives in Genesis may be somewhat surprised by the elevation of Isaac in Philo's allegorizations to a position superior to Abraham and Jacob. It is true that Isaac retains the same name throughout the narratives, has but one wife, and does not go down to Egypt. In the Bible, however, these details and others about Isaac—because of their relative sparsity and lack of variety—contribute to an impression of him as somewhat vague and indistinct. Indeed, the narrative cycles about Abraham (Gn 12–25, approximately) and Jacob (Gn 25–35, approximately) are much longer than the accounts about Isaac, who therefore seems overshadowed by his father and son.[33] How, then, did this somewhat obscure patriarch come to be associated with one who is naturally virtuous and therefore worthy of such high praise and admiration?

Contrary to what we may expect, Philo provides us with a completely straightforward explanation, albeit one that is well-folded into an aside in one of his exegetical discussions. Isaac, he writes, is self-learnt and self-taught (*automathēs kai autodidaktos*), "for (*gar*) Moses represents him as weaned, absolutely disdaining to make any use of soft and milky food suited to infants and little children, and using only strong nourishment fit for grown men, seeing that from a babe he was naturally stalwart, and

---

[32] *QG* 4.177, in which the interpretation I have presented is implicit. Abraham and Jacob are not named but are referred to indirectly (in the translation) as "those who are moderate," to whom "the middle way" is advised. (These moderate ones can also encompass Jacob's sons, who go down to Egypt as well.) See also Sarah J.K. Pearce, *The Land of the Body: Studies in Philo's Representation of Egypt* (Tübingen: Mohr Siebeck, 2007), 82–85; *Det.* 46; *Migr.* 29.

[33] Isaac's birth is foretold in Gn 17:19 and announced in Gn 21:1–8. Genesis 22 narrates the all-important episode of the binding of Isaac, but until his death is mentioned in Gn 35:29, this patriarch appears only sporadically in the narrative.

was ever attaining fresh vigour and renewing his youth" (*Somn.* 2.10).[34]
Based on Gn 21:8, which says, "And the child grew and was weaned,"
Philo understands that from his infancy, Isaac had no need of "baby food"
but was instead "naturally stalwart (*pros alkēn pephukota*)."

Further support that Isaac's weaning is the basis of his symbolic role as
naturally gifted can be found in *Migr.* 140, in an interpretation of Gn 21:7,
"Who shall tell Abraham that Sarah is suckling a child?" Philo writes, "It
does not say 'a child is being suckled by Sarah,' for the kind that is taught
without a teacher (*to autodidakton*) is nourished by no one, but is a source
of nourishment to others, being capable of teaching and not needing to
learn."[35]

Because Philo links Isaac's weaning explicitly with his being self-taught
and naturally stalwart from birth, I believe that this understanding of
Gn 21:8 is most directly behind the association of Isaac with virtue
acquired by nature. Indeed Philo frequently describes Isaac as self-learnt
(*automathēs*) and self-taught (*autodidaktos*) and often refers to him as
the *automathes genos*, "the self-learnt kind (or genus)."[36]

Although it is thus likely that Gn 21:8 is the primary source behind
the association between Isaac and nature, another possibly related verse
is Gn 21:2, which says about Sarah that "she conceived and gave birth."
In *Fug.* 167–168, Philo understands this verse allegorically to signify that
Isaac was conceived by the soul and born simultaneously:

---

[34] In *Somn.* 2.10–11, this aside occurs in a discussion whose focus is the distinction
between Isaac and Joseph. "Self-learnt" is an awkward translation for *automathēs*, which
can also be translated—and means the same thing—as "self-taught." I use "self-learnt" for
automathēs, however, to reflect the Greek root *math* and to distinguish this word from
autodidaktos, since Philo uses them both.

[35] The significance of Isaac being weaned as the basis of his association with nature
is also supported by *Migr.* 29, which refers to Isaac as "[the self-learnt, self-taught kind
(*genos to automathes, to autodidakton*)] that needs not to be fed on milk as children are
fed." A striking contrast to this interpretation and the two quoted above, however, is found
in *Sobr.* 8, in which Philo says that Isaac "ceased to be fed with milk" "at about the age of
seven."

[36] For *automathes genos*, see e.g., *Ebr.* 60; *Sobr.* 65; *Conf.* 74; *Migr.* 29; *Fug.* 168; *Mut.* 1,
137; *Somn.* 1.68, 194. For other references to Isaac as self-learnt and self-taught, see, e.g.,
Earp, "Indices," 326, notes a and b. Although Philo describes Isaac as self-taught, Philo
also speaks of him as a pupil of God (e.g., *Sacr.* 7). Since Abraham too has God as his
teacher (e.g., *Mut.* 85–87, 270; *Somn.* 1.173; *QG* 3.43), this way of speaking about Isaac
and Abraham can be somewhat confusing. See also Calvin J. Roetzel, "Theodidaktoi and
Handwork in Philo and I Thessalonians," in *L'apotre Paul: Personnalité, style et conception
du ministère*, ed. A. Vanhoye (Leuven: Leuven University Press, 1986), 328–329.

> This is he whom Holy Writ calls 'Isaac,' whom the soul did not conceive at
> one time and give birth to at another, for it says 'she conceived and gave
> birth' as though timelessly. For he that was thus born was not a man, but a
> most pure thought, beautiful not by practice but by nature.

Even though Philo understands Isaac here as a thought rather than a
man, he includes the idea that this thought was "beautiful not by practice
but by nature." This comment suggests that the interpretation that Sarah
conceived and gave birth to Isaac simultaneously—with the implication
that Isaac needed no time to develop but was naturally perfect from the
first—may thus be an additional contributing factor to the link between
this patriarch and nature.[37]

A particularly rich source of associations with Isaac, which contribute
to his extraordinary image, is Gn 21:6, in which Sarah says, "The Lord
has made laughter for me, for whosoever shall hear of it will rejoice with
me."[38] One exegetical thread based on this verse associates Isaac with
both laughter and joy, the latter understood according to Stoic terminology as "the best of the good emotions."[39] Even more remarkable, however,
is a second thread based on the detail that God Himself made the laughter. In *Leg. all.* 3.219, Philo intertwines these two threads together and
incorporates the association of Isaac with nature as well. According to
Philo, in this verse,

> [t]he 'laughter' is joy, and 'made' is equivalent to 'beget,' so that what is
> said is of this kind, the Lord begat Isaac; for He is Himself Father of the
> perfect nature (*teleia physis*), sowing and begetting happiness in men's
> souls.

In this clearly allegorical interpretation, God is said to be the Father of
perfect nature. In *Det.* 124, however, Philo again refers to this verse and
writes as follows:

> For God is the Creator of laughter that is good, and of joy, so that we
> must hold Isaac to be not a product of created beings, but a work of the
> uncreated One. For if 'Isaac' means 'laughter,' and according to Sarah's
> unerring witness God is the Maker of laughter, *God may with perfect truth
> be said to be Isaac's father.* (my emphasis)

---

[37] The same language about conceiving and giving birth is found in Gn 4:1 regarding
Eve and Cain and 4:17 regarding Cain's wife and Enoch, but Philo does not comment on
this aspect of these verses.

[38] Where the Greek has "will rejoice" (*sunchareitai*), the Hebrew has "will laugh"
(יצחק), which is Isaac's name.

[39] E.g., *Mut.* 1, 131; *Praem.* 31. On Stoic ideas about emotions, see F.H. Sandbach, *The
Stoics* (London: Chatto & Windus, 1975), 59–68.

It is tempting to explore further the various fascinating threads associated with Isaac and perhaps to compare them with Christian traditions
about Jesus.[40] For our present purposes, I would argue that these threads
should be viewed as linked to discrete verses and that the symbolism of
Isaac as naturally attaining virtue has its source in an understanding of
Gn 21:8, which says that Isaac grew and was weaned, and possibly of Gn
21:2, which says that Sarah conceived and gave birth.[41]

Jacob, "The Practicer"

With three patriarchs and three ways of acquiring virtue, one might think
that once two patriarchs have been matched with two paths to virtue, the
last match becomes inevitable and thus Jacob by default may have been
linked with practice. An obvious objection to this reasoning, however, is
that we do not know the order in which these associations were made.
Indeed, as we have seen, Colson finds the connection between Jacob
and practice to be the most understandable because of the patriarch's
"chequered career." Although this career is undoubtedly a significant
basis for the connection between Jacob and practice, however, I believe
that another factor is even more important.

In discussing practice as an avenue to virtue, Philo often uses *askēsis*
and related forms, and his most frequent epithet for Jacob is *ho askētēs*,
the practicer. While *askētēs* can describe one who practices an art or
trade, the word also has a decidedly physical nuance and is often used as
a synonym for athlete (*athlētēs*).[42] How did Jacob, known at one point in
the Bible to have been "a simple man, living at home" (Gn 25:27, based on
the Greek), acquire a reputation in Philo's works as an athlete? The answer
is plain: according to Gn 32:24–25, he was a wrestler! Indeed his successful wrestling at the Jabbok ford led to the change of his name to Israel.

---

[40] Certainly among these traditions must be included Philo's interpretation, based on
Gn 18:11, that Sarah was a virgin when she conceived Isaac; see, e.g., *Post.* 134; see also
Cher. 50. On God as Isaac's father, see also *Mut.* 130–131 in connection with Gn 17:16,
Cher. 45 in connection with Gn 21:1, and *Somn.* 1.173, which may refer to either or both
of the previous two interpretations.

[41] I therefore disagree with Colson's suggestion ("General Introduction," *Philo*, 6:xi)
that the association of Isaac with nature is linked to his association with joy. Even though
Philo brings these two associations together, I believe that they are originally separate and
based on two different verses.

[42] See *A Greek-English Lexicon*, compiled by Henry George Liddell and Robert Scott,
9th ed., revised and augmented by Henry Stuart Jones, s.v. "*askētēs*."

For Philo, then, this episode establishes Jacob as an athlete and thereby a practicer. Indeed, he often calls Jacob, the practicer, an athlete; speaks of him in relation to wrestling; and uses athletic imagery to describe him.[43] We saw this use of athletic imagery earlier, for example, in the explanation of why Jacob is still sometimes called Israel even after his name is changed (*Mut.* 84). Beyond establishing Jacob as an athlete, however, the wrestling episode carries enormous allegorical significance as "the wrestling-bout in which the Man of Practice engaged in his quest of virtue" (*Mut.* 14). Accordingly, Jacob's success in wrestling symbolizes his victory over the passions, while his new name represents his prize, the ability to see God, the height of human attainment, symbolized by the name Israel, whose very etymology is "one who sees God."

In one passage, without mentioning "practice" explicitly, Philo describes the wrestling episode as follows, with Jacob's adversary being identified as the divine word (or *logos*):

> The divine word readily listens to and accepts the athlete to be first of all a pupil, then when he has been satisfied of his fitness of nature, he fastens on the gloves as a trainer does and summons him to the exercises, then closes with him and forces him to wrestle until he has developed in him an irresistible strength, and by the breath of divine inspiration he changes ears into eyes, and gives him when remodelled in a new form the name of Israel—He who sees (*Somn.* 1.129).[44]

Although Jacob's wrestling match, then, is undoubtedly at the heart of Philo's identification of him with the practicer, Philo applies the description of Jacob as a practicer well beyond this one episode. In other contexts, Philo speaks of Jacob as a practicer of virtue (*aretē*; *Det.* 45–46, *Ebr.* 82); of excellent things (*kaloi*, *Sacr.* 17, *Migr.* 153), and of knowledge (*epistēmē*, *Det.* 3). In these noble pursuits, he is occasionally compared with Esau, who is linked with passion, folly, and practice of base things (*Leg. all.* 3.190–191, *Sacr.* 17, *Migr.* 153, *Her.* 252–253, *QG* 4.238).

The biblical account of Jacob's life offers several other details compatible with his depiction as a practicer. As we saw in the interpretation of why Jacob's name vacillates with Israel (*Mut.* 83–84), Philo

---

[43] E.g., *Leg.* 3.190; *Sobr.* 65; *Migr.* 199–200; *Mut.* 14, 44; *Somn.* 1, 129, 255; *QG* 4.228. Philo himself appears to have been an interested spectator of sports like wrestling (see, e.g., *Prob.* 26, 110).

[44] Here Philo gives only a partial etymology for Israel instead of the full one, "he who sees God;" see Birnbaum, *Place*, 94–95.

emphasizes that one who practices has uneven experiences and must persist in practice to maintain the achievement, a persistence that requires great toil (e.g., *Migr.* 213–214; *Somn.* 1.115, 168, 208; *Ios.* 223). Similarly, Rebecca advises Jacob to go to Haran, a land associated with the senses, so that the practicer might gain a wide variety of experiences (*Fug.* 23–39, *Somn.* 1.46, *QG* 4.240). The practicer's need for variety is also reflected in Philo's interpretation of why Jacob has several wives and concubines (*Congr.* 35).[45]

Colson, then, is undoubtedly correct that Jacob's "chequered career" fits nicely with his symbolic role as a practicer. Because of the unmistakable link between practice and athletics, however, and because of the great significance that Philo attributes to Jacob's wrestling match, I believe that Jacob's experience as a wrestler is the primary reason behind his identification as the practicer. Once this initial identification was made, the details of Jacob's varied life provided multiple threads with which Philo (and perhaps his predecessors) could embroider a rich and colorful tapestry of interpretation.

The Graces: A Missing Link?

So far, we have identified a number of building blocks that may have contributed to Philo's allegorization of the patriarchs as three different ways of acquiring virtue. We have seen that in philosophical and other works, learning, nature, and practice were regarded as important factors for the attainment of a range of skills and moral qualities. In Philonic exegeses of specific verses, we have also identified possible sources for the association of Abraham with learning, Isaac with nature, and Jacob with practice. A big question that remains, however, is what inspired Philo, or perhaps his predecessors, to bring the patriarchs together with the three paths to virtue in the first place.

As John Dillon and Yehoshua Amir have recognized, Philo offers a valuable hint in *Abr.* 54.[46] After explaining that Abraham, Isaac, and Jacob symbolize the three paths to virtue, Philo comments that Moses

---

[45] For other interpretations of Jacob's varied experiences (not all of which pertain to practice, however), see Earp, "Indices," 336–348.

[46] John Dillon, *The Middle Platonists, 80 BC to AD 220*, rev. ed. (Ithaca, N.Y.: Cornell University Press, 1977 and 1996), 153 (see also 163); Amir, "Transference," 18–20.

[v]ery properly … associated these three together, nominally men, but really … virtues—teaching, nature, practice. Another name is given to them by men, who call them the Graces, also three in number; either because these values are a gift of God's grace to our kind for perfecting its life, or because they have given themselves to the reasonable soul as a perfect and most excellent gift…

Philo's remark that people call the three paths to virtue by another name, the Graces (*Charites*), suggests that parallel (and maybe prior) to the allegorization of the patriarchs was a similar allegorization of the Graces. Both in Philo's thought and in Greek culture, the Graces play a significant role, and they have a long and varied history in Greek mythology.[47] Hesiod, for example, mentions them as daughters of Zeus and Eurynome (*Theogony* 907–909). Centuries later, in his essay *On Benefits*, devoted to the social and moral importance of giving and receiving, Seneca, a contemporary of Philo, preserves additional important details related to the Graces. Apparently referring in part to a visual representation of them, he reports that they are "three in number"; sisters; with interlocked hands; smiling, young, and virginal; clothed in "loose and transparent garb" (1.3.2); and engaged in a ring dance, "which returns upon itself" (1.3.4)[48]

Seneca interprets this portrayal to signify reciprocity in giving and receiving, that is, that a benefit returns to the giver and "the beauty of the whole is destroyed if the course is anywhere broken" (1.3.4). He also mocks the treatment of the Graces by Chrysippus (third century BCE), who, in Seneca's opinion, focuses too much on aspects irrelevant to "the duty itself of giving, receiving, and returning a benefit" (1.3.8). Thus, he claims that Chrysippus pays excessive attention to such particulars as names and at times even invents names for the figures he discusses. Chrysippus also attributes mistaken significance to the Graces' being daughters of Jupiter and Eurynome (1.3.9–10; 1.4.4–5). Noting that Seneca thus presents these details about Chrysippus and that the concept of the three different paths to virtue can also be found in Chrysippus, Pierre Boyancé raises the possibility that perhaps Chrysippus himself was

---

[47] See, e.g., *The Oxford Classical Dictionary*, 3rd ed., s.v. "Charites"; Bonnie MacLachlan, *The Age of Grace: Charis in Early Greek Poetry* (Princeton: Princeton University Press, 1993); James H. Oliver, *Demokratia, the Gods, and the Free World* (Baltimore: Johns Hopkins Press, 1960), 91–117.

[48] *On Benefits*, in *Seneca in Ten Volumes*, vol. 3, trans., John W. Basore (Cambridge, Mass. and London: Harvard University Press, 1989) (used for all quotations from Seneca cited here).

the source of the allegorization that eventually found its way into Philo's works.[49]

Significantly, some of Philo's allusions to the Graces also reflect an originally mythological background, such as when he speaks of them as God's virginal daughters.[50] In Philo's reference to the three patriarchs as belonging to one household and one race, Amir sees a possible allusion to the Greek portrayal of the three Graces as interconnected.[51] If he is correct, perhaps even more relevant may be Philo's remark that each patriarch possesses the three qualities of nature, teaching, and practice, since these are all interrelated.[52]

Philo's two explanations in *Abr.* 54 for why people call the three qualities Graces may be similarly illuminating. One explanation accords with what he says elsewhere about the Graces, while the second explanation contrasts with his other remarks about them. Philo observes that some people give the name of Graces to the qualities represented by the patriarchs because these qualities "are a gift of God's grace to our kind for perfecting its life." This comment accords with the idea that he expresses elsewhere that virtue itself is a gift of God's grace.[53] Here, then, the virtues symbolized by the patriarchs are seen as God's gracious gift to humanity. Indeed, in Philo's thought, the Graces generally are "an expression of benefits accorded by God to men."[54] Whether personified or not, then, in Philo's thought the Graces are under God's control.

A second explanation for calling the virtues "Graces" is that "they have given themselves to the reasonable soul as a perfect and most excellent gift." This explanation portrays the Graces, or virtues, as independent agents, that is, not explicitly under the control of God or a higher power.

---

[49] Pierre Boyancé, "Écho des exégèses de la mythologie grecque chez Philon," in *Philon d'Alexandrie* (Paris: Éditions Centre National de la Recherché Scientifique, 1967), 179–180. Because Seneca refers to Hecaton as copying from Chrysippus (*On Benefits* 1.3.9), Boyancé also wonders whether Hecaton may have served as an intermediary between Chrysippus and Seneca.

[50] *Migr.* 31, *QE* 2.61; see also *Post.* 32, *Fug.* 141. Boyancé ("Echo," 178–183) discusses these and other passages like *Mos.* 2.7 and *Plant.* 89, which buttress the notion that Philo drew his descriptions of the Graces from an originally mythological background.

[51] Amir, "Transference," 20.

[52] *Abr.* 53, quoted earlier; for a related idea, see also *Mos.* 2.7.

[53] For references and discussion, see John M.G. Barclay, " 'By the Grace of God I Am What I Am': Grace and Agency in Philo and Paul," in *Divine and Human Agency in Paul and His Cultural Environment*, ed. John M.G. Barclay and Simon J. Gathercole (London and New York: T&T Clark, 2006), 143–146. See also Dieter Zeller, *Charis bei Philon und Paulus* (Stuttgart: Verlag Katholisches Bibelwerk, 1990), 86–99.

[54] Boyancé, "Écho," 180.

Philo's allusion to this explanation may thus reflect his awareness of the Graces as divinities in Greek mythology. These two different explanations combined with mythological traces in Philo's own references to these entities suggest that the Graces may have been symbolic figures whose originally mythological lore and its interpretation by Greek thinkers were transformed and adapted for Jewish exegetical purposes. Philo may therefore have known of a parallel source that allegorized the Graces as qualities that he himself associates with the patriarchs.[55]

Although we have no direct evidence of such an allegorization, Philo's reference in *Abr.* 54, supported by Seneca's discussion of Chrysippus's treatment of the Graces, makes it seem very plausible that such an allegorization existed. If so, Philo himself—or his predecessors themselves—may not have applied directly to the patriarchs the notion that virtue is acquired through nature, learning, and/or practice. Instead he—or his predecessors—may have been influenced by an earlier allegorization in which these qualities were symbolized by the Graces. In this way, then, the Graces may have been "a missing link" between the philosophical formulation of learning, nature, and practice and its application to Abraham, Isaac, and Jacob.

Conclusion

Philo's understanding of Abraham, Isaac, and Jacob as symbols of three paths to the acquisition of virtue relies on a number of discrete elements, or exegetical building blocks. These include, on the most basic level, the notion that virtue can be attained through learning, nature, and practice and the identification of Abraham as a learner, Isaac as naturally gifted, and Jacob as a practicer. As far back as the fifth century BCE, these three factors appear in philosophical and other discussions about how to attain various skills and moral qualities.

Regarding the identification of each patriarch with each different path, I have suggested that each of these identifications is based on interpretations of specific biblical verses or episodes. Thus, Abraham is associated with learning on the basis of complex allegorizations of his mating

---

[55] In *Abr.* 54, the explanations about the Graces pertain to God's linking of His name with Abraham, Isaac, and Jacob (Exod. 3:15; see *Abr.* 50-51). If one understands the patriarchs as qualities instead of men, then the name of God, who is eternal, is thus seen as being more suitably associated with imperishable virtues rather than with perishable

with Hagar prior to his conception of Isaac with Sarah (Gn 16:1–6), his migrations from Chaldea and Haran (Gn 11:31; 12:1–7), and, secondarily, the change of this name from Abram to Abraham (Gn 17:5). Each of these interpretations is itself an intricate amalgam of building blocks that include an analogy from Homeric exegesis, a variety of etymologies, and earlier understandings of Abraham's journey. Similarly, Isaac becomes associated with natural ability on the basis of an interpretation of Gn 21:8, which says that he was weaned, and possibly of Gn 21:2, which says that Sarah conceived and gave birth. Finally, Jacob is identified with practice, which itself is linked with athletic ability, because of his successful wrestling, as narrated in Gn 32:24–25.

Although we can identify several sources for the notion that virtue is acquired via learning, nature, and practice, and although we can hypothesize about the exegetical foundations underlying the association of each patriarch with each different path, we do not know how the three paths and the three patriarchs came to be linked together in the first place. In *Abr.* 54, Philo provides a valuable hint when he remarks that some people give the name of Graces to these paths (or virtues). This comment suggests that Philo's own interpretation of the patriarchs may have been influenced by a prior allegorization of these Greek mythological figures.

Because other Jewish sources offer no evidence of the interpretation of the patriarchs as learning, nature, and practice, we cannot determine precisely when this motif originated. Nor can we ascertain whether it had a long history of development or whether Philo was responsible for contributing most of the building blocks himself. What we can say, however, is that he brought these building blocks together with dazzling ingenuity, and the resulting creation is a lasting, deeply impressive, and magnificent monument to Alexandrian Jewish exegesis.

humans. One wonders who originated the two explanations about the Graces, whether these interpreters preceded Philo or were contemporary to him, and, if the latter, what his relationship with these interpreters may have been.

EXEGETICAL TRADITIONS IN ALEXANDRIA: PHILO'S REWORKING OF THE *LETTER OF ARISTEAS* 145–149 AS A CASE STUDY[*]

HANS SVEBAKKEN

Introduction

In a revised version of his Harvard dissertation, Thomas H. Tobin considers Philo's unique contribution to a long and complex history of interpreting the biblical account of man's creation within Alexandrian Judaism.[1] Using an extensive source-critical analysis of Philo's writings, Tobin reconstructs a historical sequence of interpretations, each reflecting the efforts of a new generation of Jewish exegetes to understand Genesis 1–3 in light of prevailing trends in the philosophical milieu of their day.[2] While these interpreters naturally disagreed with the work of their predecessors on certain points, they tended not to reject it openly, because they considered themselves heirs of a venerable tradition.[3] They

---

[*] Offered with many thanks to Fr. Tom Tobin for sparking my interest in Philo, for directing my dissertation (part of which appears here, expanded and revised), and for modeling the ways of a true gentleman and scholar.

[1] Thomas H. Tobin, *The Creation of Man: Philo and the History of Interpretation* CBQMS 14 (Washington, D.C.: Catholic Biblical Association of America, 1983). On exegetical traditions in general, see Burton L. Mack, "Philo Judaeus and Exegetical Traditions in Alexandria," *ANRW* 21.1:227–271.

[2] For Tobin's methodology, see *Creation of Man*, 1–19. Chapters of Tobin's monograph treat each "level" of interpretation in turn: "Anti-Anthropomorphic Interpretations" (III), "The Single Creation of Man" (IV), "The Double Creation of Man" (V), and "Philo and the Allegory of the Soul" (VI). As a distinct line of interpretation, "Single Creation of Man" takes Gn 1:27 and Gn 2:7 as *two* references to the creation of *one* man, while "Double Creation of Man" takes them as two references to the creation of *two different* men. Consideration of the contemporary philosophical trends informing these interpretations figures prominently in Tobin's study, which—as he puts it: "involves the analysis of the thought patterns used in the interpretation, and the relationship of those thought patterns to the biblical text and to the philosophical milieu of Alexandria during that period .... [T]hese interpretations were attempts to be true both to the biblical text and to the best in the philosophical learning of the period" (idem, 9). Tobin envisions these exegetes working in the school-like setting of the Alexandrian synagogue (idem, 172–176).

[3] E.g., Tobin, *Creation of Man*, 100: "As was the case with most of the ancient world,

struck a delicate balance between continuity and change, honoring traditional interpretations by reusing them in whole or in part but often
reworking them to suit their own interests. Situating himself within this
broader tradition, Philo takes a traditional, Platonically inspired interpretation of Gn 1:27 and Gn 2:7 as the creation of two different *men*
(one heavenly, one earthly) and reworks it into the basis for a distinction between two sorts of *minds* (one heavenly, one earthly).[4] Tobin finds
"two very significant shifts" occurring at this level of interpretation, both
of which distinguish the work of Philo from the work of his predecessors.[5] First, Philo introduces the "allegory of the soul," which presumes
his exegesis of the creation of man but focuses really on the *fall* of man:

> The allegory of the soul is essentially a method of interpretation in which
> the figures described in the text of Genesis as figures in the external world
> are internalized and taken to refer to internal, spiritual realities. In this
> allegory, the man created in Gn 2:7 becomes a symbol of "mind" (νοῦς),
> the woman of "sense-perception" (αἴσθησις), and the serpent of "pleasure"
> (ἡδονή). Figures of the external world, Adam, Eve, and the serpent, are
> now taken to refer to the interior life of the individual human being.[6]

Modeled on Middle-Platonic allegorical readings of the *Odyssey*, which
depict the soul's arduous journey from the sensible to the intelligible
realm, Philo's allegory of the soul envisions the soul's struggle to escape
entanglements with the sensible realm due to the deceptive influence of
pleasure.[7] The second shift involves Philo's notable attempt (the first of

previous interpretations were to be prized. Previous interpretations were something to
which they felt a responsibility, something which therefore could not be easily or openly
rejected." Here Tobin comments on the incorporation of an earlier *Stoic* interpretation of
Gn 2:7 into a larger (and later) *Platonic* interpretation of the creation account (idem,
77–101). But he finds this sort of reverence demonstrated *throughout* the history of
interpretation.

[4] For Philo's interpretation of the creation of man, see Tobin, *Creation of Man*, 135–
145. Questions pertaining to *which man* God placed in the garden (Gn 2:15) figure
prominently in this level of interpretation (cf. *Leg.* 1.88–89, 90–96; NB *Leg.* 1.90: ὁ γὰρ
κατ᾽ εἰκόνα [νοῦς] οὐ γήινος, ἀλλ᾽ οὐράνιος).

[5] Tobin, *Creation of Man*, 145–161 (quotation from 145).

[6] Tobin, *Creation of Man*, 34. On the allegory of the soul, see esp. idem, 135–176.
Tobin notes that Burton Mack ("Weisheit und Allegorie bei Philo von Alexandrien"
SPh 5 (1979): 57–105, 80–82) also identified the "Philonic stratum" of interpretation
as the allegory of the soul in his analysis of *De congressu eruditionis gratia* (Tobin,
Creation of Man, 34, n. 22). The "technical vocabulary of allegory" appears at this level of
interpretation (e.g., ἀλληγορία, σύμβολον; see idem, 147).

[7] On Middle-Platonic parallels, see Tobin, *Creation of Man*, 150–154; cf. Robert
Lamberton, *Homer the Theologian: Neoplatonist Allegorical Reading and the Growth of the
Epic Tradition*, TCH 9 (Berkeley: University of California Press, 1986), especially 44–82.

its kind) to maintain the validity of both allegorical and non-allegorical levels of interpretation.[8] Here he departs from the standard practice of his Greek models, who tended to disregard or reject the literal significance of texts they interpreted, and who in this regard influenced at least *some* Jewish interpreters.[9]

By analyzing interpretations of a particular text (Gn 1–3), Tobin draws general conclusions about the characteristic interests and methods of Philo himself (that is, allegory of the soul, maintaining both levels) and the exegetical tradition he inherited (continuity and change, contemporary philosophy). In this way, he offers a framework for analyzing the history of interpretation of other texts—although he rightly cautions against taking the interpretation of the creation of man as "*the* paradigm" for the interpretation of other parts of the Pentateuch.[10]

In conversation with the framework derived from Tobin's research, this essay considers the list of prohibited birds in Lv 11:13–19 (which, of course, does belong to a different part of the Pentateuch) to see if Tobin's conclusions help to make sense of the way Philo uses a traditional interpretation from the *Letter of Aristeas* in his own exposition of the dietary laws.

Eleazar and Philo: Two Interpretations of Lv 11:13–19

Leviticus 11 provides dietary regulations distinguishing "clean" and lawfully edible creatures from "unclean," prohibited creatures—and among its restrictions it lists twenty species of prohibited birds:

For examples of *struggle* with the wiles of pleasure (ἡδονή) as part of the allegory of the soul, see *Opif.* 165–166, *Leg.* 3.59–64 (cf. Tobin, *Creation of Man*, 145–146). On Philo's view of pleasure, see Alain Le Boulluec, "La place des concepts philosophiques dans la réflexion de Philon sur le plaisir," in *Philon d'Alexandrie et le langage de la philosophie*, ed. Carlos Lévy (Turnhout: Brepolis, 1998), 129–152. On pleasure as deceiver in the context of Plato's philosophy, see Jessica Moss, "Pleasure and Illusion in Plato," *Ph&PhenR* 72 (2006): 503–535.

[8] Tobin, *Creation of Man*, 154–172. For Philo, allegory *proper* is the allegory of the soul, so "non-allegorical" technically means not allegory of the soul and encompasses a range of interpretations, from simplistically literal to highly sophisticated (see idem, 158–159).

[9] On Jewish allegorists who neglected laws in their literal sense (τοὺς ῥητοὺς νόμους), see *Migr.* 89–93. On this passage, see Tobin, *Creation of Man*, 155–156; also David M. Hay, "Philo's References to Other Allegorists," *SPh* 6 (1979–1980): 41–75, 47–51.

[10] Tobin, *Creation of Man*, 180.

And these you shall regard with loathing among the birds (ἀπὸ τῶν πετεινῶν). And they shall not be eaten; they are an abomination (βδέλυγμά ἐστιν): the eagle (ἀετόν) and the bearded vulture (γρύπα) and the osprey (ἁλιάετον) and the vulture (γύπα) and the kite (ἰκτῖνα) and those like it and a raven (κόρακα) and those like it and ostrich (στρουθόν) and little owl (γλαῦκα) and sea gull (λάρον) and those like it and a hawk (ἱέρακα) and those similar to it and long-eared owl (νυκτικόρακα) and diving petrel (καταράκτην) and ibis (ἴβιν) and water hen (πορφυρίωνα) and pelican (πελεκᾶνα) and swan (κύκνον) and heron (ἐρωδιόν) and water plover (χαραδριόν) and those like it and hoopoe (ἔποπα) and bat (νυκτερίδα) (Lv 11:13–19).[11]

The *Letter of Aristeas*, written a century or more before Philo lived, attributes to the high priest, Eleazar, an apologia for the Jewish dietary laws (*Let. Arist.* 128–169) including an explanation of Moses' prohibition of these birds (*Let. Arist.* 145–149).[12] Essentially, Eleazar associates their carnivorous diet with a certain character, which Moses sought to prohibit among his followers in a symbolic way through the designation "unclean."[13] Simply put, human beings ought to abstain from the violent, "unjust" behavior these creatures represent. Philo, too, considers

---

[11] *A New English Translation of the Septuagint*, trans. Dirk L. Büchner (Oxford University Press, 2007). Deut 14:11–18 lists the same birds in a slightly different order.

[12] Eleazar also explains the Mosaic criteria of cloven hooves and rumination (Lv 11:1–8; see *Let. Arist.* 150–160) and the prohibitions of mice and weasels (Lv 11:29; see *Let. Arist.* 163–167). On the *Letter of Aristeas*, see Moses Hadas, ed., trans., *Aristeas to Philocrates: Letter of Aristeas* (New York: Harper, 1951; reprint, Eugene, Oreg.: Wipf & Stock, 2007). On Eleazar's interpretation of the dietary laws, see Katell Berthelot, "L'interprétation symbolique des lois alimentaires dans la Lettre d'Aristée: une influence pythagoricienne," *JJS* 52 (2001): 253–268; also Fausto Parente, "La Lettera di Aristea come fonte per la storia del giudaismo alessandrino durante la prima metà del I secolo a.C.," *ASNSP* 3.2.1–2 (1972): 177–237 (part one), 517–567 (part two), esp. 222–231; Giovanni Maria Vian, "Purità e culto nell'esegesi giudaico-ellenistica," *ASE* 13 (1996): 67–84, 71–74. Philo most likely died ca. 50 CE (Peder Borgen, "Philo of Alexandria," *ABD* 5:333–342, 333). Hadas (*Aristeas*, 9–53) surveys the internal and external evidence for dating the *Letter of Aristeas* and suggests ca. 130 BCE (idem, 54). James G. Février considers *Let. Arist.* 83–171 an interpolation *postdating* Philo; see Février, *La date, la composition et les sources de la Lettre d'Aristée à Philocrate*, BEHE 242 (Paris: Édouard Champion, 1925). But his theory relies too heavily on arguments from silence regarding what Philo and Josephus *ought* to have said about the "interpolated" material (idem, 29). He suggests incongruities between §§ 83–171 and the rest of the letter, but they do not warrant his interpolation theory. Février dates the rest of the letter to before 30 BCE (idem, 30).

[13] The term ἀκάθαρτος does not appear in Lv 11:13–19, but in Lv 11:46–47 it clearly refers to *all* of the prohibited creatures (τὰ μὴ ἐσθιόμενα), including birds (cf. *Let. Arist.* 147: ἀκάθαρτα προσονομάσας).

the prohibited birds of Leviticus 11:13–19, but in the context of how the dietary laws function to promote observance of the Tenth Commandment, which Philo reads as "You shall not desire" (οὐκ ἐπιθυμήσεις).[14] As he expounds the laws governing clean and unclean creatures from land, sea, and sky (*Spec.* 4.100–118), Philo reproduces both Eleazar's characterization of the prohibited birds (*Spec.* 4.116–117) and his concern to explain a Mosaic prohibition of carnivores, although Philo shifts that concern from birds to land animals (*Spec.* 4.103–104). Ultimately, Philo does not so much reproduce Eleazar's line of interpretation as rework it, incorporating key elements but changing them to suit his purpose. A more detailed analysis of Philo's "reworking" of Eleazar's interpretation of Lv 11:13–19 demonstrates Philo's likely *knowledge* of that interpretation as it appears in the *Letter of Aristeas*.[15]

---

[14] Philo's exposition of the Tenth Commandment appears in *Spec.* 4.79–131 (cf. *Decal.* 142–153). On the organization of laws under rubrics defined by the Ten Commandments, see Cristina Termini, "Taxonomy of Biblical Laws and φιλοτεχνία in Philo of Alexandria: A Comparison with Josephus and Cicero," *SPhA* 16 (2004): 1–29, esp. 1–10. In terms of dietary laws considered by Eleazar, Philo treats not only birds but also the criteria of cloven hooves and rumination (*Spec.* 4.106–109). On Philo's exposition of the Tenth Commandment, see Hans Svebakken, "Philo of Alexandria's Exposition of the Tenth Commandment" (Ph.D. diss., Loyola University of Chicago, 2009). For the dietary laws in Philo, see James N. Rhodes, "Diet and Desire: The Logic of the Dietary Laws According to Philo," *ETL* 79 (2003): 122–133; also Richard D. Hecht, "Patterns of Exegesis in Philo's Interpretation of Leviticus," *SPh* 6 (1979–1980): 77–155, esp. 108–115; Isaak Heinemann, *Philons griechische und jüdische Bildung: Kulturvergleichende Untersuchungen zu Philons Darstellung der jüdischen Gesetze* (Breslau: Marcus, 1932; reprint, Darmstadt: Wissenschaftliche Buchgesellschaft, 1962), 155–166.

[15] For comparisons of Philo and Eleazar's respective treatments of the dietary laws (i.e., birds, cloven hooves, rumination), see Rhodes, "Diet and Desire;" also Février, *Lettre d'Aristée*, 59–63; Hecht, "Patterns of Exegesis," 112–114; Raffaele Tramontano, *La Lettera di Aristea a Filocrate: Introduzione, testo, versione e commento* (Naples: Ufficio succursale della civiltà cattolica, 1931), 180–184. As for Philo's knowledge of Eleazar's work in the *Letter of Aristeas*, Hadas in general considers it likely, as part of a broader consideration including the parallel accounts of Septuagint origins in *Let. Arist.* 301–311 and *Mos.* 2.26–44 (see Hadas, *Aristeas*, 25–26; cf. Rhodes, "Diet and Desire," 124, n. 10). Others attribute similarities to a common exegetical tradition, not Philo's reading the *Letter of Aristeas*; see, e.g., Berthelot, "Interprétation symbolique," 253; also Gregory E. Sterling, "'The School of Sacred Laws': The Social Setting of Philo's Treatises," *VC* 53 (1999): 148–164, esp. 153–154. Both Février and Tramontano take the similarities as highly suggestive of literary dependence, although Février's theory of interpolation presumes dependence of *Let. Arist.* on Philo (see Février, *Lettre d'Aristée*, 59–63, esp. 61; Tramontano, *Lettera di Aristea*, 180–184, esp. 184; cf. Hecht, "Patterns of Exegesis," 113, n. 51). In any case, only Tramontano makes the similar treatment of prohibited birds (Lv 11:13–19) part of his argument for literary dependence, but without extensive detail or redaction-critical analysis.

Common elements in Philo and Eleazar

Although Eleazar himself does not distinguish among them, his interpretation of Lv 11:13–19 (*Let. Arist.* 145–149) has three distinct levels:
(1) the level of (implicit) reference *to* the text, in which he lists relevant
species of winged creatures; (2) the level of observations *about* the text, in
which he characterizes the "clean" and "unclean" birds; and (3) the level
of interpretation *of* the text, in which he explains the ethical significance
of Moses' prohibition of carnivores. Philo, in the course of his exposition
regarding birds (*Spec.* 4.116–117) *and* land animals (*Spec.* 4.103–109),
reproduces key elements from each of these levels in ways that demonstrate familiarity with the *Letter of Aristeas*. In fact, comparing each level
of Eleazar's interpretation with corresponding elements in Philo's work
creates a strong case for literary dependence.

At the level of (implicit) reference *to* the text, Eleazar makes a curious omission: although he bases his entire line of interpretation on a
list of unclean birds in Lv 11:13–19, he names none of them. Instead,
he gives examples of the sorts of winged creatures Jews do eat, naming *five* species: pigeons (περιστεραί), turtledoves (τρυγόνες), locusts
(ἀττακοί), partridges (πέρδικες), and "geese and the others like them"
(ἔτι δὲ χῆνες καὶ τὰ ἄλλα ὅσα τοιαῦτα).[16] The Pentateuch has no list
of clean birds, so—with the exception of "locusts," which appear on a
list of clean insects (lit. ἑρπετὰ τῶν πετεινῶν) in Lv 11:22 (τὸν ἀττά-
κην)—Eleazar produces here a list of his own making, one undoubtedly based on his knowledge of the Jewish diet but nevertheless formulated without guidance or constraint from a biblical model.[17] When
Philo broaches the topic of unclean birds in *Spec.* 4.116–117, he follows
Eleazar by (1) naming none of the unclean birds and (2) offering instead
what the Pentateuch does not: a list of "clean" birds. Indeed, Philo's list
bears a striking resemblance to Eleazar's, containing *five* species, three of
which appear on Eleazar's list in the same order: doves (φάττας), *pigeons*
(περιστεράς), *turtledoves* (τρυγόνας), and "the tribes of cranes, *geese* and

---

[16] *Let. Arist.* 145.

[17] Pigeons (περιστεραί) and turtledoves (τρυγόνες) do appear together as birds fit
for sacrifice (e.g., Lv 1:14) and would count as "clean" for that reason, but Eleazar
notably reverses the biblical order of this pairing. Beginning with Gn 15:9 (τρυγόνα καὶ
περιστεράν), the birds are paired in the context of sacrifice eleven times, always in the
order "turtledove ... pigeon," with *one* exception (Lv 12:6). So although "Eleazar" most
likely does have the biblical pairing in mind, he reverses the order one might expect in
such an allusion (although note περιστερὰν καὶ τρυγόνα in *Spec.* 1.162).

the like" (τὰς γεράνων καὶ χηνῶν καὶ ὁμοιοτρόπων ἀγέλας).[18] Unless Philo independently produced such agreements in number, content, and sequence by happenstance, he must have used Eleazar's list as a working model.[19]

At the level of observations *about* the text, Eleazar provides the material for his interpretation by characterizing the species of birds, both the "clean" he lists and the "unclean" he does not. He again composes freely, without the guidance or constraint of any biblical model for his remarks, and again key elements of his characterizations appear in Philo's work.[20] As for the unnamed prohibited species, Eleazar calls them "wild and carnivorous" (ἄγριά τε καὶ σαρκοφάγα).[21] In his characterization of unclean birds, Philo repeats one of these labels, although he uses a slightly different term for "carnivorous" (σαρκοβόρος).[22] When Eleazar reflects further on the behavior of these birds, he notes how they use their *strength* (δύναμις) to "oppress the rest" (καταδυναστεύοντα ... τὰ λοιπά) and procure their food with injustice (μετὰ ἀδικίας).[23] Their violent behavior, he adds, affects not only other birds but also *other animals* (he lists "lambs and kids" [τοὺς ἄρνας καὶ ἐρίφους]) and *human beings* (τοὺς ἀνθρώπους). Although worded differently, Philo's remarks on the behavior of unclean birds reproduce the essential features of Eleazar's characterization: these creatures prey on (φονᾷ) *other animals* (κατ' ἄλλων) and *human beings* (κατ' ἀνθρώπων)—and they use their *strength* (δύναμις) for mischievous ends (ἐπιβούλοις).[24] As for the permitted species, Eleazar calls them "gentle" (ἥμερος), in contrast with the "wild" (ἄγριος) species prohibited by law.[25] Philo likewise considers

---

[18] Philo does *not* reproduce the "locusts" (ἀττηκοί) and "partridges" (πέρδικες) of Eleazar's list, but at least the former *could not* have appeared on Philo's list, since they belong with the "ἀκρίς" and "ὀφιομάχης" (see Lv 11:20–23) treated in a different part of his exposition (*Spec.* 4.114–115).

[19] Cf. Tramontano, *Lettera di Aristea*, 184.

[20] Lv 11:13–19 simply *lists* the birds, saying nothing *about* them. However obvious the characterizations of Eleazar (and Philo) may be, they nevertheless do not derive from the biblical text and so represent a distinct exegetical move, though not an *interpretation* per se.

[21] *Let. Arist.* 146.

[22] *Spec.* 4.116.

[23] *Let. Arist.* 146.

[24] *Spec.* 4.116. On κατ' ἄλλων as other *animals*, not other *birds*, see André Mosès, *De specialibus legibus III et IV: Introduction, traduction et notes*, PAPM 25 (Paris: Cerf, 1970), 271, n. 7.

[25] *Let. Arist.* 145–147 (3).

them part of "the tame and gentle class" (ἐν τῇ τιθασῷ καὶ ἡμέρῳ τάξει), reproducing the prominent term "gentle" (ἥμερος) from Eleazar's description.[26] When it comes, however, to Eleazar's description of the behavior of clean birds, who eat "earth's produce" (τὰ φυόμενα ... ἐπὶ γῆς) and do not oppress other creatures (οὐ καταδυναστεύει), Philo offers no comparable remarks—at least regarding *birds*.[27] Instead, he relocates his echo of Eleazar's description to a different part of his essay: to the consideration of land animals (*Spec.* 4.103–109). Philo signals this relocation in three ways: by attributing to clean land animals a diet of "earth's produce" (τροφαῖς ... αἷς ἀναδίδωσι γῆ), by describing clean land animals as "gentle" (ἥμερος)—repeating in a new context Eleazar's term for clean birds—and by commending clean land animals for abstaining from the behavior he attributes to unclean *birds*.[28] Philo's redeployment reflects his decision to shift the major element of Eleazar's line of interpretation from the domain of birds to the domain of land animals. Although Philo takes the interpretation of "carnivorous" in a new direction, his decision to capitalize on this trait exegetically must derive from a reading of Eleazar's exposition, since it otherwise defies explanation in the context of land animals.

At the level of interpretation *of* the text, Eleazar explains the significance of a Mosaic prohibition of carnivorous species. The crux and culmination of Eleazar's line of interpretation—hermeneutical reflection on the trait "carnivore"—represents his exegesis of a particular feature ("carnivore" equals "unclean") of a particular text (Lv 11:13–19) involving a particular type of animal (birds). So Philo's explanation of a Mosaic prohibition of carnivores in the context of *land animals* (not birds) makes sense as the relocation of a key feature of Eleazar's line of exegesis.[29]

---

[26] *Spec.* 4.117.

[27] *Let. Arist.* 147 (cf. 145: πυροῖς καὶ ὀσπρίοις χρώμενα πρὸς τὴν τροφήν).

[28] Eleazar (*Let. Arist.* 146–147) uses positive and negative formulations of the same terminology to note that herbivores *do not engage* (οὐ καταδυναστεύει) in certain reprehensible carnivorous behaviors (καταδυναστεύοντα ... τὰ λοίπα). Philo likewise uses positive and negative formulations of the same terminology to note in *Spec.* 4.104 (land animals) that herbivores do *not* engage (μηδὲν εἰς ἐπιβουλὴν πραγματευόμενα) in certain reprehensible carnivorous behaviors (ἐπιβούλοις κεχρημένα ταῖς δυνάμεσι) noted in *Spec.* 4.116 (birds).

[29] Philo suggests in *Spec.* 4.104 that Moses actually prohibited carnivorous land animals: ἀπαγορεῦσαι καὶ τῆς τῶν ἄλλων σαρκοβόρων ἀνὰ κράτος χρήσεως (cf. *Spec.* 1.223 [on Lv 19:7–8]: τὴν ... χρῆσιν ἀνὰ κράτος ἀπηγόρευσε; *Prov.* 2.63: ἡ τῶν τοιούτων χρῆσις ἀπηγόρευται νόμῳ). What Mosaic prohibition of carnivores does Philo have in mind if not the one in Lv 11:13–19? NB Philo's use of σαρκοβόρος both in *Spec.* 4.116

Philo *infers* such a prohibition in light of the list of ten clean land animals in Deuteronomy 14:4–5 (*Spec.* 4.104–105). But Philo's inference—unlike Eleazar's—contradicts the biblical data, which actually *names* species of unclean land animals (Lv 11:4–7). The list of camel (κάμηλος), hare (δασύπους), coney (χοιρογρύλλιος), and pig (ὗς) hardly supports the notion (inferred or otherwise) of Moses targeting carnivores among the land animals. In fact, these unclean land animals are obviously herbivores, and Lv 11:1–7 gives the reason for their unclean status: a failure to exhibit either cloven hooves or rumination. Philo's departure from the biblical evidence becomes more pronounced in light of his remarks on a hypothetical prohibition of *man-eaters* (θηρία ὅσα σαρκῶν ἀνθρωπίνων ἅπτεται).[30] Casting man-eaters as unclean creatures has no biblical warrant. Further confirming his debt to the *Letter of Aristeas*, Philo redeploys two key terms from Eleazar's discussion of birds: "wild" (ἄγριος) and "gentle" (ἥμερος).[31]

In sum, Philo's extended treatment of the dietary laws in *Spec.* 4.100–118 (which postdates the *Letter of Aristeas*) exhibits notable agreements with several distinct aspects (levels) of the exposition of Lv 11:13–19 attributed to Eleazar in *Let. Arist.* 145–149. The nature and extent of these agreements, while never amounting to block quotation, nevertheless demonstrate Philo's knowledge and considered use *of that text*.[32]

Different interpretations in Philo and Eleazar

Eleazar explains Moses' prohibition of carnivores as an ingenious design to reduce the incidence of unjust behavior—i.e., to promote justice (δικαιοσύνη)—among his followers:

---

to describe the (actually) prohibited species of Lv 11:13–19 and in *Spec.* 4.104 to describe also the (supposedly) prohibited land animals.

[30] *Spec.* 4.103. NB Μωυσῆ δὲ τῆς τούτων ἀπολαύσεως ἀνέχειν **δοκεῖ**. Hecht, "Patterns of Exegesis," rightly omits any discussion of *Spec.* 4.103–104, since his article treats Philo's interpretation of clean and unclean animals *in Leviticus 11*, which of course says nothing about "man-eaters."

[31] *Spec.* 4.103–104.

[32] Cf. Tobin's conclusion about how Philo uses earlier interpretations: "This does not mean that Philo is quoting these interpretations *verbatim*. But he does preserve the original structure, content, and key vocabulary of each of these interpretations to such an extent that these interpretations must have been available to him in their original form" (*Creation of Man*, 172–173).

Through these creatures then, by calling them "unclean," he set up a symbol (παράσημον) that those for whom the legislation was drawn up must practice righteousness in spirit (κατὰ ψυχήν ... δικαιοσύνῃ συγχρῆσθαι) and oppress no one (μηδένα καταδυναστεύειν), trusting in their own strength (πεποιθότας ἰσχύι τῇ καθ᾽ ἑαυτούς), nor rob anyone of anything (ἀφαιρεῖσθαι μηδέν), but must guide their lives in accordance with justice (ἐκ δικαίου τὰ τοῦ βίου κυβερνᾶν), just as the gentle creatures among the birds above mentioned consume pulses that grow upon the earth and do not tyrannize (καταδυναστεύει) to the destruction of their kindred (*Let. Arist.* 147).[33]

Quite simply, the unclean birds of Leviticus 11:13–19 exhibit certain behavioral traits analogous to human acts of injustice.[34] By prohibiting them, Moses packaged moral exhortations in *symbolic* language, in effect telling his followers to practice justice and eschew the use of force for violent, oppressive ends.[35] The ethical benefit of this sort of legislation comes strictly through observance *at the symbolic level*, since people must first decipher the exhortation in the symbol and then obey *it* (the moral exhortation), not the dietary restriction.[36] Abstinence from the proscribed birds does not in itself fulfill Moses' purpose, since the unenlightened could in theory avoid the meat and practice injustice. Conversely, eating one of the proscribed birds would not violate Moses' intent, since it would not necessarily involve unjust behavior. In this respect, Eleazar disregards the literal observance of the laws regarding

---

[33] Trans. M. Hadas. On the concern for justice, see also *Let. Arist.* 148 (εἶναι δικαίους); *Let. Arist.* 144 (δικαιοσύνης ἕνεκεν); *Let. Arist.* 169 (πρὸς δικαιοσύνην).

[34] Note the analogy in *Let. Arist.* 149 between animal *disposition* (διάθεσις) and human *ways* (τρόποι) (cf. *Let. Arist.* 163: κακοποιητικὸς γὰρ ὁ τρόπος).

[35] Eleazar actually uses the terminology of "sign," not "symbol": note (for example) διὰ τῶν τοιούτων ... σημειοῦσθαι (*Let. Arist.* 148); σημεῖον (*Let. Arist.* 150); τὸ σημειοῦσθαι διὰ τούτων (*Let. Arist.* 151) (cf. *Let. Arist.* 150: τροπολογῶν). On Eleazar's method and its Pythagorean provenance, see Berthelot, "Interprétation symbolique;" also on method, see Folker Siegert, "Early Jewish Interpretation in a Hellenistic Style," in *Hebrew Bible/Old Testament: The History of Its Interpretation*, ed. Magne Sæbø, vol. 1.1 (Göttingen: Vandenhoeck & Ruprecht, 1996), 130–198, esp. 144–154. Since Eleazar's signs ultimately point to human *behavior*, and thus realities in the external world, he does not engage in "allegorical" interpretation by Philo's definition (see Tobin, *Creation of Man*, 158–159). Even Eleazar's discussion of *memory* (symbolized by rumination) highlights actions in the *external world*, not inner realities of the soul (*Let. Arist.* 153–160; e.g., 158: τιθέναι τὰ λόγια, πρὸς τὸ μνείαν εἶναι θεοῦ).

[36] *Let. Arist.* 148 (trans. Hadas): "By such examples (διὰ τῶν τοιούτων), then, the lawgiver has commended *to men of understanding* a symbol (παραδέδωκεν ... σημειοῦσθαι τοῖς συνετοῖς) that they must be just ..." (emphasis added). In other words, failure to perceive Moses' symbolic exhortation would preclude obedience to the *real* prohibition, which governs habits of character, not diet.

unclean birds, taking them instead as purely symbolic efforts on Moses' part to commend a particular virtue, the virtue of justice (δικαιοσύνη).[37]

Philo, by contrast, explains Moses' prohibition of carnivores as an ingenious design to reduce the incidence of passion—i.e., to promote self-control (ἐγκράτεια)—among his followers:

> Possibly it might be thought just (δίκαιον) that all wild beasts that feed on human flesh (θηρία ὅσα σαρκῶν ἀνθρωπίνων ἅπτεται) should suffer from men what men have suffered from them. But Moses would have us abstain from the enjoyment of such, even though they provide a very appetizing and delectable repast. He was considering what is suitable to a gentle-mannered soul (λογιζόμενος τὸ πρέπον ἡμέρῳ ψυχῇ), for though it is fitting enough that one should suffer for what one has done, it is not fitting conduct for the sufferers to retaliate it on the wrongdoers, lest the savage passion of anger should turn them unawares into beasts (μὴ λάθωσιν ὑπ' ὀργῆς, ἀγρίου πάθους, θηριωθέντες). So careful is he against this danger (τοσαύτῃ χρῆται προφυλακῇ τοῦ πράγματος) that wishing to restrain preemptively the impulse for revenge against man-eaters (ὥστε μακρόθεν ἀνεῖρξαι βουλόμενος τὴν ἐπὶ τὰ λεχθέντα ὁρμήν), he also strictly forbade them to eat the other carnivorous animals. (*Spec.* 4.103–104)[38]

---

[37] Eleazar disregards literal observance insofar as it has *in itself* no bearing on the achievement (or not) of Moses' purpose in prohibiting certain birds (cf. *Let. Arist.* 144, where Eleazar rejects the "debased idea" [καταπεπτωκότα λόγον] of Moses formulating the dietary laws for the sake of mice, weasels, etc. [Lv 11:29]). Parente ("La *Lettera di Aristea*," 222–231) takes this relative disregard as evidence for the *Letter of Aristeas* approving (if not promoting) the *discontinuance* of literal observance. He even suggests the influence of the *Letter of Aristeas* on the exegetes chided by Philo in *Migr.* 89–93 for neglecting the literal sense of the laws (idem, 230–231). But the *Letter of Aristeas* nowhere speaks *against* observing the law—in fact, it seems to credit literal observance with preservation of the Jewish community (e.g., *Let. Arist.* 139: ὁ νομοθέτης ... περιέφραξεν ἡμᾶς; cf. 142). The ambivalence reflects a desire both to maintain group identity and embrace the broader culture; cf. Reinhard Feldmeier, "Weise hinter 'eisernen Mauern': Tora und jüdisches Selbstverständnis zwischen Akkulturation und Absonderung im Aristeasbrief," in *Die Septuaginta zwischen Judentum und Christentum*, ed. Martin Hengel and Anna Maria Schwemer, WUNT 72 (Tübingen: Mohr, 1994), 20–37; also Victor Tcherikover, "The Ideology of the *Letter of Aristeas*," HTR 51 (1958): 59–85. Parente, however, correctly notes the *compatibility* of Eleazar's mode of interpretation with abandonment of literal observance.

[38] F.H. Colson's translation, with the exception of μακρόθεν ἀνεῖρξαι βουλόμενος τὴν ἐπὶ τὰ λεχθέντα ὁρμήν, which he translates: "wishing to restrain by implication the appetite for the food just mentioned." Clearly τὰ λεχθέντα refers to the man-eating θηρία mentioned at the beginning of § 103. But ἐπί in this case indicates not just an impulse "for" these creatures, as in a desire *for* their meat. Instead, ἐπί indicates an impulse "against" these creatures, as in a desire for revenge indulged by slaughtering them for food. Colson himself acknowledges this sense when he suggests "tendency to such vindictiveness" as another translation for τὴν ἐπὶ τὰ λεχθέντα ὁρμήν (see 70, n. a).

Although his reference to a Mosaic prohibition of carnivores signals a
debt to Eleazar's exegesis of Lv 11:13–19, Philo explains such a prohibition on entirely different grounds. According to Eleazar's interpretation,
carnivores have an intrinsically objectionable disposition, which Moses
used as the symbolic basis for prohibiting analogous and likewise objectionable behavior among human beings. According to Philo's interpretation, Moses finds nothing wrong with carnivores per se. He restricts them
categorically only to keep his followers far from the moral danger posed
by one class of carnivores, the man-eaters (θηρία ὅσα σαρκῶν ἀνθρωπίνων ἅπτεται). Lions, for example, are as a species guilty of eating human
beings, so the law of retribution warrants their being eaten in return.[39]
Moses realized that the victims (human beings) ought not to adminis-
ter the punishment (eating lions) because of their compromised ability
to function as dispassionate agents of justice. Instead of acting from a
strictly rational motive to see justice done, they might overstep the dic-
tates of reason and act from a personal, impassioned motive to avenge the
brutal deaths of their human comrades.[40] In other words, Moses prohibited man-eaters because of their unique potential for inciting a particular
sort of internal reaction among those who might slaughter them for food.
As Philo puts it, they might become beasts (θηριωθέντες) by indulging
the "savage passion" (ἄγριος πάθος) of anger (ὀργή).

The danger, in Philo's view, cannot lie in anger itself, which he elsewhere characterizes as a beneficial "weapon of defense" (ἀμυντήριον
ὅπλον) created to help mankind.[41] Rather, the danger lies in the otherwise useful emotion of anger usurping reason to become "savage"
(ἄγριος) and immoderate instead of "gentle" (ἥμερος) and measured.[42]

---

[39] Philo lists bears (ἄρκτους), lions (λέοντας), and panthers (παρδάλεις) among τά
... γένη τῶν ἀτιθάσων θηρίων, ἃ σαρκῶν ἀνθρωπείων ἅπτεται (Mos. 1.109).

[40] For a Middle-Platonic discussion of delivering punishment on the basis of reason,
not passion, see Plutarch, Cohib. ira 460 A–C; on Plutarch, see John Dillon, The Middle
Platonists, rev. ed. (Ithaca: Cornell University Press, 1996), 184–230.

[41] Leg. 2.8 (cf. Leg. 2.9, where Philo equates τὰ θηρία of Gn 2:19 allegorically with τὰ
πάθη τῆς ψυχῆς, which God created as "helpers"; Philo tempers—but does not reject
entirely—this positive image in Leg. 2.10–11). In addition, Philo's reference to righteous
ὀργή (e.g., Fug. 90, Mos. 1.302) and God's ὀργή (e.g., Somn. 2.179, Mos. 1.6) argues against
his considering the emotion objectionable in itself.

[42] In Migr. 210, Philo speaks of τό ... ὀργῆς πάθος becoming "wild" (ἐξηγριωμένον)
and causing beastly behavior (ἐκθηριώσης); he recommends not its elimination but its
"taming" (ἡμέρωσον) through reduction of excess (ἄγαν). In other words, a gentle emotion becomes "wild" when it gets out of control, opposing the moderating force of reason. True opposition between reason (λόγος) and emotion (πάθος) of course presumes
their belonging to different parts of the soul. Philo follows his Middle-Platonic contem-

This resonates with the concern in Philo's exposition of the Tenth Commandment (*Spec.* 4.79–131) for the moderation of desire (ἐπιθυμία) through the exercise of self-control (ἐγκράτεια), especially since Philo most likely has in mind the definition of anger (ὀργή) as a *desire* (ἐπιθυμία) for retribution (τιμωρία).[43] In fact, Philo's discussion of man-eaters reflects an effort to find a semblance of the logic he attributes to all of Moses' legislation regarding "unclean" creatures: their especially delicious meat.

According to Philo, Moses selected for prohibition the animals whose flesh is "finest" (εὐσαρκότατα) and "fattest" (πιότατα) and so yields the tastiest meats.[44] Such meats arouse pleasure (ἡδονή) and so can incite an overwhelming, excessive desire (ἐπιθυμία)—by avoiding them the moral agent cultivates a life of self-control (ἐγκράτεια).[45] Philo finds the premier example of this principle in pork, a meat acknowledged by all who partake as "most delicious" (ἥδιστον).[46] So in order for carnivores to illustrate the principle supposedly at work in *all* restrictions of "unclean" animals, Philo must show how this class of creatures tastes especially good. He implies that the lion, like the pig, represents a delectable meal, but in a fundamentally different sense. The pig incites desire by

---

poraries in making emotion (πάθος) a function of the soul's *non-rational* (ἄλογος) part (e.g., *Leg.* 3.116; cf. Plutarch, *Virt. mor.*)—i.e., *not* (contra orthodox Stoicism) a function of the rational faculty; see Svebakken, "Tenth Commandment," 40–99, esp. 69–72; attributing emotion to a non-rational faculty distinguishes Philo *also* from the "unorthodox" Posidonius: see John Cooper, "Posidonius on Emotions," in *Reason and Emotion: Essays on Ancient Moral Psychology and Ethical Theory* (Princeton: Princeton University Press, 1999), 449–484.

[43] E.g., Ps.-Andronicus Περὶ παθῶν 231.81, ed. Gilbert-Thirry: Ὀργή ... ἐστιν ἐπιθυμία τιμωρίας τοῦ ἠδικηκέναι δοκοῦντος (cf. Aristotle, *Rhetoric* 1378a30–1378b10: ὀργή = ὄρεξις τιμωρίας). In other words, Philo had reasonable grounds for including a discussion of ὀργή (ἐπιθυμία τιμωρίας) in his broader exposition of οὐκ ἐπιθυμήσεις, and the exposition's overarching concern for moderation through self-control (ἐγκράτεια) would apply: e.g., *Spec.* 4.79: μέτρα ταῖς ὁρμαῖς ὁρίζει; *Spec.* 4.97: ἐπεστόμισε διατάγμασι ... πρὸς ἐγκράτειαν; *Spec.* 4.99: πρὸς ἄσκησιν ... ἐγκρατείας; *Spec.* 4.101: πρός ... ἐγκράτειαν; *Spec.* 4.124: πάλιν εἰς διδασκαλίαν ἐγκρατείας (on Philo's view of ἐγκράτεια, see Svebakken, "Tenth Commandment," 100–138).

[44] *Spec.* 4.100.

[45] Especially pleasurable foods encourage eating *for the sake of* pleasure, which leads to overindulgence (*Spec.* 4.100). By avoiding them, the moral agent learns "frugality and simple contentedness" (ὀλιγοδεΐα καὶ εὐκολία), which characterize the life of ἐγκράτεια insofar as the motives of reason (e.g., eating for health and well being) predominate over desire's invariable motive of pleasure (NB the association of ὀλιγοδεΐα, εὐκολία, and ἐγκράτεια in *Spec.* 4.101 [cf. *Spec.* 1.173]). For ἐγκράτεια as predominance of rational motivation, see Svebakken, "Tenth Commandment," 118–123.

[46] *Spec.* 4.101.

promising abundant pleasure through the sweet taste of delicious meat. The lion incites desire by promising abundant pleasure, too, but through the sweet taste of *revenge*.[47] Moses, understanding the meat of man-eating animals to be especially pleasurable in this unique sense, recognized a danger and did not allow his followers to consider them a source of food. In fact, Moses was so eager to protect against the dangerous "impulse" (ὁρμή) to kill and eat *with a vengeance*, that he forbade the consumption of any animal that kills and eats other animals, let alone human beings.[48] Herbivores, Moses reasoned, "never plot mischief against anyone" (μηδὲν εἰς ἐπιβουλὴν πραγματευόμενα), man or animal, so no one runs the risk of eating them with a vengeance.[49] No one could reasonably see herbivores as reprehensible aggressors, so no one could reasonably harbor a dangerous, potentially overwhelming desire to punish them. By fashioning the legislation regarding carnivores in this way—as a matter of self-control (ἐγκράτεια) and not justice (δικαιοσύνη)—Philo clearly differs with Eleazar as to the purpose of such restrictions, but Philo also differs in his conception of how Moses designed these restrictions to *work*.

Whereas Eleazar attributes the ethical benefit of a restriction on carnivores to observance at the *symbolic* level, Philo attributes it to observance at the *literal* level.[50] Man-eating animals are not, in Philo's view, the rep-

---

[47] On the *pleasure* of retribution, cf. *Spec.* 3.85 (ἀντεφησθῆναι). In his discussion of anger (and the pleasure of retribution), Aristotle cites *Iliad* 18.109: "Wherefore it has been well said of anger, that *Far sweeter than dripping honey down the throat it spreads in men's hearts*" (*Rhetoric* 1378b4–7; trans. J.H. Freese). In *Cohib. ira* 460 C, Plutarch describes "gorging oneself" with retribution (τιμωρίας ἐμφορεῖσθαι) for the sake of pleasure (πρὸς ἡδονήν) as "beastlike" (θηριῶδες).

[48] *Spec.* 4.104: ὥστε μακρόθεν ἀνεῖξαι βουλόμενος τὴν ἐπὶ τὰ λεχθέντα ὁρμήν.

[49] *Spec.* 4.104.

[50] In other words, Philo does *not* engage in a symbolic (or "allegorical") interpretation like Eleazar's when he considers the carnivore-herbivore distinction in *Spec.* 4.103–104 (*pace* Rhodes, "Diet and Desire," 123–125; Vian, "Purità e culto," 78). Philo *does* engage in symbolic interpretations comparable to Eleazar's elsewhere in *Spec.* 4.100–118: namely, §§ 106–109 (criteria for clean land animals), §§ 110–112 (criteria for clean aquatic animals), §§ 113–115 (clean and unclean "creeping" animals). But he invariably *announces* this sort of interpretation: ταυτὶ δὲ τὰ σημεῖα ἀμφότερα **σύμβολα** (§ 106), **σύμβολα** δὲ καὶ ταῦτ' ἐστί (§ 112), πάλιν **αἰνιττόμενος** διὰ μὲν ἑρπετῶν (§ 113), πάλιν διὰ **συμβόλων** (§ 114). He makes no such announcement in *Spec.* 4.103–105. Heinemann (*Bildung*, 161) notes Philo's acknowledgement of both "allegorische und wörtliche Begründungen" for the dietary laws, giving examples of the two approaches (161–166). Under "wörtliche Begründungen" Heinemann mentions first the prohibition of "besonders wohlschmeckende Tiere" (such as pork), recognizing Moses' goal: "zur Selbstbeherrschung anregen" (163). In Heinemann's view, the prohibition of man-eaters involves "wörtliche Begründungen" as well, but he does not relate it either to the prohibition of tasty meats or the larger context of self-control in service to the Tenth Commandment.

resentation of a character trait, which the wise must first understand and then avoid. By (hypothetically) calling these creatures "unclean," Moses was *not* symbolically packaging an exhortation to eschew the beastly ways of man-eating animals. Man-eaters actually eat human beings, who might actually eat them in return, indulging a vengeance that overshadows reason. By actually abstaining from the meat of man-eaters, the soul avoids a troublesome passion.

As for herbivores, both Eleazar and Philo commend them as "gentle" (ἥμερος) creatures, but they again differ as to the symbolic or literal significance of such a disposition. For Eleazar, a person who merely follows the instruction to eat only herbivores misses Moses' true purpose: to promote the gentle life of justice these creatures represent. For Philo, the person who eats only herbivores—even without reflection on the significance of the rule—fulfills Moses' purpose: to safeguard his followers from a passionate desire for revenge by allowing them to eat only harmless creatures.[51]

In sum, Eleazar explained the appearance of carnivores on a list of "unclean" birds as Moses' ingenious way of telling his followers to practice *justice*. Philo relocates Eleazar's concern to the context of *land animals*, where it becomes an example (albeit strained) of Moses' ingenious way of cultivating self-control among his followers. By practicing this dietary law, they will become better managers of desire and so become obedient to the Decalogue's categorical restriction on desire (οὐκ ἐπιθυμήσεις).

Philo's Use of Aristeas in light of Tobin's Research

How do the results of this case study concerning the interpretation of Lv 11:13–19 fit (or not) within the framework for analyzing histories of interpretation offered by Tobin's research? Do these results reveal an interest on Philo's part either to promote the allegory of the soul or to maintain the validity of non-allegorical levels of interpretation? Do these

---

[51] In this legislation, Moses had in mind what suited a "tame" soul (*Spec.* 4.103: λογιζομένος τὸ πρέπον ἡμέρῳ ψυχῇ). But ἥμερος in this case does not involve mirroring the gentle habits of herbivores but keeping emotion under control; cf. the Middle-Platonic *Handbook of Platonism* (*Didaskalikos*), which defines ἥμερος πάθος as natural emotion kept within moderate bounds (σύμμετρα); see 186.14–24 in *Alcinoos: Enseignement des doctrines de Platon*, ed. John Whittaker, trans. Pierre Louis, 2nd ed. (Paris: Belles Lettres, 2002); also 32.4 in *Alcinous: The Handbook of Platonism*, trans. John Dillon (Oxford: Clarendon, 1993).

results reflect an exegetical *tradition* inclined to correlate interpretations with prevailing philosophical trends and respect traditional interpretations? Philo indeed reflects all of these interests.

Philo's own interests emerge in (1) his development of a *non*-allegorical interpretation of the Mosaic prohibition of carnivores that (2) nevertheless resonates with his allegory of the soul. Philo is in fact creating a *new* "literal" interpretation, not preserving an earlier one, as he does in regard to traditional interpretations of Gn 1–2.[52] But Philo develops a sophisticated notion of how literal observance affects what Tobin notes as the crux of the allegory of the soul: "the interior life of the individual human being."[53] Philo frames the (hypothetical) prohibition of man-eaters as a safeguard against pleasure (ἡδονή), whose deceptive influence figures prominently in his allegory of the soul under the guise of "serpent." His line of interpretation includes technical terms from the realm of moral psychology, "impulse" (ὁρμή) and "emotion" (πάθος), situated in the context of acquiring the moral virtue of self-control (ἐγκράτεια).[54] Concern with interior life at the level of "literal" interpretation in *Spec.* 4.103–104 appears elsewhere at a "symbolic" level, for example in Philo's discussion of the "snake-fighter" (*Spec.* 4.114–115).[55] So Philo achieves to some degree a consistent and mutually

---

[52] See Tobin, *Creation of Man*, 162–172. As Tobin explains, Philo could preserve earlier (and in his view *inspired*) "literal" (non-allegorical) interpretations of the creation of man intact, since his allegory of the soul functioned not as a *competing* interpretation at the "literal" (non-allegorical) level but as an *additional* interpretation at a brand new level. In the case of Lv 11:13–19 (a legal text), Philo does not deploy the allegory of the soul, so he cannot simply place his new interpretation alongside the earlier work of Eleazar. Instead, he must displace Eleazar's "literal" (non-allegorical) interpretation with a new one better suited to the exegetical agenda of his exposition of the Tenth Commandment.

[53] Idem, 34.

[54] Such terms reflect the concern for interiority underlying Philo's allegory of the soul, only expressed in the different context of non-allegorical interpretation. Interpreting a text in terms of "emotion" (πάθος), for example, demonstrates a concern for the inner life of the soul. In *Spec.* 4.103–104, Philo introduces "emotion" (πάθος) into his displaced interpretation of Lv 11:13–19 as an elaboration on the value of literal observance. In *Leg.* 2.9–11, Philo introduces "emotion" (πάθος) into his interpretation of Gn 2:19 (τὰ θηρία = τὰ πάθη τῆς ψυχῆς) as an elaboration on his allegory of the soul (see Tobin, *Creation of Man*, 121–122).

[55] The "snake-fighter" (ὀφιομάχης) appears among the clean "creeping things with wings that walk on all fours" in Lv 11:21–22. In his interpretation, Philo approximates Eleazar's *technique* by correlating a trait of this creature ("legs above the feet," which enable leaping off of the ground [ὥστε πηδᾶν ἀπὸ τῆς γῆς δύνασθαι]) with an analogous human trait, but he *uses* the technique to address a different realm of human experience. Whereas Eleazar interprets animal traits in terms of human *behavior* (external world), Philo interprets this trait in terms of the *inner life* of the soul. He speaks in *Spec.* 4.114–

reinforcing affirmation of *both* levels of interpretation, although practical observance serves as the actual means to acquiring self-control. In this way, he works out an elegant defense of the position he takes in *Migr.* 89–93, where he stresses the importance of actually observing Mosaic ordinances regarding, for example, Sabbath and circumcision, instead of attending *only* to their deeper symbolic significance:

> [E]xactly as we have to take thought for the body, because it is the abode of the soul, so we must pay heed to the letter of the laws (τῶν ῥητῶν νόμων ἐπιμελητέον). If we keep and observe these (φυλαττομένων γὰρ τούτων), we shall gain a clearer conception (ἀριδηλότερον κἀκεῖνα γνωρισθήσεται) of those things of which these are the symbols (ὧν εἰσιν οὗτοι σύμβολα); and besides that we shall not incur the censure of the many and the charges they are sure to bring against us. (*Migr.* 93)[56]

If certain dietary laws are symbols (σύμβολα) of self-control (ἐγκράτεια), and if the observance of certain dietary laws inculcates self-control (ἐγκράτεια), then actual observance not only *illuminates* symbolic significance—it also truly *embodies* symbolic significance.

A hint of Philo's reverence for tradition appears in his notably different approach to the regulations concerning birds (*Spec.* 4.116–117) over against the regulations concerning land animals (*Spec.* 4.103–109), aquatic animals (*Spec.* 4.110–112), and "creeping" things (*Spec.* 4.113–115): he offers *no* explanation of their significance in terms of his broader exposition of the Tenth Commandment.[57] Like Eleazar, he *characterizes* the carnivorous species prohibited in Lv 11:13–19, but he stops short of

---

115 of a soul (ψυχή) able to "leap up" from the earth (ἄνω πηδᾶν ... ἀπὸ γῆς) escaping the entanglements of bodily life to achieve a heavenly vision. The tone suggests Philo's deployment of the allegory of the soul (cf. Tobin, *Creation of Man*, 150–154), and so does the use of σύμβολον, one of the technical terms of true allegory (see idem, 147). In fact, Philo's understanding of the snake-fighter makes sense *only* in light of his allegory of the soul: Philo implicitly links the ὀφιομάχης with self-control in *Spec.* 4.114–115 (NB κραταιοτέρᾳ δυνάμει), but he does it *explicitly* elsewhere (*Opif.* 164: συμβολικῶς ἐγκράτεια εἶναί μοι δοκεῖ), because this creature "fights" pleasure (*Opif.* 164: μάχην ... ἡδονήν). Such an interpretation hinges entirely on Philo's *allegorical* equation of "snake" with "pleasure" (e.g., *Opif.* 157) (cf. Hecht, "Patterns of Exegesis," 111–112). Cf. Philo's interpretation of aquatic creatures (*Spec.* 4.110–112).

56 Trans. F.H. Colson. In regard to the legal ordinances mentioned in *Migr.* 89–93, Tobin notes the affirmation of both the level of literal observance and the level of interpretations "consistent with Philo's allegory of the soul" (Tobin, *Creation of Man*, 156).

57 In his summary of laws regarding clean and unclean creatures (*Spec.* 4.118), Philo suggests that Moses prohibited certain birds to withdraw fuel from a fire and "extinguish desire" (σβέσιν τῆς ἐπιθυμίας ἀπεργάζεται), but he has made *no argument* to that effect in his actual discussion of birds.

explaining how these prohibitions fit into Moses' plan to regulate desire through the dietary laws. This omission becomes more striking in light of *Spec.* 4.103–104, since Philo's contrived rationale involving man-eaters— their "tasty" meat can incite an overwhelming desire (for vengeance)— would work just as well with birds as it does with land animals. Both Philo and Eleazar comment on the harm done to human beings by some of the unclean birds, so human beings could arguably eat them with a vengeance.[58] So why does Philo relocate to land animals an exegetical move better suited to a discussion of birds? The explanation suggested by Tobin's research makes the most sense: Philo inherited a tradition that venerated the work of its predecessors, and rather than openly reject Eleazar's interpretation of Lv 11:13–19, he chooses to offer no interpretation at all, relocating the (transformed) final step of Eleazar's exegesis to a different part of his exposition.[59] As for contemporary philosophy, the notion of Mosaic laws enjoining a certain behavior to achieve a certain moral end—in this case abstinence from especially pleasurable foods to engender self-control—allows Philo to correlate his work with a similar *philosophical* notion of improving the soul through deliberate *exercises*.[60]

While Philo undoubtedly knew of such exercises from a variety of sources, his exposition of the Tenth Commandment exhibits the form and function of a type of treatise appearing among Plutarch's works, which aims first to "diagnose" (κρίσις) a troublesome passion and then to prescribe a set of practical exercises as "treatment" (ἄσκησις).[61] In

---

[58] *Let. Arist.* 146: τοὺς ἀνθρώπους δὲ ἀδικοῦσι νεκρούς τε καὶ ζῶντας; *Spec.* 4.116: ὅσα … κατ' ἀνθρώπων φονᾷ.

[59] Typically Philo does *not* revise earlier interpretations, but circumstances required it in this case (see above, n. 52). When he does revise, he follows the practice of the tradition he inherited.

[60] Such *Mosaic* exercises would fit the definition of "sittliches Exerzitium" (also "sittliche Übung"), the term used by Paul Rabbow to describe a type of methodical practice popular among philosophers of the early Roman Era: "a particular exertion, a calculated act of self-influence, carried out with the express purpose of achieving a specific ethical effect; it always transcends itself, insofar is it is either repeated or forms part of a larger network of acts designed for the same purpose" (my translation of Paul Rabbow, *Seelenführung: Methodik der Exerzitien in der Antike* [München: Kösel, 1954], 18). Cf. Pierre Hadot, "Spiritual Exercises," in *Philosophy as a Way of Life: Spiritual Exercises from Socrates to Foucault*, ed. Arnold I. Davidson, trans. Michael Chase (Malden, Mass.: Blackwell, 1995), 81–125.

[61] See Svebakken, "Tenth Commandment," 144–151. For an example among Plutarch's works, see *De garrulitate* (*Garr.*); for analysis of the genre, see Heinz Gerd Ingenkamp, *Plutarchs Schriften über die Heilung der Seele* (Hypomnemata 34; Göttingen: Vandenhoeck & Ruprecht, 1971). On the nature and purpose of "diagnosis" (κρίσις) and "treatment" (ἄσκησις), see *Garr.* 510 C–D (cf. Rabbow, *Seelenfürung*, 340: "Plutarchs System

part one of his exposition (*Spec.* 4.79–94), Philo offers a "diagnosis" of passionate desire (ἐπιθυμία), explaining how it works and how it harms both the individual and society.[62] In part two (*Spec.* 4.95–131), Philo casts the dietary laws as Moses' method for "treating" passionate desire, namely, as modes of *practice* (ἄσκησις) comparable to the exercises found in Plutarch's treatises.[63] In fact, the very principle Philo finds at work in Moses' (hypothetical) prohibition of man-eaters appears as one of the "exercises" prescribed in *De garrulitate*, where Plutarch recommends avoiding especially pleasurable *topics* to promote self-control in regard to *speaking*.[64] So Philo proves himself an heir of the Alexandrian tradition of exegesis by demonstrating reverence for both the work of contemporary philosophers *and* the traditional interpretations of his predecessors.

Conclusion

Evidence for Philo's interaction with a tradition of exegesis exists not only in connection with the creation account(s) of Genesis, which Tobin considers in *The Creation of Man*, but also in connection with legal texts from the Pentateuch, such as the list of prohibited birds in Lv 11:13–19. The *Letter of Aristeas* contains the traditional line of interpretation, which Philo incorporates into his own exposition of the dietary laws with three significant modifications: first, he relocates the crux of the interpretation

---

der Seelenheilung scheidet κρίσις und ἄσκησις; die κρίσις gibt die Erkenntnis des Übels in seinem Wesen, seiner Schädlichkeit; die ἄσκησις die praktische Übung gegen das Übel"). Of course, Plutarch (b. ca. 45 CE) postdated Philo, but the milieu of Plutarch's *teacher*, Ammonius, would account for Philo's knowledge of the genre. On Ammonius see C.P. Jones, "The Teacher of Plutarch," *HSCP* 71 (1967), 205–213; also Dillon, *Middle Platonists*, 189–192. Jones suggests dates for Ammonius of 20 to 70–80 CE ("Teacher of Plutarch," 208). Dillon calls Ammonius "a product of Alexandrian Platonism" (*Middle Platonists*, 190), even though he taught and died in Athens. John Glucker believes, concerning Ammonius' career as a teacher and arrival in Athens, that "[w]hatever philosophy he knew he had already learnt in Egypt;" see Glucker, *Antiochus and the Late Academy*, Hypomnemata 56 (Göttingen: Vandenhoeck & Ruprecht, 1978), 133. In regard to the allegory of the soul, Tobin suggests a similar connection between the work of Philo and the milieu of Ammonius (Tobin, *Creation of Man*, 151–153).

[62] E.g., *Spec.* 4.84 (NB τοσοῦτον ἄρα καὶ οὕτως κακὸν ὑπερβάλλον ἐστὶν ἐπιθυμία).

[63] E.g., *Spec.* 4.99 (NB πρὸς ἄσκησιν … ἐγκρατείας).

[64] See *Garr.* 513 D. The notion of self-control appears throughout the treatise: e.g., ἐγκράτεια in 505 D, 506 A–B; ἀκρασία in 503 C, 507 E, 508 F (cf. 503 C: ἀχαλίων … στομάτων). Cf. Jacques Boulogne, "L'intempérance verbale: L'imaginaire de Plutarche dans la thérapie des maladies de l'âme," in *Les passions antiques et médiévales*, ed. Bernard Besnier et al. (Paris: Presses universitaires de France, 2003), 161–169.

from the context of birds to the context of land animals; second, he explains the prohibition as an attempt on Moses' part to promote self-control (ἐγκράτεια), not justice (δικαιοσύνη); and third, he highlights observance of the prohibition at the literal (not symbolic) level. Each of these modifications makes sense in light of the results of Tobin's research.

The opening chapters of Genesis tell a story, and Jewish exegetes in Alexandria used appropriate sources of comparative philosophical material (e.g., Plato's *Timaeus*) to articulate the deeper meaning of this story. In his own interpretations of the creation narrative, Philo continued this trend but took a decidedly inward turn, finding a way through allegory for Genesis 1–3 (esp. Gn 3) to tell a story about the inner life of the soul. By contrast, the dietary laws of Leviticus 11 do not tell a story— they prescribe certain types of *behavior*. In order to articulate the deeper meaning of legal sections of the Pentateuch in terms of contemporary philosophy, Philo needed suitable models, such as the type of treatise Plutarch later used to prescribe certain types of *behavior* for the treatment of passion(s). So Philo's move to an emphasis on self-control (ἐγκράτεια)—while clearly serving the agenda of his exposition of the Tenth Commandment—reflects his effort to credit Mosaic legislation with the concern for self-control characteristic of contemporary moral essays. Philo's emphasis on *actual* observance likewise reflects a conviction that the moral agent acquires self-control through practical exercises. Philo notably does *not* deploy the allegory of the soul, which Tobin identified as his chief concern in regard to Gn 1–3. But this does not indicate the loss of such a concern on Philo's part, only a different way of expressing it in regard to legal material. Philo does in fact demonstrate the interest in the inner life of the soul characteristic of his allegory, but he does it by framing his interpretation in terms of moral psychology. Philo has an overarching interest in interior life: with *narrative* texts it appears as the allegory of the soul and with *legal* texts—at least in this case—it appears as the discourse of moral psychology, where Mosaic precepts become practical exercises for managing desire.

PART TWO

FOUNDATIONS AMID FLUX:
CHRISTIAN RESPONSES TO A TRANSITORY WORLD

THE SECOND TEMPLE AND THE ARTS OF RESISTANCE

Adela Yarbro Collins

Various kinds of events are perceived as catastrophes by human societies. Some are natural disasters; others are social upheavals. The latter type of catastrophe is the focus of this study.[1]

It once seemed to me obvious that the destruction of the second temple and the city of Jerusalem by the Romans in 70 CE was a catastrophic social upheaval from the point of view of all Jews living at the time, as it so clearly was for the author of 4 Ezra.[2] It now seems that attitudes toward the temple and its imagined or actual destruction were more complex. One reason for this change in perspective is the argument by James C. Scott that non-elite groups often resist dominant groups in subtle and indirect ways.[3]

A likely example of this phenomenon is a work dubbed "the Animal Apocalypse" by scholars. It is an allegorical composition in which different types of animals represent various nations or ethnic groups, and angels signify human beings. This work was composed several hundred years after the destruction of the first temple and long before the demolition of the second temple. It was given its present form in the time of Judas Maccabeus, who continued the revolt against the Greco-Syrian king begun by his father.[4] An earlier form of the work may have been composed near the end of the third century or the beginning of the second century BCE.[5] The text envisages a time of judgment to be followed

---

[1] It is a pleasure to dedicate this study to Tom Tobin in appreciation of his friendship and colleagueship as well as his contributions to scholarship.

[2] 4 Ezra is a Jewish apocalyptic work preserved in 2 Esdras 3–14, a book included in the Old Testament apocrypha. For an interpretation of this work, see Michael Edward Stone, Fourth Ezra, Hermeneia (Minneapolis, Minn.: Fortress, 1990).

[3] James C. Scott, Domination and the Arts of Resistance: Hidden Transcripts (New Haven and London: Yale University Press, 1990).

[4] I.e., around 165 BCE; George W.E. Nickelsburg, 1 Enoch 1: A Commentary on the Book of 1 Enoch Chapters 1–36, 81–108, Hermeneia (Minneapolis, Minn.: Fortress, 2001) 8; Patrick A. Tiller, A Commentary on the Animal Apocalypse of 1 Enoch, Early Judaism and Its Literature 4 (Atlanta, Ga.: SBL Scholars Press, 1993), 78–79. "The Animal Apocalypse" has been incorporated in the composite work known as 1 Enoch or Ethiopic Enoch as the second dream vision of Enoch in chapters 85–90; Nickelsburg, 1 Enoch 1, 354–408.

[5] Nickelsburg, 1 Enoch 1, 8.

by a new beginning.[6] In this new age, there will be a new Jerusalem, more beautiful than the first. The city will become the center of a new political order, led by the people of Israel to whom all the nations of the earth will be subject. It is surprising, however, that there will be no temple in the new Jerusalem.[7]

In the allegorical account of the history of Israel in this work, the first temple is positively portrayed under the image of a high "tower" built on the first "house," the first Jerusalem.[8] The second temple, however, is negatively described as polluted and impure.[9] This view of the temple is probably due to differences in the interpretation of biblical law between the author of the work and his audience, on the one hand, and the priests who controlled the temple cult in the second temple period up to the time of the defilement of the temple by Antiochus IV, on the other.[10] These priests were also the political rulers of Judea under the authority of first the Persians and then the Macedonians and their successors. Thus, differences concerning legal interpretation and administration of the temple cult were not only "religious" issues, but they also reflect social and political conflict.[11] The depiction of the new Jerusalem without a temple, a "house" without a "tower," may be understood, at least in part, as reflecting resistance to the dominant orders of society in the second temple period up to the crisis of Hellenization. This resistance may have come from dissident priests or from alienated scribes.

If this inference of resistance to the dominant group is correct, it may have a bearing on the choice of the technique of allegorical composition. The resistance may be disguised as part of a "hidden transcript," a body of speech, gestures, and texts in which a subordinate group expresses its criticism of and resistance to the dominant group. As James Scott has written:

> what permits subordinate groups to undercut the authorized cultural norms is the fact that cultural expression by virtue of its polyvalent symbolism and metaphor lends itself to disguise. By the subtle use of codes one can insinuate into a ritual, a pattern of dress, a song, a story, meanings that

---

[6] *1 Enoch* 90:20–38; Nickelsburg, *1 Enoch 1*, 402.

[7] *1 Enoch* 90:28–36.

[8] *1 Enoch* 89:50; Nickelsburg, *1 Enoch 1*, 366–367, 384. See also Tiller, *Animal Apocalypse*, 37–38.

[9] *1 Enoch* 89:72–73; Nickelsburg, *1 Enoch 1*, 387, 394–395.

[10] Tiller, *Animal Apocalypse*, 39–40.

[11] Tiller concludes that the legal objections were probably "intertwined with social and political opposition as well" (*Animal Apocalypse*, 40).

are accessible to one intended audience and opaque to another audience the actors wish to exclude. Alternatively, the excluded (and in this case, powerful) may grasp the seditious message in the performance but find it difficult to react because that sedition is clothed in terms that also can lay claim to a perfectly innocent construction.[12]

Those who used the Animal Apocalypse, for example, could claim that the altar was polluted because of violations of the law by individual, negligent priests, rather than by the current members of the whole dominant group.

Another interesting case is the book of Daniel. The form of the work that has come down to us was composed between 167 and 164 BCE, although it is presented as originating in Babylon in the sixth century BCE.[13] Chapter 7 contains a vision of four beasts that rise from the sea. The fourth beast is the most powerful and terrifying. It is put to death by an enthroned human figure, the Ancient of Days, who also takes dominion away from the other three beasts and gives it to another figure in human form, the "one like a son of man." Whereas the Animal Apocalypse has no explicit interpretation, Daniel asks one of those attending the throne of the Ancient of Days to explain the vision. This figure states that the four beasts signify four kings. The transfer of dominion from the four beasts to the "one like a son of man" is associated with the rule of "the holy ones of the Most High." The "little horn" of the fourth beast is interpreted as a king who will "speak words against the Most High."

Analogously to the Animal Apocalypse, the vision of the four beasts in Daniel seems to be a written representation of an aspect of the "hidden transcript" of those resisting the rule of Antiochus IV and his program of Hellenization and imposed worship of gods foreign to the Judeans. Although Antiochus is not named, those in the know realize that he is being portrayed as a beast and that his downfall is predicted. The allusions to Antiochus are clear enough, yet the indirect language provides deniability. It also provides the king with the option of ignoring the story. It is not after all a case of open rebellion. Further, the portrayal of Antiochus and his demise are presented as divinely revealed. The claim that the depiction of Antiochus as a beast and his downfall were divinely revealed to a wise man of the distant past is also a deterrent to the exercise of punishment on the part of the dominant group against the protesters. Theoretically, the king may fear the deity and leave those

---

[12] Scott, *Arts of Resistance*, 158.
[13] John J. Collins, *Daniel*, Hermeneia (Minneapolis, Minn.: Fortress, 1993), 38.

resisting indirectly alone. More likely in this case, he may disdain the power of the god of his subjects.

This vision and its interpretation are influenced by ancient Near Eastern combat myths. These typically portray a god doing battle with a beast. When the beast is defeated, the god's kingship is established. Such stories were told and written down in order to legitimate the human king who is associated with the victorious god.[14] The vision attributed to Daniel, however, turns the usual type of combat myth on its head. The current king is analogous to the defeated beast, rather than the divine victor. The Ancient of Days and the "one like a son of man," the victorious divine beings in human form, represent the opponents of the current king, who win the battle rather than being subdued.[15]

The approach taken so far in this paper is the consideration of certain Jewish texts in the context of power relations, namely, the exercise of power and resistance to it. It is also interesting, and I hope illuminating, to consider from this point of view the attitude toward the temple taken by the Essenes, or the Covenanters, a name implied by their self-descriptions.[16] The Dead Sea Scrolls have confirmed Josephus' description of the group as consisting of two orders, one that avoided marriage and another that practiced it.[17] The *Damascus Rule* apparently provides a set of guidelines for the organization and practices of those Covenanters who did marry. The *Community Rule* does the same for those who did not.[18] The *Damascus Rule* most frequently refers to those who did

----

[14] Richard J. Clifford, "The Roots of Apocalypticism in Near Eastern Myth," in *The Encyclopedia of Apocalypticism*, ed. Bernard McGinn, John J. Collins, and Stephen J. Stein, 3 vols. (New York: Continuum, 1998) 1.3–38.

[15] Cf. Adela Yarbro Collins, "Pergamon in Early Christian Literature," in *Pergamon, Citadel of the Gods: Archaeological Record, Literary Description, and Religious Development*, ed. Helmut Koester, Harvard Theological Studies 46 (Harrisburg, Penn.: Trinity Press International, 1998), 164–184, especially 176–184.

[16] The name "Covenanters" is suggested by Yonder Gillihan, "Civic Ideology among the Covenanters of the Dead Sea Scrolls and Other Greco-Roman Voluntary Associations" (Ph.D. diss., University of Chicago, 2007). On the identification of the group related to the Dead Sea Scrolls with the Essenes, see James C. VanderKam, *The Dead Sea Scrolls Today* (Grand Rapids, Mich.: Eerdmans, 1994), 71–98.

[17] Josephus *Bell.* 2.8.2, 13 §§ 120, 160. For a Greek text and English translation, see Geza Vermes and Martin D. Goodman, eds., *The Essenes according to the Classical Sources* (Sheffield, United Kingdom: JSOT Press for the Oxford Centre for Postgraduate Hebrew Studies, 1989), 36–39, 46–47.

[18] John J. Collins, "Forms of Community in the Dead Sea Scrolls," in *Emanuel: Studies in Hebrew Bible, Septuagint, and Dead Sea Scrolls in Honor of Emanuel Tov*, ed. Shalom M. Paul, Robert A. Kraft, Lawrence H. Schiffman, and Weston W. Fields, Supplements to Vetus Testamentum 94 (Leiden and Boston: Brill, 2003), 97–111, especially 104.

marry as "the congregation," whereas the *Community Rule* describes the non-marrying order as "the union" or "the community."[19]

The elite group, the "community," is also called the "council of the community." The council may be defined as a group of twelve men and three priests, "perfect in everything that has been revealed from all the law." The council has the task of atoning "for sin by doing justice and undergoing trials."[20] It is also described as "a holy house for Israel and the foundation of the holy of holies for Aaron," which is "to atone for the land." It is "the most holy dwelling for Aaron with eternal knowledge of the covenant of justice in order to offer a pleasant aroma; and it will be a house of perfection and truth in Israel."[21] The council will "atone for the guilt of iniquity and for the unfaithfulness of sin … without the flesh of burnt offerings and without the fat of sacrifice—the offering of the lips in compliance with the decree will be like the pleasant aroma of justice, and the perfectedness of behaviour will be acceptable like a freewill offering."[22]

This portrayal of the "council of the community" makes clear that it is a substitute for the temple in Jerusalem. Like the author and implied audience of the Animal Apocalypse, the Covenanters rejected the temple in Jerusalem because the priestly group in charge of it was not administering it properly. In the case of the Covenanters, one reason for rejecting the temple was that its cult was based on the wrong calendar, the lunar instead of the solar.[23] Ordinary Covenanters were free to use the temple for purposes that did not depend on the calendar.[24] The elite group, however, the "union" or "community," apparently avoided the temple altogether. Since they regarded all those outside their group as apostates and sinners (in the strongest sense), they no doubt rejected the ruling priestly families as unfit in a more general sense as well.

Although religious language is used to criticize the current temple administration and to depict the council of the community as an

---

[19] E.g., *CD* 10:4–8; 13:10–13; 1QS 1:1, 12.

[20] 1QS 8:1–4 in *The Dead Sea Scrolls Study Edition*, trans. and ed. Florentino García Martínez and Eibert J.C. Tigchelaar, 2 vols. (Leiden: Brill, 1997–1998) 1.89.

[21] 1QS 8:5–9; *Study Edition*, (translation slightly modified), 1.89.

[22] 1QS 9:4–5; *Study Edition*, (slightly modified), 1.91.

[23] VanderKam, *Dead Sea Scrolls Today*, 102–103, 114–116. Also mentioned in *CD* 4:12–21 are "fornication," "wealth," and "defilement of the temple." For discussion of the significance of "fornication" here, see "Divorce in the Cultural Contexts of Mark" in the commentary on Mark 10:1–12 in Adela Yarbro Collins, *Mark*, Hermeneia (Minneapolis, Minn.: Fortress, 2007).

[24] *CD* 6:11–14; 11:17–21. For discussion, see Gillihan, "Civic Ideology," 221–222.

alternative temple, it is clear that the conflict was also political. An important factor in the community's rejection of the temple may have been the appointment of Jonathan as high priest by the Seleucid Alexander Balas in 152 BCE.[25] Jonathan was one of the brothers of Judas Maccabeus and his military successor. The Maccabees, also known as the Hasmonean family, held the office of high priest until 37 BCE.[26] The Covenanters may have opposed their role as high priests because the Hasmoneans were not descendants of Zadok, as were the high priests from the exile to the crisis under Antiochus IV.[27] In addition, Jonathan may have usurped a position to which the Teacher of Righteousness, the virtual founder of the Covenanters, had a claim. In any case, the Hasmoneans were also the political leaders of Judea. After Simon succeeded his brother Jonathan and established the autonomy of the Jewish state, Antiochus VII recognized him as "ethnarch of the Judeans."[28] Later Hasmonean rulers took the title "king."[29]

The temple and its cult were thus integral parts of the Hasmonean state.[30] Instead of rejoicing in the establishment of an autonomous Jewish state, the Covenanters opposed it. Yonder Gillihan has interpreted the Covenanters as a voluntary association. He has argued that there were two types of voluntary associations in the Greco-Roman world: those with an assimilationist civic ideology and those with an alternative

---

[25] VanderKam, *Dead Sea Scrolls Today*, 100–104.

[26] James C. VanderKam, *From Joshua to Caiaphas: High Priests after the Exile* (Minneapolis, Minn.: Augsburg Fortress / Assen, the Netherlands: Royal van Gorcum, 2004), 240–393.

[27] See *CD* 4:1–6. See also VanderKam, *High Priests after the Exile*, 19, 44–45, 124, 137–138, 147–153, 157, 167–168, 181–182, 188, 197. The break in the Zadokite line may have occurred when Menelaus was appointed high priest, since he was the first high priest after the exile who was not a descendant of Joshua. Nevertheless, he does seem to have been a member of a priestly clan (Ibid., 189–191, 203). Alice Hunt remarks that the Zadokites are "[r]ecognized concurrently as critical figures for historical understanding and as historically elusive"; *Missing Priests: The Zadokites in Tradition and History*, Library of Hebrew Bible / Old Testament Studies 452 (New York and London: T & T Clark, 2006), 11.

[28] 1 Maccabees 15:1–2.

[29] The first Hasmonean to adopt the title "king" was either Aristobulus (104 BCE) or Janneus (103–76 BCE); see Scott T. Carroll, "Aristobulus 3," *ABD*, ed. David Noel Freedman (New Haven, Conn.: Yale University Press, 1992) 1:382; idem, "Janneus," *ABD*, 3:640.

[30] The cult of the temple in Jerusalem already had some features of a state cult in the Persian and Greek periods. It was customary for the Persian and Seleucid kings to "pay at least part of the expenses involved in the Jerusalem cult" (VanderKam, *High Priests after the Exile*, 189).

civic ideology. Although even alternative associations could not avoid replicating some of the organizational features and values of the state in which they were active, the goal reflected in their ideologies and practices was to provide an alternative state for their members. In the case of the Covenanters, their goal was ultimately to replace the current state with one that expressed and practiced their own values.[31]

Given these attitudes and practices, the Covenanters supported the temple cult in principle, but had no great affection for or loyalty to the current temple building. In fact, if they had had the power and the resources, they would have removed the current structure and replaced it with their ideal temple, which is described in the *Temple Scroll*.[32] Finally, they expected and hoped for a new temple to be created by God, which would endure forever. This temple is mentioned in the *Temple Scroll* in a speech attributed to God:

> I shall accept them (the offerings of the children of Israel) and they shall be my people and I shall be for them for ever. I will dwell with them for ever and ever and will sanctify my [sa]nctuary by my glory. I will cause my glory to rest on it until the day of creation, on which I shall create my sanctuary, establishing it for myself for all time according to the covenant which I have made with Jacob in Bethel.[33]

This definitive, eschatological temple is also mentioned in the *Florilegium*.[34]

Josephus says that the Essenes swear "to reveal nothing to outsiders even though violence unto death be used against [them]."[35] This practice of secrecy is confirmed by the *Community Rule*, which states that one

---

[31] Gillihan, "Civic Ideology," chapters 2–7.

[32] 11Q19; 11Q20; and 4Q524; for discussion, see Adela Yarbro Collins, "The Dream of a New Jerusalem at Qumran," in *The Bible and the Dead Sea Scrolls*, ed. James H. Charlesworth, 3 vols. (Waco, Tex.: Baylor University Press, 2006) 1.231–254, especially 239–244.

[33] 11Q19 29:6–10; *The Complete Dead Sea Scrolls in English*, trans. Geza Vermes, rev. ed. (London: Penguin Books, 2004), 201; Yarbro Collins, "New Jerusalem," 244.

[34] 4Q174 1:1–13. See Yarbro Collins, "New Jerusalem," 244–245 for a translation from Vermes (*Complete Dead Sea Scrolls*, 525–526) with modifications based on the translation of Michael O. Wise, "4QFlorilegium and the Temple of Adam," *RevQ* 15 (1991): 105–106. For discussion, see Yarbro Collins, "New Jerusalem," 245–246. The final temple, made by God, may also be the one described in a text dubbed "Description of the New Jerusalem" by scholars (see Yarbro Collins, ibid., 246–248).

[35] Josephus *Bell.* 2.8.7 § 141; *Essenes*, trans. Vermes and Goodman, 43; for the Greek text, see ibid., 42.

of the practices of the sons of light is "concealment concerning the truth of the mysteries of knowledge" (1QS 4:6).[36] The Instructor of the community "should not reproach or argue with the men of the pit but instead hide the counsel of the law in the midst of the men of injustice" (1QS 9:16–17).[37] Such secrecy may have had a variety of motivations, but it is compatible with the notion of a "hidden transcript" of the powerless. Speaking openly about their ideology, which involved the radical reform or replacement of the current political order, could have been dangerous. To outsiders they seemed to be more like a philosophical school than an apocalyptic sect preparing for the overthrow of the ruling Jewish group and their foreign allies.

The community of the Dead Sea Scrolls survived until the first Jewish war with Rome, during which the second temple was destroyed. The most likely scenarios explaining the group's disappearance are that they disbanded in disillusionment or that they resisted the Romans, who killed many if not all of them. The two explanations are not mutually exclusive. In any case, the group continued to exist when Pompey submitted Palestine to Roman oversight by making it part of the province of Syria[38] and when the Hasmonean dynasty came to an end and Herod came to power. They no doubt updated their interpretations of biblical texts as well as their own sometimes cryptic and ambiguous works.

Because of Mark Antony's influence on the Senate, Herod was formally crowned king of Judea in Rome in 40 BCE.[39] It was only in 37 BCE, however, that he actually gained control over his territory.[40] Taxation of the people of Judea (including Galilee and Perea)[41] during his rule was not excessive by ancient standards but was no doubt resisted by some of the people.[42] These taxes were levied on agricultural produce, on public

---

[36] García Martínez and Tigchelaar, *Study Edition*, 1.77.

[37] García Martínez and Tigchelaar, *Study Edition*, 1.93.

[38] Fabian E. Udoh, *To Caesar What Is Caesar's: Tribute, Taxes, and Imperial Administration in Early Roman Palestine (63 BCE – 70 CE)*, Brown Judaic Studies 343 (Providence, R.I.: Brown Judaic Studies, 2005), 9–30.

[39] Josephus *Bell.* 1.14.4 §§ 282–285; see also Lee I. Levine, "Herod the Great," in *ABD*, 3:161–169, especially 161.

[40] Josephus *Bell.* 1.17.3 §§ 328–357; Levine, "Herod," 161.

[41] Levine, "Herod," 165.

[42] Note that after Herod's death, some of the people petitioned his son and successor, Archelaus, for a reduction of taxes, and others for the abolition of duties (on sales); Josephus *Bell.* 2.1.2 § 4.

purchases and sales, and they included customs duties imposed for the use of trade routes.[43] There was at this time, no poll tax.[44]

Herod's rule was repugnant to some of his people because of his identification with a foreign power, and many were dismayed at the rapid increase in the introduction of Hellenistic architecture and customs into Jerusalem and other parts of his territory.[45] During his rule, Herod appointed the high priests in ways that supported his own interests.[46]

As a client king under the patronage first of Mark Antony and then of the emperor Augustus and his son-in-law Agrippa, Herod named buildings and even whole cities after his patrons.[47] One of his ambitious building projects was the rebuilding of the second temple. He doubled the size of the temple mount by extending the artificial podium toward the south, west, and north. The new plan of the temple mount was similar to other *temenoi* (sacred areas) in the early empire.[48] By enlarging the temple mount, Herod greatly increased the degree to which the outer court served as a profane civic center. Its status was thus ambiguous: it was sacred space and also a great civic esplanade.[49] The closest analogy to the design of Herod's temple is an Egyptian Hellenistic type of porticoed enclosure dedicated to the ruler cult. Julius Caesar and Cleopatra employed it for a complex dedicated to the worship of Caesar in Alexandria. Later this complex was rededicated to Augustus. Caesar brought this architectural form, an enclosure with four porticoes, to Rome. It became one of the favorite types used in the official building programs of Augustus, Herod's patron. Although it was used both for religious and civic buildings, it maintained its association with ruler cult until the time of Domitian.[50]

Such associations, to the extent that they were known in Judea, suggested that the refashioned temple was indirectly dedicated to Herod and honored him as much or more than the God of Israel. In any case, there is evidence for a minority view that the outer court of the temple should

[43] Levine, "Herod," 164.
[44] Udoh, *Tribute, Taxes, and Imperial Administration*, 164–171, 180–206.
[45] Levine, "Herod," 165.
[46] Ibid., 164.
[47] Ibid., 166.
[48] Ibid., 167.
[49] Adela Yarbro Collins, "Jesus' Action in Herod's Temple," in *Antiquity and Humanity: Essays on Ancient Religion and Philosophy Presented to Hans Dieter Betz on His 70th Birthday*, ed. eadem and Margaret M. Mitchell (Tübingen: Mohr Siebeck, 2001), 45–61, especially 57.
[50] Ibid., 57.

not be profane public space, but rather should be holy and set apart for worship, like the inner courts. The book of Ezekiel and the *Temple Scroll* from the Dead Sea provide such evidence.[51]

The Gospel of Mark portrays Jesus driving out those who were buying and selling on the temple mount and overturning the tables of the money-changers. It is likely that this portrayal is based on an incident in the life of Jesus.[52] His actions seem to express resistance to changes brought about by Herod's remodeling of the temple. He had made the Royal Portico on the south side of the temple a focus of juridical and commercial activity.[53] These activities probably took place elsewhere before Herod's rebuilding program. Jesus apparently shared the minority view that the outer court should be holy, just like the inner courts.

Mark also portrays Jesus as predicting the destruction of the temple in 13:2. In the trial before the Sanhedrin, that is, the Judean council, "false witnesses" accuse Jesus of saying that he would destroy this temple made with hands and build another not made with hands (14:58). The primary reason that the witnesses are labeled "false" is that Jesus did not say that he himself would do these things. The passive voice in the saying of 13:2 suggests that the agent of destruction will be God. If the saying at the trial has a basis in the teaching of Jesus, as seems likely, it probably expressed an expectation analogous to those expressed in the Dead Sea Scrolls. The current temple is problematic because of its inappropriate current administration and the corresponding improper practices. This temple will be removed, in accordance with divine will, and replaced by a temple "not made with hands," that is, a glorious, definitive temple created by the deity.

It seems to me unlikely that Jesus openly opposed the temple as "an instrument of imperial legitimation and control of a subjected people," as Richard Horsley has argued.[54] His temple-actions and temple-talk employ religious language and express religious values in opposing certain abuses. Yet, given the intricate interweaving of the religious and the political at the time, his religious talk, not least his teaching about the coming of the kingdom of God, may be seen as an expression of a "hidden transcript" that included the overthrow of the current

---

[51] Ibid., 54–57.
[52] Ibid., 45–48.
[53] Ibid., 53, n. 46.
[54] Richard A. Horsley, *Jesus and the Spiral of Violence: Popular Jewish Resistance in Roman Palestine* (San Francisco: Harper & Row, 1987), 286.

political order and the establishment of another in which his audience of ordinary people would have a better life.

As noted above, the book of Daniel was already part of a "hidden transcript" in its original context. Its role as an aspect of the "hidden transcript" of those inclined to resist Roman power over Palestine is evident in Josephus' discussion of the book in his *Antiquities of the Jews*. He accepted the ostensible date of the work, the time of the Babylonian exile in the sixth century BCE. He rewrote Daniel's interpretation of Nebuchadnezzar's dream in Daniel 2, in which the statue's head of gold represents the Babylonian kingdom. Like Daniel itself, he passes over the second kingdom quickly. He adds the comment that the third kingdom will be inaugurated by "a king from the west, clad in bronze." The reference to the west makes it likely that he refers to Alexander and the empire he founded.[55] He goes on to say:

> "... and this power will be ended by still another, like iron, that will have dominion for ever through its iron nature," which (Daniel) said is harder than that of gold or silver or bronze. And Daniel also revealed to the king the meaning of the stone, but I have not thought it proper to relate this, since I am expected to write of what is past and done and not what is to be; if, however, there is anyone who has so keen a desire for exact information that he will not stop short of inquiring more closely but wishes to learn about the hidden things that are to come, let him take the trouble to read the Book of Daniel, which he will find among the sacred writings.[56]

As Ralph Marcus points out, Josephus omits the description of the feet of the statue as consisting of iron and clay (Dn 2:33–34) and its characterization as divided (2:41) and as partly strong and partly brittle (2:42). The reason appears to be that his Roman audience will recognize the fourth kingdom as Rome and he does not want to cause offense.[57] Even more striking is Josephus' refusal to identify the significance of the stone that will break the statue into pieces. The reason surely is that his fellow Jews interpreted the stone as the messiah who would defeat and replace the Roman empire and establish the kingdom of God in which Israel would rule over all the nations.[58]

---

[55] Josephus *Ant.* 10.10.4 § 209; in *Josephus: The Jewish Antiquities, Books IX–XI*, trans. Ralph Marcus, LCL (Cambridge, Mass.: Harvard University Press / London: Heinemann, 1937), 6.273; on the interpretation, see n. i (ibid.).

[56] Josephus *Ant.* 10.10.4 §§ 209–210; in *Josephus*, trans. Ralph Marcus, 6.273, 275.

[57] Ibid., 274–275, n. a.

[58] Ibid., 275, n. c.

This kingdom is also alluded to in the vision of the four beasts from the sea and the "one like a son of man" in Daniel 7. It is striking that Josephus does not discuss this vision. He skips from a discussion of Daniel in the lions' den (chapter 6)[59] to his vision of a ram and a goat in chapter 8.[60] In his treatment of chapter 8, he conflates 8:14 and 12:11, both of which deal with the length of time that the sanctuary will be desolate. He refers explicitly to both the misfortunes caused by Antiochus IV and the destruction of Jerusalem and the temple by the Romans.[61]

It seems likely that he avoided mention of chapter 7 because his fellow Jews interpreted the fourth beast and its kingdom as Rome. Unlike Josephus' rewritten description of the fourth kingdom in Daniel 2, the description of the fourth kingdom in chapter 7 is highly unflattering. Furthermore, the kingdom associated with the dominion of the "one like a son of man" in heaven is also linked to the kingdom of "the people of the Most High" in 7:27. Josephus may have considered these elements so improper that they should not be mentioned at all.

The book of Daniel is clearly part of the "hidden transcript" that was shared by the author of Mark and his ideal audience. Daniel plays an important role in the apocalyptic discourse of Jesus in Mark 13.[62] Most spectacularly, the phrase "the desolating sacrilege," or more literally, "the abomination of desolation" in v. 14 either alludes to the book of Daniel or to an apocalyptic tradition inspired by it.[63] For the author of the book of Daniel, Daniel's prophecy of a "desolating sacrilege" had already been fulfilled by the pagan altar built by the agents of Antiochus IV over the altar of burnt offering in the temple in Jerusalem. For the author of Mark, that prophecy was yet to be fulfilled. The most satisfactory interpretation of the author's expectation is that he expected the Romans, when they got control of the temple, to set up a statue in it of Zeus/Jupiter or of the emperor as Zeus/Jupiter, as Gaius Caligula had attempted to do.[64]

---

[59] Josephus *Ant.* 10.11.5–7 §§ 250–263.

[60] Ibid., 10.11.7 §§ 264–276.

[61] As Marcus reconstructs the text (*Josephus*, 6.310, textual note 3, and 310–311, note c). He infers that Josephus interprets Daniel 11–12 as a prophecy of Roman conquest, as did the rabbis.

[62] Lars Hartman, *Prophecy Interpreted: The Formation of Some Jewish Apocalyptic Texts and of the Eschatological Discourse Mark 13 Par.*, CBNTS 1 (Lund: Gleerup, 1966), 172–174.

[63] The wording of the phrase in Mark 13:14 is closest to Dn 12:11; cf. Dn 9:27, 11:31; 1 Mc 1:54.

[64] Philo *Legat.* 29 § 188; cf. Josephus *Ant.* 18.8.2 § 261. For discussion, see the commentary on 13:14–20 in Yarbro Collins, *Mark*.

The lack of explicit mention of Daniel and the cryptic "Let the reader understand" in v. 14 show that the author is hinting at things that ought not to be discussed openly.

As we have seen, a reading of Daniel 2 and 7 that seems to have been widespread among Jews in the first century CE interprets the fourth kingdom of those chapters as the Roman empire. The defeat of the Roman empire is to be followed by an eternal kingdom to be established by divine power. This reading of Daniel seems to underlie the argument of 2 Thessalonians, which was probably not written by Paul.[65]

The body of the letter opens with a statement that appears to reveal the occasion for writing:

> We entreat you, brothers and sisters, concerning the coming of our Lord Jesus Christ and our being gathered to him, not to be too easily shaken from the composure of your minds or to be frightened, neither through a spirit nor discourse nor a letter supposed to be from us, as if the Day of the Lord were upon us (2 Thes 2:1–2).

Why was the author concerned about his addressees thinking that the Day of the Lord was imminent?[66] In the context of Jewish apocalyptic expectations at the time, including those of followers of Jesus, it is likely that the Jewish war with Rome, before its disastrous conclusion, led many to think that the end of the fourth kingdom was near. "The coming of our Lord Jesus Christ" was associated with the end of that kingdom as the event prophesied by Daniel in terms of the stone that would smash the statue and the kingdom taken from the four beasts and given to the "one like a son of man."

The author of the letter, however, argues that the Day of the Lord cannot come until "the rebellion" takes place, which is associated with the revelation of "the man of lawlessness, the son of perdition" (2:3). This man is, in effect, an evil king, who will oppose and exalt himself above every so-called god or object of worship, so that he takes his seat in the temple of God, declaring himself to be God (2:4). The man of lawlessness was ready to burst on the scene, since the mystery or secret

---

[65] Glenn S. Holland, *The Tradition that You Received from Us: 2 Thessalonians in the Pauline Tradition*, Hermeneutische Untersuchungen zur Theologie 24 (Tübingen: Mohr Siebeck, 1988), 129–158; Maarten J.J. Menken, *2 Thessalonians: Facing the End with Sobriety*, New Testament Readings (London and New York: Routledge, 1994), 146–149.

[66] For discussion of the phrase "Day of the Lord," see Adela Yarbro Collins, "Christian Messianism and the First Jewish War with Rome," in *Biblical Traditions in Transmission: Essays in Honour of Michael A. Knibb*, ed. Charlotte Hempel and Judith M. Lieu, Supplements to the Journal for the Study of Judaism 111 (Leiden: Brill, 2006), 333–343.

of lawlessness was already at work (2:7). It was only "the restraining force" that prevented his appearance (2:6). There is "one who restrains" that appearance until he himself is removed from the scene (2:7). This language is highly ambiguous and has been interpreted in a variety of ways.[67]

In any case, the "man of lawlessness" will be accepted by many who are destined to perish. This acceptance is part of the "rebellion" that must occur before the Day of the Lord.[68] A similar theme occurs in Mark 13. False messiahs and false prophets will appear and deceive many, immediately before the revelation of the Son of Man.[69] But the main difference between Mark 13 and 2 Thessalonians seems to result from different interpretations of the prophecy of the "abomination of desolation" in Daniel. Whereas Mark expected the Romans to fulfill this prophecy by setting up a statue in the temple, the author of 2 Thessalonians expected the prophecy to be fulfilled even more dramatically by an evil king. The portrait of this wicked deceiver (2:4) resembles the veiled description of Antiochus IV in Daniel 7–12, especially his self-exaltation in 11:36–37.

The idea that he will take his seat in the temple of God and declare himself to be God is reminiscent of the "desolating sacrilege" of Daniel 9:27 and Mark 13:14. For Mark and the author of 2 Thessalonians, the motif recalls not only Antiochus but also Gaius Caligula's attempt to install his statue in the temple of Jerusalem in particular and the imperial cult of the deified emperors in general.[70]

It is tempting to speculate about the identity of "the man of lawlessness" from the point of view of the author of 2 Thessalonians. Did he think of this evil king as the Roman emperor or his agent who would expect divine honors after winning the war against the Jews? The text does not reveal this secret. It seems likely, however, that this teaching about an evil king who would be destroyed by the breath of the Lord, the risen Jesus, when he comes (2:8) gives us a glimpse of a hidden transcript of resistance that dares not speak its name.

---

[67] For an argument that "the restraining force" is divine and "the one who restrains" is an angel, acting as God's agent, see Yarbro Collins, "Christian Messianism."

[68] Cf. 2 Thes 2:9–12 with 2:3.

[69] See Mark 13:21–22 for the warning about false messiahs and false prophets and 13:24–27 for the revelation of the Son of Man. On the theme of deception, cf. Mark 13:5–6, 21–22 with 2 Thes 2:10–13.

[70] Josephus says of Caligula: "he wished to be considered a god and to be hailed as such" (*Bell.* 2.10.1 § 184).

The Essenes, apparently, and certainly many other Jews of Palestine, including at first Josephus, did engage in open rebellion against Rome.[71] The authors of Mark and 2 Thessalonians and their audiences do not seem to have rebelled, but the glimpses we can get of their "hidden transcripts" suggest that they hoped for the overthrow of dominant groups by divine means.

---

[71] Scott, *Arts of Resistance*, 79, argues that the "hidden transcript" sometimes led subordinate groups to have an exaggerated sense of their own power.

MAMMONA INIQUITATIS:
CAN WE MAKE SENSE OF THE PARABLE
OF THE DISHONEST STEWARD?

Edmondo Lupieri

At the beginning of what is now chapter 15, Luke sets the scene:[1] "All the tax collectors and the sinners" are there to "listen" to Jesus, but there are also "the Pharisees and the scribes," who "murmur"[2] against him "because he accepts the sinners and eats with them" (Luke 15:1–2).[3] Luke

---

[1] Apparently, Luke has begun a new section of his narrative at what is now 14:1, having Jesus enter the "house of a chief of the Pharisees on a Shabbat day to eat." The following discussion centers around the issue of the people who should be invited: "the beggars, the poor, the blind and the lame," both in the present time (14:13) and in the eschaton (14:21). This is the new "justice" (14:14), even if its practice creates problems for some halakic interpretations of sabbatical prohibitions (14:2–6, centered on curing the sick or saving "a son or an ox" fallen "into a well ... on the day of Shabbat"). The new justice, though, defines a new exclusion: the "men" who had been "invited" will not touch the food (14:24). Up to this point, the criticism of this passage against observant Pharisees seems quite clear to me. Without interruption of the narrative flow, Luke says that "large crowds" join him and that Jesus "turn[s] to them" (14:25; is Jesus still inside the house? In the similar scene of 12:1, Jesus has just left the house of the Pharisee who had invited him to dine: compare 11:53 and 11:37). Here Jesus explains what it means to be a true disciple, in negative terms ("whoever does not ... is not capable of being my disciple:" 14:26–33). It appears quite logical that Jesus is not talking directly to the Pharisees any more but to "crowds" which could more easily accept his preaching. Again, this section ends with some exclusion: "also the salt," indeed, can get "rotten" and become useless (even as "manure") and therefore must be "thrown outside" (14:34–35). If it has to be thrown "outside," then it was "inside" beforehand. I see also here a strong criticism of observant Pharisees, destined to be excluded in the eschatological time (notice the use of future tenses in 14:14, 14:24 and 14:35, and the mention of the "resurrection of the righteous" in the first passage).

[2] Or "grumble," in more modern translations (in my own translation of the text I occasionally go back to the wording of the King James, especially when it seems more literal than that of the RSV or other versions). When Jesus accepts the contiguity with "sinners and tax collectors ... Pharisees and scribes murmur"; when Jesus enters the house of one of them (Zacchaeus) to stay with them, then "all ... murmur" with similar words: see Luke 19:7. These are the only two occurrences of the verb *diagogguzō* in Luke and in the NT (but *gogguzō* is used in the very similar passage of 5:30). The model of all these *goggusmoi* is obviously biblical, as 1 Corinthians 10 explains.

[3] "Tax collectors" and "sinners" may be part of the "crowds" of 14:25. They also come to "listen to him." Luke needs to have all of the actors present at the same time in the same place and therefore does not seem to change the background of the scene until the

then puts three parables on the lips of Jesus, all of them regarding the acceptance of lost elements: one out of hundred (the "lost sheep": Luke 15:3–7), one out of ten (the "lost drachma": Luke 15:8–10), and one out of two (the "lost son": Luke 15:11–32).

Immediately after the words of the father to his oldest and now jealous and grumbling son, at the beginning of what is now his chapter 16, Luke says that Jesus spoke "also to (his) disciples" (Luke 16:1). This may signify that the words that follow are thought to address the problems of the early communities of followers of Jesus, but the word "also" shows that the new addressees are not alone. Indeed, the whole of Luke 16 is organized as a "circular" or chiastic unit, rotating around the ironic reaction of the Pharisees (Luke 16:14), which roughly stands in the middle of the chapter. The "first wing" of this new unit is composed of a parable regarding the administration of unrighteous richness (the "Dishonest Steward": Luke 16:1–9), and of a group of apparently loose logia regarding faithfulness and richness ("mammon": Luke 16:10–13; cf. 16:9). After the reaction of the Pharisees, we find the "second wing," composed of a group of apparently loose logia regarding justification and the Law (Luke 16:15–18), and of a parable regarding unrighteous richness ("Dives and the Poor Lazarus": Luke 16:19–31).

This last parable ends with a sentence about the incapability of conversion for people (Jews) who do not listen to the real words of Moses nor to those of the prophets: They do not seem to be able to "believe" in any case, not even if "someone is resurrected from the dead" (Luke 16:31).[4] Immediately afterwards, Jesus talks "to his disciples" (apparently only to them) with a group of logia regarding "scandals" and true "faith" inside the community,[5] whose members are described as the "useless ser-

---

end of the whole section. (If this is true, as strange as it may sound, Jesus is still in the house of the Pharisee and the criticism that he "eats with" the sinners may be considered a generic statement—see the parallel passage of 5:29–30—and not a reaction to the present behavior of Jesus.) No "prostitutes" are mentioned here, together with the tax collectors, but they might be included among the "sinners" thanks to 7:37 (notice the very similar context of dining in the house of a Pharisee).

[4] This may reflect the conscience of early followers of Jesus, incapable of converting many among the other Jews, in spite of the proclamation of Jesus' resurrection. For a possibly similar "mood," see 18:8b (and even 5:39?).

[5] Apparently, regarding the "faith" Luke uses here an image which runs parallel to Mark 11:23. After the "Withering of the Barren Fig-Tree," in Mark there is a logion according to which "this mountain" (possibly the Zion or the Mount of Olives) can be removed from its place and thrown into the sea by the power of prayer. In Luke there is no account of a withered fig-tree. Instead, the Lukan barren fig-tree receives an extra

vants / slaves" of the "Lord" (Luke 17:1–10).[6] Then Luke changes the scene and begins a new section: recalling 9:51, he depicts Jesus and his disciples walking towards Jerusalem and passing through Samaria and Galilee (Luke 17:11).[7]

As usual, then, Luke carefully has crafted the whole section, and its various parts have their own narrative function in their contexts. The three parables on the acceptance of "lost individuals of a group" rebuke the objection of scribes and Pharisees to Jesus' acceptance of sinners and tax-collectors. The parable of the "Dishonest Steward" and the following logia on dishonest richness address both the disciples and the Pharisees, who indeed react against Jesus' words. Then, with the logia on justification and the Law and the following parable of "Dives and the Poor Lazarus," Jesus seems to conclude his discussion with the Pharisees, who are absolutely incapable of believing. Finally, he addresses only his disciples with a set of logia ending with the sentence on the "useless servants," in a context apparently oriented towards the early communities of believers. The parable of the "Dishonest Steward," therefore, should be understood, together with the following group of logia, in this polemical and catechetical context.

There is no doubt that this parable is one of the most difficult to be interpreted in this Gospel, as demonstrated by the plethora of conflicting interpretations offered through the history of its exegesis.[8] Nevertheless,

---

year of care in Luke 13:6–9. In our context "[this] sycamore" (therefore still some kind of "fig-tree") is told to be eradicated and transplanted in the sea (Luke 17:6). In Mt 21:21, we are told that the disciples can do the same as Jesus did to "the fig-tree," but also that "this mountain" (possibly the Zion or the Mount of Olives), according to their prayers, can be removed and thrown into the sea. We also find "this mountain" in Mt 17:20, but in a different context as "this mountain" (in this case probably the Mount of the Transfiguration, last mentioned at Mt 17:9) can move from one place to another according to prayer, without any reference to a sea into which it could be thrown. It seems to me that Matt is conflating and harmonizing the various passages he found in his sources.

[6] It seems therefore that Luke wants to conclude the section with a deeper explanation of what it really means to be Jesus' disciple. This should be an answer to questions left opened at 14:26–33 (see above n. 1) and especially the explanation of what kind of "servitude" is expected from the faithful as their response to Jesus' *diakonia* (see Luke 12:37 and below n. 29). Mt 25:30 may be a reaction to this kind of reflections.

[7] Quite logically, then, even if there are always Pharisees on the scene (17:20), the main point is now explicitly the salvation of the non-Judeans (17:16.18).

[8] See the "Appendix" by Brian Dennert. I got the idea of writing this note when I had the chance to hear the presentation of a new interpretation, according to which the parable contains some teachings on "Early Christian Fundraising;" D. Burkett, "Make Friends with Unrighteous Mammon (Luke 16:9): A Form of Early Christian Fundraising" (paper

it seems to me that the Lukan context can guide us to understand at least something.[9]

Above all, even if it is not explicitly stated, we should be quite confident that 16:1–9 is a parable, with a traditional incipit, introducing "a certain man," and a conclusion which turns into teaching addressed to both present disciples and future followers. If this is a parable, then, we are allowed to look for at least two levels of interpretation: the surface story and its more or less allegorical meaning, which is usually explained in the ending of the story, with or without an explicit interpretation (which may be an original part of the story or be added to clarify or re-interpret the text).

The core discussion of the Lukan context rotates around salvation and, particularly, about "who saves whom." This is a common discussion in the whole NT and stems from the proselytizing activity by specific groups of early communities of believers. Apparently, the ones whose ideas are reflected here had to face a series of problems and of conflicting situations, which I would summarize as follows: a) most observant Jews did not convert; b) the observant Jews who did convert created problems inside the communities, since they wanted to keep their halakic rules; c) both non-converted and converted observant Jews strongly criticized the converted individuals and groups who did not want to accept their rules (nor recognize their leadership); d) all involved groups had competing proselytizing activities among the Gentiles and accused each other to impede their salvation; e) among the non-converted observant Jews, the Pharisees were the ones most active in proselytizing among the Gentiles.

All these elements were essential in the world of the early generations of Jesus' followers, are present in almost all the strata of the NT,[10] and are particularly strong and evident already in Paul. The confrontations were so virulent that they produced passages like 1 Thes 2:14–16, which

---

presented at the Annual Meeting of the SBL, New Orleans, La., November 22, 2009). If I understand this proposal correctly, the "steward" symbolizes the rich, converted or sympathizers (who do not really own anything, since everything belongs to God), while the "debtors" are the poor among the followers of Jesus, who will own "the eternal dwellings" (of 16:9) thanks to their conversion. In certain ways, my reading is a reappraisal of interpretations which appeared every once in a while in the past: see the "Appendix" by Dennert, n. 30 and n. 14 (Tertullian).

[9] Generally speaking, I am quite skeptical about the possibility of identifying "original" meanings of this and of other Gospel passages, whether a narrative or a speech of Jesus. I would be glad and satisfied if I could simply understand what the evangelist meant with each passage.

[10] For Luke, see esp. 11:52.

some contemporary exegetes find so violent and so oriented towards the destruction of Jerusalem that they do not think Paul could possibly have written it.[11] All considered, though, these struggles contributed to the construction of diversified Jewish identities among the followers of Jesus and finally to the constitution of diversified Christian identities.[12]

The theological reinterpretation of salvation history by many early followers of Jesus likely was as follows. God had freely donated salvation to Israel. Through his merciful act, God wanted to save not only the whole of the Jewish people, including the sinners, but also, via the Jews, all the Gentiles. The followers of Jesus had to reinterpret and understand the "universalistic" passages of the Bible[13] in light of this kind of "radical inclusivity." Unfortunately, the Jewish leaders did not donate to everybody the salvation they had freely received but considered it a sort of private property,[14] creating a caste of privileged people inside Israel and constructing obstacles to the conversion of the Gentiles. They had tried to keep for themselves the fruits they were supposed to give back to their Lord.[15] When the Lord, in his mercy, sent his "slaves" and finally his "son" to collect the fruits of the vineyard, they repelled the prophets and killed Jesus (Luke 20:9–19).

---

[11] See B.A. Pearson, "1 Thessalonians 2:13–16: A Deutero-Pauline Interpolation," *HTR* 69 (1971): 79–94, who traces back the idea to F.C. Baur (and already A. Ritschl, though only for one verse). Although not untenable, given the possibly composite nature of the Pauline correspondence to the Thessalonians, the hypothesis is uninfluential upon our discussion. What matters is that ideas of this kind were present in different streams of Early Christianity towards the end of the first century CE.

[12] To the point that the same old polemical images, like the one depicting the Pharisees as "a dog in the manger," who does not nourish himself and impedes the oxen from eating, are still utilized by a Gnostic community in their polemic against the "greater Church" (*Gos. Thom.* 102, NHC II, 50, 2–5).

[13] As an example, I would suggest the reinterpretation of traditional biblical lore (esp. Isaiah 60) in Rv 21:24–27; see E. Lupieri, *A Commentary on the Apocalypse of John* (Grand Rapids: Eerdmans, 2006), 348–352.

[14] Since it was not their own, they must be considered "bandits" or "thieves" (Luke 19:48).

[15] As Luke explains by the sending of the "other seventy [two]" disciples (Luke 10:1), the "harvest" is the conversion that the new "workers" are reaping (Luke 10:2). The workers sent by Jesus at Luke 10 are not the "workers of injustice" of Luke 13:37 nor the "farmers" of the vineyard. While Luke 10 seems to be a prophetic allusion to the universalistic mission of the Christian church, the parable of the vineyard is more oriented towards the failure of the Jewish leadership (see esp. Luke 20:19, where both "scribes and high priests" understand that the parable is "addressed to them"). In both instances, I believe the collection of the fruit (grapes or wheat) is the salvation of the categories of people God was expecting the "workers" would save, since he had given them the knowledge / authority for doing so.

If this is the logical and historical background of the Lukan section we are analyzing,[16] then the general meaning of the parable and of its narrative context seems to be coherent and quite understandable.

In Luke 15, the first three parables represent the extension of salvation to the "lost" elements among the Jews.[17] These are the "sinners,"[18] who are not "righteous" and therefore the ones who are not observant, at least not according to the halakah established by the Pharisees.[19] After having so represented, against the Pharisees, the reintegration of the "lost sheep of the house of Israel,"[20] the Lukan Jesus, as we noticed above, turns also to the disciples, and therefore probably also to the believers of the time of Luke. The parable of the Dishonest Steward seems to be at home among believers who have full conscience of the end of the old "economy" (16:2) and seems to be designed to show what the correct behavior of the religious leaders should be—or should have been—in a moment of dramatic change.

The "lord" of the parable is a "rich man,"[21] whose steward has been accused of "squandering" his possessions. We are not told whether the

---

[16] And, I would say, one of the reasons for the writing of this and other Gospels and NT texts.

[17] The three groups in the parables are "genetically homogeneous": the hundred sheep are all sheep, the ten drachmai are all drachmai, and the two sons are both sons of the same father.

[18] Luke 15:7, 10 and 21. In the narrative framework, these are the tax collectors and sinners who came to listen to Jesus (15:1). By opposing the "first son," who always works as a "servant" for his father, whose "commandment" he never infringes, to the second son, who goes to a far away and foreign country and loses everything with prostitutes, the third parable seems to pave the way smoothly towards the discussion of the extension of salvation to the Gentiles.

[19] The almost synonymity of "righteous" and "observant" (of the Torah and/or a specific halakic teaching) is common in some Jewish sources, like Josephus. There were other Jews, though, who did not accept the idea that the observance of the Torah, intended as a "righteous/just" behavior, was capable of salvation. They felt the necessity for a "justifying" intervention of God, the only one able to "make just" a human, since the correct observance was either impossible or useless. We find such positions usually expressed in Jewish apocalyptic writings and the early followers of Jesus mostly sided with them.

[20] As Mt 10:6 would have put it. Curiously, Luke does not explicitly mention "sheep" anywhere else in the Gospel and Acts 8:32 is a quotation from Is 53:7. Similarly, Rom 8:6, with the only occurrence of the word in Paul, is a quotation of Ps 43:23. It seems that, differently from the communities represented by Matthew and John, those of Pauline and Lukan tradition did not use the term as a depiction for the believers.

[21] This is the first difficulty. Given the usual Lukan criticism of richness (even in the immediate context of 16:14) and given the fact that the "rich man" of the next parable (at 16:19) is a negative human figure, most exegetes have abandoned the idea that the "rich man" of 16:1 may represent God. In spite of this, I think that we should go back

accusations are grounded or not. As a matter of fact, the accusation of "squandering the belongings" (of the lord) applies more to the behavior of the Prodigal Son[22] than to that of our steward. Instead, a relative "squandering" appears in his new behavior, the one which the lord praises and seems to run in the direction opposite to the behavior praised in Luke 19:12–27 (and to the interpretation of 16:1–9 I am defending here). As with the concept of "justice,"[23] "keeping" and "squandering" acquire opposite meanings when the subjects of the actions are the traditionally observant Jews (Pharisees) or the believers in Jesus. If the steward, before his transformation, used to increase the interest rates, adding extra weights to those prescribed by the Law of Moses, he did not bring a real gain to his lord,[24] but "squandered" the opportunity to save the sinners (and then the Gentiles). With the coming of Jesus, Jewish richness must be brought outside and/or given away to bring fruit.[25] The destiny of the non-converted Jews, though, is sealed: The lord has already decided to take away the administration from his steward and presumably to give it to someone else. There is nothing the steward can do to change his lord's decision: he is fired.

I would read this in parallel with the other parables in which some goods (e.g., the vineyard [20:16, 19], the house [13:24–27], the kingdom [13:28–29], the inheritance [20:14], or even the invitation to a banquet [14:24]) are taken away from those to whom they had originally been given or promised or to whom they belonged from hereditary rights and are given to someone else.[26] In other words, this is another case in which

---

to an old way of interpreting the passage and accept that this "rich man," together with other unpleasant figures of Lukan parables, represents God. Indeed, even if Luke does not describe God as a "rich man" elsewhere, God usually appears as a powerful male human, often called a/the "lord." He is objectively rich and owns land, houses, slaves, cattle; he can even be a "noble man" who "takes for himself a/the kingdom" (or the "kingly power") in a far away region and acts in apparently cruel or pitiless ways. These last details belong to a story explicitly described as a "parable" by Luke at 19:11–27 and which shows many points of contact with ours and with our context.

[22] In a "land far away," he "squandered his own goods" according to Luke 15:13.

[23] Which we will analyze in the next pages.

[24] Even if he did not put the extras in his pocket.

[25] In this way, there is no contradiction with Luke 19:12–27. This last passage seems to be a further explanation of the same subject, including a historical reflection on the punishment of those of the People who did not recognize the will of God in Jesus' interpretation of the Law.

[26] This kind of supersessionism is a strong presence in the Gospel, from the beginning of the Galilean ministry of Jesus: Luke 4:26–27. The fate of Jewish leadership, of losing their power and being substituted by others, seems to me one concrete example—possibly

the evangelist describes the transition from the old "economy" to the new one, the one which we now call Christian. Luke's description, though, is carefully nuanced. The steward still has some kind of authority, for a very short time, over his lord's belongings. He does not seem to be a slave (no "slaves" appear in this parable) to be punished nor an "enemy" to be killed:[27] he can change his behavior. Obliged by necessity, he now makes it easier for other people to obtain the goods of his lord.[28] In so doing, he does exactly what his lord wanted him to do, and this is why his lord praises him. The steward has finally learnt to act in a "wise" way,[29] not

the most resounding at his time—of Luke's meditation about the reversal of human destiny, variously stressed in his Gospel (*e. g.* the *Magnificat* at 1:52–53 and the "Dirges" at 6:24–26).

[27] As in the above mentioned parable of 19:12–27.

[28] Luke explains at 11:46 that the correct behavior of the scribes should be that of lightening the weights of the observance. This could also explain why the steward does not condone completely the debt to the debtors. Maybe Luke thinks that, being still a person of the old economy, the steward does not have the power to do so (only the creditor, owner of the riches, can completely condone the debts, the amount being irrelevant to him: Luke 7:41–42). Some exegetes think that the "discount" applied by the steward is in reality the restitution of a percentage that the steward had unjustly required before, for his own advantage and not for his lord's. While I do not see a clear indication in the text that this is the right way to go, the metaphor still could be applied to the additional weight the Pharisees and other observant Jewish leaders were accused to have added to the requirements of the Torah (see also Luke 6:1–2 and 11:38).

[29] I see no reason for translating *phronimos* as "shrewd" here and as "wise" at 12:42, as the context and wording are extremely similar. I deem probable that Luke deepens or adapts the teaching already presented in chapter 12 to a slightly different context in our passage. There Jesus addresses only his disciples (12:22) and we can therefore expect that Luke is addressing problems primarily faced by his own communities. At 12:35–38, the Lukan Jesus tells the disciples to be "ready," like "those slaves" who are "awake" when their "lord" comes back at night, and therefore are "blessed." Then, at 12:41, Peter asks "the Lord" whether that "parable" is for them or "for everyone." Jesus answers with another parable (12:42–46), which is about a "faithful and wise steward," whom we realize is a "slave" and who is found behaving correctly by his lord. Therefore, he is proclaimed "blessed" and receives authority "over all his [lord's] possessions." That same slave, though, seeing that his lord is not coming, could "begin to beat the menservants and maidens, and to eat and drink and get drunk." The result is expressed vividly: "The lord of that slave will come on a day when he does not expect him and at an hour that he does not know, and he will divide him into two and will put his part with the unbelievers." In this context, the behavior of the lord is not particularly merciful, but the explanation comes in the following verses (12:47–53: the fact that at v. 54 Jesus turns "also to the crowds" and therefore is not talking exclusively to his disciples any more should prove that these are the concluding verses). Apparently, Luke organizes the explanation on different levels. The first one (vv. 47–48a) tells us of a slave who knowingly disobeys his lord and who is therefore beaten more than a slave who does the same but does not know what the lord expects from him. This seems to be a quite traditional explanation of why Israel receives a greater punishment than the Gentiles, a question that became of extreme

keeping the goods covered or shut away like the "foolish (*aphron*) rich man" (12:16–21) or the frightened slave (19:20) do.

If these other figures represent observant Jews or Jewish leaders, incapable of doing what God had expected them to do, our steward is someone who understands that salvation must be at the disposal of others. But who are the others, the "debtors" of the lord? The fact that they will have "everlasting habitations," where they can "receive" the steward once he has lost his job, is quite illuminating. It is not impossible that these are the converted Gentiles,[30] who will come from the four directions of the

---

actuality after the year 70 CE and that we find largely debated in an apocalyptical work like 4 *Ezra*. With the following sentence, though (v. 48b–c), Luke introduces another contraposition, between those to whom a lot "was given" and those to whom a lot "was entrusted": the second ones will be requested for more than the first ones. If the ones who were "entrusted" are the followers of Jesus (simple faithful or authorities?) then the traditional material regarding Jews and Gentiles is reoriented towards believers (in Jesus) and non-believers. That this is the case, it should be explained by the following words of Jesus (12:49–53). He says that "the fire" he came to "throw upon the earth," probably as the result of his own "baptism" (which should be his death), will cause "division … in the earth," even in the same "house" and family. This should be the result of what we would call conversion to the beliefs in Jesus. But this should also explain the "division into two" of the guilty slave-steward. The whole imagery of the preceding passages, indeed, comes from the traditional Jewish lore depicting the visitation by God (even the fact that the "lord" is coming "from the wedding," probably reflecting "Christian" symbology, could still imply that that lord is the "father," since it is not explained whose wedding is the one mentioned and it could be the wedding of the lord's son), but the detail that the "lord" will "serve (food)" to his own "slaves" obliges us to identify this "lord" with Jesus (with strong eucharistic echoes in the text: see above n. 6 and the discussion of 17:7–8). It is the coming of Jesus which causes the division into two fields or "parts" of both "the land" (of Israel) and of the whole "earth." The "part" which does not accept conversion, whatever its ethnical origin, will be "with the unbelievers." Finally, the long Lukan explanation seems also to be oriented towards a reduction of the eschatological meaning of the "coming of the son of man" (12:40): the sudden coming of the Lord could also be interpreted as the eschatological realization of the triumph of the cross and of the diffusion of the true faith in the Land and on the earth. To sum up, it seems that Luke has a large amount of traditional material regarding the visitation of God, the coming of the Son of Man and the second coming of Jesus, and that he organizes it in a way that is coherent with his own ecclesiological eschatology.

[30] The interpretation of the passage is connected to the explanation of 16:8b, where "sons of this eon" are "wiser than the sons of light, towards (?) their own generation." In the other Lukan passage where the expression "sons of this eon" appears, these seem to be simply the people who live normally in this world and not in the future one, the eon of the resurrection (Luke 20:34). They marry and get married; maybe their life is not perfect, but there is no explicit blame (nor anachronistic exaltation of asceticism). If they are subject to the Law of Moses (20:28), they are Jews. In our parable, then, who are the "sons of light"? Does the steward belong originally to this second category? Which is the relationship between the debtors and the "sons of this eon"? If the "sons of this

earth to sit and eat with the patriarchs and all the prophets in the kingdom, while the ones who expected to be inside (the "you" of the story) can only knock at the door and be "thrown outside" (13:25–29).[31] If not Gentiles (or not only), they are yet again the excluded of Israel, those outcast whom Jesus had "received" at 15:2 and who will be able, in the eschaton as well in the Lukan church, to "receive" those observant Jews who were able to change their habit.

The passage we have just quoted (13:25–29) can help us to better understand our context, since Luke 13:23 explicitly states that the discussion is about "salvation," while the people who were listening to Jesus in that moment are considered to be "workers of injustice" (*ergatai adikias*: 13:27). Also our steward is called "the administrator of (the) injustice" (*ton oikonomon tēs adikias*: 16:8) and the richness he is supposed to handle, the goods of his lord, is also called "the mammon of (the) injustice" (*tou mammōna tēs adikias*: 16:9). The contraposition to the justice / righteousness of the Pharisees should now be quite obvious, but what does it mean in a concrete sense?

The discussion by the evangelist centers around the true and real "righteousness," which is not that offered by the halakah of the Pharisees (18:9–14a). Real righteousness is doing the will of God, the Lord, Father, Householder, Slaveowner, and so forth. According to most NT texts, especially in the Pauline and Lukan writings, the will of God is the gratuitous extension of salvation to everybody, particularly the excluded

---

eon" are either Gentiles or the not-so-observant Jews, they are probably "wiser" because they are open to repentance and conversion "in front of their generation," which is the generation of the unrepentant at the time of Jesus and John the Baptist (see esp. 7:31; 9:41; 11:29–30, 31–32, 50–51; 17:25; Acts 2:40). If this is the case, "sons of light" would not be a definition of the believers (as e.g. in 1 Thes 5:5, Eph 5:8, John 12:36) but maybe a self definition (used ironically by Luke?) of observant Jews. That all Jews are "sons" (of Abraham: 3:8; 13:16; 16:24; 19:9, and therefore of God: 3:48) is always recognized by Luke; if they can keep the rights of their sonship is a different problem. The steward, then, possibly belongs to the sons of light because he is born in the house of Israel and / or is originally convinced to be a son of light because of his observance but then gets wiser, like the sons of this eon, who are able to repent and convert, in front of their generation of unrepentant.

[31] The possibility of a radical inclusion of the Gentiles has brought some to theorize that the "steward" is no one else than Paul (cf. Eph 3:2; but see above n. 28). If we want to identify a specific historical figure under the persona of the steward, the fact that after all the inclusion is not so radical or gratuitous could allow us to think of several Jewish reformers, from John the Baptist to Peter or any of Jesus' disciples. Luke, though, probably wants to keep the discussion at a more general level, given the presence of the Pharisees and the address to all the disciples.

of the house of Israel and the Gentiles. Whoever helps expand salvation outside the borders of the observance is a "righteous" person.[32]

If this expansion beyond the traditional borders of Jewish (Pharisaic) observance is "righteousness," the Pharisaic observance, which usually helps define a person as "righteous," becomes "unrighteous," even if not applied. All the goods that God had donated to Israel become "unrighteous," as long as the Jewish authorities jealously keep them under their "unrighteous" control. The "richness" donated by God has become the "mammon of injustice."

At least in the mind of some early groups of followers of Jesus, if not for Jesus himself, the epiphany of this transformation was the economic dimension of cultic Jewish life. According to their view, anything useful for salvation could be "sold," even in the temple of Jerusalem (Luke 19:45), under the control of the "high priests" and with the complicity of "scribes ... and the leaders of the people" (19:47). Or, at least, this was the accusation: by putting monetary value on and selling the instruments of salvation, religion had become a business.[33]

This allows the Lukan Jesus to expand his teaching with a series of sentences apparently loosely connected with the context but actually strictly bound to it. First, he opposes "faithful" and "unjust / unrighteous" behaviors in a "very small thing" and in the "great one" (16:10). The "great thing" should be the new announcement of salvation brought by Jesus and proclaimed by his church, while the "very small one," in comparison, is the old economy again. But the old economy, in the hands of the observant leaders, has become an "unjust mammon," in the use of which they were not "faithful / trustworthy" (16:11). Further, what they were administering was not theirs because it belonged to someone else (God; 16:12). In this way, they will be unable to take any advantage from the change brought by the new economy, since they will be incapable of being entrusted the "true" richness that actually should have been "theirs." In conclusion, they could not be "servants of two lords" (16:13).

According to Luke, the Pharisees, "who love money," understand perfectly well that Jesus was talking about them and react "sneer[ing] at him" (16:14). The four following sentences are the first part of Jesus'

---

[32] The model is Jesus, whose "righteousness" is recognized also by the Gentiles, thanks to his death: Luke 23:47.

[33] See E. Lupieri, "'Businessmen and Merchants Will Not Enter the Places of My Father' (Gos. Thom. 64 [NHC II, 2; 44:34 f.]): Early Christianity and Market Mentality," in *The Standardized Monetarization of the Market and the Impact on Religion, Politics, Law and Ethics*, ed. M. Welker and J. von Hagen (forthcoming).

answer. He begins accusing them of "justifying themselves" and deny-
ing the true observance of the Law, therefore bypassing the only instrument of justification (before the coming of Jesus). The basis for their
justice/righteousness is human "abomination,"[34] against the judgment
of God (16:15). To the wrong observance of the Pharisees, Jesus then
opposes the presence of the evangelization, in an apparent contraposition to the Law of past (16:16). Nevertheless, the "gospel," which is the
new way for justification and salvation, does not abolish the Law.

To cancel that impression, Luke immediately stresses the validity of the
Law in all its detail, at least until the end of the eon (16:17). The teaching
about the divorce, however, explains how to understand its validity: the
real meaning of the Law is not the interpretation usually offered by the
Pharisees but the one variously attributed to Jesus in different NT strata
(16:18; see 1 Cor 7:10–11). Therefore, the "novelty" brought by Jesus and
his followers is the real and true interpretation of the Law, against the
traditional reading of the Pharisees.[35]

The second part of Jesus' answer is the parable of Dives and the Poor
Lazarus. Comments on a few details will suffice for our discussion. The
actors are both Jews and the Abrahamic sonship of the rich man is
stressed several times in few lines (Luke 16:24, 25, 30). Being a "child" of
Abraham, though, does not save the sinful (as underlined already at 3:8),
nor Dives' relatives, while the outcast Lazarus rests in Abraham's bosom.
Both here and in the parable of the two sons, the "lost" individual finds
himself in a state of contiguity with animals, there "pigs" and "dogs" here,
and their food,[36] for which he craves (Luke 15:15–16 and 16:21). Needless
to say, pigs and dogs are animals that, although not contaminating while
alive, were not particularly loved by observant Jews and appear together
as a symbol of contamination in another famous sentence attributed
to Jesus by Matthew (7:6). Luke, then, rehashes the same idea of the

---

[34] The word "abomination" (*bdelugma*) has a long history in apocalyptical contexts. A
key term in Mark 13:14, it derives from Dn 9:27, 11:31 and 12:11, and is reused in Mt
24:15, but avoided—I think intentionally—in Luke 21:20–24. Luke uses it here to give it,
I suppose, a more general meaning and function, although still loosely connected to the
fall of Jerusalem, as the beginning of the punishment for the sinful behavior of Jewish
religious authorities.

[35] In general, the whole work of Luke has the aim to defend a moderate version of
Pauline "Christianity" and to render it more acceptable for other groups of believing Jews
and early "Christ worshipers." This context seems to me an example of his program.

[36] "Crumbs" from the tables of the "children" [of Israel] are food for the "little dogs"
[the children of the Gentiles] according to Mark 7:27–28. Luke apparently avoids the
insulting detail.

reintegration of the outcast of Israel from different points of view: at the beginning of the section the discussion deals primarily with exclusion caused by the observance and by strict religious norms while at the end, having referred to the "marketizing" of salvation, Luke is able to take the narration to a subject he loves, the negative power of "richness" in its socio-economic dimension.[37]

If all this is plausible, the parable of the Dishonest Steward, brought back to its Lukan narrative context, becomes understandable and makes good sense. This does not mean, though, that the parable is "easy." Some passages remain obscure: why does the steward say that he is "not strong enough to dig" and "ashamed to beg" (Luke 16:3)? Does it mean that he does not have the strength necessary to work in the vineyard of the Lord and that he is too proud to ask others to donate him the instruments of salvation? It could also be that we have here simply some narrative elements, deprived of allegorical meaning, which function to embellish the story or entertain the audience.[38] A healthy balance between the opposing risks of missing an important clue or of overestimating secondary details is always difficult to obtain. In any case, with or without the Lukan irony, the whole Lukan discussion wants to bring the faithful to the realization that the inclusion of the outcast, both in its religious and social dimensions, although a necessity hard to swallow, is the will of God.

---

[37] The parable still stresses the potential impurity of social exclusion through the presence of the "dogs." Similar in their behavior to the Samaritan (who does not observe the rules of purity of the Judeans and does not care about the potential contamination brought by contact with a body which looks like a cadaver and therefore is able to save the life of a human being: Luke 10:30–37) these potentially contaminating animals are able to show more compassion than Dives, to the point of "licking" the almost certainly contaminating "sores" of the poor Lazarus.

[38] This is what T. Bednarz, a specialist of humor in ancient literature, keeps saying; see her "Lukan Humor and the Parable of the Dishonest Household Manager (Luke 16:1–17)" (paper presented at the annual meeting of the SBL, New Orleans, La., November 22, 2009).

APPENDIX:
A SURVEY OF THE INTERPRETATIVE HISTORY OF THE PARABLE OF THE DISHONEST STEWARD (LUKE 16:1–9)

Brian C. Dennert

Perhaps no parable offers scholars as much difficulty in interpretation and as many opportunities for research than the parable of the Dishonest Steward (Luke 16:1–9). The master's praise of an "unrighteous" (*adikia*) steward and Jesus' use of him as an example has prompted a voluminous number of proposals, the sheer magnitude of which can overwhelm the perspective interpreter. Therefore, this brief summary of the parable's interpretative history cannot attempt to be exhaustive.[1] Instead, it seeks to be representative of the major interpretations in the early church, medieval Catholicism, the Protestant Reformation, and contemporary scholars in order to reveal the different approaches adopted in studying this parable.

Interpretation in the Early Church:
A Tradition of Almsgiving Emerges

Early Christian writers from multiple regions interpreted the parable as an exhortation to almsgiving in light of the accompanying comments (vv. 8b–13), particularly v. 9. Clement of Alexandria used this parable in his discussion of how the rich should be generous with their wealth,

---

[1] For a more comprehensive discussion of modern interpretation of this parable, see Dennis J. Ireland, "A History of Recent Interpretation of the Parable of the Unjust Steward (Luke 16:1–13)," *WTJ* (1989): 293–318, and the discussion of works appearing after Ireland's work in Dave L.T. Mathewson, "The Parable of the Unjust Steward (Luke 16:1–13): A Reexamination of the Traditional View in Light of Recent Challenges," *JETS* 38 (1995): 29–39. An abbreviated collection of early church interpretation of the parable appears in Arthur A. Just, *Luke* (ACCS 3; Downers Grove, Ill: InterVarsity, 2003), 253–256. The concise list of views in Klyne Snodgrass, *Stories with Intent: A Comprehensive Guide to the Parables of Jesus* (Grand Rapids: Eerdmans, 2008), 406–410, and extensive bibliography on the parable in Arland Hultgren, *The Parables of Jesus: A Commentary* (Grand Rapids: Eerdmans, 2000), 154–157, also prove helpful as overviews of the scholarship on this parable.

an interpretation Cyril of Alexandria echoed a few centuries later.[2] An economic sense also appears in Tertullian's view that the parable teaches that one should not be controlled by money,[3] with John Chrysostom, Ambrose, Augustine, and Jerome noting it as a call for almsgiving.[4] That the servant's generosity was with money belonging to the master rather than his own money did not trouble interpreters, as Clement of Alexandria noted that the steward's generosity with his master's goods serves as a reminder that God is the owner of one's possessions,[5] a point Augustine reiterated in discussing the "agency" of Christians over things that are not their own.[6] John Chrysostom and Augustine further observed that the actions of the steward teach that even if one has gained money through dishonest means, one can still use it for the kingdom,[7] with Gregory of Nazianzus comparing this use of money to Israel "plundering the Egyptians."[8]

Many of these early interpreters saw the conduct of the steward as immoral, stating that Jesus endorses his wisdom, not his behavior.[9] In fact, Cyprian argued that Jesus used this worldly example to teach those who would not listen to godly examples.[10] The perception that the steward represents the world's wisdom also occurs in Origen's comparison of the wisdom of the steward with the wisdom of the serpent[11] and Athanasius' use of 16:8 to describe the Arians.[12]

---

[2] Clement of Alexandria *Quis div.* 13 (*ANF* 2:594); Cyril of Alexandria, *Commentary on the Gospel of Saint Luke*, trans. R. Payne Smith (Astoria, N.Y.: Studion, 1983), 439–441.

[3] Tertullian *Marc.* 4.33.1 (*ANF* 3.402–403); *Pat.* 7 (*ANF* 3:721).

[4] Chrysostom *Hom. Matt.* 5.8 (*NPNF¹* 10:35), 52.5 (*NPNF¹*10:325); *Hom. Rom.* 18 (*NPNF¹* 11:484); Ambrose *Exp. Luc.* 7.244–245 (Just, *Luke*, 256); Augustine *Serm.* 359A; see Augustine, *Sermons (341–400) on Various Subjects*, pt. 3, vol. 10, *The Works of Saint Augustine: A Translation for the 21st Century*, ed. John Rotelle, trans. Edmund Hill (Hyde Park, N.Y.: New City, 1995), 209–221; Jerome *Epist.* 54.12 (*NPNF²* 6:106), 72.4 (*NPNF²* 6:153), 77.11 (*NPNF²* 6:162), 108.16 (*NPNF²* 6:203), 118.4 (*NPNF²* 6:222), 121 (*NPNF²* 6:224), 123.6 (*NPNF²* 6:232), 130.7 (*NPNF²* 6:264). In *Serm.* 359A.11, Augustine argues that the parable directs one to give twenty percent instead of the ten percent of the Pharisees (*Sermons*, 216).

[5] Clement of Alexandria *Quis div* 32 (*ANF* 2:600).

[6] Augustine *Serm.* 359A.11 (*Sermons*, 217).

[7] Chrysostom *Hom. Matt.* 5.8 (*NPNF¹*10:35); Augustine *Serm.* 359A.15 (*Sermons*, 219–220).

[8] Gregory Nazianzus *Homilies* 45.20 (*NPNF²* 7:430).

[9] For example, see Augustine *Serm.* 359A.10 (*Sermons*, 216); and Jerome *Ruf.* I.24 (*NPNF²* 3:496).

[10] Cyprian *Epistles* 73.19 (FC 51:280–281).

[11] Origen *Hom. Jer.* 17.3.2 (FC 97:182–183).

[12] Athanasius *Ep. Aeg. Lib.* 18 (*NPNF²* 4:232).

While the most common interpretation in the early church saw the parable as an example and exhortation to almsgiving, writers such as Tertullian and Origen also found elements of the text that lent towards allegorical interpretation. Origen connected the debts owed to the master (not the steward) and the documentation of these debts to the recording of sin in Dn 7:10 and Col 2:14, with the reckoning referring to judgment and the stewardship pointing to the ministry of the Word of God.[13] Tertullian grounded an allegorical meaning upon the address of the parable to the Jewish people who were facing removal of their stewardship in the service of God, wherein they were to help deliver people from their debt of sin. Instead of becoming friends with the Gentiles, as the dishonest steward did, the Jews had treated them harshly, which caused them not to be welcomed into "eternal habitations" when they lost this grace of stewardship.[14]

Medieval and Reformation Interpretations: The Tradition Deepens

Both prominent medieval Catholic interpreters and the Protestant Reformers continued to view the parable as an exhortation to generosity without endorsing the actions of steward based upon the comments following the parable. According to Bonaventure, the parable is partly an explicit example and partly an allegory, with the exhortation of v. 8 as the example and the "detestable" behavior of the steward explained through allegory.[15] That is, Jesus used the steward's prudence as an example to imitate like the wisdom of serpents, with the steward's actions allegorically demonstrating the mercy that is to characterize Christians before the final judgment, as they have squandered the mercy and gifts of God like this steward. While Martin Luther and John Calvin rejected allegorical interpretation, they both argued that the point of the parable is the need for generosity among Christians. The generosity commanded differs from the steward's dishonest actions because it is to be both shrewd and righteous.[16] Interestingly, Luther did not see the main difficulty of

---

[13] See Origen Hom. Gen. 13 (FC 71:194); Comm. Matt. 14.8 (ANF 9:499). Augustine also seems to have detected elements of allegory in comparing the fact of death to the removal of the steward from his post (Serm. 359A.8–11; see Sermons, 215–217).

[14] Tertullian Fug. 13 (ANF 4:125).

[15] Bonaventure, Commentary on the Gospel of Luke, 3 vols., trans. Robert J. Karris (St. Bonaventure, N.Y.: Franciscan Institute Publications, 2001–2004), 2:1470–1489.

[16] Martin Luther, Sermons of Martin Luther, 8 vols., ed. John Nicholas Lenker, trans.

the text as the immoral action of the steward but the passage's potential for teaching salvation by works and the existence of other mediators, causing him to move quickly from explaining why one should not imitate the steward literally to how this passage illustrates works of compassion springing from faith like Matthew 25.[17]

Modern Interpretations: The Tradition Challenged—and Scattered

The rise of critical methods in biblical studies altered the discussion of this parable in two major ways, as some have sought to determine the meaning of the original parable told by Jesus while others have pursued its meaning in its Lukan redaction beyond the attached remarks of vv. 8b–13.[18] The distinction between the historical Jesus and the teachings of the early church in the Gospels led to many scholars seeing some or all of vv. 8b–13 as early church commentary on a parable that most likely stems from the historical Jesus.[19] This reopened interpretation of the parable beyond the economic sense indicated by these concluding comments.

Although some scholars retained the traditional interpretation of the parable being at least in part about generosity or almsgiving by reaffirming the connection between the parable and the comments that

---

John Nicholas Lenker, et. al. (Minneapolis: Lutherans in All Lands, 1904; reprint, Grand Rapids: Baker, 1983), 4: 291–315; and John Calvin, *Commentary on Harmony of the Gospels*, vol. 17, Calvin's Commentaries (Grand Rapids: Baker Book House, 2005), 175–183.

[17] Luther, *Sermons*, 4:292–300.

[18] This division is not absolute, as some scholars will discuss both elements. However, interpreters usually favor one issue over the other.

[19] The nearly unanimous acceptance of the authenticity of the parable (16:1–8a) includes the Jesus Seminar; see Robert Funk, *The Five Gospels: The Search for the Authentic Words of Jesus* (New York: Polebridge, 1993), 358–359. Furthermore, scholars began to detect different and conflicting applications even within vv. 8b–13, as vv. 8b–9 appear to use the steward as positive example while vv. 10–12 presents the steward as a negative example; see John S. Kloppenborg, "The Dishonoured Master (Luke 16:1–8a)," *Bib* 70 (1989): 474–475. The differences between the comments in vv. 9–13 leads Dodd's often quoted statement that these are three separate sermons applying the passage; see C.H. Dodd, *The Parables of the Kingdom*, rev. ed. (New York: Charles Scribner's Sons, 1961), 17. In contrast, see Craig Blomberg, *The Parables of Jesus* (Downers Grove, Ill.: InterVarsity, 1990), 243–247, and Darrell Bock, *Luke*, 2 vols., BECNT 3 (Grand Rapids: Baker, 1994–1996), 1323–1343, who argue that a parable can make multiple points, with vv. 8b–13 unpacking the multiple points of the parable.

follow,[20] numerous scholars have proposed alternative meanings for the parable as told by Jesus. One approach redefines the boundaries of the original parable unit, such as viewing the original parable ending at v. 7 to illustrate eschatological prudence[21] or arguing that v. 8b accompanied the parable, making the parable a lesson on embodying the values of the kingdom to which one belongs.[22] Many scholars end the parable at v. 8a,[23] which prompts the question of why the master would praise the actions of the steward. Notable ways to solve this problem include an economic explanation that the steward's actions did not injure the master,[24] a sociological view that the steward restored the master's honor,[25] a

---

[20] In addition to arguments of Blomberg and Bock (see n. 19), some scholars see vv. 10–13 as secondary comments and vv. 8b–9 containing the original application. See Paul Gätcher, "The Parable of the Dishonest Steward after Oriental Conceptions," *CBQ* 12 (1950): 121–131; Francis E. Williams, "Is Almsgiving the Point of the 'Unjust Steward'?" *JBL* 83 (1964): 293–297; I. Howard Marshall, *The Gospel of Luke: A Commentary on the Greek Text*, NIGTC (Grand Rapids: Eerdmans, 1978), 614–622; David Wenham, *The Parables of Jesus* (Downers Grove, Ill.: InterVarsity, 1989), 161–171; Ireland, "Parable," 315–318; and Joel B. Green, *The Gospel of Luke*, NICNT (Grand Rapids: Eerdmans, 1998), 586–595.

[21] See Rudolf Bultmann, *History of the Synoptic Tradition*, trans. John Marsh, rev. ed. (Oxford: Blackwell, 1972), 175–176, 199–200; Joachim Jeremias, *The Parables of Jesus*, trans. S.H. Hooke, rev. ed. (New York: Charles Scribner's Son, 1963), 45–48, 181–182; Dodd, *Parables*, 17–18; and Norman Perrin, *Rediscovering the Teaching of Jesus* (New York: Harper & Row, 1967), 114–115. While ending the parable at v. 7, a different line of argumentation occurs in J. Dominic Crossan, *In Parables: The Challenge of the Historical Jesus*, 2nd ed. (Sonoma: Polebridge Press, 1992), 108–111.

[22] See Hultgren, *Parables*, 146–154.

[23] See the discussion below for the different approaches taken by Joseph A. Fitzmyer, "The Story of the Dishonest Manager (Luke 16:1–13)," *TS* 25 (1964): 23–42; Brandon Bernard Scott, "A Master's Praise: Luke 16:1–8a," *Bib* 64 (1983): 173–188; and Kloppenborg, "The Dishonoured Master," 474–495, all of whom hold that the original parable unit ends at v. 8a.

[24] Gätcher, "Parable," 121–131; J. Duncan M. Derrett, "Fresh Light on St. Luke 16," *NTS* 7 (1961): 198–219; idem, "'Take thy Bond … and Write Fifty,' (Luke xvi.6): The Nature of the Bond," *JTS* 23 (1972): 438–440; and Fitzmyer, "The Story," 23–42. A significant difference appears between Derrett's view that the steward eliminated the usury forbidden in the Torah and Fitzmyer's position that the steward eliminated his personal profits in these debts.

[25] Scholars taking this approach with various nuances include Kenneth E. Bailey, *Poet and Peasant: A Literary-Cultural Approach to the Parables in Luke* (Grand Rapids: Eerdmans, 1976), 86–110; William R. Herzog II, *Parables as Subversive Speech* (Louisville: Westminster/John Knox, 1994), 233–258; Kloppenborg, "The Dishonoured Master," 474–495; David T. Landry and Ben May, "Honor Restored: New Light on the Parable of the Prudent Steward (Luke 16:1–8a)," *JBL* 119 (2000): 287–309. Although focusing on the charges against the steward, the discussion in John G. Lyre, "Of What Charges? (Luke 16:1–2)," *BTB* 32 (2002): 21–28, follows a similar approach.

Christological proposal to defend Jesus' inclusion of "sinners,"[26] or justifications using literary conventions or forms.[27] Scholars using the same background often reach different conclusions, typically influenced by their integration of insights from other views.

Meanwhile, the rise of redaction criticism and use of literary methods in biblical interpretation caused other scholars to develop a greater concern for how Luke uses the parable within the Gospel, potentially developing Lukan redactional themes besides generosity and care for the poor. Analyzing the relationship of the parable in its broader context or relating it to other parables and passages in the Gospel has produced these alternative readings. For example, reading this parable in tandem with the preceding parable of the Lost Son could show it illustrating teachings about God's grace or the nature of repentance.[28] The dispute with the Pharisees leads some to view the parable as a defense of Jesus' ministry of forgiveness and an invitation to participate this program of "debt

---

[26] William R.G. Loader, "Jesus and the Rogue in Luke 16,1–8a: The Parable of the Unjust Steward," *RB* 96 (1989): 518–532; and Colin Brown, "The Unjust Steward: A New Twist?" in *Worship, Theology, and Ministry in the Early Church: Essays in Honor of Ralph P. Martin*, ed. Michael J. Wilkins and Terence Paige, JSNTSup 87 (Sheffield: Sheffield Academic Press, 1992), 121–145.

[27] This category includes various proposals. For the view that the praise of v. 9 is meant as irony, see Paul G. Bretscher, "Brief Studies: The Parable of the Unjust Steward—A New Approach to Luke 16:1–9," *CTM* 22 (1951): 756–762; Donald R. Fletcher, "The Riddle of the Unjust Steward: Is Irony the Key?" *JBL* 92 (1963): 15–30; Stanly E. Porter, "The Parable of the Unjust Steward (Luke 16:1–13): Irony as the Key," in *The Bible in Three Dimensions: Essays in Celebration of Forty Years of Biblical Studies in the University of Sheffield*, ed. David J.A. Clines, et al., JSOTSup 87 (Sheffield: JSOT Press, 1990), 127–153; and I.J. du Pleisss, "Philanthropy or Sarcasm? Another Look at the Parable of the Dishonest Manager (Luke 16:1–13)," *Neot* 24 (1990): 1–20. The story is seen as "comic relief" in Dan O. Via, *The Parables: Their Literary and Existential Dimensions* (Philadelphia: Fortress, 1967), 155–162. The "rogue" story of revenge is the key to interpretation in Crossan, *In Parables*, 108–111; Scott "A Master's Praise," 173–188; and Mary Ann Beavis, "Ancient Slavery as an Interpretive Context for the New Testament Servant Parables with Special Reference to the Unjust Steward (Luke 16:1–8)," *JBL* 111 (1992): 37–54, though all these writers come to vastly different conclusions from this same background.

[28] John R. Donahue, *The Gospel in Parable* (Philadelphia: Fortress, 1988), 162–169, argues that the parable presents the "foolish" character of God as the master after the Lost Son shows him as father, drawing on the connections observed in Bailey, *Poet*, 109. In comparing the parable to the rest of the parables in the Lukan *Sondergut*, Douglas M. Parrott, "The Dishonest Steward (Luke 16:1–8a) and Luke's Special Parable Collection," *NTS* 37 (1991): 499–515, maintains that the lost original ending to this parable would present the steward showing a lack of repentance to serve as a foil to the repentant son. A comparison to the Lost Son also appears in the concluding section of Landry and May, "Honor Restored," 305–308, where they discuss the broader Lukan context of the parable after refining the sociological view of Kloppenborg.

relief" as described in Luke.[29] Another trajectory within this approach sees the parable as a call to reduce the burden of the ceremonial laws on others and exercise flexibility in relation to the Gentiles.[30]

Conclusion: One Parable, Three Ways, No Consensus

This history of interpretation reveals three major approaches to interpreting the parable of the dishonest steward. The traditional approach utilized the comments of vv. 8b–13 to ground a meaning of almsgiving or generosity, an interpretation still defended by some today. The opinion of many modern scholars that vv. 8b–13 present the early church's interpretation of the parable leads to the second approach, which seeks to determine the meaning of the parable as told by the historical Jesus through a deeper understanding of the economic, social, or literary background to the parable. The ever expanding pool of interpretations offered by this second approach[31] leads to some scholars adopting a third approach, which attempts to find the meaning of the parable as redacted by Luke in light of its context and the major interests of his gospel.

Of these three approaches, it seems that the third approach offers the greatest potential for future study of the parable. If the problem of the first approach is that it confined the meaning of the parable to the words that follow it, then the problem with the second approach is that there is no clear or universal standard for evaluation of interpretations. The third approach integrates the work produced by the other approaches while offering a clear standard to evaluate different proposals—the Gospel of Luke and the parable's wider context. This standard is wide enough

---

[29] For various ways of arguing this point, see L. John Topel, "On the Injustice of the Unjust Steward: Lk 16:1–13," *CBQ* 37 (1975): 216–227; Loader, "Jesus and the Rogue," 518–532; and Ryan S. Schellenberg, "Which Master? Whose Steward? Metalepsis and Lordship in the Parable of the Prudent Steward (Lk 16.1–13)," *JSNT* 30 (2008): 263–288.

[30] Examples of this approach would be Ehrhard Kamlah, "Die Parabel vom ungerechten Verwalter (Lk 16:1 ff.) im Rahmen der Knechtsgleichnisse," in *Abraham unser Vater*, ed. O. Betz, M. Hengel, and P. Schmidt (Leiden: Brill, 1963), 276–294; Ronald G. Lunt, "Expounding the Parables: III. The Parable of the Unjust Steward (Luke xvi.1–15)," *ExpTim* 77, no. 5 (1965–1966): 132–136; and C.S. Mann, "Unjust Steward or Prudent Manager?" *ExpTim* 102, no. 8 (1990–1991): 234–235, although Mann bases his conclusions on an emendation of the text.

[31] Perhaps the wide ranging number of proposals for the original parable confirms Bultmann's observation that the original meaning of the parable has been forever lost (*History of Synoptic Tradition*, 199–200).

to promote study that generates new insights while narrow enough to appraise the merit of new proposals. Therefore, while the interpretation of this parable is not easy, it is not impossible.

GALATIANS 3:28 AND THE PROBLEM OF
EQUALITY IN THE CHURCH AND SOCIETY

David E. Aune

I. *Introduction*

The ancient Mediterranean world was redolent with economic, national, racial, social, and gender hierarchies, divisions, and inequalities, like many societies in the modern world. While the kinds of human rights that have developed in the West during the past two centuries, influenced by the Enlightenment, have roots in the ancient world, those rights were based not on *secular* conceptions of the human person that have flourished in modern liberal democratic regimes, but rather on the *religious* ideologies of various ancient ethnolinguistic groups.[1] This essay, dedicated to my friend and former colleague, Tom Tobin, S.J., will focus on the evidence for the theoretical and practical conceptions of *equality* in early Christianity, with emphasis on equality in the three areas of nationality, social status and gender, under the assumption that equality is a basic constituent of human rights everywhere.

Since ancient societies had an essentially religious orientation, conceptions of equality that have modern analogues were based on religious rather than secular or rational presuppositions. Monotheism (the belief that one God exists and no others), for example, appears to have functioned as a necessary, though insufficient, cause for the development of the conception of equality between major ethnolinguistic groups. In post-exilic period (i.e., following the mid-sixth century BCE), Judaism developed an ethnocentric form of ethical monotheism in which the God of Israel was identified with the one God of the cosmos with the

---

[1] The phrase "ethnolinguistic group" indicates a society that typically shares a common language and a common ethnicity (i.e., according to Weber a social construct and so distinct from race) and consequently have a common self-designation, sense of common identity, a common history (real or imagined) and kinship ties. The traditional conception of "race" has not proven to be helpful in recent years and has been replaced by more accurate descriptions of people that share many physical and cultural features such as "bio-geographical ancestry."

implication that the gods worshiped by Gentiles were idols with no reality. While some Jews maintained that all people would eventually share
the blessings attendant on recognizing the God of Israel as the one and
only God (particularly in the latter days), other Jews were negative about
the access that the Gentiles could have to God and expected that they
would finally be excluded from his presence and annihilated.[2]

Another form of monotheism was developed in Stoicism, founded
in the late fourth century BCE by Zeno of Citium (334–262 BCE). Stoics
formulated a strikingly non-ethnocentric form of materialistic monism
in which God and the material world were considered identical.[3] God
was also regarded as identical with Reason or Mind, which pervades
the cosmos and is also present in gods and human beings. One social
implication of this form of monotheism that helped to break down
national and social barriers is that individual human natures are parts
of universal nature.[4] Stoics were famously cosmopolitans who held that
all people are equal and should live in mutual love and understanding.[5]

In addition to having an essentially religious orientation, ancient societies had conceptions of the human person that differed from notions of
the autonomous self that developed in the west beginning with Augustine's *Confessions* through the Enlightenment to modern western liberal democracies. The differences between ancient and modern western conceptions of the person are often understood in terms of the
dichotomous models of "individualism-collectivism" (describing cultures) or "idiocentrism-allocentrism" (describing individuals who are
part of those cultures).[6] Individualistic cultures and idiocentric persons
emphasize values that serve the interests of the self (by making the
self feel good, distinguished, independent), while collectivist cultures
emphasize values that subordinate personal goals to the values of the

---

[2] The variegated view that Jews had of gentiles from the Hebrew Bible to the early
rabbinic period is discussed by E.P. Sanders, *Jesus and Judaism* (Philadelphia: Fortress
Press, 1985), 212–218.

[3] Zeno and Chrysippus according to Diogenes Laertius 7.148–149 (*Stoicorum Veterum Fragmenta* 2.1022, 1132); Seneca *Epistulae morales* 92.30.

[4] Chrysippus according to Diogenes Laertius 7.87–89 (*Stoicorum Veterum Fragmenta*
3.178).

[5] Epictetus *Discourses* 2.5.26.

[6] H.C. Triandis, R. Bontempo, M.J. Villareal, M. Asai and N. Lucca, "Individualism
and Collectivism: Cross-Cultural Perspectives on Self-Ingroup Relationships," *Journal of
Personality and Social Psychology* 54 (1988): 323–338; Shalom H. Schwartz, "Individualism-Collectivism: Critique and Proposed Refinements," *Journal of Cross-Cultural Psychology* 21 (1990).

group. Types of individualism (ancient or modern) and types of collectivism (ancient or modern) contrasted with modern conceptions of self as group-oriented.[7] The notion of *individual* rights is a modern Western conception centered on a post-Christian society made up of people who are largely of northern European ancestry living in modern liberal democracies.

Early "Christianity"—the terms "Christian" and "Christianity" are actually anachronistic when used of the followers of Jesus before ca. 120 CE[8]—began as a sectarian movement within Palestinian Judaism originally limited to Aramaic-speaking Palestinian Jews. Within ten to fifteen years after the death of Jesus (ca. 29 CE), the Jesus movement had begun expanding outside Palestine to Jewish communities in the Levantine diaspora, in cities such as Samaria, cities on the island of Cyprus and Antioch on the Orontes in Syria (the third largest city of the Roman Empire). Paul was the central figure in the mission to the Gentiles and some time before he began writing letters to communities he had founded, the followers of Jesus somehow adopted the innovative designation "church" (ἐκκλησία) for individual local assemblies of believers.[9] This conception, which included people of various nationalities, social

---

[7] Bruce J. Malina and Jerome H. Neyrey, *Portraits of Paul: An Archeology of Ancient Personality* (Louisville: Westminster John Knox, 1996), 1–18, 153–201; Bruce J. Malina, "Understanding New Testament Persons," *The Social Sciences and New Testament Interpretation*, ed. Richard Rohrbaugh (Peabody: Hendrickson, 1996), 41–61; Bruce J. Malina and Jerome H. Neyrey, "First-Century Personality: Dyadic Not Individual," *The Social World of Luke-Acts: Models for Interpretation*, ed. Jerome H. Neyrey (Peabody: Hendrickson, 1991), 67–96.

[8] The term "Christian" (a Latinism formed with the adjectival ending *-anus* ["belonging to"] and therefore in all likelihood coined by Roman authorities) occurs three times in the New Testament: Acts 11:26 (the passage claims that the disciples were first called "Christians" in Antioch); 26:28; 1 Peter 4:16; both documents were written ca. 90 CE. According to 1 Peter 4:16, followers of Jesus had suffered persecution for "the name of Christ," suggesting that the label "Christian" was a term of abuse. The terms "Christian" and "Christianity" appear frequently in the letters of Ignatius of Antioch (died ca. 115 CE). The plural form *Christiani* occurs in three Roman authors in works that appeared in the early second century: Tacitus *Annals* 15.44 (written ca. 116 CE); Pliny, *Epistulae.* 10.96.1 (written between 98 and 110 CE); Suetonius *Nero* 16.2 (written early in the second century). By ca. 120 CE, the term *Christianos* is found from Antioch in Syria (Acts 11:26; Ignatius of Antioch), to Caesarea (Acts 26:28), to Anatolia (1 Peter 4:16; Pliny the Younger; *Martyrdom of Polycarp* 12.2), to Rome (Tacitus, Suetonius).

[9] Wilfred Cantwell Smith, *The Meaning and End of Religion* (New York: Macmillan, 1962; Minneapolis: Fortress Press, 1991), 24. The term ἐκκλησία is used in the Septuagint to refer to the people of God (e.g., Dt 23:2–3; 1 Chr 28:8; Neh 13:1), and it is likely that the term was adopted for group of the followers of Jesus understood as the new people of God.

statuses as well as both men and women, had no close analogy in the ancient world. The earliest work in the New Testament, 1 Thessalonians (written ca. 49 CE), is addressed "To the church of the Thessalonians in God the Father and the Lord Jesus Christ" (1:1), and later Paul has occasion to refer to "the churches of God in Christ Jesus which are in Judea" (2:14) in the plural (see also 1 Cor 11:16; 2 Thes 1:4). Both uses of the term "church" suggest that it is already traditional and widespread usage. Even more striking is the fact that "church" is used in the singular to refer to the global community of believers.[10] In the ancient world, religious identity and ethnicity were virtually inseparable. After struggling for years with the particularity of its original Jewish identity, Christianity was somehow able to conceptualize itself on analogy to the ancient philosophical schools, as primarily a system of belief and practice unconnected in any essential way with ethnicity and nationality.

II. *Jesus of Nazareth and Human Rights*

Raising the question of what Jesus said and did during his brief ministry in the early first century (ca. 26–29 CE) is a historical problem with which generations of scholars have wrestled. Yet there are two quite different ways of examining the influence that Jesus had on the socio-religious movement that he inspired.

First, it is possible to emphasize the importance of reconstructing the teachings and activities of the historical Jesus using the historical critical method.[11] While this is certainly a legitimate enterprise, one complication of the approach is the fact that there are major disagreements among critical scholars when it comes to deciding what the historical Jesus actually said and did. Currently there are two competing models of the historical Jesus. According to the older model, Jesus was an apocalyptic prophet, who proclaimed the imminent arrival of the Kingdom of God and taught an ethic (based in part on conventional Jewish moral teaching) appropriate for living under the reign of God (following in the tradition of Johannes Weiss and Albert Schweitzer).[12] Viewing Jesus as an

---

[10] 1 Cor 10:32; 12:28; 15:9; Gal 1:13; Phil 3:6; Acts 20:28.
[11] For a masterful use of the historical method to reconstruct the life and teachings of Jesus, see John P. Meier, *A Marginal Jew: Rethinking the Historical Jesus*, Anchor Bible Reference Library, 4 vols. (New York: Doubleday, 1991–2009). A fifth volume is in preparation.
[12] This view is well-represented by the works of three scholars: E.P. Sanders, *Jesus*

apocalyptic prophet tends to emphasize the *distance* between Jesus and the modern world.

The other model is that of Jesus as a prophet and teacher of subversive wisdom, a view that argues that apocalyptic features of the teaching of Jesus were a product of the early church (in the tradition of liberal Protestantism).[13] The view that understands Jesus primarily as a prophetic teacher of a this-worldly wisdom tends to lessen the historical distance between Jesus and the modern world. Those who have understood Jesus using this model have frequently exhibited a strong interest in the social relevance of Jesus' mission for the modern world. John Dominic Crossan, for example, presents Jesus as a revolutionary who preached social equality. Crossan regards the Jesus movement that emerged after the death of Jesus as a social movement that emerged from the subjugated peoples of the Roman Empire, immersed in poverty and misery, which sought to transform a violent and predatory empire into an egalitarian society.[14] Elisabeth Schüssler Fiorenza describes the movement in which Jesus and his companions participated as an egalitarian movement that formed an inclusive community of the downtrodden and powerless.[15]

Second, it is important to recognize the fact that the four Gospels *in their present written form* (admittedly combining history with legend and myth) have continued to exert influence on Christian belief and practice from the time of their origin and initial circulation (ca. 70–100 CE) to the present. In other words, what the historical Jesus actually said and did (to the extent that can be reconstructed using various criteria of historicity) is not as important as what his followers *thought* that he said and did. In other words, the *Wirkungsgeschichte* ("history of influence")

---

and Judaism (Philadelphia: Fortress Press, 1985); *idem, The Historical Figure of* Jesus (London: Penguin Books, 1993); Dale C. Allison, *Jesus of Nazareth: Millenarian Prophet* (Minneapolis: Fortress Press, 1998); and Bart D. Ehrman, *Jesus: Apocalyptic Prophet of the New Millennium* (Oxford and New York: Oxford University Press, 1999).

[13] This approach is represented by Marcus J. Borg, *Jesus, A New Vision: Spirit, Culture and The Life of Discipleship* (New York: HarperCollins, 1987); *idem, Meeting Jesus Again for the First Time: The Historical Jesus and the Heart of Contemporary Faith* (New York: HarperCollins, 1994); John Dominic Crossan, *The Historical Jesus: The Life of a Mediterranean Jewish Peasant* (New York: HarperCollins, 1991), *idem, Jesus: A Revolutionary Biography* (New York: HarperCollins, 1994), in many ways a summary of his 1991 book; and *idem, The Essential Jesus: Original Sayings and Earliest Images* (New York: HarperCollins, 1994).

[14] See John Dominic Crossan, *Jesus: A Revolutionary Biography* (New York: HarperCollins, 1994).

[15] Elisabeth Schüssler Fiorenza, *Jesus and the Politics of Interpretation* (London and New York: Continuum, 1997).

of the canonical Gospels has been more important and influential for the thinking of the church than the relatively recent attempts to reconstruct the historical Jesus or the "real" Jesus.

The learned liberal Protestant historian of early Christianity, Adolf von Harnack (1851–1930), proposed that the core teaching of the historical Jesus had three emphases: (1) the fatherhood of God (i.e., the father of all people), which implies (2) the brotherhood of man and (3) the worth of the individual.[16] These are all basic principles of nineteenth century religious liberalism that provided a Christian theological basis for human rights. Since it was important for Harnack that the teaching of Jesus be preserved in Christianity, the faith he founded, Harnack regarded these three core beliefs as the permanent heart of Christian faith and life from the beginning through to the modern period, even though these essentials were often lost sight of during the Middle Ages. More than a century after Harnack's book *What is Christianity?* appeared, few if any scholars concerned with reconstructing the teachings of the historical Jesus accept any of Harnack's postulates as primary emphases of the teaching of Jesus. What Harnack did, like many others before and after him, was to read his own conception of Christianity (which he considered the most enlightened conception of religion that had yet appeared in the world) back into the teaching of Jesus. Had Jesus actually held these views, it would certainly be appropriate to regard Jesus as the founder of a human rights tradition that would reach fruition in the modern period. Unfortunately, neither the historical Jesus (as reconstructed by modern scholars) nor the Jesus presented by an uncritical reading of the Gospels held the views ascribed to him by Harnack.

Let us now turn to a more sophisticated reading of the Jesus of the Gospels and yet one that takes seriously the basic thrust of the narratives. As the founder of a revitalization movement, Jesus was primarily interested in the restoration of all Israel in the end time (this program is symbolized by the fact that the twelve disciples were intentionally chosen by Jesus to represent the restoration of the Twelve Tribes Israel).[17] To that extent his proclamation of the imminent arrival of the Kingdom of God was an ethnocentric message, for Jesus did not regard either himself or his disciples as having a mission to the Gentiles. At the same time,

---

[16] Adolf von Harnack, *What is Christianity? Lectures delivered in the University of Berlin during the Winter-Term 1899–1900*, trans. T.B. Saunders, 2nd ed., rev. (New York: G.P. Putnam's Sons; London: Williams and Norgate, 1908).

[17] Sanders, *Jesus and Judaism*, 61–119.

his proclamation emphasized an eschatological social reversal, in which, for example, God accepted the poor and rejected the rich (Mark 10:23): "Then Jesus looked around and said to his disciples, 'How hard it will be for those who have wealth to enter the kingdom of God!'" This eschatological reversal had an important rhetorical function, for it signaled a subversion of the typical religious values and conceptions that characterized the Jewish religious establishment. The conception of an eschatological social reversal is central to the Beatitudes, the first of which focuses on the plight of the poor (Luke 6:20; Mt 5:3): "Blessed are you poor, for yours is the kingdom of God."

Another significant aspect of the eschatological reversal is God's rejection of Israel (doubtless because of their rejection of the message of Jesus) and acceptance of the Gentiles, a theme found in Luke 13:28–29, a passage with a strong claim to historicity:[18]

> [Those Jews addressed will be thrown out of the kingdom and] There you will weep and gnash your teeth, when you see Abraham and Isaac and Jacob and all the prophets in the kingdom of God and you yourselves thrust out. And men will come from east and west, and from north and south, and sit at table in the kingdom of God.

This kind of eschatological reversal, in which Israel, the traditional people of God, is rejected and replaced by Gentiles is found in other sayings of Jesus including the allegorical Parable of the Wicked Tenants (Mark 12:1–11 and parallels), in which the tenants (Israel) will be destroyed by the owner (God), who will turn the vineyard over to others (Gentiles).[19] While Jesus did not pursue a mission to the Gentiles, neither did he accept the ritual separation of Jews from Gentiles that was characteristic of Jewish religious practice.

Another striking characteristic of the ministry of Jesus is the fact that he rejected the "caste system" of official Judaism during the first century CE as well as the purity system on which it was based; he both accepted and associated with those whom official Judaism excluded. As Udo Schnelle has recently observed:[20]

---

[18] John P. Meier, *Mentor, Message and Miracles*, vol. 2 of *A Marginal Jew: Rethinking the Historical Jesus*, Anchor Bible Reference Library (New York: Doubleday, 1994), 309–317.

[19] Arland J. Hultgren, *The Parables of Jesus: A Commentary* (Grand Rapids: Eerdmans, 2000), 351–382.

[20] Udo Schnelle, *Theology of the New Testament*, trans. M.E. Boring (Grand Rapids: Baker Academic, 2009), 108.

Jesus draws no boundaries within Israel: he sets the marginalized in the center—the poor, the women who have suffered discrimination, children, tax collectors, prostitutes; he integrates the sick, the ritually unclean, the lepers, those possessed by demons, and even Samaritans into the holy people of God.

The following statement is particularly provocative (Mt 21:31): "Truly I tell you, the tax collectors and the prostitutes are going into the kingdom of God ahead of you." Jesus consciously dramatized God's acceptance of social outcasts by having table fellowship with them, ignoring Jewish food and ritual purity laws and thereby implicitly rejecting an unjust social structure. (Parenthetically, it should be mentioned that the Gospels contributed powerfully to Mahatma Gandhi's practice of nonviolence, which was then picked up by Martin Luther King, Jr.).[21]

The kind of company Jesus kept is reflected in Mt 11:18–19:

> For John came neither eating nor drinking, and they say, 'He has a demon'; the Son of man came eating and drinking, and they say, 'Behold, a glutton and a drunkard, a friend of tax collectors and sinners!' Yet wisdom is justified by her deeds.

Finally, a story found in Mark 2:15–17 dramatizes Jesus' counter-cultural practice:

> And as he sat at table in his house, many tax collectors and sinners were sitting with Jesus and his disciples, for there were many who followed him. And the scribes of the Pharisees, when they saw that he was eating with sinners and tax collectors, said to his disciples, 'Why does he eat with tax collectors and sinners?' And when Jesus heard it, he said to them, 'Those who are well have no need of a physician, but those who are sick; I came not to call the righteous, but sinners.'

We have already mentioned the fact that the Four Gospels agree that Jesus undertook no programmatic ministry directed toward the Gentiles as a group.[22] When universalizing features are found in the Gospels, they are typically late and legendary additions reflecting developments in the Jesus movement from the late first century CE, though only critical scholars have been aware of this fact. The absence of a Gentile mission is epitomized by the statement attributed to Jesus before sending his disciples out on a mission to the people of Israel (Mt 10:5): "Go nowhere

---

[21] Terrence J. Rynne, *Gandhi and Jesus: The Saving Power of Nonviolence* (Maryknoll: Orbis Books, 2008); Michael J. Nojeim, *Gandhi and King: The Power of Nonviolent Resistance* (Westport: Praeger, 2004).

[22] Meier, *Mentor, Message and Miracles*, vol. 2 of *A Marginal Jew*, 660.

among the Gentiles, and enter no town of the Samaritans, but rather to the lost sheep of the house of Israel." Yet at the end of Matthew, the risen Lord tells the disciples (28:19–20):

> Go therefore and make disciples of all nations, baptizing them in the name of the Father and of the Son and of the Holy Spirit, teaching them too observe all that I have commanded you; and lo, I am with you always, to the close of the age.

This passage in fact reflects the fact that following the death of Jesus, his followers did inaugurate a mission to the Gentiles, which the author of Matthew wanted to trace back to Jesus.

Rather than reaching out to Gentiles as a group, there are three stories involving Jesus' outreach out to various distressed non-Jews: the Gerasene demoniac (Mark 5:1–20), the Syrophoenician woman (Mark 7:24–30; Mt 15:21–28), the Centurion's Servant (Matt 8:5–13; Luke 7:1–10). The story of the Syrophoenician woman, while probably not authentic, contains an emphasis on universality, but does not reflect very well on him.[23] Mark 7:24–30 contains the story of the healing of the demon-possessed daughter of a Gentile. Like many others, she had heard that a famous and effective healer was in the area, so she appealed directly to Jesus (v. 26): "Now the woman was a Greek, a Syrophoenician by birth. And she begged him to cast the demon out of her daughter." This gives way to a thrust-and-parry bit of dialogue (vv. 27–30):

> And he said to her, "Let the children first be fed, for it is not right to take the children's bread and throw it to the dogs." But she answered him, "Yes, Lord; yet even the dogs under the table eat the children's crumbs." And he said to her, "For this saying you may go your way; the demon has left your daughter." And she went home, and found the child lying in bed, and the demon gone.

This story is striking for the harsh and insulting language used by Jesus, including characterizing Gentiles as "dogs" (using the so-called "criterion of embarrassment" one might argue for the authenticity of this story). The story also portrays Jesus' focus on Israel to the virtual exclusion of Gentiles, even those with pressing physical and emotional needs.

Jesus had a central concern for the equality of all Jewish people before God in his vision of the restoration of the Twelve Tribes of Israel, regardless of their social station, gender, or occupations and whether or not they maintained the requisite state of ritual purity demanded by traditional

---

[23] Ibid., 59–61.

Judaism. Though Jesus did not pursue a mission to the Gentiles, neither did he argue that Jews keep separate from Gentiles because of the danger of ritual pollution. Jesus pursued an ethnocentric mission to Israel, but in so doing he disregarded the social rules that separated Jews from one another as well as from God. While the later mission to the Gentiles, pursued by the followers of Jesus after his death, was not part of a program envisaged by Jesus, it can be argued that such a universal mission is based on the inherent logic of the message of Jesus.

III. *Pauline Conceptions of Equality and Their Influence*

The earliest surviving Christian writings are the seven genuine letters of Paul, written from ca. AD 49–58.[24] One of Paul's central emphases, particularly in Romans and Galatians, is that the traditional God of Israel is no respecter of persons and has therefore prepared a way of salvation not only for Jews, but also for Gentiles.[25] Taking a page from the ministry of Jesus, Paul ignored ethnic particularities, especially Jewish ritual regulations that made the close association of Jews with Gentiles virtually impossible. Paul understood faith in Jesus Christ to be the only requirement for salvation.

Perhaps the most radical statement of this idea is found in Paul's letter to the Galatians (3:26–28):

> For you are all sons of God through faith in Christ Jesus.
> For as many of you as were baptized into Christ have put on Christ.
> There is neither Jew nor Greek,
> There is neither slave nor free,
> There is neither male nor female;
> For you are all one in Christ Jesus.

This is a quite astonishing conception that seems to abolish, in principle, all inequities based on nationality, social status and gender.[26] Since ca. 1970, scholarly discussions of the meaning and implications of Gal 3:28 (and the close parallels mentioned below) have proliferated, in large part because of the importance of the passage for Christian feminism.[27]

---

[24] Romans, 1–2 Corinthians, Galatians, Philippians, 1 Thessalonians, Philemon.

[25] Jouette M. Bassler, *Divine Impartiality: Paul and a Theological Axiom* (Chico: Scholars Press, 1981).

[26] Elisabeth Schüssler Fiorenza, *In Memory of Her: A Feminist Theological Reconstruction of Christian Origins* (New York: Crossroad, 1983), 205–241.

[27] Rebecca Merrill Groothuis, for example, regards Gal 3:28 as probably the most

Here Paul does not use the conventional language of equality, but calls for the erasing of the distinguishing marks between people.[28]

While Gal 3:28 is the most comprehensive Pauline statement on universalism, it is not an isolated statement. 1 Cor. 12:13, for example, mentions both nationality and social status in two parallel lines formulated antithetically as in Gal 3:28:

> For it is by one Spirit we were all baptized into one body,
> Whether Jews or Greeks,
> Whether slaves or free,
> And all were made to drink of one Spirit.

The same two areas of equality are mentioned in Col 3:9–11 (a Deutero-Pauline letter written under the influence of Pauline thought):

> Do not lie to one another, seeing that you have put off the old nature with its practices and have put on the new nature [a metaphor for baptism], which is being renewed in knowledge after the image of its creator. Here there is not Greek and Jew, circumcised and uncircumcised, barbarian, Scythian, slave, free man, but Christ is all, and in all.

Here the antithesis focusing on nationality, "Greek and Jew," is replicated with another common antithesis found in Pauline rhetoric: "circumcised [Jew] and uncircumcised [i.e., Greek]," expanded with "barbarian, Scythian [found nowhere else]." "Slave, free person" are also included, as in Gal 3:28.

It is widely but not universally agreed that Gal 3:28 is a traditional baptismal formula (baptism is explicitly mentioned in v. 27), but whether or not that is so actually makes little difference in how the passage is interpreted.[29] In the parallel in 1 Cor 12:13, baptism is again explicitly

---

important biblical text supporting gender equality (*Good News for Women: A Biblical Picture of Gender Equality* [Grand Rapids: Eerdmans, 1997], 25.

[28] Pamela M. Eisenbaum, "Is Paul the Father of Misogyny and Antisemitism?" *Cross Currents* 50 (2000–2001): 506–524 (here 512).

[29] Those who think that Gal 3:28 does not entirely fit its present context typically argue that it is a liturgical tradition cited by Paul, though he is really only interested in the abolition of the distinction between Jew and Greek; e.g., J. Louis Martyn, *Galatians: A New Translation with Introduction and Commentary*, Anchor Bible 33A (New York: Doubleday, 1997), 376. On the other hand, others argue that Gal 3:28 is entirely suited to its context and that it is probably not a traditional liturgical formulation; e.g. Troy Martin, "The Covenant of Circumcision (Genesis 17:9–14) and the Situational Antithesis in Galatians 3:28," *Journal of Biblical Literature* 122 (2003): 111–125. These either/or positions are problematic. Here I follow Brigitte Kahl, "No Longer Male: Masculinity Struggles behind Galatians 3.28?" *Journal for the Study of the New Testament* 79 (2000): 38: "Pre-Pauline in origin, the baptismal formula nevertheless is genuinely Pauline in its present rhetorical embedding and literary shape."

mentioned and it is referred to obliquely through use of the baptismal "put off" / "put on" metaphor is used in Col 3:9–11.[30] Yet since ethnicity, social status, and gender were obviously not somehow eliminated in the real world for those who believed and were baptized, the question is, what did Gal 3:28 mean to Paul, regardless of whether or not it had a liturgical origin? Some understand Gal 3:28 (and parallels) as a theological rather than a social statement that refers, not to ethnicity, social status, and gender relationships *within the church between members*, but only to the fact that baptism into the body of Christ is available to all regardless of ethnicity, social status, and gender.[31] That is, according to Paul's understanding of the new covenant, salvation is available to people of all nationalities, social statuses and genders, who are all equal *coram deo* ("in the sight of God").[32] A similar position is articulated by Troy Martin:[33]

> When Gal 3:28 proclaims that in Christ there is neither Jew nor Greek, slave nor free, and that in Christ there is no male and female, the proclamation only pertains to the absence of these distinctions as requirements for baptism in contrast to the requirements in the covenant of circumcision. This verse does not proclaim the absolute abolition of these distinctions but only their irrelevance for participation in Christian baptism and full membership in the Christian community.

Yet this reading of Gal 3:28, at least in my view, does not go far enough. Paul is not only concerned with the irrelevance of nationality, social status, and gender for entry into the church through baptism, he is equally concerned to emphasize that after entry, believers continue to be "one in Christ Jesus," i.e., brothers and sisters in the new family of God. According to Elisabeth Schüssler Fiorenza, "the Christian movement was based not on racial and national inheritance and kinship lines, but on a new kinship in Jesus Christ."[34] Further, in declaring the end of ethnic, social, and gender polarities in the new creation (Gal 6:15), Paul does not contemplate the abolition of ethnic, social, and gender differences in the real world, but rather the end of all social hierarchies; in Gal 3:28, Paul rejects hierarchy but not difference as such.[35]

---

[30] Schüssler Fiorenza, *In Memory of Her*, 208.
[31] Ronald Y.K. Fung, "Ministry in the New Testament," *The Church and the Bible and the World*, ed. D.A. Carson (Grand Rapids: Baker, 1987), 183–184.
[32] Eisenbaum, "Is Paul the Father of Misogyny and Antisemitism?" 511.
[33] Martin, "The Covenant of circumcision," 122.
[34] Schüssler Fiorenza, *In Memory of Her*, 210.
[35] Kahl, "No Longer Male," 44–45.

For Paul, nationality, social status and gender continue to be of no consequence in the church. Richard W. Hove argues at length that "you are all one" does not mean "you are all equal," since he is convinced that the phrase "there is no longer male or female" is a *theological* statement that has nothing to do with the elimination of social gender roles.[36] In my view, however, the phrase has *everything* to do with gender roles. *Spiritually*, all who have been baptized are "one in Christ Jesus" and are brothers and sisters in the family of God, which is a new spiritual reality, even though *physically* they remain what they were before baptism. There is an inevitable tension between physical reality and spiritual reality that Paul has not fully worked out as we shall see as we discuss each of the antithetical phrases in Gal 3:28 (and parallels), particularly in our discussion of 1 Cor 7:21–24 and Philemon.

1. *"There is neither Jew nor Greek"*

Paul often used the ethnic terms "Jew" and "Greek" in tandem (collective singulars), with the latter term meaning "Gentiles."[37] "Jew and Greek" was used as an ethnocentric designation of everyone in the world, analogous to the equally ethnocentric Greek phrase "Hellenes and *barbaroi*," i.e., Greeks and non-Greeks. When Paul uses the phrase "neither Jew nor Greek," however, he is not simply referring to the eradication of ethnic differences generally, but rather to the abolition of Jewish ritual law as a primary means of eliminating the differences between Jew and Greek.[38] In Rom 10:12–13, Paul expresses his view about ethnic divisions in very specific terms: "For there is no distinction between Jew and Greek; the same Lord is Lord of all and bestows his riches upon all who call upon him. For, 'every one who calls upon the name of the Lord will be saved.'" When Paul uses the phrase "Jew and Greek," and particularly in the form "the Jew first and also the Greek," he is referring to Jewish chronological priority in the history of salvation.[39] The phrases "circumcised and uncircumcised" (Col 3:11) and "circumcision and uncircumcision" (always in that order) are examples of synecdoche parallel to "Jew and Greek" that

---

[36] Richard W. Hove, *Equality in Christ? Galatians 3:28 and the Gender Dispute* (Wheaton: Crossway Books, 1999), 107–116.

[37] Rom 1:16; 2:9, 10; 3:9; 10:12; 1 Cor 1:22–24; 10:32; 12:13; Gal 3:28; cf. Col 3:11.

[38] Eisenbaum, "Is Paul the Father of Misogyny and Antisemitism?" 514.

[39] Ibid.

occur several times in the genuine Pauline letters.[40] A close parallel to Rom 10:12–13, cited above, is found in Gal 6:15: "For neither circumcision counts for anything, nor uncircumcision, but a new creation." In the OT and early Judaism, circumcision was occasionally given a religious interpretation, i.e., "circumcision of the heart,"[41] a view picked up by Paul and later Christian authors (Rom 2:28–29) or baptism referred to as a "circumcision made without hands" (Col 2:11–12).[42]

In Gal 3:28, then, when Paul says that there is neither Jew nor Greek, does he refer only to the fact that the initiatory rite of baptism is open to those of all ethnic groups, or does he mean, in addition, that equality among ethnic groups continues to characterize the behavior of all of those who are "one in Christ Jesus"? A clear answer to this question can be found earlier in Galatians, where Paul recounts his confrontation with Peter (Gal 2:11–14). Paul tells us that Peter, along with other Jewish followers of Jesus, ate with Gentiles in Antioch. When a group of the "circumcision party" (meaning Jewish followers of Jesus who require circumcision, a sign of ethnic identity, signaling conversion to Judaism, and of all Gentile converts to the Jesus movement) arrived from Jerusalem, sent by James the Just, Peter along with Barnabas and other Jewish believers, separated themselves from Gentiles believers in conformity with the requirements of Jewish ritual requirements. Paul, at least according to his own autobiographical account, opposed Peter for living like a Gentile, yet trying to compel the Gentiles to live like Jews. What this brief narrative reveals is that for Paul, the principle of "there is no Jew or Gentle" not only applies those who enter the church through baptism, but also ought to be the attitude of those Jews and Gentiles who are members of the community of faith. Paul expresses this conviction differently in 1 Cor 10:17: "Because there is one loaf, we who are many are one body, for we all partake of the one loaf." The traditional Jewish attitude toward eating with Gentiles is expressed in part of a blessing given by Abraham to Jacob (*Jubilees* 22:16):[43]

---

[40] Circumcised and uncircumcised: Rom 3:30; 4:9; 1 Cor 7:18; circumcision and uncircumcision: Rom 2:25, 26; 1 Cor 7:19; Gal 5:6; 6:15; cf. Eph 2:11.

[41] Dt 10:16; 30:6; Jer 4:4; 9:26; Ez 44:7, 9; 1QpHab 11.13; cf. 1QS 5.5.

[42] *Barnabas* 6:4–5; Justin *Dialog.* 14:4.

[43] Orville Wintermute, "Jubilees," *The Old Testament Pseudepigrapha*, ed. James H. Charlesworth, 2 vols. (Garden City, New York: Doubleday and Company, 1985), 2.98.

And you also, my son, Jacob, remember my words,
and keep the commandments of Abraham your father.
Separate yourself from the gentiles,
and do not eat with them,[44]
and do not perform deeds like theirs,
And do not become associates of theirs.
Because their deeds are defiled,
And all of their ways are contaminated, and despicable, and abominable.

The expansion of the Jesus movement from a sect within Judaism to a social-religious movement composed of both Jews and Gentiles was the cause of lasting conflict between these two ethno-linguistic entities. The central issue was the role played by Jewish ritual law (circumcision, food regulations, purity laws, Sabbath observance), i.e., symbolic markers of Jewish national identity. The Pauline affirmation that "there is neither Jew nor Greek" (Gal 3:28) and the parallel expression "where there is no Greek and Jew, circumcised and uncircumcised" (Col 3:11) is a concept of national or ethnic parity with which not all first century Jewish followers of Jesus would have agreed. By the end of the first century the Jewish Christian groups in the eastern Mediterranean that insisted on combining ritually observant Judaism with belief in Jesus as the Messiah had effectively marginalized themselves and are now remembered only as isolated heretical sects that soon disappeared from the pages of history.[45] Also by the end of the first century, Christianity had spread throughout the Mediterranean world as an unparalleled socio-religious movement that accepted people from all ethnic groups, the rich and the poor, men and women, slaves and free.

The issue of whether or not Gentile followers of Jesus should be circumcised was the centrally divisive issue, with "circumcision" understood as an abbreviation for conversion to Judaism. The Book of Acts narrates the growing tension between observant Jews who were followers of Jesus and an increasing number of Gentile converts (Acts 15:3). At least initially, these Gentile converts were probably largely drawn from those whom the author of Acts designates "God-fearers," i.e., non-Jews

---

[44] The supposition here is that food prepared by Gentiles is not prepared in accordance with Jewish purity laws.

[45] Hans-Joachim Schoeps, *Jewish Christianity: Factional Disputes in the Early Church*, trans. Douglas R.A. Hare (Philadelphia: Fortress Press, 1969); Simon Claude Mimouni, *Le Judéo-Christianisme Ancien: Essais Historiques* (Paris: Éditions du Cerf, 1998); Oskar Skarsaune and Reidar Hvalvik (eds.), *Jewish Believers in Jesus: The Early Centuries* (Peabody: Hendrickson Publishers, 2007); Matt Jackson-McCabe (ed.), *Jewish Christianity Reconsidered: Rethinking Ancient Groups and Texts* (Minneapolis: Fortress Press, 2007).

who were attracted to the ethical monotheism of Judaism and who participated in local synagogue services, but who did not observe the ritual regulations based on the Torah with any consistency, nor did they submit to circumcision (Acts 11:19–21; 15:1).[46]

A major emphasis of the Book of Acts is the conflict between Jewish and Gentile followers of Jesus and the apparent compromise reached by the two groups in the Apostolic Council of Acts 15 (Acts 15:6–29), a passage described by C.K. Barrett as "the centre of Acts."[47] In Acts 15:1–6, the author of Acts provides an introduction to the narrative of the council and the decision reached with v. 1 framing the issue in this way:

> Then certain individuals came down from Judea and were teaching the brothers, "Unless you are circumcised according to the custom of Moses, you cannot be saved."

Here salvation is explicitly made dependent on circumcision, i.e., conversion to Judaism. This issue is repeated with variations in Acts 15:5:

> But some of the believers who belonged to the sect of the Pharisees stood up and said, "It is necessary for them [i.e., Gentiles who had been converted to the Jesus movement] to be circumcised and ordered to keep the law of Moses."

These converted Pharisees required Gentile followers of Jesus to be circumcised, i.e., to become converted to Judaism, with the result that they are then obligated to observe the ritual requirements of Judaism (i.e., Sabbath observance and *kashrut*, or purity regulations).

At this Apostolic Council, an apparent compromise was reached between the two groups, represented by "the apostles and elders" led by James the Just on the one hand, and on the other, Paul and Barnabas, the Jewish leaders of the Gentile mission. The resultant "Apostolic Decree" formulated by the apostles and elders was based on the assumption that Jewish followers of Jesus would continue to observe the Mosaic Law, while Gentile believers were only obligated to observe certain rules, i.e., commands given to Noah by God that applied to all humankind, negatively formulated as four ritual requirements (Acts 15:29; 21:25): the prohibition of eating the meat of animals that had been sacrificed to idols, blood (i.e., eating animals that had not been ritually slaughtered),

---

[46] A bibliography on "God-fearers" to 1997 may be found in Joseph A. Fitzmyer, S.J., *The Acts of the Apostles: A New Translation and Commentary*, Anchor Bible, 18C (New York: Doubleday, 1998), 450.

[47] C.K. Barrett, *The Acts of the Apostles in Two Volumes*, International Critical Commentary (London: T & T Clark, 1998), 2.709.

strangled animals (i.e., those ensnared and killed), and fornication.[48] These rules are patterned after the Mosaic requirements for Gentiles living among Jews found in Lv 17–18 as well as in the Jewish Christian version of the Noachide minimum obligation of the law.[49]

David Catchpole has argued that there are three theological presuppositions behind the Apostolic Decree: (1) Christian theology is fundamentally Mosaic, (2) the theology reflected in the Decree does nothing about the distinction between Jew and Gentile, and (3) since Lev 17–18 is concerned with the cleanness of the land, the cleanness / uncleanness distinction still remains in effect and in proscribing what Jewish followers of Jesus required of Gentile followers of Jesus, the Decree demands what non-believing Jews already required of Gentiles.[50] Paul would have disagreed vehemently with all of these theological presuppositions, which suggests that historically he could not have been a participant in the Jerusalem council. Paul absence from the Council is hinted at by the awkward insertion of Acts 21:25 (where Paul is informed about the substance of the Apostolic Decree by James as if he were ignorant of it), and to that extent the narrative of Acts 15 is inaccurate.[51] The Decree, then, cannot be traced back to the apostolic conference referred to in Gal 2:1–10, but must have been promulgated later. Further, the absence of any mention of the possible circumcision of Gentiles in Acts 15:6–29, though specifically presented at the central issue needing resolution in Acts 15:1–5 (partly quoted above), assumes that this critical issue has already been dealt with, though nothing about this has been mentioned earlier in Acts.

2. *"There is neither slave nor free"*

Paul's declaration in various versions that "there is neither slave nor free" (Gal 3:28; 1 Cor 12:13; cf. Col 3:11) is expressed more forcefully than related sentiments current during the second half of the fourth century BCE. Aristotle, after reviewing various contemporary views of the master / slave relationship, mentions one view, probably that of the

---

[48] Hans-Joachim Schoeps, *Paul: The Theology of the Apostle in the Light of Jewish Religious History* (Philadelphia: Westminster Press, 1959), 66–67.

[49] The Noachide laws represent a legendary development of the demands stipulated by God in the covenant with Noah briefly mentioned in Genesis 9.

[50] David Catchpole, "Paul, James and the Apostolic Decree," *New Testament Studies* 23 (1977): 429–430.

[51] Ibid., 431.

Sophists, who used natural law to oppose custom, i.e., the *physis / nomos*
antithesis (Aristotle *Politics* 1253b [1.2.3]; LCL trans.):[52]

> Others, however, maintain that for one man to be another man's master is
> contrary to nature [παρὰ φύσιν], because it is only convention [νόμῳ] that
> makes the one a slave and the other a freemen and there is no difference
> between them by nature, and that therefore it is unjust, for it is based on
> force.

Aristotle himself maintains that slavery is "natural" (he repeatedly speaks
of a person who is φύσει δοῦλος, "a slave by nature") rather than conventional and that slavery was both just and good for both the slave and the
master (*Politics* 1252a–1255b [1.1.1–2.23]).[53] According to the Roman
law of persons, which is primarily concerned with legal status rather than
theoretical arguments, "all men are either free or slaves,"[54] so that under
Roman jurisdiction, slavery and freedom are legal statuses.

Paul discusses slavery at greater length in 1 Cor 7:21–24 and Philemon
and the relation of slaves to masters is mentioned in several of the
Deutero-Pauline household codes (Col 3:22–24; 4:1; Eph 6:5–9; 1 Tm
6:1–2; Titus 2:9–10). In 1 Cor 7:21–24 (in the same chapter, marriage as
well as circumcision and uncircumcision are discussed), Paul argues that
members of the church should remain in the same social station they had
when they became part of the people of God (italics added):

> Were you a slave when called? Never mind. But if you can gain your
> freedom, avail yourself of the opportunity. *For he who was called in the Lord
> as a slave is a freedman of the Lord. Likewise he who was free when called
> is a slave of Christ.* You were bought with a price; do not become slaves of
> men. So, brethren, in whatever state each was called, there let him remain
> with God.

Here the phrase "he who was called in the Lord as a slave is a freedman
in the Lord" is clearly an example of freedom *coram Christo*; external circumstances are relatively unimportant compared with the new spiritual
reality of being in Christ.[55] As De Ste. Croix observes: "the equality exists

---

[52] Slavery was theoretically defended by some Greeks on the basis that non-Greeks
(barbarians) were naturally inferior. For a brief treatment of the critique of slavery during
the fourth century BCE in the Greek world, see W.K.C. Guthrie, *The Sophists* (Cambridge:
Cambridge University Press, 1971), 155–160.

[53] On the Greek theory of "natural slavery," see G.E.M. de Ste. Croix, *The Class Struggle
in the Ancient Greek World from the Archaic Age to the Arab Conquest* (Ithaca: Cornell
University Press, 1981), 416–418.

[54] Gaius *Institutes* 1.9; Justinian *Institutes* 1.3 (identical statements): "omnes homini
aut liberi sunt aut servi."

[55] De Ste. Croix, *Class Struggle*, 419.

'in the sight of God' and has no relation whatever to temporal affairs."[56] In antiquity there was a widespread view, expressed by Epicureans, Stoics, and Christians, that slavery (like poverty and war, wealth and peace) is a matter of indifference affecting externals only (Lucretius *De rerum natura* 1.455–458). The good and wise man is never really a slave even though he may actually be one; it is the bad man who is really a slave, since he lives in bondage to his own desires.[57] This ancient paradoxical commonplace is applied by Paul to followers of Jesus: those who are free are really slaves of Christ, while those who are slaves are really free in the Lord.

In 1 Corinthians 7, Paul also discusses the social situations of the married and the single (vv. 1–16, 25–28, 32–40) and the circumcised and uncircumcised (vv. 17–20), covering all three of the antitheses in Gal 3:28. Paul's advice on all three issues is based on his expectation of the imminent end of the world, discussed in an explanatory digression in 1 Cor 7:29–31 (italics added), which applies directly to marriage and indirectly to slavery and circumcision:

> I mean, brethren, *the appointed time has grown very short*; from now only, let those who have wives live as though they had none, and those who mourn as though they were not mourning, and those who rejoice as though they were not rejoicing, and those who buy as though they had no goods, and those who deal with the world as though they had no dealings with it. *For the form of this world is passing away.*

Therefore, Paul expects slaves as well as the married and single, the circumcised and the uncircumcised to consider their present situation in life within an *eschatological framework*, i.e., time is short and the form of this world is passing away. Slavery, like marriage or celibacy, circumcision or uncircumcision, belongs to "the present scheme of things that is

---

[56] Ibid.

[57] See A.J. Malherbe, *The Cynic Epistles: A Study Edition* (Missoula, Mont.: Scholars Press, 1977), 87, for Bion in Stobaeus, *Anthologium* 3.187.5: "Slaves who are morally good are free; masters who are morally evil are slaves of their desires." Cf. Epictetus *Dissertationes* 1.19.8–9. Ps.-Crates *Ep.* 34: "And he [Diogenes] said that he was skilled at ruling men. 'So if any of you needs a master, let him come forward and strike a bargain with the sellers.' But they laughed at him and said, 'And who is there who, since he is free, needs a master?' 'All,' he said, 'who are base and who honor pleasure and despise toil, the greatest incitements to evils.'" A later formulation of this principle is found in Augustine, *City of God*, trans. William M. Green, LCL 412 (Cambridge, Mass.: Harvard University Press, 1963) 4.3: "Hence even if a good man be a slave, he is free; whereas is a wicked man rule, he is a slave—and a slave not to one man but, what is worse, to as many masters as he has vices."

already on its way out."[58] This eschatological motivation for not attempting to change one's status overlays the primary reason Paul gives for slaves
remaining slaves, i.e., the one sold as slave is master and free, while the
masters are really slaves.

Though there are several ways of reconstructing the situation behind
Paul's Letter to Philemon, the basic facts are that Onesimus is a slave
owned by Philemon (or Archippus), but who has for some unstated
reason left or been sent from home in Colossae and has made contact
with Paul who is in prison (perhaps in Ephesus) and was apparently
converted by him. While Onesimus has traditionally been regarded as
a runaway slave, there is actually little support in this short letter for
such a reading, though that view still finds widespread support.[59] More
probably, Onesimus had somehow wronged or injured Philemon (v. 18).
Onesimus, who knew about Philemon's relationship with Paul, had come
to Paul in prison, hoping that he would act as an *amicus domini* ("friend
of the master") by interceding for him with Philemon to heal whatever
breach had arisen between master and slave.[60] Onesimus had clearly
become one of Paul's valued coworkers, as v. 12 indicates:

> I am sending him back to you, sending my very heart. I would have been
> glad to keep him with me, in order that he might serve me on your behalf
> during my imprisonment for the gospel.

Paul's Letter to Philemon provides a tantalizing snapshot of a master-
slave relationship within the early church that has important implications
for understanding the meaning of the baptismal formula in Gal 3:28.
Though the entire letter revolves about the issue of slavery, the term
"slave" occurs just twice, both instances in v. 16. In vv. 15–16, Paul tells
Philemon (italics added):

> Perhaps this is why he was parted from you for a while, that you might have
> him back for ever, *no longer as a slave but more than a slave, as a beloved
> brother*, especially to me but how much more to you, both in the flesh and
> in the Lord.

---

[58] Gordon Fee, *The First Epistle to the Corinthians*, The New International Commentary on the New Testament (Grand Rapids, Mich.: Eerdmans, 1987), 342.

[59] There is still widespread support for this reading: cf. J.G. Nordling, "*Onesimus
Fugitivus*: A Defense of the Runaway Slave Hypothesis in Philemon," *Journal for the Study
of the New Testament* 41 (1991): 97–119.

[60] John R. Levison, "Paul's Letter to Philemon," *The Blackwell Companion to the
New Testament*, ed. David E. Aune (Oxford: Wiley-Blackwell, 2010), 526–531; Joseph
A. Fitzmyer, *The Letter to Philemon*, Anchor Bible 34C (New York: Doubleday, 2000),
17–18, 20–23.

The italicized portion indicates that though Paul is sending Onesimus back to Philemon "as a slave," since he has been converted to the faith after departing from his owner, he is now at the same time also a "beloved brother," i.e., using the language of Gal 3:28, they are now "one in Christ Jesus."[61] While this passage has been construed in a variety of ways,[62] this reading coheres well with Paul's intentions in Gal 3:28. For Philemon to have regarded Onesimus as both a slave "in the flesh" (i.e., physically) and yet as also a beloved brother "in the Lord" (i.e., spiritually)—the latter phrase understood as an equivalent to "in Christ Jesus" in Gal 3:28—would inevitably have involved a degree of tension and conflict between the two roles, a tension that Paul neither acknowledges nor explores.[63]

Regarding a slave as a brother has a precedent in the Old Testament (Lv 25:39–46; Dt 15:12–18; Jer 34:8–17); all these passages, however, express the incongruity of Israelites owning fellow Israelites as slaves and the notion of "brotherhood" is ethnic.[64] In Greek thought on slavery, there was similarly a widespread discomfort with enslaving fellow Greeks, which was similarly an ethnic sentiment.[65] In both cultures, most slaves were gotten through war or raids on non-Israelites and non-Greeks, implicitly connecting slavery with assumptions of racial inferiority.[66] In contrast to traditional Greek thought, there were Roman Stoics who regarded slaves as brothers. According to Epictetus (*Dissertationes* 1.13.3–4), for example, all people are family, brothers and sisters by nature [ἀδελφῶν φύσει] and offspring of Zeus.[67] Philo also attributes the Stoic conception of universal brotherhood to the Essenes, whom he presents as a utopian community (*Quod omnis probus liber sit* 79):[68]

---

[61] Fitzmyer, *Philemon*, 114.

[62] Various ways of construing the passage are reviewed by John M.G. Barclay, "Paul, Philemon and the Dilemma of Christian Slave-Ownership," *New Testament Studies* 37 (1991): 170–175.

[63] The tensions between the two roles are explored by Barclay, "Paul, Philemon and the Dilemma of Christian Slave-Ownership," 177–182.

[64] Philo discusses Deut 15:12–18 in *De specialibus legibus* 2.18.79–85, where among other things he construes the word "slaves" to really mean "laborers."

[65] Guthrie, *The Sophists*, 156. Note the widespread view placed in the mouth of Iphigeneia addressing her mother, Clytemnestra, in Euripides, *Iphigenia Aulidensis* 1400: "It is right for Greeks to rule over barbarians, but not barbarians over Greeks, mother, for they are slaves, but we are free."

[66] Moses I. Finley, *Ancient Slavery and Modern Ideology* (New York: The Viking Press, 1980), 119.

[67] See also the letter of Seneca on master/slave relations: *Epistulae morales* 40.1, 10.

[68] Translated with modifications; see Philo, *Questions and Answers on Exodus*, trans.

No single slave is to be found among them, but all are free, exchanging services with each other, and they denounce the owners of slaves, not merely for their injustice in outraging the law of equality [ἰσότητα], but also for their impiety in annulling the law of nature [θεσμὸν φύσεως], who like a mother has born and reared all men alike, and created them genuine brothers [ἀδελφοὺς γνησίους], not in mere name, but in very reality [ὄντως] ....

The suggestion has been made that in his Letter to Philemon, Paul is hinting, very obliquely, that Philemon manumit Onesimus.[69] Modern Christian readers often express disappointment that Paul does not forthrightly condemn slavery, advocate manumission or propose a social program for abolishing slavery.[70] On the other hand, Paul does not justify slavery or suggest that it is an institution ordained by God or sanctioned by nature.[71] In the ancient world, slavery was concentrated primarily in Roman Italy, mainland Greece, and Greek settlements overseas; in these areas the idea of life without slavery would have been unthinkable. While a few fragments of debates on the subject among Greek thinkers have survived, no one, pagan or Christian, advocated the abolition of slavery.[72] Both the Roman Stoics and Church Fathers argued for the human treatment of slaves, but at the same time "preached obedience to the slaves."[73]

In view of the fact that both Philemon and Onesimus, master and slave, are "one in Christ Jesus" (to use the phrase from Gal 3:28), the institution of slavery is transcended by the special relationship that Philemon and Onesimus share as "beloved brothers." As in the case of 1 Cor 7:21–24, members of the church who happen to be slaves are free "in Christ." From an exterior perspective, some who are members of the church are slaves and masters. However, as Troels Engberg-Pedersen has argued:[74]

Ralph Marcus, Loeb Classical Library 401 (Cambridge, Mass.: Harvard University Press, 1953).

[69] Aristotle, *Politics 1330a* [7.9], maintained that all slaves should be offered the ultimate goal of emancipation.

[70] A strikingly large number of slaves were freed in Roman Italy, where slaves constituted nearly half the population; see Keith Hopkins, *Conquerors and Slaves* (Cambridge: Cambridge University Press, 1978), 115–118.

[71] Wolfgang Schrage, *The Ethics of the New Testament*, trans. David E. Green (Philadelphia: Fortress Press, 1988), 233.

[72] Finley, *Ancient Slavery*, 120.

[73] Finley, *Ancient Slavery*, 121.

[74] Troels Engberg-Pedersen, *Paul and the Stoics* (Edinburgh: T. & T. Clark, 2000), 150.

[Jews and Greeks, slave and free, male and female] ... will no longer let these properties play any normative role whatever in their own self-definition. Instead, they will see themselves as all one—in Christ Jesus. That is, for their normative self-identification they will focus on no other self-defining characteristic than the one which they all equally share, that of being 'in Christ Jesus'.

According to Engberg-Pedersen,[75] Paul's construction of the self is not individualistic in any modern sense, but rather a communitarian one so that being "in Christ" is not only some kind of spiritual reality, but is also how one sees oneself as identical with Christ.

Apart from 1 Corinthians 7 and Paul's Letter to Philemon, there are brief mentions of the respective duties of slaves to masters and master to slaves in the Deutero-Pauline household codes (Col 3:22–24; 4:1; Eph 6:5–9; 1 Tm 6:1–2; Titus 2:9–10), primarily emphasizing the duties of slaves, but is also concerned to prevent the mistreatment of slaves. Yet these texts are arguably not written by Paul himself and deal primarily with the coexistence of slave and free in the church. Later Christian texts on the subject of slavery are relatively disappointing. One relatively early example is Ignatius of Antioch (died ca. 115 CE) who recommends to Polycarp that he not free male or female slaves at the expense of the church (*Polyc.* 4.3). Yet, on the positive side, this text suggests that the manumission of slaves owned by members of the church was not an unusual practice.

3. "There is neither male nor female"

The phrase "there is neither male nor female" in Gal 3:28 (missing from 1 Cor 12:13 and Col 3:9–11), has attracted a great deal of interpretive interest since the rise of feminism and its influence on Biblical interpretation. Elisabeth Schüssler Fiorenza has referred to it aptly as "a focal point of feminist debate."[76] Feminist criticism is used by New Testament scholars in the modern church as a reading strategy that focuses on, among other things, the roles of women, their lives, and voices as well as the ideological views of sexuality in the New Testament, early church and the ancient world in the interest of contributing to the liberation of women in the church as well as in society.[77] While the ancient

---

[75] Ibid., 6–8, 149–151.

[76] Elisabeth Schüssler Fiorenza, *Rhetoric and Ethic: The Politics of Biblical Studies* (Minneapolis: Fortress, 1999), 159; see also the discussion of Gal 3:28 on 159–173.

[77] For a recent discussion of feminist criticism used in the study of the New Testa-

Mediterranean world was a male-dominated hierarchical society,[78] there
is evidence that during the first century some members of the Jesus movement took counter-cultural stances on the public roles of women in the
church. This was facilitated in part by the sectarian nature of the new
movement, which needed to establish its own identity, norms, and values
over against those of pagan culture and society generally. The ideological
stance of Paul's statement "there is neither male nor female," unlike the
companion antithesis of "neither Jew nor Greek" and "neither slave nor
free," has few parallels in the rest of Paul's letters, though 1 Cor 11:11–12 is
an exception, for it is a parenthetical remark in which Paul relativizes the
relationship between men and women, an insight expressed more fully
in Gal 3:28:[79]

> Nevertheless, in the Lord woman is not independent of man nor man of
> woman; for as woman was made from man, so man is now born of woman.
> And all things are of God.

It is important to observe that in this passage the hierarchical relationship
between men and women is relativized only *in the Lord*, a parallel to the
concluding phrase *all things are of God*. It is not only that men and women
are equal *coram deo*, but that the preceding injunction in 1 Cor 11:9–10,
should not be read in a subordinationist way.[80]

If we examine what can be known about the *realia* of gender roles
in the early church, it becomes immediately obvious that there was
ambivalence over the issue. There is fragmentary evidence that women
held significant leadership positions in the churches, including the roles
of apostle (see below on Junia in Rom 16:7), deacon (see below on Phoebe
in Rom 16:1–2),[81] leaders of house churches (Mary the mother of John

---

ment, see Amy-Jill Levine, "Feminist Criticism," in *The Blackwell Companion to the New Testament* (Oxford: Wiley-Blackwell, 2010), 156–165.

[78] Dale B. Martin, *The Corinthian Body* (New Haven and London: Yale University Press, 1995), 3–135.

[79] Krister Stendahl, *The Bible and the Role of Women* (Philadelphia: Fortress, 1966), 35.

[80] Fee, *Corinthians*, 522–524.

[81] See A.N. Sherwin-White, *The Letters of Pliny: A Historical and Social Commentary* (Oxford: Clarendon Press, 1966), 708. In a letter written by Pliny the Younger, the Roman governor of Bithynia at the beginning of the second century, to the emperor Trajan, we learn that two women slaves (*ancillis*) were "deacons" (*ministrae*) in the church of Bithynia (Pliny *Ep.* 10.96.8), indicating that in this region and time, being a slave and being a woman were not obstacles to enjoying status in the Christian communities (Schüssler Fiorenza, *In Memory of Her*, 209).

Mark in Acts 12:12; Lydia in Acts 16:14–15, 40; Nympha in Col 4:15) as well teachers and prophets (1 Cor 11:4–16).[82] Yet there is also evidence to indicated that there were frequent attempts to emphasize or reinstate traditional gender values by silencing women in public (1 Cor 14:33–35)[83] and by exhorting them to play a more conventional subordinate role in the family (Eph 5:22–6:4; Col 3:18–4:1; 1 Tm 2:11–15; Titus 2:1–10). However, since Ephesians, Colossians and the Pastoral Letters (1–2 Timothy and Titus) are widely regarded as Deutero-Pauline,[84] the subordinate role for women recommended by the unknown authors of these letters probably reflects post-Pauline developments during the late first and early second century. For whatever reason, the role of women in the church became increasing assimilated toward the hierarchical gender conception of the broader Greco-Roman world during the early second century.

Let us look for a moment at two interesting important texts on the roles of women in the early church found in Romans 16. First, in Rom 16:1–2, Paul mentions Phoebe the deaconess (NRSV):

> I commend to you our sister Phoebe, a deacon [διάκονον] of the church at Cenchreae [the seaport of Corinth], so that you may welcome her in the Lord as is fitting for the saints, and help her in whatever she may require from you, for she has been a benefactor [προστάτις] of many and of myself as well.

As with several other New Testament texts relating to women in ministry, the plain meaning of this passage has frequently been subverted,[85] most easily by translating *diakonos* as "servant."[86] But although many earlier commentaries have tried to downplay Phoebe's role in the church in

---

[82] S. Heine, "Diakoninnen—Frauen und Ämter in den ersten christlichen Jahrhunderten," *Internationale Kirchliche Zeitschrift* 78 (1988): 213–227.

[83] This passage is widely, and I think correctly, understood as a reactionary interpolation into 1 Corinthians; a view held even by a conservative Evangelical scholar; see Fee, *Corinthians*, 699–708.

[84] For recent treatments of the pseudepigraphal character of these Pauline letters see Jörg Frey, Jens Herzer, Martina Janssen and Clare K. Rithschild, eds., *Pseudepigraphie und Verfasserfiktion in frühchristlichen Briefen*, WUNT, 236 (Tübingen: Mohr Siebeck, 2009), which contains essays on all the Pauline letters considered by critical scholars to be pseudepigraphal.

[85] According to K. Romaniuk, "Was Phoebe in Rom 16,1 a Deaconess?" *Zeitschrift für die Neutestamentliche Wissenschaft* 81 (1990): 132–134, Paul courteously exaggerates the position of Phoebe in the community by likening her role to that of an official deacon.

[86] For arguments against translating *diakonos* as "servant," see J.D.G. Dunn, *Romans 9–16*, Word Biblical Commentary 38b (Dallas: Word Books, 1988), 886–887.

Cenchraea, "it now seems more likely that she functioned as the leader of the congregation."[87] In addition, her role of "benefactor" or "patron" (commentators frequently fail to give *prostates* its most natural and obvious sense of "patron"), suggests that she was a woman of wealth and a person of prominence in the ancient world,[88] one who personally sponsored projects of vital significance to Paul.[89]

In Rom 16:7, two people are mentioned that Paul considers "prominent among the apostles." One of them is Andronicus (a masculine name) and, for the name of the other, there are two different readings in the Greek manuscripts, one of which is Junia (a feminine name) or Junias (a masculine name). In a recent monograph by New Testament textual critic Eldon Jay Epp, the author argues convincingly that the name originally written by Paul was "Junia."[90] He makes the following points: (1) While "Junia" was a common name that occurs hundreds of times in ancient sources, the masculine form "Junias" (possibly an abbreviation of "Junianus") is not attested in any Greco-Roman sources. (2) Contextually, several women are commended warmly by Paul in Romans 16, including Prisca. (3) The name "Junia" was the unanimous choice of interpreters during the first 1300 years in the history of interpretation of Rom 16:7 (often as the wife of Andronicus). (4) The name "Junia" was chosen as the correct reading in all editions of the Greek New Testament until the early 20th century, though from 1927 through 1998, critical editions of the Greek New Testament by Nestle, Nestle-Aland and the United Bible Society chose the masculine form "Junias." English translations of the New Testament produced during the 19th and 20th centuries, on the other hand, favored the masculine form "Junias." The choice of the masculine name in these instances appears to be the result of prejudice rather than reason.

---

[87] Robert Jewett, *Romans: A Commentary*, Hermeneia (Minneapolis: Fortress, 2007), 944; see the analysis of διάκονος (a word of common gender) by Bengt Holmberg, *Paul and Power: The Structure of Authority in the Primitive Church as Reflected in the Pauline Epistles* (Philadelphia: Fortress, 1978), 99–100, especially n. 30.

[88] Joseph A. Fitzmyer, S.J., *Romans: A New Translation and Commentary*, Anchor Bible 33 (New York: Doubleday, 1993), 731. For a more detailed discussion of the social and cultural significance of a *prostates*, see R.A. Kearsley, "Women in public life in the Roman east: Iunia Theodora, Claudia Metrodora and Phoebe, benefactress of Paul," *Tyndale Bulletin* 50 (1999): 189–211.

[89] Jewett, *Romans*, 945–948.

[90] Eldon Jay Epp, *Junia: The First Woman Apostle* (Minneapolis: Fortress, 2005). See also the comments of Schüssler Fiorenza, *In Memory of Her*, 47–48, 172.

While Paul's declaration that "there is neither male nor female" (Gal 3:28), an allusion both to Gen 1:27,[91] has no parallel in the other two New Testament passages that are variant forms of the baptismal formula in Gal 3:28 (1 Cor 12:13 and Col 3:11), a "no male nor female" antithesis is found in an interesting text that represents a conflation of Gal 3:28, 1 Cor 12:13 and Col 3:9–11 in the relatively late Valentinian *Tripartite Tractate* (I, 5) 132.23–28 (composed ca. early third to the mid-fourth century CE):[92]

> For the end will receive a unitary existence just as the beginning is unitary, where there is no male nor female, nor slave and free, nor circumcision and uncircumcision, neither angel nor man, but Christ is all in all.

In this eschatological vision, the human divisions reflected in gender, legal, and social status and nationality will be transcended when the original unitary mode of existence is restored at the end. In this construal of the tradition found in Gal 3:28, no contemporary social application of "there is no male nor female" in terms of gender equality is contemplated; the restoration of primal unity is understood as entirely an eschatological occurrence. While Gal 3:28 has also been interpreted eschatologically by modern scholars, that does not seem to reflect the original intention of Paul.[93]

One striking text dealing with the male / female dichotomy is found in the early second century in a text that concludes the *Gospel of Thomas*, logion 114:

> Simon Peter said to them, "Let Mary leave us, for women are not worthy of Life!" Jesus said, "I myself shall lead her in order to make her male so that she may become a living spirit resembling you males. For every woman who will make herself male will enter the Kingdom of Heaven."

---

[91] Mary Rose D'Angelo, "Gender Refusers in the Early Christian Mission; Gal 2:28 as an Interpretation of Gen 1:27b," *Reading in Christian Communities*," ed. Charles A. Bobertz and David Brakke (Notre Dame: University of Notre Dame Press, 2002), 149–173. D'Angelo (161) adds that the phrase "male and female" is also found in Gen 5:1–5 (perhaps an alternate version or restatement of Gen 1:27); 6:19–20; 7:2–3, 15–16.

[92] Harold W. Attridge and Elaine H. Pagels, "The Tripartite Tractate (I, 5)," *The Nag Hammadi Library in English*, ed. James M. Robinson, 3rd ed. (San Francisco: Harper & Row, 1988), 58, 101. A brief commentary on this passage is found in Harold W. Attridge and Elaine H. Pagels, "The Tripartite Tractate (I, 5)," *Nag Hammadi Codex I (The Jung Codex): Notes*, ed. Harold W. Attridge, Nag Hammadi Studies 23 (Leiden: E.J. Brill, 1985), 487.

[93] Martin, "The Covenant of Circumcision," 123–124.

This strange dialogue, which shows no signs of having been influenced by the Pauline letters, occurs in the same text in which Salome calls herself to discipleship (*Gos. Thom.* 61). Despite the clearly misogynistic opening remark of Simon Peter, demanding the exclusion of Mary (probably Mary Magdalene) from the circle of disciples, (which should probably be interpreted as an attack on the leadership roles of women in the early church), the emphasis is on the defense that Jesus provides against the exclusion of women.[94] Yet the price is high. Salvation is dependent on females (by definition excluded from salvation) being transformed into males. *Gospel of Thomas* 114, then, reflects a "backward" creation, reversing the creation of a living spirit from the dust by God (Gen 2:7), after which the rib of the male Adam was transformed into the first woman.[95] Scholars have tended to read this text as a reference to the restoration of primal androgeny.[96] According to Elaine Pagels, this saying assumes "that men form the legitimate body of the community, while women are allowed to participate only when they assimilate themselves to men."[97] Yet it is likely that the conception of "maleness" here reflects a widespread symbolic understanding in which it is actually detached from sexuality. A parallel text from the Jewish interpreter Philo of Alexandria is found in *Quaestiones in Exodum* 1.8, where he tries to explain why a male sheep is chosen for sacrifice in Ex 12:5b:

> For progress is indeed nothing else than the giving up of the female gender by changing into the male, since the female gender is material, passive, corporeal and sense-perceptible, while the male is active, rational, incorporeal and more akin to mind and thought.

Of course, this symbolic understanding of maleness and femaleness is only possible because of the hierarchical and subordinationist view sanctioned by the social and cultural mores of the Greco-Roman world (e.g. Aristotle *Politics* 1254b [1.2.12]: "Also, as between the sexes, the male is by nature superior and the female inferior, the male ruler and the female subject").

---

[94] Uwe-Karsten Plisch, *The Gospel of Thomas: Original Text with Commentary* (Stuttgart: Deutsche Bibelgesellschat, 2008), 243–247.
[95] Jorunn Jacobsen Buckley, *Female Fault and Fulfillment in Gnosticism* (Chapel Hill: University of North Carolina Press, 1986), 85.
[96] Various interpretations of Gos. Thom. 14 are reviewed by Buckley, *Female Fault and Fulfillment in Gnosticism*, 85–87.
[97] Elaine Pagels, *The Gnostic Gospels* (New York: Random House, 1979), 49.

IV. *Summary*

While historians like Adolf von Harnack confidently reconstructed the teaching of Jesus in a way that was friendly to modern human rights, emphasizing the universal fatherhood of God, the brotherhood of man and the infinite worth of the individual, that reconstruction was an anachronistic illusion. By the mid-twentieth century, New Testament scholars were making serious efforts to acknowledge and correct the problems of subjectivism inherent in reconstructing the life and teaching of Jesus. While it is legitimate to inquire whether particular sayings or deeds of Jesus are historical or not, the Gospels have been read as realistic narratives throughout the history of the church, and it is primarily this commonsense reading that has influenced the church down through the centuries. Jesus is presented in the Gospels was one who proclaimed the coming of the Kingdom of God and the coincident restoration of the Twelve Tribes of Israel. While Jesus is not presented as engaging in a mission to Gentiles, he did emphasize a great eschatological social reversal in which the poor would not only be accepted by God and the rich rejected, but Israel as the people of God would be rejected, while the Gentiles would be accepted. Within Judaism itself, Jesus rejected the "caste system" that separated the non-observant from the observant Jews, those considered ritually unclean from those that considered themselves ritually pure. His proclamation of the Kingdom of God was in effect a democratizing of salvation in that he did not discriminate against the poor, the outcasts, Samaritans, Roman soldiers, prostitutes, and tax collectors. He dramatized the new conception of equality before God that he was proclaiming by sharing table fellowship with whoever accepted his message of the imminent Kingdom of God and its moral implications for daily living. In doing this, he ignored the rigid system of purity laws that often functioned to exclude ordinary Jews from the Temple, where God was present and where salvation could be obtained through the sacrificial system.

In our discussion of the ideology and practice of equality advocated by Paul, we used the three consecutive phrases found in Gal 3:28 as a springboard for examining various types of equality in the Pauline letters and other early Christian literature. While Paul's conception of aspects of human equality is not ethnocentric, neither is it universal in the sense advocated by the Roman Stoics. For Paul, human equality is limited to the church of God, though any one who believes and is baptized can be a member. The phrase "there is neither Jew nor Greek" indicates that Paul thought that entry into the people of God by baptism was equally accessible to people of all nationalities, but particularly that Jews had no advantage over Gentiles. Yet it is clear that Paul did not consider equality as a reality only *coram deo* ("before God"), since he was convinced that Jewish believers and Gentile believers were obligated to share table fellowship (strongly reminiscent of the practice of Jesus) as part of their shared life "in Christ Jesus." The very fact that Paul thought that national differences were irrelevant for those who belonged to the new people of God suggests that the two other areas of equality, "neither slave nor free" and "neither male nor female," not only reflect equal status before God, they also signal changed attitudes toward others that ought to prevail in the life of the church.

The statement "there is neither slave nor free" is somewhat more ambivalent. In Paul's relatively brief discussion of slavery in 1 Corinthians 7, he gives his version of the paradoxical saying widely found in antiquity (v. 22): "For he who was called in the Lord as a slave is a freedman of the Lord. Likewise he who was free when called is a slave of Christ." Here equality exists *coram deo* ("before God") and has no relationship to actual social status.[98] Elsewhere in 1 Cor 7, Paul advises slaves, like the unmarried, to keep the social status that they had when they became believers (based on the argument that the present world is about to pass away), but if they have the chance to become free they should take advantage of it (v. 21). In Paul's letter to Philemon, he tells his friend to consider Onesimus as both a slave "in the flesh" (i.e., physically) and yet as also a beloved brother "in the Lord" (i.e., spiritually). While Paul does not resolve the tension that would have existed between those two quite different roles, a transformation of social relationships is certainly in view.

When Paul maintains that "there is neither male nor female" in Gal 3:28, he is not speaking of society in general, but only of the transformed relationship between men and women that characterized life "in Christ Jesus." Obviously, Paul is not claiming that the physical characteristics of females and males will be eliminated or that the biological character of human beings will be nullified, but he is claiming that gender equality in the church is part of the new life in Christ. While Paul still shows the influence of the gender hierarchy that dominated Greco-Roman society, it is nevertheless true, as Martin has observed, that "Paul assigns women a

---

[98] De Ste. Croix, *Class Struggle*, 419.

larger role and more respect in his churches and in his theology than they would have enjoyed in many other areas of Greco-Roman Society."[99] In the long history of Pauline interpretation in the church, it is remarkable how frequently in the last century and a half the ideology of gender hierarchy has obscured and downplayed the role of Phoebe, the deacon and patron of Paul (Rom 16:1–2), or turned Junia, the apostle, into a male figure (Rom 16:7). Now, perhaps more than every before, it is possible to let Paul's views of the roles of men and women in the church be treated honestly and objectively.

---

[99] Martin, *The Corinthian Body*, 199.

"WELCOME HIM AS YOU WOULD WELCOME ME" (PHILEMON 17): DOES PAUL CALL FOR VIRTUE OR THE ACTUALIZATION OF A VISION?*

Wendy Cotter, C.S.J.

Introduction

Paul's expectation of Philemon in vv. 16–17 holds significance for the portrait of the apostle himself. What are Paul's expectations of Philemon's relationship with Onesimus, the slave, when after asserting that Onesimus is now Philemon's beloved brother in the flesh and in the Lord (v. 16), he issues a test of partnership in Philemon's willingness to welcome Onesimus as he would welcome Paul? Is this a call to exert the virtues of forbearance and mercy towards Onesimus? Or is he asking for Philemon to recognize the end of the master-slave relationship that obtained before Onesimus was transformed through his conversion, becoming Paul's child (10)? Since the Letter to Philemon has no set of master-slave directives, scholars usually rely on the Letter to the Colossians which is thought to be connected and which does have master-slave regulations (Col 3:22–4:1). But is Colossians a reliable lens for Paul?

This essay reopens the meaning of Philemon 16–17, an undisputed letter of Paul, and of necessity reopens the question of Colossians 3:22–4:1 as representative of Paul's views on masters and slaves. Before the question of Paul's expectation for this runaway slave commences, however, recent challenges to the identity of Onesimus as a runaway slave must be addressed.

---

* I am honored to say that I have been a colleague and friend of Fr. Thomas H. Tobin, S.J., at Loyola University Chicago since 1991. His great scholarship combines with his unfailing kindness toward colleagues and students alike in an inspiring manner. This article is dedicated to him with my sincerest thanks and to wish him every blessing on his sixty-fifth birthday.

Onesimus: A Runaway Slave?

Perhaps the most extreme of modern proposals is that of Allen Dwyer Callaghan who claims Onesimus is not a slave at all but the estranged brother of Philemon.[1] The foundations of his argument occur in v. 16 where Callaghan claims a metaphorical meaning for ὡς ("as") when Paul states, "no longer as (ὡς) a slave but more than a slave, a beloved brother." For Callaghan, Paul is reminding Philemon that this estrangement cannot continue, and his brother must not be treated like a slave any longer but as "a beloved brother—especially to me, but how much more to you, both in the flesh and in the Lord." Callaghan dismisses the literal interpretation of "slave" on the grounds that Paul writes no other letter like this one:

> In fact, we have no letters of intercession on behalf of a runaway slave that may be compared to Philemon, and scholars consequently have grasped at straws to argue for the relevance of purported parallels.[2]

The reason Callaghan's theory has been unpersuasive is that it rests on special pleading, since there is no other instance in any of Paul's letter where ὡς is used in a metaphorical way.[3]

While most scholars agree that Philemon 16 identifies Onesimus as a slave, a few theories hold that the letter does not support the conclusion he had run away. J.H. Houldan observes there is no mention of it by Paul or of anything concerning the slave's repentance. Rather, Paul seems to indicate in vv. 13–14 that his purpose in writing is to ask Philemon to be generous enough to allow Onesimus to stay with Paul. Thus, Houldan proposes that Philemon had probably sent Onesimus to Paul on some errand and, while there, the slave had been converted and proved himself helpful to Paul.[4] In response to this, N.T. Wright summarizes four main

---

[1] Allen Dwight Callaghan, *Embassy of Onesimus: The Letter of Paul to Philemon* (Valley Forge, Pa.: Trinity Press International, 1997), 44–54.

[2] Ibid., 8. Callaghan's critique of Pliny's letters to Sabinianus and others show this plainly.

[3] See the detailed critique in Ben Witherington III, *Letters to Philemon, the Colossians, and the Ephesians: A Socio-Rhetorical Commentary on the Captivity Epistles* (Grand Rapids, Mich.: Eerdmans, 2007), 62–64.

[4] J.H. Houlden, *Paul's Letters from Prison* (London: SCM, 1970), 226; see variations on this idea in F.F. Bruce, *The Epistle to the Colossians, to Philemon and to the Ephesians* (Grand Rapids: Eerdmans, 1984), 197. S.C. Winter, "Paul's Letter to Philemon," *NTS* 33 (1987), 1–15, objects that the opening of the letter does not describe a situation of a runaway slave, so Philemon must know (and have permitted) that Onesimus to be there. It is, however, one thing to say that Philemon had found out, and another to say that he

problems.[5] First, Paul's statement in v. 21 that he is sure Philemon will do even more than Paul says is puzzling if what Philemon wants is the return of Onesimus. Second, one notes that in v. 15 Paul assures Philemon that he will have Onesimus back forever. Third, the overall evidence in the letter's rhetoric focuses on reconciliation between Philemon and Onesimus that would otherwise be confusing. Finally, in seeking a parallel to this letter among those of Greco-Roman antiquity, the closest is that of Pliny the Younger to Sabinianus, a letter of intercession for a freedman who had come to Pliny begging for reconciliation with Sabinianus.[6] Besides these, we might also ask why Paul would go to such lengths asking to keep Onesimus and involving the whole Church as listeners, when Paul knew he would soon be with them (v. 22) and could ask Philemon in person.

The letter is given another purpose by J. Albert Harrill, who is impressed by the similarity of language between slave-apprentice contracts and Paul's letter to Philemon. The partnership language holds outstanding parallels:

> Paul addresses Philemon with affective language—'coworker,' 'friend,' and 'brother' (1 and 7) and expresses 'joy' over the love (7) upon which Paul bases the whole proposition. Paul asks, 'let me have this benefit' (20) asserting confidence in success (21) and the concrete expectation of a meeting (22).[7]

Other similarities include (A) assurance of the obedience of the slave-apprentice (v. 8); (B) the expressed willingness of the apprentice to serve (v. 13); (C) the apprentice becoming a useful servant (v. 11); and (D) the presence of a common penalty clause in which the master craftsman promises to pay the debts of the apprentice (v. 19).

> These parallels suggest that the Epistle to Philemon is a letter of recommendation: Paul recommends Onesimus for apprenticeship in the service of the gospel, and explicit 'appeal' (10) .... In short, Paul wants Philemon to entrust the slave with new responsibilities, as a business partner.[8]

---

had allowed Onesimus to be there. Paul's rhetoric suggests that he anticipates trouble. The letter is aimed at reconciliation.

[5] N.T. Wright, *Colossians and Philemon*, Tyndale New Testament Commentaries 12 (Nottingham, U.K.: Intervarsity Press, 1986), 71–72.

[6] Pliny the Younger, *Letters of Pliny*, 9.21.

[7] J. Albert Harrill, *Slaves in the New Testament* (Minneapolis: Fortress, 2006), esp. 14–15. See also Brook W.R. Pearson, *Corresponding Sense: Paul, Dialectic & Gadamer* (Leiden; Boston; Köln: Brill, 2001), esp. 61–62, who holds that the evidence points to Onesimus having been sent to Paul by Philemon and that scholars have accepted a traditional interpretation without testing for the evidence to support it.

[8] Harrill, *Slaves*, 15.

The problem is that Harrill does not follow Paul's partnership language all the way through the letter to Paul's reminders to Philemon of his rights to command him. That is, Paul does indeed use language of equality in the greeting ("coworker," "friend," and "brother:" vv. 1 and 7, and "joy" over the love: v. 7), but then signals to Philemon the diplomatic method he is going to employ in the letter, "Though I am bold enough in Christ to command you to do your duty, yet I would rather appeal to you on the basis of love" (vv. 8–9). The very use of "do your duty" is hardly partnership talk. Paul seems to be putting his foot down. Again, in vv. 18–19b, when Paul promises to cover Onesimus' debts, Harrill's identification of this as a master's usual assurance to pay the debts incurred by the apprentice is countered by Paul's broad reminder that any debt of Onesimus could never equal what Philemon owes Paul, his very self (v. 19), (something he mentions that he won't mention). Finally, Harrill's proposal that v. 20's plea, "let me have this benefit," like the summation of the slave-apprentice partnership agreements has to account for v. 21, "Confident of your obedience, I am writing to you, knowing that you will do even more than I say."[9]

John M. Barclay sums up Paul's appeal well when he states:

> Paul's request is presented as an appeal rather than a command on two occasions (vv. 8, 14), but each time the more brutal alternative is mentioned as a non-too-subtle indication of the hierarchical relationship between Paul and Philemon; the closing reference to 'obedience' finally makes that quite clear (v. 21).[10]

Other signs of Paul's efforts to pressure Philemon may be seen in Paul's decision to establish the whole church, which meets in Philemon's house, as the audience to hear Paul's wishes. This in itself signals that Paul does not trust Philemon enough in this matter to send a completely private letter. Despite the turns of phrase and efforts to be charming, Paul keeps showing he thinks he must alert Philemon that they are not equal partners and Philemon may not do what he wishes. Paul wants him to do his duty out of love, but in the end Paul tells him what that duty is.

The theories that Onesimus had not run away but had Philemon's permission and those that claim Paul is writing a letter of partner-to-partner contract or agreement to accept Onesimus address only portions

---

[9] Emphases in these quotations of Paul are mine.
[10] John M.G. Barclay, *Colossians and Philemon* (Sheffield, U.K.: Sheffield, 1996), 103.

of the letter. The overall evidence, as Wright has summarized it, appeals for reconciliation; the situation that best fits Paul's rhetoric is that the slave, Onesimus, had run away.

Paul's Rhetoric in Returning the Transformed Onesimus

If vv. 13–14 do not represent the reason for Paul's letter, namely, to request the service of Onesimus, how do the verses function? Lightfoot comments, "With delicate tact the Apostle assumes that Philemon would have wished to perform these friendly offices in person, if it had been possible."[11] While Lightfoot's translation of ὑπὲϱ σοῦ ("in person") may express the real jab Paul intended, it is unlikely Paul actually would have expected Philemon himself to attend to Paul's daily needs in prison. The rendering of the NRSV "in your place" is probably what Philemon heard. Either way, Paul is bringing attention to the fact that Philemon had never thought to send anyone in the first place. This is all the more poignant since Paul just described himself with pathos as "an old man and now also as a prisoner of Christ Jesus" (v. 9). What Paul is really saying is that, however Onesimus came to be here with him, his outstanding performance has brought honor to the house of Philemon, which Onesimus is understood to represent.[12] Paul's claiming he wants to keep Onesimus with him testifies to Philemon the superlative service of Onesimus as well as the affection Paul has for him, this new child of his. Paul's statement that he does not want to force an act of generosity communicates Philemon's lack of concern to send anyone on his own, and therefore discouraging any presumption of Paul to request that Onesimus stay.

After this side-ways admonishment, Paul lifts the tone in v. 14 to a reflection on the workings of Providence, which have turned the "parting" for "an hour" into a return that will last forever (v. 15). Paul is reassuring Philemon this will never happen again.

---

[11] J.B. Lightfoot, *St. Paul's Epistle to the Colossians and to Philemon* (London: Macmillan and Company, 1895), 407.

[12] Lightfoot notes that Paul uses the imperfect ἐβουλόμην to express what Lightfoot calls "tentative wishing" as he states, "I wanted to keep him with me," but uses the aorist ἠθέλησα for "but I did not want to do anything without your consent" (v. 14). As Lightfoot, *Colossians and Philemon*, 407, interprets it, "The will stepped in and put an end to the inclination of the mind."

What Then Does Paul Request of Philemon?

The expectation of Paul occurs in vv. 15b–17:

> … so that you might have him back forever, no longer as a slave but more than a slave, a beloved brother—especially to me but how much more to you, both in the flesh and in the Lord. So if you consider me your partner, welcome him as you would welcome me.

The interpretation of this text has been overshadowed by the greater Letter to the Colossians and the presumed connection between them. Similarities in names in both letters have led some scholars such as John Nordling to conclude that Colossians is also an authentic letter of Paul:

> Since so many of the names and epithets mentioned in Philemon 23–24 and Col 4:10–14 refer to the same individuals, it is probable that Paul wrote *both* letters at about the same time for two distinct, yet related epistolary audiences at Colossae.[13]

The name, Onesimus, occurs in Col 4:9: "He [Tychius] is coming with Onesimus, the faithful and beloved brother, who is one of you. They will tell you about everything here." Thus, Nordling and scholars who claim Paul's authorship for Colossians turn to the master-slave instructions in Col 3:22–4:1 to define Paul's expectations for Philemon and Onesimus:

> Slaves, obey your earthly masters in everything, not only while being watched and in order to please them, but whole-heartedly, fearing the Lord. Whatever your task, put yourselves into it, as done for the Lord and not for your masters, since you know that from the Lord you will receive the inheritance as your reward: you serve the Lord Christ for the wrongdoing will be paid back for whatever wrong has been done, and there is no partiality. Masters, treat your slaves justly and fairly, for you know that you also have a Master in heaven.

Based on Colossians' teaching, as F.F. Scott warns, Philemon 16–17 must not be misunderstood as a plea for Onesimus' freedom:

> It is not suggested that Onesimus, because he was now a Christian, should be given his freedom. We miss the point of the letter altogether if we conceive of Paul as dealing with a serious offence in a purely sentimental fashion. He insists that the deserter should return to the post of duty and henceforth show himself faithful, and even face punishment if it should be dealt out to him.[14]

---

[13] John G. Nordling, *Philemon* (St. Louis, Mo.: Concordia University Press, 2004), 8.

[14] F.F. Scott, *The Epistles to the Colossians, to Philemon and to the Ephesians* (1930; reprint, London: Hodder and Stoughton, 1958), 110.

For this reason, Scott understands Paul's use of "in the flesh" and "in the Lord" to represent two separate categories so that "in the flesh" is meant to reinforce Onesimus' role as Philemon's slave:

> The bond between Philemon and Onesimus will henceforth be a double one. They will be related 'in the flesh' (i.e., in matters of the world) as master and servant, and they will also be related as brothers in Christ. These two relationships will strengthen and enrich one another.[15]

Wright agrees and cites 1 Cor 7:22 as a confirming teaching to Col 3:22–4:1:

> "This is not a request for emancipation. It simply applies what was said about relations between Christian masters and slaves in, e.g., 1 Corinthians 7:22 or Colossians 3:22–4:1."[16]

Actually, the inclusion of 1 Cor 7:22 as supportive to Colossians 3:22–4:1 is maintained by scholars such as Markus Barth and Matthew Blanke, who admit separate authorship of Colossians, but hold that it represents Paul's views just the same.[17]

Their interpretation of Philemon 16 is argued in an excursus, "To Be a Sibling *and* a Slave or Master,"[18] where Barth and Blanke first establish the point that Col 4:1 reminds the masters they too have a "lord" in heaven, just as Paul asserts in 1 Cor 7:22, "whoever was free when called is a slave of Christ." From this, they conclude, "Here the behavior of the *Lord* Christ with his slaves ought to be taken as a model for the behavior of earthly lords with their slaves [cf. Mt 18:21–35]."[19] Since Paul does not explicate exactly how to express that proper role of master in Philemon 16, Barth and Blanke argue that Paul is trusting Philemon with the way to exert this virtue:

---

[15] Ibid.

[16] Wright, *Colossians and Philemon*, 192; emphasis mine.

[17] Markus Barth and Helmut Blanke, *The Letter to Philemon: a New Translation with Notes and Commentary* (Grand Rapids, Mich.: Eerdmans, 2000), 201: "Since even in undisputed letters Paul takes a conservative stance, there is no reason for assuming that the *Haustafeln* essentially contradict the apostle's own proclamation and ethical directives."

[18] "If Colossians is an authentic Pauline letter, then its statements acquire special meaning in a framework of the presentation of the Letter to Philemon, since Philemon and Colossians were both addressed to Christians of the same place and are very nearly contemporary. If Colossians is a pseudo-Pauline letter, in any case it has been composed almost at the same time, and probably is very nearly Pauline in its content. It reveals, then, an early step in the further development of Pauline thought by the young Church," (Ibid., 477–478).

[19] Ibid., 480.

Clear statements formulating this thought in the behavioral instructions to the 'lords' are lacking. The admonition to slaveholders remains extremely terse. Consequences to be drawn from the details of the house tables are left to them, as Paul too, leaves to Philemon to translate his 'general' admonishments into concrete conduct where Onesimus is concerned.[20]

James D.G. Dunn likewise concludes separate authorship for Colossians, even noting it may have written by a disciple who had a different theology, but Dunn still appeals to Colossians throughout his commentary on Philemon, for example:

> [The relationship between master and slave] will have a double dimension ("in the flesh" and "in the Lord"), and by broader implication of such passages as Gal 3:28 that relationships "in Christ" transcended even if they did not abolish distinctions of race, status and gender (see also on Col 3:11 and 4:1; cf. the also ambiguous 1 Cor 7:20–24).[21]

Since Dunn (and others) depend on Col 3:22–4:1 for the meaning of Philemon 16–17, it only follows that they conclude Paul's teaching in Gal 3:28 concerning the dissolution of distinctions was left a spiritual reflection and not actualized practically.

Paul's "Lack of Concern" for Actual Slavery?

Assumptions that Philemon 16–17 must discount ideas of freedom and that Paul himself was indifferent to actual slavery are reinforced by the notion supplied by Colossians as well as the corroborating texts of Ephesians (6:5–8) and the pastorals (1 Timothy 6:1; Titus 2:9–10), which are disputed Pauline letters. The influence of these associations is seen in the work of classical historian, Peter Garnsey,[22] who instructs his audience that actual slavery was of no concern to Paul, but only salvation:

---

[20] Ibid. See also F.F. Scott, *Colossians, Philemon and Ephesians*, 113 ("Paul leaves his friend to decide for himself how he will act towards the return slave"); Michael Weed, *The Letters of Paul to the Ephesians, the Colossians and Philemon* (Austin, Tex.: R.B. Sweet, 1971), 25; Eduard Lohse, *Colossians and Philemon* (Philadelphia, Pa.: Fortress, 1971), 203; and John Nordling, *Philemon* (Concordia, Kans.: St. Louis, 2004), 249 ("Paul did not intend to tell Philemon exactly which course of action he envisioned ... We can't tell what he wanted").

[21] James D.G. Dunn, *The Epistles to Colossians and Philemon* (Grand Rapids, Mich.: Eerdmans, 1996), 335.

[22] See Peter Garnsey, *Ideas of Slavery from Aristotle to Augustine* (Cambridge: Cambridge University Press, 1996), 173 n. 1: "For 'Paul' read 'Paul and some of his followers'."

Paul and Seneca advised masters to be humane to their slaves, and Paul instructed slaves to obey their masters (and wives their husbands) as if they were serving God. Such quietism was born of the conviction that physical slavery was a matter of no importance alongside virtue (Stoic) and salvation (for the Christian).[23]

In the statement below, notice that Garnsey cites Philemon, an undisputed Pauline letter, among the disputed letters, a sign of the command these letters hold over the interpretation of Philemon:

> The Ephesians passage [Eph 6:5–8[24]] is completely consistent with a number of other texts composed by Paul or his followers [Col 3:22–4:1; Titus 2:9–10; Philemon; 1 Tm 6:1] … uncritical of slavery.[25]

The response to Paul's "uncritical" position on slavery causes Garnsey to lament, "It is deeply troubling that people with a positive view of human nature and its potential were unable to resolve, once and for all, that slaves were persons and not things."[26]

Not so for the scholars who endorse Paul's teachings in Colossians. Wright reflects it was only sensible for Paul to refrain from protesting a master-slave relationship: first, out of a sense of fairness since he had no slaves of his own and would never feel the inconvenience of being bereft of their aid; and, second, more importantly, because it would certainly result in a persecution of the churches. Wright sees Paul's choice to invoke virtuous behavior among slave owners as the beginning, a planting of a mustard seed that would grow into the concept of freedom for slaves one day:

Not all the works attributed to Paul were composed by him. Ephesians, 1 Timothy and Titus are not by Paul. These verses I cite from these letters convey essentially the same message on slavery as is presented in authentic Pauline letters, and are not far removed from him in time. I follow Kümmel (1975) in these matters." Garnsey does not supply a page reference to Kümmel, but see W.G. Kümmel, *Introduction to the New Testament*, trans. Howard Kee, rev. ed. (Nashville: Abingdon, 1975), 366–384, especially 384. It is only fair to note that while Kümmel argues for Pauline authorship for Colossians, he takes pains to show the distinction in vocabulary and especially the theology of Ephesians and the pastorals, noting, "If the pastorals are incorporated in the presentation of Pauline thought, the result is in any case, an adulteration of Pauline theology."

[23] Garnsey, *Ideas of Slavery*, 19.

[24] Eph. 6:5–8: "Slaves, obey your earthly masters with fear and trembling, in singleness of heart, as you obey Christ; not only while being watched, and in order to please them, but as slaves of Christ, doing the will of God from the heart."

[25] Garnsey, *Ideas of Slavery*, 31.

[26] Ibid., 19.

His way of changing the world was to plant a grain of mustard seed, which
inconspicuous at first grows into a spreading tree. And in the meantime
(see Col 3:22–4:1) he teaches masters and slaves to treat themselves and
each other as human beings. Like an artist or poet, he does some of his
finest work, not by the obscure clarity of direct statement, but by veiled
allusion and teasing suggestion.[27]

Dunn too defends Paul with the argument that Paul could not be expected to imagine a world without slaves; expectations of such vision
belong to our own history and modern realizations. Even if Paul had this
vision, he would not have protested for fear of bringing violent repercus-
sions on the churches. Thus, for Paul, "the most effective amelioration
depended on the master's kindly treatment."[28]

Barth and Blanke, influenced by some modern treatments of Greco-
Roman slavery that illustrate the better conditions for slaves,[29] claim
Paul saw benefit in slaves remaining so, since many freedmen were
homeless and hungry. Enduring the evils known might be better than
the unknown. The worldly freedoms are not the ones that count in any
case, "and never in other letters does the apostle presume that everything
will be all right if only and as soon as a person gains economical, political
and social freedom."[30]

---

[27] N.T. Wright, *Colossians and Ephesians*, 174. Like Dunn, he uses the statements in
Colossians 3:22–4:1 to reflect Paul's approach in Phil. 16–17.

[28] Dunn, *Colossians and Philemon*, 306–307, and again, although of separate authorship, Colossians 3:11, 22 and 4:1 as reflective of Paul's message in Philemon 16.

[29] Scholars such as W.L. Westerman, *The Slave Systems of Greek and Roman Antiquity*
(Philadelphia, Pa.: The American Philosophical Society, 1955); John Crook, *Law and Life
in Rome* (Ithaca, N.Y.: Cornell University Press, 1967); and Scott S. Bartchy, *MAΛΛON
XPEΣAI*: First Century Slavery and 1 Corinthians 7:21, SBLDS 11 (Missoula, Mont.:
Society of Biblical Literature, 1973) draw attention to the improvements in slaves' treatment and possibilities for a better life in the Greco-Roman period. Certain laws pro-
tected them as had not been the case in the past, and they were cared for by their owners, while the freedmen and free born were poor and often died due to their inability to
support themselves. Moreover, slaves could hold positions of authority in households in
spite of their state. Scholars are divided on this matter, and several have illustrated how
the cruelty to slaves has ample evidence; see, e.g., Orlando Paterson, *Slavery and Social
Death: A Comparative Study* (Cambridge, Mass.: Harvard University Press, 1982); Keith
R. Bradley, *Slaves and Masters in the Roman Empire: A Study in Social Control* (New York:
Oxford University Press, 1984); Richard Horsley, "Paul and Slavery: A Critical Alternative
to Recent Readings," in *Semeia 83/84: Slavery in Text and Interpretation*, ed. Allen Dwight
Callaghan, Richard A. Horsley, and Abraham Smith (Atlanta: Scholars Press, 1998), 153–
200. Thanks to John Byron, *Recent Research on Paul and Slavery* (Sheffield, U.K.: Sheffield
University Press, 2008), 22–34.

[30] Barth and Blanke, *Colossians and Philemon*, 368–369. See also R. McL. Wilson,

These few examples indicate how Colossians as well as Ephesians, 1 and 2 Timothy, and Titus have bolstered each other in their definition of Paul's own view on slavery, whether he wrote the letters or not. Not only does this affect the interpretation of Philemon 16–17, but also that of the two texts from undisputed Paul letters, which belong as backdrop to the Philemon letter, namely, 1 Cor 7:20–24 and Gal 3:28. The question is whether Colossians is a reliable lens for Paul.

Colossians, a Reliable Lens for Paul's Teachings on Slavery?

Paul's authorship of Colossians was first questioned by Edward Evanston in 1805 but argued in a detailed manner by Ernst Mayeroff in 1838.[31] In comparison to the undisputed letters of Paul, Colossians shows differences in vocabulary,[32] style,[33] manner of argumentation, themes, theology, Christology, and eschatology.[34] For scholars who defend Paul's

---

Colossians and Philemon: A Critical and Exegetical Commentary (New York: T & T. Clark, 2005), 328, n. 28: "The life of the slave was not necessarily one of hardship."

[31] Edward Evanston, *The Dissonance of the Four Generally Received Evangelists and the Evidence of Their Respective Authenticity Examined*, 2nd ed. (Ipswich: G. Jermym, 1805). Yet the challenge is based on Evanston's insistence that authenticity of the canonical documents can be shown by their coherence with Luke's gospel and Acts. Colossians is dismissed as unreliable because in 2:1 the writer indicates that he has not met the church in Laodicea, when Acts 16:6–18:23 claim that Paul visited Phrygia, which would include both Colossae and Laodicea (313–314); see also Ernst Mayerhoff, *Der Brief an der Colosser, mit vernehmlicher Beruchsichtigung der Drei Pastoralbriefe kritisch geprüft* (Berlin: Mayerhoff, 1838), who concluded that Colossians was dependent on Ephesians. Note that the research for this discussion on the debate over the authenticity of Colossians reflects the work of Raymond F. Collins, *Letters Paul Did Not Write: The Letter to the Hebrews and the Pauline Pseudepigrapha* (Wilmington, Del.: 1988), 171–208.

[32] Eighty-six words not found in Paul's undisputed letters combine with thirty hapaxlegomenae.

[33] John L. Mackenzie, *Dictionary of the Bible* (New York: Bruce; London: Collier-Macmillan, 1965), *s.v.* "Letter to the Colossians," 146, describes it as "hieratic and liturgical, indeed it is often obscure and overloaded."

[34] See Marianne Meye Thompson, *Colossians & Philemon* (Grand Rapids, Mich.: Eerdmans, 2005), 2–4, who compares Colossians with Paul's undisputed letters: "Gone are the sharp polemics, the rapid-fire series of biting questions (Rom 3:27–4:1; 6:1–3; 7:7; 8:31–35; 1 Cor 3:3–5; Gal 3:1–5), and the direct and pointed appeals to the readers such as 'O foolish Galatians!' (3:1), 'Already you are filled! Already you have become rich! Without us you have become kings!' (1 Cor 4:8), and 'We have spoken freely to you Corinthians!' (2 Cor 6:11). In Colossians Paul's ire is not aroused as it is in these other epistles, and the tone and style he adopts here pale in fervor when compared to Galatians or Corinthians" (Ibid., 2–3). Thompson questions whether the issues in Colossians may

authorship, the vocabularic and stylistic differences may be explained by the theory of Paul's use of an amanuensis.[35] Marianne Meye Thompson finds the reason for the absence in Colossians of Paul's usual passionate and direct argumentation in the possibility Paul does not know the community as well as he knows the Corinthian and Galatian membership.[36] Scholars such as Dunn appeal to a "Pauline School"[37] or to a disciple who knew Paul but had a different theology.[38]

The differences in theology and Christology recognized by Dunn and Thompson are explained away by Wright as developments in Paul's own thinking. Special features of the letter to the Colossians may find echoes in Paul's undisputed letters; for example, the hymn in Col 1:15–20, emphasizing Christ as Redeemer, connects with Phil 2:6–11; 1 Cor 8:6; 2 Cor 4:4; 8:9.[39] True, the Paul of Corinthians sees the whole Church as the total body of Christ, while Colossians distinguishes Christ as its head, and members as the body (Col 1:18, 24; 2:19), but for Wright this is

---

not be as grievous as those and answers herself, "And yet, that is scarcely the case. In Colossians, the significance of the person of Christ and the sufficiency of his death on the cross for Christian faith and conduct are at stake. It is hard to imagine that Paul thought the issues were of lesser importance that those troubling the Galatians or other churches founded in the course of his mission" (Ibid., 3). Further, "There are curious theological differences between Colossians and some of Paul's other letters ... Lacking treatments of justification or the Law, the role of the Spirit, and the overarching eschatological framework that is foundational to Pauline thought" (Ibid.). Finally, "The problem is not that Colossians fails to treat a typical Pauline theme, but that Colossians fails to treat the theme in a typically Pauline manner" (Ibid., 2–3).

[35] For Timothy as the amanuensis, see Heinrich Ewald, *Die Sendschriften des Apostels-Paulus* (Göttingen, 1857); Eduard Schweitzer, "The Letter to the Colossians Neither Pauline nor Postpauline?" in *Pluralisme et oecumenisme en recherches théologiques*, ed. R.E. Hoeckman, BETL 43 (Louvain: Peeters, 1976), 3–16; and more recently Thompson, *Colossians & Philemon*, 3. For Epaphras as the amanuensis, see Albert Klöpper, *Der Brief an die Colosser, kritsch untersucht und in seinem Verhältnisse zum paulinischen Lehrbegriff exegetisch und biblisch-theologisch erortet* (Berlin: G. Reimer, 1882); and Mark Kiley, *Colossians as Pseudepigraphy*, JSOT (Sheffield, UK: Sheffield Press, 1986). For an unknown amanuensis, see Pierre Benoit, "Rapports littéraires entre les épîtres aux Colossiens et aux Ephésiens," in *Neutestamentliche Aufsätze* (Regensberg: Pustet, 1963), 11–22. See also Collins, *Letters Paul did Not Write*, 176–177.

[36] Thompson, *Colossians & Philemon*, 3.

[37] Eduard Lohse, *Die Briefe an die Philipper, an die Kolosser und an Philemon*, KEK 14 (Göttingen: Vandenhoeck & Ruprecht, 1968); idem, *Colossians and Philemon*, Hermeneia (Philadelphia: Fortress, 1971); Helmut Merklein, "Paulische Theologie in der Rezeption der Kolosser- und Epheserbriefes," in *Paulus in den neutestamentliche Spätschriften: Zur Paulusrezeption im Neuen Testament*, QD 89 (Freiburg: Herder, 1981), 25–69.

[38] Dunn, *The Epistles to Colossians and Philemon*, 36–37.

[39] Wright, *Colossians and Philemon*, 36.

only a different metaphor for the same concept. Further, the theme of justification by faith is not found in Colossians, but Wright points out it only occurs in Romans, Galatians and Phil 3:2 ff.[40] In fact, in the end, as has been seen, even scholars who disagree with Wright and hold for separate authorship in Colossians maintain that the letter still reflects Paul's views.

The area far less addressed as a difference between Colossians and the undisputed letters is the eschatology that typifies Paul's undisputed letters, which Marianne Meye Thompson admits in her examination of Colossians, "Lacking is the ... overarching eschatological framework that is foundational to Pauline thought."[41]

The Eschatology of Paul

Raymond Collins describes the eschatology of Colossians:

> The temporal categories of Paul have given way to spatial categories. Although there are a few cases of consequent eschatology in Colossians (cf. 3:4, 6, 24; 4:11), the "already" but "not yet" schema typical of Paul is absent in Colossians.[42]

Barclay further explains Colossians' realized eschatology,

> The Colossian Christians are assured that they have been rescued from the power of darkness and transferred into the kingdom of God's Son (1:3), and later they are described as having been both buried *and raised* with Christian baptism (2:12), a motif that governs 3:1–4.[43]

This he contrasts with the "already but not yet" eschatology of Paul's undisputed letters:

> As is well known, Paul expresses himself far more cautiously in 1 Corinthians, emphasizing the 'not yet' at least as often as the 'already' (e.g., 1 Cor 4:8–10; 13:8–13) and in his reflection on baptism in Romans 6 he seems to go out of his way to *avoid* saying that the baptized have been raised with Christ; they have 'newness of life' (6:4) and *will* be united with him in a resurrection like him (6:6), but are not described as already raised.[44]

---

[40] Ibid.
[41] Thompson, *Colossians and Ephesians*, 3.
[42] Collins, *Letters Paul Did Not Write*, 187.
[43] Barclay, *Colossians and Philemon*, 26; emphasis mine.
[44] Ibid.

Barclay's study leads him to conclude, while Colossians has some:

> forward-looking references (e.g., 3:4, 6, 24), the Christian life is no longer
> lived under the shadow of the future as radically as in Paul. The dominant
> metaphors have become spatial (below and above, e.g., 3:1–4) rather than
> temporal (now and then).[45]

Unlike Colossians, Ephesians, and the Pastorals, every undisputed letter
of Paul alerts the communities that the time is short, the Kingdom is near,
and the community should be vigilant in its expectation of the coming
of the Lord.[46] In fact, David E. Aune claims that it is apocalypticism that
represents "the framework of his thought."

> Whether or not apocalypticism is the *center* of Pauline thought, the apoc-
> alyptic world view certainly provides a framework for his thought … and
> it is from this perspective that the *gospel*, the central theological emphasis
> of his letters, must be understood.[47]

Aune brings out Paul's vivid awareness of the two ages:

> a dualistic contrast between the present and future age or aeon (Gal 1:4;
> Rom 8:18; 1 Cor 7:26, cf. Eph 2:2) and speaks of the evil supernatural
> powers which dominate it (1 Cor 2:6; 2 Cor 4:4).[48]

Aune explains what had been referred to as the Day of the Lord in
the prophets "became the basis for Paul's conception of the impending
eschatological judgment of the world (1 Thes 5:2; Rom 2:16)."[49]

Implications for the Use of Colossians for Philemon 16–17

In the light of this "almost but not yet" apocalyptic eschatological lens
of Paul, Wright's representation of him as someone planting a seed to be
developed later into full freedom for slaves rather presupposes the realized eschatology of Colossians (and Matt 28:16–20). The similar arguments of Barth and Blanke, of Dunne and Thompson, which presume a
Paul who is envisioning the successful settling into society of Christian
communities, fail to reflect Paul's conviction that anytime soon this evil

---

[45] Ibid.
[46] Rom 13:11–12; 1 Cor 15:51; 16:22; 2 Cor 5: 4–5; Gal 6:7–9, 15; Phil 1:6, 9–10; 2:14–
15; 3:18–20; 4:4–5; 1 Thes 4:16–18.
[47] David E. Aune, *ABD*, *s.v.* "Eschatology (Early Christian)," 2.602.
[48] Ibid.
[49] Ibid.

world will be destroyed to make way for the new city of God where his faithful "brothers and sisters" will find their πολίτευμα (Phil 3:20).[50]

Paul's Teachings in 1 Cor 7:21, Gal 3:28, and Slavery

Paul's remarks to and about slaves require the eschatological backdrop that features the imminent arrival for the Kingdom, which results in a different posture of Paul toward the larger society.

1 Cor 7:21

δοῦλος ἐκλήθης, μή σοι μελέτω· ἀλλ᾽ εἰ καὶ δύνασαι ἐλεύθερος γενέσθαι, μᾶλλον χρῆσαι.

In the text's translation, the imperative clause holds greatest importance. The usual rendering in English is represented by the RSV: "Were you a slave when called? Never mind. But if you can gain your freedom, avail yourself of the opportunity."[51] The NRSV, however, returns to a translation found in some of the fathers of the Church, where μᾶλλον χρῆσαι is translated to refer to the condition of slavery: "make use of your *present condition* now more than ever."[52] A footnote reads, "or avail yourself of the opportunity." Which of these is assigned to Paul's intent has crucial implications.

The Church Father, John Chrysostom, argued that Paul's imperative refers to slavery on the grounds it was more logical in the sentence:

---

[50] A fuller discussion of Paul's image is found in Wendy Cotter, "Our *Politeuma* is in Heaven," in *Origins and Method: Toward a New Understanding of Judaism and Christianity*, ed. Bradley McLean, JSNT Supplement Series 86 (Sheffield, U.K.: JSOT Press, 1993), 92–104.

[51] "Were you a slave when you were called? Don't let it trouble you—although if you can gain your freedom, do so" (NIV); Were you called while a slave? Do not worry about it; but if you are able also to become free, rather do that (NASB); Were you a slave when called? Do not be concerned about it. But if you can gain your freedom, avail yourself of the opportunity (ESV). Were you called *while* a slave? Do not be concerned about it; but if you can be made free, rather use *it* (NKJV).

[52] Emphasis mine. Cf. Theodoret of Cyrrhus (393–457 CE), who in his commentary on 1 Corinthians translates and comments on 1 Cor 7:21, "Are you who have been called by Christ a slave? It shouldn't concern you; even if you are able to gain manumission, you should accept your slave status all the more;" "God's grace recognizes no differences between a slave and being a master. So you should not try to escape from your status as a slave on the grounds that it is degrading for the Christian faith ... he is telling you not to use religion as a pretext for running away from slavery." My thanks for this excerpt go to Thomas Wiedemann, *Greek and Roman Slavery* (Baltimore and London: The Johns Hopkins University Press, 1981) 241, 245.

> Now we are not ignorant that some say, the words, "use it rather," are
> spoken with regard to liberty: interpreting it, 'if you can become free,
> become free'. But the expression would be very contrary to Paul's manner if
> he intended this. For he would not, when consoling the slave and signifying
> that he was in no respect injured, have told him to get free …[53]

This explains why Chrysostom understood the next verse, 1 Cor 7:22
("For whoever was called in the Lord as a slave is a freed person belonging
to the Lord, just as whoever was free when called is a slave of Christ"), to
mean that actual slavery was of no importance. J.B. Lightfoot, however,
holds the opposite view based on the pattern of the rhetoric in vv. 10–11
and 15, where Paul introduces the possibility of change and deals with it
as accepted.[54]

> vv. 10: To the married I give this command—not I but the Lord—that the
> wife should not separate from her husband, 11: but if she does separate,
> let her remain unmarried or else be reconciled to her husband (ἐὰν δὲ καὶ
> χωρισθῇ, μενέτω ἄγαμος ἢ τῷ ἀνδρὶ καταλλαγήτω), ….
>
> v. 15: But if the unbelieving partner separates, let it be so (εἰ δὲ ὁ ἄπιστος
> χωρίζεται, χωριζέσθω); in such a case the brother or sister is not bound.
> It is to peace that God has called you.

Besides these examples, which occur prior to Paul's address to the slaves,
the same pattern is repeated in vv. 27–28, where Paul speaks to those
married and unmarried:

> v. 27: Are you bound to a wife? Do not seek to be free. Are you free from
> a wife? Do not seek a wife. 28 But if you marry (ἐὰν δὲ καὶ γαμήσῃς), you
> do not sin, and if a virgin marries, she does not sin.

Based on this pattern that both precedes and follows v. 21, the lis-
tener could only conclude that Paul's imperative to the slaves addresses
their possible freedom.[55] That meaning being clear, Paul's μή σοι μελέτω
should be recognized not as a dismissal of any importance to the mis-

---

[53] John Chrysostom, *Homily* 19: in *Epistle1 ad Cor* PG 61:164.

[54] Lightfoot, *St. Paul's Epistle to the Colossians and to Philemon* (London: Macmillan,
1895), 390–391, n. 2.

[55] Scott Bartchy makes the observation that if a slave were given freedom by his
master / mistress, there would have been no possibility of the slave to refuse that freedom;
see S.S. Bartchy, *ΜΑΛΛΟΝ ΧΡΗΣΑΙ: First Century Slavery and the Interpretation of
1 Cor 7:21*, SBL Dissertation Series 11 (Missoula, Mont.: Scholars Press, 1973), 96–
144, esp. 97–98. This is certainly true of a slave surprised with the granting of his / her
liberation. Paul seems to indicate cases where the slave was in a position to finally "buy"
his or her freedom from the owner. In fact, Paul's articulation seems to cover the situation
generally, ἀλλ' εἰ καὶ δύνασαι ἐλεύθερος γενέσθαι. Paul's imperative though, addresses
the obligation on the slave however freedom should happen to be offered.

ery of slavery, but just the opposite. There is no other author in the New Testament who seeks to comfort the slaves in recognizing the pain of ignominy in their state. There is also no letter other than the one to Philemon among the undisputed Pauline letters, in which owners of slaves are identified. This suggests that when Paul addresses the slaves in 1 Cor 7:21 they have non-Christian owners. Paul's statement in 1 Cor 7:21 to the "free" may well be his attempt to remind them there is to be no superiority of attitude towards the actual slaves, but to have them remember that all true Christians are slaves, slaves to Christ.

The key to understanding Paul's teaching in 1 Cor 7, namely, that everyone should remain in the state he or she was when called, if at all possible, is found in vv. 29–31:

> I mean, brothers and sisters, the appointed time has grown short; from now on, let even those who have wives be as though they had none, and those who mourn as though they were not mourning, and those who rejoice as though they were not rejoicing, and those who buy as though they had no possessions, and those who deal with the world as though they had no dealings with it. For the present form of this world is passing away.

Thus, the reason for the married and unmarried to remain so, and for slaves to accept their state and not be upset, is because the whole world will soon be judged. This is a far different context than Col 3:18–21, where the point is to settle well into society. We do not notice the author of Colossians enjoining the unmarried to stay that way, as Paul does, because in fact the community of Colossians is a settled community dealing with the larger society. Thus, one cannot call on 1 Cor 7:21–22 as a parallel to Col 3:21–4:1.

Galatians 3:25–28

v. 25: But now that faith has come, we are no longer subject to a disciplinarian, for in Christ Jesus 26 you are all children of God through faith. 27 As many of you as were baptized into Christ have clothed yourself with Christ. 28 There is no longer Jew or Greek, there is no longer slave or free, there is no longer male and female; for all of you are one in Christ Jesus (25 ἐλθούσης δὲ τῆς πίστεως οὐκέτι ὑπὸ παιδαγωγόν ἐσμεν. 26 Πάντες γὰρ υἱοὶ θεοῦ ἐστε διὰ τῆς πίστεως ἐν Χριστῷ Ἰησοῦ· 27 ὅσοι γὰρ εἰς Χριστὸν ἐβαπτίσθητε, Χριστὸν ἐνεδύσασθε. 28 οὐκ ἔνι Ἰουδαῖος οὐδὲ Ἕλλην, οὐκ ἔνι δοῦλος οὐδὲ ἐλεύθερος, οὐκ ἔνι ἄρσεν καὶ θῆλυ· πάντες γὰρ ὑμεῖς εἷς ἐστε ἐν Χριστῷ Ἰησοῦ.)

Once it is seen that Colossians cannot be the interpretive lens for Paul's meaning in 1 Cor 7:21, it is no longer possible to conclude from the master-slave instructions in Colossians that Paul avoided the dissolution of divisions among his converts (Gal 3:27–28), which had obtained before their incorporation into Christ as brothers and sisters through baptism.

In Raymond Collins' most recent book, *The Power of Images in Paul*,[56] which examines only the undisputed letters of Paul, Collins remarks on Paul's pronounced use of kinship language wherever there are social divisions. Interestingly, both Galatians and Philemon stand out for the abundance of kinship language:

> Were it not for the letter to the Galatians, one might say that in no other text of the New Testament does kinship language have such importance as it does in the Letter to Philemon and the church in his house.[57]

In regard to Galatians, Thomas H. Tobin, S.J., explains Paul's teaching in Gal 3:27–28, where putting on the risen Christ in baptism results in the dissolution of distinctions:

> The interpretation of baptism in Gal 3:27–28 is that, in this rite, believers put on the risen Christ and are united with him to such an extent that they are now all 'one in Christ Jesus' (Gal 3:28). Because of this, all other distinctions between human beings are relativized, even those between Jew and Greek, slave and free, and male and female.[58]

But do we have any proof that Paul tried to actualize this freedom from division in his communities or does Gal 3:28 reflect a spiritual reality meant to remain as such? When one seeks evidence that suggests Paul worked to actualize his "no longer Jew or Greek," his very argument in Rom 3:28–4:1 indicates Paul's refusal to support the difference between Jew and Greek shows it was a problematic issue for the Roman church. Tobin reflects:

> However reformulated his arguments might have been [from his Letter to the Galatians] Paul still refused to compromise his basic convictions about the present manifestation of God's righteousness in Christ for Jews and Gentiles alike through faith apart from the Law.[59]

Further proof that this conviction reflects his expectation an actual reality is found in Paul's description of Peter's visit to Antioch in Gal 2:11–14. The compromise articulated in Gal 2:7, that Peter would be assigned

---

[56] Raymond F. Collins, *The Power of Images in Paul* (Collegeville, Minn.: Michael Glazier, 2008).

[57] Ibid., 76.

[58] Thomas H. Tobin, *Paul's Rhetoric in its Contexts: The Argument of Romans* (Peabody, Mass.: Hendrickson, 2004), 200.

[59] Ibid., 153.

to the circumcised and Paul to the uncircumcised, could only function in Judea. Outside Judea, mixed populations would result in divided Christian communities if the policy were to hold. In Antioch, it is clear that Jews and Gentiles were eating together and that Peter followed the custom there (Gal 2:12a–b). Only when certain people came from James did Peter withdraw with the other Jews of the community to eat separately from the Gentiles, offending what Paul calls "the truth of the gospel" (Gal 2:14). Paul is furious at the division that resulted. For the Galatian community to whom Paul is writing, such divisions were opposed by Paul as Hans Dieter Betz states:

> For them [the Galatian Christians] 'freedom' was not merely a theological notion, but they regarded themselves as free from 'this evil world' with its repressive social, religious, and cultural laws and conventions. They had left behind the cultural and social distinctions between Greeks and non-Greeks, the religious distinction between Jews and non-Jews, the social systems of slavery and the subordination of women.[60]

If Paul's letter to the Galatians shows that the community actualized the dissolution of the divisions between Jew and Greek, what evidence supports the conclusion that Paul's communities were also trying to dissolve the social strictures dividing men and women? In fact, women appear in positions of authority in Cenchrae (Rom 16:1–2: Phoebe, deacon of Cenchrae), in Corinth (1 Cor 1: 11: Chloe) and in Philippi (Phil 4:2–3: Euodia and Syntyche).[61] Paul could take advantage of the greater latitude in Roman culture for women's roles in the home to introduce their mutual leadership in the churches which were obliged to meet in homes.[62] Margaret MacDonald's, "Reading Real Women Through the Undisputed Letters of Paul,"[63] reinforces the impression both sexes may lead, teach, minister, delegate, and serve each other. It is important to note here that, even

---

[60] Hans Dieter Betz, *Galatians*, Hermeneia (Philadelphia: Fortress, 1979), 29. With thanks for this reference to Tatha Wiley, *Paul and Gentile Women: Reframing Galatians* (New York; London: Continuum, 2005), 55.

[61] Also in Rom 16:3–4, Prisca, who with her husband work with Paul and risk their necks for Paul's life, (Rom 16:3–4, see 1 Cor 16:19); Mary "who has worked very hard among you" (v. 6); Junias, who with Andonicus are relatives of Paul and in prison with him, "prominent among the apostles, and they were in Christ before I was" (v. 7); Tryphaena and Tryphosa "workers in the Lord" (v. 12); and Aphia, "our sister" (Philemon 2).

[62] I explore this subject in Wendy Cotter, "Women's Authority Roles in Paul's Churches: Countercultural or Conventional," *NovT* 36 (1994): 350–372.

[63] Margaret Y. MacDonald, "Rereading Real Women Through the Undisputed Letters of Paul," *Women & Christian Origins*, ed. Ross Shepard Kraemer and Mary Rose D'Angelo (New York: Oxford University Press, 1999), 199–220.

though it was the case that the wife was the *domina* of the home, evidence of Roman culture does not allow one to suppose that it was commonplace or conventional for women to head up heterosexual groups or
collegia even if they did congregate in a home. The evidence that women
were leaders of an ἐκκλησία, the official civic gathering of the citizens
of God's kingdom, is something that still would have been unconven-
tional.

"No longer Slave or Free" and Philemon 16–17

The evidence from Paul's undisputed letters supports the conclusion that
he tried to actualize the dissolution of the distinctions between Jew
and Greek as well as male and female to feature an equality of persons
as brothers and sisters in Christ. Thus, the third division, "no longer
slave or free" is open to the possibility that Paul also tried to actualize
the dissolution of that division as well. 1 Cor 7:21 speaks to his keen
awareness of the sufferings slaves felt about the ignominy of their state.
As stated above, in the light of Paul's teaching, 1 Cor 7:22 reminds the
community that everyone is a slave, a slave of Christ. This erases any
lingering smugness over the social status of being "free," as superior to
actual slaves. Only in the Letter to Philemon does Paul takes on the
personal problem of the slave-free issue up close, in the heated situation
of a slave who has run away from a baptized Christian slave owner and
who in that renegade action met Paul and received baptism. The other
six undisputed letters of Paul address policies and principles that answer
a variety of questions. Here, Paul himself is the one involved with the
transformed slave and must now face down Philemon's ingrained and
socially recognized right to discipline his renegade slave as he sees fit. The
manner in which Paul first compliments Philemon and then, as discussed
earlier, reminds him of the obedience gives every indication of Paul's
awareness of the conventions he is challenging, the enormity of what he
is asking of Philemon. If it were only a plea to be kind, his pressing on
his authority would not be expected to be so constant and the coercive
language for Philemon's acceptance not so pronounced. Also, as noted
earlier, Paul's decision to create a public audience by greeting the leaders
and the church as listeners indicates the degree to which Paul dares not
allow Philemon the idea that he may make whatever decision he pleases
and be in communion with the church, of which Paul is the founder. This
swing between compliment and coercive reminder better fits a situation

where Paul is nervous that what he asks runs the risk of being understood as an option, not an obligation. In v. 16, Paul demands that Philemon regard Onesimus as a slave no longer, but as far more, a beloved brother. The emphasis on "in the flesh" as well as "in the Lord" conveys the idea that now Onesimus has joined this family and must be seen as an actual brother. Why else would Paul care to stipulate that the brotherhood was not merely "spiritual" but actual? Finally, v. 17 is where Paul sets out a test for Philemon, one that will show unequivocally whether he shares Paul's vision, the new reality that comes with baptism, the kinship that replaces the world's divisions. With the whole church listening, he writes in v. 17, "So if you consider me your partner, welcome him as you would welcome me." The test is extremely practical. Carolyn Osiek explains:

> What Philemon is to prepare for Paul is a *xenia* usually understood here as lodging (as in Acts 28:23), but its meaning is broader: a hospitable reception with all the amenities that good hospitality entails.[64]

This is attached to his previous expression of surety that Philemon will do even more than Paul says. Note the addition "One thing more, prepare a guest room for me, for I am hoping through your prayers to be granted to you" (v. 22). Thus the welcome of Onesimus and the welcome of Paul may be close to each other, and according to v. 17, both welcomes should be the same. In *Entertaining Angels: Early Christian Hospitality in its Mediterranean Setting*,[65] Andrew Arterbury draws from an exhaustive source of ancient literature, both Jewish and non-Jewish, to itemize features of hospitality just for strangers. Of course, one must allow for more intimacy and genuine emotion in the welcome if the person who arrives is a returning relative or dear friend: the host goes out to welcome the visitor; after a small exchange in conversation; the guest is invited into the house and often the host would lead the person in by the hand; the host makes arrangements for the traveler to have a bath, or depending on the circumstances, to have servants wash the guest's feet; the host seats the guest at the table and provides a meals which is often extravagant; the host provides lodging; the host takes care of the traveler's animal; the guest is often offered new clothes; entertainment is often provided;

---

[64] Carolyn Osiek, *Philippians; Philemon*, ANTC (Nashville, Tenn.: Abingdon, Press, 2000), 142. For this reference, thanks to Andrew Arterbury, *Entertaining Angels: Early Christian Hospitality in its Mediterranean Setting* (Sheffield, U.K.: University of Sheffield, 2005), 103.

[65] For the Arterbury reference, see previous note.

and as the guest leaves the host often supplies material goods to help the person on their way.[66]

These are the elements that will surely be offered to Paul when he arrives, and as we see, Paul announces he will soon be with them (v. 22). When one considers the usual elements of hospitality summarized by Arterbury, such a welcome would be completely incompatible with a returning renegade slave or, indeed, any slave at all. Thus, Paul's actual promise of an imminent visit provides the immediate model of how Onesimus is to be welcomed. If Philemon really shares Paul's understanding of the power of baptism, then he will be able to see Onesimus no longer as a slave, but as a beloved brother. The old relationship is over. Scholarly questions as to whether Paul is asking for Onesimus' manumission miss the point: Paul has just told Philemon that Onesimus is no longer a slave. Baptism into Christ resulted in the manumission of Onesimus. The question is whether Philemon will accept that truth and show he endorses it. Paul is not asking for virtuous mercy for Onesimus but the recognition and acceptance of his new brother in the flesh and in the Lord, as the community waits for the παρουσία of the Lord.

---

[66] Ibid., 182–186. Many of these elements are seen, for example, in the Lukan parable of the Prodigal Son (Lk 15:11–32) where the father receives the returning boy: "But while he was still far off, his father saw him, had compassion; he ran and put his arms around him and kissed him" (v. 20); "Then the son said to him, 'Father I have sinned against heaven and against you; I am not longer worthy to be called your son'" (v. 21); "But the father said to his slaves, 'Quickly bring a new robe—the best one, and put it on him; put a ring on his finger and sandals on his feet'" (v. 22); "get the fatted calf and kill it, and let us eat and celebrate" (v. 23); and "when he [the older son] came and approached the house, he heard music and dancing" (v. 25b).

THE GOD TRANSFORMED:
GRECO-ROMAN LITERARY ANTECEDENTS
TO THE INCARNATION

Lawrence DiPaolo, Jr.

This article sets out to trace the language of transformation in Greco-Roman religious literature from the time of Homer to the first century of the Common Era.[1] It is the contention of the author that both the manner by which a god was transformed (the method of transformation) as well as the end stage of the transformation as it is described in the Greco-Roman religious literary corpus is the proper literary antecedent for understanding similar descriptions in the material normally designated as Christ Hymns in the New Testament.

Introduction

I would like to begin, if I may, with a story. In Herodotus' *Histories* (written sometime between 446 and 425 BCE) we find this particularly odd vignette in which he recounts a somewhat embarrassing public spectacle surrounding the return of the disgraced tyrant of Athens, Pisistratus (546–527 BCE):

> The Greeks have never been simpletons; for centuries past they have been distinguished from other nations by superior wits; and of all Greeks the Athenians are allowed to be the most intelligent: yet it was at the Athenians' expense that this ridiculous trick was played. In the village of Paeania there was a handsome woman called Phye, nearly six feet tall, whom they fitted out in a suit of armor and mounted in a chariot; then, after getting her to pose in the most striking attitude, they drove into Athens, where messengers who had preceded them were already, according to their instructions, talking to the people and urging them to welcome Pisistratus back, because the goddess Athene herself had shown him extraordinary honour and was bringing him home to her own acropolis. They spread

---

[1] Portions of this article originally appeared in my book, *Hymn Fragments Embedded in the New Testament: Hellenistic Jewish and Greco-Roman Parallels* (New York: Edwin Mellen Press, 2008).

this nonsense all over the town, and it was not long before rumour reached the outlying villages that Athene was bringing Pisistratus back, and both villagers and townsfolk, convinced that the woman Phye was indeed the goddess, offered her prayers and received Psistratus with open arms.[2]

Placing the contempt that Herodotus held for the Athenians aside, this story illustrates that, at least in the countryside of Athens in the sixth century BCE, the idea that a goddess could appear to mortals was a real one. The belief in the transformation of a god or goddess into a form recognizable to humans was part of the religious landscape of classical Greece and it was an idea which had a long literary provenance. Even at this relatively late date in the Greek religious tradition of the sixth century BCE, assuming the presences of portions of the pantheon as early as the second millennium BCE, we see a people convinced, albeit mistakenly, that a goddess had dwelled among them. For the common Greeks, the idea of the incarnation of a divinity, the idea that a member of the Olympian pantheon could dwell among them, was real. Granted, the philosophically minded Greeks ascribed such stories to a mythological age or to the "lies of the poets."[3] Yet, when one examines the breadth of the literary evidence concerning how the Greeks and later the Romans described their incarnate divinities, we see that in addition to this being an idea which permeated religious thought from the time of Homer to Christ, it was also an idea that was expressed differently throughout time. We cannot expect the words used by Hesiod to describe an incarnate god to be as applicable when someone like Plutarch takes up the topic some eight hundred years later. This article will examine how the language of transformation in regard to the incarnation of divinities changed over time in the Greek and Roman religious literature leading up to the first century CE. Starting with Homer and Hesiod and working up to and slightly beyond the time of composition of the New Testament, we will see how both the Greeks and Romans modified the ways they described the incarnation of divinities over time. We will also show how these depictions of incarnate divinities, especially those in the Hellenistic period, are decidedly similar to what we see in the Christ hymns which deal with the Incarnation of Christ (Philippians 2:6–7, John 1:14, and 1 Timothy 3:16). It is the contention of the author

---

[2] Herodotus, *The Histories*, trans. Aubrey de Sélincourt (Middlesex, England: Penguin Books, 1972), 1.61.

[3] Plato, *The Republic*, trans. Paul Shorey, LCL 237, Rev. ed. (Cambridge, Mass.: Harvard University Press, 1930), 377d.

that depictions of incarnate divinities in Hellenistic and Greco-Roman literature, both religious and secular, were the most probable font for the images of the Incarnate Christ that we have in the New Testament.

The God in Human Form

Although it seems almost too obvious to mention, the Greeks, from their earliest known writings, assumed their divinities existed primarily in human form. Whether the god or goddess changed this primary form into something non-human (normally some animal or in the case of Zeus a meteorological occurrence) never detracted from the belief that, on Mt. Olympus, the family of gods were decidedly human in appearance as we see in this excerpt from the opening chapter of Hesiod's *Theogony*:[4]

> From the Heliconian Muses let us begin to sing, who hold the great and holy mount of Helicon, and dance on soft feet about the deep-blue spring and the altar of the almighty son of Cronos, and, when they have washed their tender bodies in Permessus or in the Horse's Spring or Olmeius, make their fair, lovely dances upon highest Helicon and move with vigorous feet. Thence they arise and go abroad by night, veiled in thick mist, and utter their song with lovely voice, praising Zeus the aegis-holder, and queenly Hera of Argos who walks on golden sandals, and the daughter of Zeus the aegis-holder bright-eyed Athena, and Phoebus Apollo, and Artemis who delights in arrows, and Poseidon the earth holder who shakes the earth, and revered Themis, and quick-glancing Aphrodite, and Hebe with the crown of gold, and fair Dione, Leto, Iapetus, and Cronos the crafty counselor, Eos, and great Helius, and bright Selene, Earth, too, and great Oceanus, and dark Night, and the holy race of all the other deathless ones that are for ever.[5]

In this, one of our earliest examples of Greek literature, we see gods who have children, have bodies with which to dance, sing, give praise, walk, and shake the earth. There is no question that they are of a different substance than humankind, their deathless nature attests to this. But they are, at least in terms of their form, appearance, and actions, decidedly human. Granted, the gods of the Greeks and Romans could take other forms as the situation dictated but this was done normally (at least in the case of Zeus) when the god was acting decidedly less divinely than

---

[4] Unless otherwise indicated all translations are from the LCL volumes.

[5] Hesiod, *Theogony*, in *Homeric Hymns and Homerica*, trans. Hugh G. Evelyn-White, LCL 57 (Cambridge, Mass.: Harvard University Press, 1977), 1.4–21.

normal. Often, in the case of Zeus in pursuit of one of his many amorous conquests, the thunder god would assume various forms to obtain the object of his desires. Whether in the form of a bull or swan or any other number of countless metamorphoses, the father of the gods regularly changed his human form for another, more often than not the form of a powerful or majestic animal in an attempt to secure his prey.

Far more common, however, is the transformation of a god or more often goddess into a form recognizable as a human one. The gods of the Greeks and the Romans more often than not chose to take the form of specific humans, usually to convey messages, deceive those around them or in general participate in whatever battle or intrigue lay before them. From Homer to Virgil, the gods of the Greek and Roman pantheon often descended from Olympus to appear in the guise most comfortable to human observers such as a trusted friend, a beloved relative, a comrade in arms, or a non-descript stranger. The manner by which this transformation is described in Greek and later Latin is a complex one and it is to this examination that we now turn.

Homer

The epic poet Homer often recounted how a god or more often a goddess would appear in the guise or form of someone else. This transformation was usually undertaken to aid in one intrigue or another in the world of humans. One notable example from the *Iliad* has the goddess Aphrodite assuming the form of an old woman:

> Then with her hand the goddess laid hold of her fragrant robe, and plucked it, and spoke to her in the likeness (ἐϊκυῖα) of an ancient dame, a woolcomber, who had been wont to card the fair wool for her when she dwelt in Lacedaemon, and who was well loved of her; in her likeness (ἐεισαμένη) fair Aphrodite spoke.[6]

What is notable about this example is that Homer is not terribly concerned with the mechanism of transformation, i.e., the "how." We are not given any detailed descriptions of how the goddess changed. He is more concerned with the effect the transformation has on the observers. This example from the *Iliad* demonstrates the somewhat fluid language of transformation employed by Homer. In the first instance, a particip-

---

[6] Homer, *Iliad: Books 1–12*, trans. A.T. Murray, LCL 170 (Cambridge, Mass.: Harvard University Press, 1924), 3.388.

ial form of ἔοικα is used, a verb which is normally translated as "to be like." In the second instance we see a participial form of εἴδω, a verb normally translated as "to be seen." The use of a form of εἴδω to describe appearance of transformed gods is quite common in Homer's descriptions of Athena such as when she takes the form of Phoenix,[7] Mentor,[8] Dymas' daughter,[9] or the form of one of Alkinoos' servants.[10] On occasion, however, Homer deviates from using solely a form of εἴδω and uses the aforementioned ἔοικα as in the second part of the example above. A similar example occurs when Odysseus, finally back home in Ithaca, again encounters Athena in the guise of a beautiful woman:

> Then she took the form of a woman (δέμας δ' ἤϊκτο γυναικὶ), fair, stately, and wise, "He must be indeed a shifty and deceitful person," said she, "who could surpass you in all manner of craft."[11]

As with the previous example, which used this form of ἔοικα, i.e. to be like, Homer has given a hint at a somewhat less elastic meaning, i.e. the god no longer simply looks like but *is* alike in form to someone else.[12] One, however, would not wish to push this interpretation too far as both terms seem to be suitably elastic to allow for various interpretations.

The Homeric Hymn to Demeter

Written at roughly the same time as the *Iliad* and the *Odyssey*,[13] the *Homeric Hymn to Demeter* also describes a god in the state of transformation. This hymn in dactylic hexameter is important to our study for as it sheds light on the inherent difficulty in seeing the true "form" of a god

---

[7] Homer, *Iliad: Books 13–24*, trans. A.T. Murray, LCL 171 (Cambridge, Mass.: Harvard University Press, 1924), 17.550.

[8] Homer, *Odyssey: Books 1–12*, trans. A.T. Murray, LCL 104 (Cambridge, Mass.: Harvard University Press, 1925), 2.393.

[9] Homer, *Od.*, 6.15.

[10] Homer, *Od.*, 8.1.

[11] Homer, *Odyssey: Books 13–24*, trans. A.T. Murray, LCL 105 (Cambridge, Mass.: Harvard University Press, 1925), 13.288.

[12] W.B. Stanford has commented that this example is particularly interesting in that this particular transformation could indicate the "true" form of Athena, i.e. the young woman *sans* her armor as in Archaic Greek art. See W.M. Stanford, ed., *The Odyssey of Homer* (London: Macmillan and New York: St. Martin's Press, 1965), 210, nn. 288, 289.

[13] Apostolos N. Athanassakis, *The Homeric Hymns* (Baltimore: Johns Hopkins University Press, 1984), xii–xiii.

or in this case goddess. In one of the first descriptions of the appearance of Demeter we are told the following:

> There the daughters of Celeus, son of Eleusis, saw her as they were coming for easy drawn water, to carry it in pitchers of bronze to their dear father's house: Four were they and like goddesses in the flower of their girlhood, Callidice and Cleisidice and lovely Demo and Callithoë who was the eldest of them all. They knew her not-for the gods are not easily discerned by mortals (χαλεποὶ δὲ θεοὶ θνητοῖσιν ὁρᾶσθαι).[14]

What is important about this passage is the idea that the true form of a god or goddess is something not easily perceived by the human observer. It was an a priori assumption during an encounter with a deity that there is and always will be in the mind of the observer a difficulty in terms of perception, that is to say, whatever the "true" form of a god or goddess might be, humans would be invariably unable to perceive it. Thus, what humans see when they gaze upon Demeter, in this case an old woman, is not the true form of the goddess but simply an appearance. We shall see this ambiguity in terms of human perception often.

The Homeric Hymn to Demeter gives us yet another early example of a god or goddess transforming when Metaneira, the mother of Demophoön, surprises the goddess as she thrusts the infant into the purifying fire:

> Thus speaking, the goddess changed her size and appearance (μέγεθος καὶ εἶδος ἄμειψε) thrusting off old age. Beauty breathed about her and from her sweet robes a delicious fragrance spread; a light beamed far out from the goddesses' immortal skin, and her golden hair flowed over her shoulders. The well built house flooded with her radiance like lightening.[15]

In this passage we are confronted with a more active idea of transformation through the use of the verb ἀμείβω, meaning to change or exchange. We are now truly encountering not the appearance of transformation but the *mechanics* of transformation, i.e., the "how." The verb is paired with εἶδος, normally translated as that which is seen, form, shape or figure, but here we are confronted with a goddess actually changing here appearance. We are again dealing with the *appearance* of the goddess, and, as can be expected, no mention is made of her "true" form. However, there is a

---

[14] Hesiod, *The Homeric Hymn to Demeter*, in *Homeric Hymns and Homerica*, trans. Hugh G. Evelyn-White, LCL 57 (Cambridge, Mass.: Harvard University Press, 1977), ll. 105–111.

[15] Helene P. Foley, ed., *The Homeric Hymn to Demeter* (Princeton: Princeton University Press, 1994), ll. 275–280.

subtle shift in this transformation relative to the examples from the *Iliad* and the *Odyssey* in that the author of the *Homeric Hymns* is ascribing a greater deal of activity to the deity, namely, it is the deity who changes her appearance.

Euripides

In the works of Euripides (480–406 BCE), we see a similar approach to the god taking human form as we saw in the *Homeric Hymns* with the use of verbs which convey greater action and describe the transformation. We see this most clearly in the following famous example from *The Bacchae* in the opening lines where the god, Dionysus, recounts his origins:

> I am come, the son of Zeus, to this Theban land, Dionysis, to whom the daughter of Kadmos gave birth, Semele, midwived by lightening born fire. And having changed my form from god to mortal (μορφὴν δ' ἀμείψας ἐκ θεοῦ βροτησιάν) I am here at the streams of Dirke and the water of Ismenus.[16]

A similar preference for words which convey action is seen in Euripides' *Helen*, where the heroine similarly recounts her parentage:

> For me, not fameless is my fatherland Sparta: My sire was Tyndarus. The tale telleth that to my mother Zeus flew, who had stolen the likeness of a swan (κύκνου μορφώματ' ὄρνιθος λαβών), and fleeing from a chasing eagle, wrought by guile his pleasure, if the tale be true.[17]

Euripides, unlike Homer and closer to the usage in the *Homeric Hymn to Demeter*, seems to prefer greater action (λαβών, ἀμείψας) in recounting the transition from god to mortal or god to animal. Whereas Homer most often prefers words which at least imply the act of observation by another (εἴδω), more often than not in the middle voice, Euripides stresses the action of the god and emphasizes the transition from one state to another. This may stem from the necessity of crafting dialogue for the stage or may simply be the preference of the great playwright. Whether the transformation is actively described or not, however, the end result is always the same; it is simply the outward form or appearance that is transformed. What is clear is that in the period from Homer, Hesiod

---

[16] Euripides, *Bacchae*, ed. Richard Seaford (Warminster, England: Aris & Phillips, Ltd., 1996), ll. 1–4.

[17] Euripides, *Helen*, trans. David Kovacs, vol. 5, LCL 11 (Cambridge, Mass.: Harvard University Press, 2002), ll. 16–21.

and the Homeric Hymns to the time of Euripides, there seem to have been two relatively complimentary ways of describing the transformation of a god or goddess. One recounted that the divinity simple looked like or appeared as something else (*The Iliad* and *The Odyssey*) or one described the god or goddess taking or exchanging (*The Homeric Hymns* and Euripides) their form or appearance for that of another.

Apollodorus, Isidorus, Plutarch, Pausanias

When Apollodorus recounts the same myth as the one found in Euripides' *Helen* in his *Library* sometime in the second century BC we see yet another way of describing the transformation of Zeus from god to swan in that the author uses the aorist passive participle from ὁμοιόω, ὁμοιοθέντος meaning to be made like or be like:

> But Zeus in the form of a swan consorted with Leda (Διὸς δὲ Λήδᾳ συνελθόντος ὁμοιωθέντος κύκνῳ) ... But some say that Helen was a daughter of Nemesis and Zeus; for that she, flying from the arms of Zeus changed herself into a goose (εἰς χῆνα τὴν μορφὴν μεταβαλεῖν) but Zeus in his turn took the likeness of a swan (ὁμοιωθέντα δὲ καὶ Δία κύκνῳ σθνελθεῖν) and so he enjoyed her.[18]

As with the previous examples, we are still dealing with a god (and in this case also a goddess) transforming themselves. However, Apollodorus has described the transformation somewhat differently than his literary forbearers opting for participial formations of ὁμοιόω to convey his meaning in addition to the by now familiar formulations of transformation (μορφὴν μεταβαλεῖν) seen previously.

One of the more interesting examples of a god, or in this case god-king, assuming mortal form comes from the *Hymns of Isidorus*.[19] The author of these hymns, ca. 80 BCE, recounts in primitive hexameter the salvific acts attributed to Isis. In the fourth hymn, however, the author digresses from praise of Isis to laud a certain Porramanres, a god-king considered to have been the XIIth Dynasty Pharaoh, son of Senosis, who was the center of a popular folk cult in the Fayyum area during the Ptolemies:[20]

---

[18] Apollodorus, *The Library*, vol. 2, trans. J.G. Frazer, LCL (Cambridge, Mass.: Harvard University Press, 1921), 3.10.7.

[19] Vanderlip, "The Hymn to Porramanres," in *Four Greek Hymns of Isidorus* (Toronto: A.M. Hakkert, 1972), ll. 7–9, 33–34.

[20] Vanderlip, *Four Greek Hymns of Isidorus*, 66–67, n. 6.

A certain one, they say was born (γενέσθαι) a divine king of Egypt, he appeared (ἐξεφάνη) on earth as Lord of All the World, rich, righteous and omnipotent (lines 7–9).

When the Egyptians say his name (in their language) they call (him) Porramanres, the Great, Deathless (ἀθάνατον) (lines 33–34).

What is interesting about this example, notwithstanding the "birth" of a god as well as his "deathless" nature, is the way in which the god appears in the mortal realm. We have an example in which the entry of this personage onto the scene of the mortal world is expressed via a derivative of the Greek verb φαίνω, here meaning appeared or manifested, a decidedly different way of describing the appearance of a god than we have seen previously.

As we get closer to the time of the writing of the New Testament, we find that the variety in describing the transformation from god to mortal, whether human or animal, has continued unabated. It must be noted, however, that, with the later Greek writers, one gets a distinct impression: however they describe the transformation, the authors regarded all such miraculous occurrences as pure fable or mere superstition. In each case greater emphasis seems to be placed on the perceptions of those relaying the information, perceptions that each author is clear to assign to someone else. Plutarch (45–125 CE) in recounting the divine origins of Alexander describes the process in this manner:

> However, after his vision, as we are told, Philip sent Chaeron of Megalopolis to Delphi, by whom an oracle was brought him from Apollo, who bade him sacrifice to Ammon and hold that god in greatest reverence, but told him he was to lose that one of his eyes which he had applied to the chink in the door when he espied the god, in the form of a serpent (ἐν μορφῇ δράκοντος), sharing the couch of his wife.[21]

Plutarch, although using the common word for form (μορφή), nevertheless fails to recount the actual transformation of the god. Pausanias, writing in the early to mid-second century CE, recounts the similar circumstances surrounding the birth of a little known Messenian, Aristomenes:

> Of the young men who had grown up in Messenia the best and most numerous were round Andania, and among them was Aristomenes, who to this day is worshipped as a hero among the Messenians. They think that even the circumstances of his birth were notable, for they assert that a

---

[21] Plutarch, *Alexander*, in *Lives*, vol. 7, trans. Bernadotte Perrin, LCL (Cambridge, Mass.: Harvard University Press, 1919), 3.4–6.

spirit or a god united with his mother, Nicoteleia, in the form of a serpent (δράκοντι εἰκασμένον σθγγενέσθαι λέγουσι).[22]

Pausanias, perhaps faintly nechoing Homer, has opted for a somewhat more subtle depiction, choosing a form of εἰκάζω which means to make like or portray. Finally, Dio Cassius (ca. 165–229 CE) relegates reports of the miraculous birth of the future Emperor to the fevered incubations of his mother in the temple of Asclepius. The transformation of the god into the form of a snake is not detailed, simply alluded to by recounting the perceptions of Attia, the mother of Augustus:

> He was influenced largely by Attia's emphatic declaration that the youth had been engendered by Apollo; for while sleeping once in his temple, she said, she thought she had intercourse with a serpent, and it was this that caused her at the end of the allotted time to bear a son.[23]

Latin Writers: Suetonius, Virgil, and Ovid

We would be remiss in our investigation if we did not examine, however briefly, some of the Latin sources of our time period. Historians like Suetonius (69–122 CE) often describe gods in human or animal form, yet one gets the impression that they treat the occurrences as mostly hearsay. In recounting the circumstances surrounding the birth of Augustus, Suetonius describes his divine birth in this manner:

> I have read the following story in the books of Asclepias of Mendes entitled Theologumena. When Attia had come in the middle of the night to the solemn service of Apollo, she had her litter set down in the temple and fell asleep, while the rest of the matrons also slept. On a sudden [sic] a serpent glided up to her and shortly went away. When she awoke, she purified herself, as if after the embraces of her husband, and at once there appeared on her body a mark in colours like a serpent, and she could never get rid of it; so that presently she ceased ever to go to the public baths. In the tenth month after that Augustus was born and was therefore regarded as the son of Apollo. Atia too, before she gave him birth, dreamed that her vitals were borne up to the stars and spread over the whole extent of land and sea, while Octavius dreamed that the sun rose from Attia's womb.[24]

---

[22] Pausanias, *Description of Greece*, vol. 2, trans. W.H.S. Jones and H.A. Omerod, LCL 188 (Cambridge, Mass.: Harvard University Press), 4.14.7 (Jones / Omerod, LCL).

[23] Dio Cassius, *Roman History*, vol. 2, trans. Earnest Cary, LCL (Cambridge, Mass.: Harvard University Press, 1955), 15.2.

[24] Suetonius, Augustus, in *The Lives of the Caesars*, vol. 1, trans. J.C. Rolfe and K.R. Bradley, LCL 31 (Cambridge, Mass.: Harvard University Press, 1914), 94.4.

Suetonius does not recount that Apollo in the form of a serpent slept with Attia the mother of Augustus. Instead, he relates that, as a result of a visitation of a serpent in a dream and a subsequent mark on her body, the mother of the future Emperor believed she had been visited by Apollo. Later Latin historians like Suetonius tend to eschew language which implies the transfer from one state to another by simply stating that individuals thought or simply believed that they had been touched by a god in another form. When we turn to the Latin epic poets such as Virgil and Ovid, however, we see similar language to that which we have seen before, namely, an emphasis on the active transformation of a god from one state to another. As both authors were conscientiously modeling themselves on earlier Greek models, this should surprise no one.

Virgil's *Aeneid*, written between 29–19 BCE, in telling the exploits of Aeneas on his journey home after the Trojan War, also recounts gods taking human form:

> Then he changes the fashion of his features to those of aged Butes (*Forma tum vertitur oris antiquum in Buten*), who aforetime was armour-bearer to Dardan Anchises, trusty watcher at his gate.[25]

Using a form of *verto*, "to turn up, turn, turn back, direct," Virgil opts for a similar way of describing this transformation as some of the more active depictions examined above. The change is clearly in the hand of the god.

Finally with Ovid, we find perhaps a work uniquely suited to our current task. It is an epic poem which is concerned expressly with transformations from one state to the other. In *Metamorphoses*, written between 2–8 CE, we find countless examples of gods changing into mortal and animal form as well as mortals changing into gods, fertile ground for our investigation. In his retelling of the myth of Apollo's servitude we read:

> There, Apollo saw Laomedon building the foundations of the new city of Troy. The great undertaking prospering with difficulty, and demanding no little [sic] resources, he, and Neptune, trident-bearing father of the swelling sea, put on mortal form (*mortalem induitur forma*), and built the walls of the city for the Phrygian king for an agreed amount in gold.[26]

As with the transformation in Virgil, the emphasis is on the action of the god who "puts on, assumes, or dresses in" the form of a mortal.

---

[25] Virgil, *Aeneid*, vol. 2, ed. G.P. Goold, trans. H.R. Fairclough, LCL 64 (Cambridge, Mass.: Harvard University Press, 1965), 9.645.

[26] Ovid, *Metamorpheses*, vol. 4, ed. G.P. Goold, trans. F.J. Miller, LCL 43 (Cambridge, Mass.: Harvard University Press, 1916), 11.196–197.

The Language of Transformation: New
Testament Hymnic Fragments Compared

The language that surrounded the transformation of a god in classical literature can be described as decidedly ambiguous. Authors from Homer to Ovid never really came down on one side or the other as to the final state of the god post-transformation. In general, the classical authors were content to describe the transformed god as something that only "seemed like" or "looked like" this new form, whether human or animal. In the later classical period with Euripides, even though the transformation takes on a more active timbre with the use of words such as μετα-βαλεῖν, "to throw into a different position," we are still confronted with simply the form of the god or goddess as we the audience perceives it. When we turn to our examples from the New Testament, we can see that these authors as well left a certain amount of ambiguity in their depictions of the transformation process by which a God became man.

Philippians 2:7b

ἐν ὁμοιώματι ἀνθρώπον γενόμενος καὶ σχήματι εὑρεθεὶς ὡς ἀνθρώπος

The author of the Philippians hymnic fragment describes the "likeness" of man as the end result of the transformation similarly to the way Apollodorus described the transformation of Zeus (ὁμοιώματι/ ὁμοιωθέν-τος). Similarly, it is the outward appearance (σχήματι) in which Christ is found as man. In both cases, the elasticity of the language concerning what exactly has occurred is maintained as we are not dealing unambiguously with the transformation of the god, simply how that likeness is perceived by the onlookers.

1 Timothy 3:16b

Ὃς ἐφανερώθη ἐν σαρκί ...

The author of the hymnic fragment found in 1 Tm 3:16 makes use of a similar verb (φαίνω) to describe the manifestation of Christ as what we find in Isidorus. As with the *Hymn to Isidorus*, we are dealing here with the "manifestation" of the god alone, and "manifestation" normally deals in the realm of the perception of the onlookers, preserving the ambiguity. Yet, this ambiguity is tempered to a great extent by other words used in close proximity to the descriptions of transformation, and it is here where our New Testament authors begin to diverge from their Greek and Roman literary forbears to a great extent. Indeed, here the end stage of flesh, σαρκί, is something almost unheard of in classical literature.

This move toward a more concrete language of transformation is in two places in particular in the New Testament. Both Phil 2:7b and John 1:14 tend to eschew the language of ambiguity by the use of γίνομαι, to be, in describing the transformation of Christ. In the case of Phil 2:7b, γίνομαι is used near the aforementioned ὁμοιώματι ("being in the likeness of man") and allows room for interpretation; there is, however, the sense of a greater existential element to the description—we are at least approaching the idea of "being" as opposed to "seeming." In the second instance, John 1:14, we have the decidedly theologically complex "the word became flesh" (ὁ λόγος ἐγένετο σὰρξ), which also opts for the more concrete γίνομαι and, unlike the Philippians example, does not combine this word with any of our aforementioned elastic terms such as ὁμοιώματι ("likeness"). Our aforementioned example, 1 Tim 3:16b, similarly pairs an elastic term such as ἐφανερώθη (was manifested) alongside the decidedly inelastic term ἐν σαρκί (in flesh).

What then can we say about these descriptions? It appears that our New Testament authors, in describing the transformation of Christ from God to man drew upon language common to the Greek literary tradition yet modified these descriptions of transformation through either the use of γίνομαι which tempers the ambiguity greatly or by describing the endpoint of the transformation as flesh (σὰρξ), which leaves little doubt as to the final outcome of the transformation. The authors of the New Testament use language similar to what we have seen in Greco-Roman works that describe transforming gods yet add something new, something different, something subtle, but which changes the meaning greatly from what had come before. Some of the elasticity of meaning attached to the transformation has been preserved yet things are decidedly more real, slightly less ambiguous as we approach the end stage of the transformation.

In describing this new Christian reality of the incarnation, the New Testament authors stood squarely in the literary tradition, which had described transforming gods for over a millennium. Yet, when confronted with the new reality, the reality of the god who dwelled among them, they made it clear that they were not simply describing a vision of a divinity but one who lived along side them in the flesh.

THE JOHANNINE LITERATURE AND GNOSTICISM:
NEW LIGHT ON THEIR RELATIONSHIP?

Urban C. von Wahlde

Past Attempts to Articulate the Relation
of the Gospel of John to Gnosticism[1]

Throughout early Christianity, the Gospel of John held a special attraction for Gnostics. In the past, this has been regularly espoused by scholars and explained in a variety of ways. The most famous of the proposals seeking to explain this relationship was that of R. Bultmann, who was convinced that a major component of the Gospel was a series of discourses that had been taken over from a "Gnostic discourse source" by the Evangelist and modified in such a way as to be, in the end, anti-Gnostic.[2] The Gnosticism that Bultmann spoke of was not the "Hellenized Gnosticism" found in many of the Nag Hammadi documents, but a reconstructed, pre-Christian Gnosticism, mainly on the basis of the then recently-discovered Mandean and Manichean documents.[3] In this view, the background of the Gospel was at the same time Gnostic and anti-Gnostic.[4]

Bultmann brought this view to bear in the famous commentary he wrote on the Gospel of John (1941). This commentary went through many editions in German before being translated into English (1971).[5] In

---

[1] This essay is dedicated to Tom Tobin, S.J., a tremendous example of a first-rate scholar but also a thoughtful colleague and a close friend throughout our twenty-nine years together at Loyola University.

[2] As the title of his first discussion indicates, Bultmann made use of the then-recently discovered Mandean and Manichean documents as the basis of his analysis. See his "Die Bedeutung der neuerschlossenen mandäischen und manichäischen Quellen für das Verständis des Johannesevangeliums," *ZNW* 24 (1925): 100–146.

[3] M. Lidzbarski, *Ginza: Der Schatz oder das Große Buch der Mandäer* (Göttingen: Vandenhoeck & Ruprecht; Leipzig: J.C. Hinrichs, 1925).

[4] R. Bultmann, *Primitive Christianity in Its Contemporary Setting* (New York: Meridian Books, 1956).

[5] R. Bultmann, *The Gospel of John* (ET; Philadelphia, Pa.: Westminster, 1971).

it, Bultmann claimed that the discourses of the Gospel were Gnostic in orientation and had been derived from a Gnostic source.[6] The discourses were taken over by the evangelist (i.e. the author of the Gospel) and were "Christianized" and thus made to refer to Jesus rather than to the Gnostic god. All of this was done in order to lure Gnostics away from their viewpoint and to show them that Christianity could fulfill their hopes even better than Gnosticism. Although this view held sway among scholars, particularly German ones, for decades, scholarship eventually came to view the position of Bultmann as too extreme. No only was there no actual text that Bultmann could point to as the "source" from which these discourses had derived but the texts Bultmann did refer to were Mandean and came from a time much later than the first century. Nevertheless, although Bultmann's specific proposal was abandoned, the seeming affinities between the Gospel and Gnosticism continued to attract scholars.

In the 1970s, after the widespread dissemination of the Nag Hammadi documents, the conviction that the Fourth Gospel was Gnostic or influenced by Gnosticism experienced something of a rebirth and, in some respects flourished, even though the documents from Nag Hammadi were recognized to be later copies of documents which themselves were almost certainly post-Christian.[7] For example, Louise Schatz declared that the Gospel of John was the first document that showed how Gnosticism absorbed and articulated the Christian message. In Schatz's view, the Jesus of the Gospel "is to be called without restriction a Gnostic revealer."[8] Kurt Rudolph, in his masterful survey of Gnosticism, believed that the Gospel was not immune to Gnostic influence.[9]

In the 1980s, Raymond E. Brown became the most famous proponent of another approach to the question of the relationship between Gnosticism and the Gospel. In 1981, Brown published a commentary on

---

[6] For a succinct summary-discussion of Bultmann's approach, see E. Haenchen, *John 1*, Hermeneia (Philadelphia: Fortress, 1984), 34–37. For a more detailed discussion, see D.M. Smith, *The Composition and Order of the Fourth Gospel: Bultmann's Literary Theory* (New Haven: Yale University Press, 1965).

[7] See, for example, the dating proposed by B. Pearson, *Ancient Gnosticism: Traditions and Literature* (Minneapolis: Fortress, 2007).

[8] L. Schatz, *Der Glaubende und die Feindliche Welt. Beobachtungen zum Gnostichen Dualismus und seiner Bedeutung für Paulus und das Joahnnesevangelium.* WMANT 37 (Neukirchen-Vluyn: Neukirchener Verlag, 1970); quoted by K. Rudolph, *Gnosis* (ET; Edinburgh: T&T Clark, 1983), 159.

[9] See, for example, Rudolph, *Gnosis*, 159.

the Johannine Epistles that is now generally accepted as one of the most thorough and most thought-provoking yet composed. In it, he suggested another relationship between the Gospel and Gnosticism. He argued that, at the time of the writing of 1 John, the community was experiencing a schism. One group proposed an "orthodox" view of the tradition while the other group proposed a more radical interpretation. According to Brown, this second group left the community and moved toward becoming a Gnostic movement.[10] Brown summarized his own view by proposing "that the adversaries eventually *became* Gnostics and, indeed, that their Johannine background may have catalyzed the development of early Gnostic systems."[11] In this view, it is not the Gospel itself that has Gnostic elements but rather one group within the Johannine community interpreted the Gospel in a way that had Gnostic affinities and eventually drifted into Gnosticism.

In the 1990's, a third approach to the question of the Gospel and Gnosticism emerged and is exemplified in the work of Pheme Perkins. In her book *Gnosticism and the New Testament*, Perkins devoted two chapters to a discussion of similarities between the Fourth Gospel and Gnosticism.[12] In her discussion of discourse material, Perkins pointed out similarities between the discourses of the Fourth Gospel and Gnostic writings and also between the various "I am" sayings in both. Perkins argued that, in spite of the striking similarities, "the Gnostic material has developed independently of the Fourth Gospel." Nevertheless, "[r]econstruction of the sources and patterns of discourse used in Gnostic texts provides important clues about the conventions employed in the Fourth Gospel. ... Johannine discourses draw upon a tradition of Jesus' sayings as well as a style of revelation discourse that has been more extensively developed

---

[10] R.E. Brown, *The Epistles of John*. Anchor Bible 30 (Garden City: Doubleday, 1982), 55–68, 104–106.

[11] (Italics in the original.) Brown, *Epistles*, 65, goes on to express his surprise that "while second-century Gnostics used GJohn (almost to the point of appropriating it), there is no clear evidence that they drew upon I John as a source for reflection. Indeed, as I shall point out ..., I John became a tool of the orthodox church writers in their arguments again the Gnostic interpretations of GJohn. This would indicate that, whether or not he was combating proto-Gnostics, the thought of the author of I John was oriented in a direction that Gnostics could not find amenable."

[12] P. Perkins, *Gnosticism and the New Testament* (Minneapolis: Fortress, 1993). In chapter 9, Perkins discusses the dialogue form. In chapter 8, she discusses the Prologue of the Gospel and its relation to Gnosticism.

in Gnostic circles."[13] Thus for Perkins, it was not a question of Johannine
dependence upon Gnosticism—or the reverse. Rather it was a matter
of both the Gospel of John and the Gnostic documents drawing from
a common milieu but each developing differently, in distinctive ways.

In 2005, two essays were published in a volume deriving from the
Johannine seminar of the Society for New Testament Studies, both attempting to discover relationships between parts of the Gospel and various Gnostic documents. Once again Pheme Perkins explored similarities between the *Apocryphon of John* and 1 John, arguing that similarities
exist between Gnosticism and the Johannine tradition but that appropriate paradigms that would account satisfactorily for the complexity of the
relationships had not yet been articulated.[14] In the same volume, John
Turner proposed a somewhat stronger thesis of "a common history-of-
religions background for two early second century sectarian movements,
namely Johannine Christianity and ... 'Sethian Gnosticism.'"[15]

Although many other scholars have addressed the relation between
the Gospel and Gnosticism, the scholars mentioned above exhibit representative approaches to the question of this relationship. From this brief
survey it is evident that, through time, scholars have reformulated their
proposals regarding the relationship in such a way that the relationship is
seen to be less and less direct: from a belief in dependence upon Gnostic
texts to the proposal that both simply share a common milieu.

This topic has been further, and more seriously, complicated by the
fact that, as scholars have continued to understand these documents
more precisely, they have come to recognize that documents that were
previously considered to express essentially the same system of thought
are in fact quite different. The result is that the phenomenon once thought
to be homogeneous is now understood to be far from such. In its most
thorough-going form, some scholars now call into question whether
there is (or was) an actual phenomenon known as Gnosticism.[16]

---

[13] Perkins, *Gnosticism*, 141.

[14] P. Perkins, "Gnostic Revelation and Johannine Sectarianism: Reading 1 John from
the Perspective of Nag Hammadi," in *Theology and Christology in the Fourth Gospel: Essays
by the Members of the SNTS Johannine Writings Seminar*, BETL 184 (Leuven: Peeters,
2005), 245–276.

[15] J. Turner, "Sethian Gnosticism and Johannine Christianity," in *Theology and Christology in the Fourth Gospel: Essays by the Members of the SNTS Johannine Writings Seminar*, BETL 184 (Leuven: Peeters, 2005) 399–433.

[16] See, for example, M. Williams, *Rethinking "Gnosticism": An Argument for Dismantling a Dubious Category* (Princeton: Princeton University Press, 1996). Williams represents a more radical skepticism. But see also K. King, *What is Gnosticism?* (Cambridge,

Because of this on-going debate, the question also arises whether it is still possible to address, in any form, the relation of the Gospel of John and its world view to the group of documents that have traditionally be identified as Gnostic. The full range of features commonly thought to be Gnostic does not appear in any one single Gnostic document. By picking and choosing, one can find elements of similarity between the Gospel and various Gnostic documents, but a central, unifying element of thought and world view that would bring these elements into a unity is not found in the Gospel of John nor does any single document in the collection found at Nag Hammadi match closely the thought and world view of the Gospel. In its most optimistic form, it is as if one can identify various "spokes" of the Gnostic "wheel" but not the unifying "hub." Consequently no satisfactory proposal that the Gospel is somehow related, in any significant way, to Gnosticism (or to the milieu of Gnosticism) has been found.[17]

A New Perspective

In this article, I propose that another approach to this problem is possible, one that seems to offer some possibility of providing more clarity to the question of the relation between Gnosticism and the Gospel of John. If we were able to demonstrate that the thought of the Gospel does have within it not only the "spokes" but also a "hub" that explains the phenomena in question thoroughly, then recourse to Gnosticism would be no longer necessary or, I would argue, even possible. If it is possible to show that the thought of the Gospel is a coherent whole without recourse to Gnosticism and that the features of the Gospel that were previously thought to be

---

Mass.: Harvard University Press, 2003). While this question is an important one, it is also important to realize that this may be a purely modern question and that in the ancient world there may have been more toleration for diversity of viewpoints within a given group than would be considered acceptable today. This is evident in varying degrees not only in the "library" of Qumran but also in the "canon" of the New Testament itself.

[17] The second drawback to this theory, but one that is related to the first, is that scholars regularly point to other features in the Gospel that are considered to be most similar to the thought and world view of Judaism in general as well as to the sectarian documents from Qumran (SDQ) and the Testaments of the Twelve Patriarchs (T12P) in particular. How these features are to be related to and integrated with others that are said to be Gnostic is not explained. Thus scholarship has been making it more and more difficult to hope to explain the relationship between the Gospel of John and Gnosticism in any significant way.

"spokes" from the "wheel" of Gnosticism can be better accounted for in another way, then we will have perhaps laid a significant foundation for understanding in a more nuanced way the special relationship between the Gospel and Gnosticism without positing a dependence in either direction.

In a commentary I have recently finished, I have attempted to explain in detail the literary and theological development of the Johannine Gospel together with that of the three letters.[18] In it, I have proposed that the Gospel has gone through three editions in reaching its present form. Moreover, I have proposed that 1 John was written after the second edition of the Gospel and attempted to correct an interpretation of the second edition that the author of 1 John understood to be erroneous. Sometime after the writing of 1 John, the views proposed in 1 John were incorporated into the text of the Gospel. These additions, together with some additional material not directly related to the crisis,[19] gave birth to the third edition of the Gospel, i.e. the Gospel in its present form.[20]

While the first edition presents the basic narrative framework of the Gospel,[21] the second edition provides the theological core of the tradition. In it, the primary purpose of Jesus' ministry is understood to be the offering of the (eschatological) Spirit of God to those who believe in Jesus. This theology is conveyed through a series of passages composed by the second author. For example, in 1:30, John the baptizer testified that the Spirit has descended on Jesus himself. In 3:3–10, Jesus explains to Nicodemus that what is "born of the flesh is flesh and that which is born

---

[18] U.C. von Wahlde, *A Commentary on the Gospel and Letters of John*, 3 vols. (Eerdmans Critical Commentary; Grand Rapids: Eerdmans, 2010).

[19] Much of this additional material seems to have attempted to correlate the Johannine tradition with that of the Synoptics.

[20] Any analysis such as the one in the commentary is open to the accusation of attributing material on the basis of "what works." To avoid that accusation, I have provided as objective an analysis as I believe is possible of the features of the various editions. Volume 1 of the commentary is dedicated entirely to this analysis. For each edition, the characteristics are listed together with a synthetic discussion of all instances of each feature. Following this, there is a discussion of the structure of the Gospel as it appeared in that edition together with a survey of its theology. For the first edition, there are twenty-eight characteristics; for the second edition, there are thirty-four characteristics and for the third edition there are fifty-six.

[21] This narrative includes all of the miracles (designated "signs" in this edition) together with additional material constituting a complete narrative, not only of the public ministry but also the basic narrative of the Passion and Resurrection. A preliminary analysis of this material (much modified and expanded in my commentary) appeared in my *The Earliest Version of John's Gospel* (Wilmington, Del.: M. Glazier, 1989).

of the Spirit is Spirit" and that Nicodemus himself must be "born again" of the Spirit.[22] In 4:10–15, Jesus offers the Samaritan woman "living water," which we later (7:38–39) find out is an image for the Spirit. Likewise in 4:20–24, Jesus explains to the woman that to worship on Gerizim or in Jerusalem is insignificant since the true worshiper will worship God "in Spirit and truth."

In 7:37–39, on the last day of the feast of Tabernacles, Jesus proclaims to the festival crowds that he will give "living water" from his side as is predicted in Scripture and the author indicates that this "living water" refers to the Spirit which those who believe in Jesus are to receive.

In 19:30, the author of the second edition reports that, at his death, Jesus inclined his head and "gave over the Spirit." While this can refer simply to death (i.e. giving over the natural spirit), in the context, it very likely was intended to refer to the "release" of the Spirit now that Jesus had been glorified. Finally in 20:19, in the upper room on the evening of the day he rose from the dead, Jesus appears in the presence of his disciples and bestows the hoped-for Spirit upon them. This is the departure of Jesus to the Father, a departure that did not involve an understanding of the death as an atonement but only as a departure to the Father.

This brief summary may be said to reflect the "core" understanding of the ministry of Jesus in the second edition. But it is also important to recognize that this gift of the Spirit—and the prerogatives deriving from the possession of the eschatological Spirit—*were understood completely within the context of the Jewish tradition.*[23]

However, this presentation of the ministry came to be interpreted in two ways within the community and so resulted in a schism. As a result, a member of the community ("the Elder") composed the document that has come to be known as "1 John" in order to refute the views of the one group and to put forward the correct interpretation of the tradition. The author of 1 John accepted the basic thrust of the second edition but argued that it needed to be corrected in some ways and to be nuanced and clarified in others. In addition, this author, in a radical departure from previous editions, couched his understanding of the ministry of Jesus

---

[22] The words "water and" were not part of the second edition as becomes clear from the second edition's conviction that the material world is of no importance. See for example 3:6, and 4:20–24 (quoted in the text) and especially 6:63 ("The Spirit is what gives life; the flesh is useless").

[23] For a detailed defense of this view, the reader is directed to Volume 1, Part 4, Section 3, "The Background of the Presentation of the Spirit in the Second Edition".

in the worldview of apocalyptic dualism, something not present in the previous editions of the Gospel.

Sometime after the composition of 1 John, the community modified the Gospel to incorporate the correctives introduced by 1 John, but at the same time incorporating the apocalyptic world view. This resulted in the Gospel of John as we know it today.

When the three editions of the Gospel are separated and viewed individually, it becomes clear that each of the editions presents its own coherent theology, worldview, and literary structure. However, the interweaving of these features in the process of editing has resulted in the many awkward disjunctures and breaks in thought that have made interpretation of the Gospel so difficult.

My purpose in recounting something of the perspective of my commentary here is to suggest that this commentary does in fact present a view of the Gospel in which all of the material of the Gospel can be gathered consistently around three "hubs." These three hubs are the three editions and the worldview and theology characteristic of each.

I would propose that the features commonly thought to reflect a Gnostic world view can be accounted for more consistently and systematically by seeing them as prerogatives of the eschatological outpouring of God's Spirit as this is articulated within non-apocalyptic, OT Judaism and presented in the second edition of the Gospel. Moreover, because of the material introduced at the third stage of the Gospel's formation, a clear perception of the worldview of the Gospel became all the more difficult, confusion arose, and the apparent similarity to Gnosticism increased.

The Prerogatives of the Eschatological Outpouring of the Spirit

As was described above, in the second edition of the Gospel Jesus is presented as the Son endowed by the Spirit and sent by the Father to offer the eschatological Spirit to those who believe in him. According to the OT, this outpouring of the eschatological Spirit had a number of prerogatives associated with it.[24] For example, by receiving the Spirit, the individual would come to possess the very life of God. All the other prerogatives were essentially derivative of this new life. The believer, by

---

[24] These prerogatives are discussed in a more comprehensive way in Vol. 1 of my commentary. I also discussed these prerogatives in my book *The Johannine Commandments: 1 John and the Struggle for the Johannine Tradition* (Mahwah, N.J.: Paulist, 1990), 105–198.

receiving God's life would come to truly know God. The person would have no need for teaching from others but would be "taught by God." The reception of the Spirit would free the individual from past sins and so transform the person that future sin would be impossible. Because of this, the person would not come into judgment but upon death would pass immediately into a spiritual existence with God.

A Means of Proceeding

It is the purpose of this article to examine once again several aspects of the Gospel that are often thought to reflect Gnostic thought and to compare the Johannine view (distinguishing between the viewpoint in the second and third editions of the Gospel) with similar features found in Gnosticism.[25] I have selected eleven elements of the Gospel that are most often thought to reflect Gnostic thought and theology and will discuss each in what follows. This, I think, will help set the possible relationship of the Gospel to Gnosticism in a clearer light.[26]

Gnosticism as an overall phenomenon is notoriously difficult to define and the Nag Hammadi documents demonstrate well the considerable variety of forms that it can take.[27] Here I am less concerned to define the phenomenon than to discuss features found in Gnosticism that are said be paralleled in the Johannine literature. In a study such as this, it is impossible to discuss all the unique features of the various systems but it should be apparent as the study progresses that the features discussed are generally those found most widely in "Gnostic" literature.[28]

---

[25] That the Gospel reflects Gnostic thought is to a certain extent an anachronism. The Gospel precedes all of the Gnostic documents from Nag Hammadi by two or more centuries. Yet the writings of Irenaeus clearly indicate that a developed form of Gnosticism existed by the last third of the second century CE.

[26] The eleven elements I have selected are intended to reflect some of the most basic tenets of Gnosticism and at the same time call attention to features of the Gospel that are said to reflect Gnosticism even if some of these features are not found in all forms of Gnosticism.

[27] Some scholars prefer to abandon the overall term and to speak only of specific systems such as Sethianism, Valentinianism (distinguishing between "eastern" and "western" types), Basilidian gnosis, etc. While many of the Nag Hammadi documents reveal an affiliation with one or other of these more clearly defined "systems," it is difficult to determine the affiliation of a number of the other documents in that Coptic collection.

[28] In order to provide an objective control on this list of features, I have chosen to base it on the definition of Gnosticism presented by Birger Pearson in his recent (2007) book

230 URBAN C. VON WAHLDE

Prominent Features of the Gospel Commonly
Thought to Be Related to Gnosticism

1. The Importance of Knowing and Knowledge

In the Gospel of John, the Greek verbs for "knowing" (*oidan* and *gignōs-kein*) occur over seventy times.[29] This is a frequency much greater than in any other book of the New Testament. John the Baptist admits that he did not "know" Jesus (1:31, 33) but that the one who sent him to baptize revealed to him who Jesus was. The Father "knows" Jesus (10:15) and Jesus knows the Father (7:29; 8:55, 55; 10:15; 17:25). Jesus also knows his own (10:14) and his own "know" Jesus (10:4, 5, 14, 27).

However, the Samaritan woman does not "know" (4:10). But by far it is "the Jews" who do not "know". They do not "know" the Father (7:28; 8:19, 27, 55; 16:3; 17:25) nor do they "know" Jesus (8:19; 16:3). They do not "know" what Jesus is saying (3:10) or the parable about the sheep and the shepherd (10:6). "The Jews" say they "know" the father and mother of Jesus (6:42). They also claim to "know" Jesus, but actually they do not (7:28); and they claim to "know" where Jesus is from, but actually they do not (7:28). In addition to "the Jews," "the world" should "know" that the Father has sent Jesus (17:23) but it does not "know" the Father (17:25).

The disciples are urged to "know" the Father (14:7, 7) and to "know" Jesus (14:7). They will "know" that Jesus is in the Father and the Father in him (14:20); they "know" the way Jesus is going (14:4). They "know" that the Father sent Jesus (17:25), that Jesus has come forth from the Father (17:8), and that all Jesus has the Father has given him (17:7). Yet in spite of this the disciples' knowing is still incomplete before Jesus' glorification (12:16; 13:7, 7; 14:9; 16:18, 30).

This emphasis on knowing is one of the features that first caught the attention of scholars, who suggested that the usage had a Gnostic background.[30] In Gnosticism, knowledge of the soul's true situation in the world and its heavenly origin with God is necessary in order to begin the

---

on the topic. To this list I will add certain other features of the Johannine tradition that bear a similarity to Gnosticism.

[29] However the noun *gnosis* never appears.

[30] Pearson, *Ancient Gnosticism*, 12, begins his definition of the essential features of Gnosticism by stating that "knowledge (*gnosis*) is of central importance in Gnosticism; indeed, it is a prerequisite for salvation." He then goes on describe the type of knowledge he is talking about: "a knowledge of God and a knowledge of the true nature of the human self."

escape from this material world and to return to its heavenly abode. The very name of the movement reflects the importance of this knowledge for salvation.[31] One example of such orientation is found in *The Book of Thomas the Contender* (II.138.7–18), where the Savior says:

> ... examine yourself that you may understand who you are, in what way you exist, and how you will come to be. Since you are called my brother, it is not fitting that you be ignorant of yourself. And I know that you have understood, because you had already understood that I am the knowledge of the truth. So while you accompany me, although you are uncomprehending, you have (in fact) already known, and you will be called 'the one who knows himself.' For he who has not known himself has known nothing, but he who has known himself has at the same time already achieved knowledge about the Depth of the All.[32]

However, close analysis of the notion of "knowing" in the Gospel of John shows it has little in common with Gnostic notions. Knowledge for the Johannine believer is knowledge of God not knowledge of self. Moreover, in Gnostic systems, the possession of knowledge and its "effects" vary. In some Gnostic systems, it is said that there are three types of persons: the "spiritual" or "pneumatic" (*pneumatikos*), the "psychic" (*psychikos*) and the "fleshly" (*sarkikos*), who were also called "earthly" (*choikos*) or "hylic" (*hylikos*). For pneumatics, the ability to "know" is connatural and, once knowledge is attained, salvation is assured.[33]

At times, such knowledge is conceived of as a gift from God given also to psychics.[34] Yet in some systems, the psychics, even with the gift of knowledge, are not capable of entering into the Pleroma.[35]

---

[31] Rudolph, *Gnosis*, 55, 113–118, with multiple examples.

[32] Ibid.

[33] For example, *The Gospel of Truth* 21.5–22.15. A general description of the myth appears, in various forms, in Irenaeus *Against Heresies* 1.1–8; Clement's *Excerpts from Theodotus* 45.2–65.2; Hyppolytus, *Refutation of All Heresies* 6.29.2–6.36.4. However, in other works such as the *Tripartite Tractate* (125.1–10), psychics may also attain salvation but not as easily as pneumatics.

[34] This was the view of the "western" Valentinian school. Heracleon's commentary on the Gospel of John (fragments 17, 40) interprets the Samaritan woman as "pneumatic" and the story of the healing of the official's son as an allegory of the salvation of "psychic" individuals. With this gift, salvation is assured even for the psychic. See Pearson, *Ancient Gnosticism*, 163–164.

[35] This was typical of western Valentinianism. See Pearson, *Ancient Gnosticism*, 156–158, 188. However, according to documents such as the *Tripartite Tractate* (122.12–129.34), in the end the psychics who respond properly will achieve the same salvation as the spirituals. Again see Pearson, *Ancient Gnosticism*, 186–187. On the development of

In their basic conception, these ideas have almost nothing in common with the Johannine conception of the ability to know. At the same time, it is easy to see how, on a superficial level, the Johannine contrast between the insufficiency of the flesh and the importance of the Spirit (cf. John 3:6; 6:63) could appeal to Gnostics, who held to the existence of different "types" of persons. Moreover, the conviction that salvation was assured to the pneumatic person was similar in some respects to the "realized eschatology" of the Gospel inasmuch as the believer who possessed the eschatological Spirit already possessed eternal life in its fullness and so would not come into judgment.

However, the Johannine concept is completely different in origin and nature from the Gnostic notion. In the Gospel of John, the background of the failure to "know" and the ability to "know" is derived from the OT portrayal that, throughout their history, Israel had not "known" God.[36] This had led them into sin and idolatry.[37] But the prophets had promised that "in the last days," all this would change and the Israelites would know God fully.[38]

This knowledge of Yahweh is an eschatological gift; it is not something that the people have achieved or were born with as was the case with Gnostics. Second, this knowledge of God will be direct. That is, the people will not be dependent upon intermediaries for attaining this knowledge. They will not need teachers (Jer 31:34). Third, this knowledge is not only an intellectual comprehension but a comprehension that is directly linked to correct action (Jer 24:7).[39]

While the similarities to this OT conception of eschatological "knowledge" are implicit as they appear in the second edition, in 1 John it

---

Valentinian theology and the distinctions between western and eastern Valentinianism, see especially Einar Thomassen, *The Spiritual Seed, the Church of the Valentinians*, Nag Hammadi and Manichaean Studies 60 (Leiden: Brill, 2006).

[36] Is 1:2–4 says: "The ox knows its owner, and the donkey its master's crib; but Israel does not know, my people do not understand" (NRSV).

[37] Jer 9:2–3: "For they are all adulterers, a band of traitors. They bend their tongues like bows; they have grown strong in the land for falsehood, and not for truth; for they proceed from evil to evil, and they do not know me, says the Lord" (NRSV).

[38] Jer 31:33–34: "But this is the covenant that I will make with the house of Israel after those days, says the Lord: I will put my law within them; and I will write it on their hearts; and I will be their God, and they shall be my people. No longer shall they teach one another, or say to each other, 'Know the Lord,' for they shall all know me, from the least of them to the greatest, says the Lord" (NRSV).

[39] The fact that Jeremiah says "they will return to me" implies the action consequent upon this knowledge. See also the discussion of "Spirit and Experience" in J.D.G. Dunn, *Unity and Diversity in the New Testament*, 2nd ed. (Philadelphia: Trinity, 1990), 174–202.

becomes explicit that the author and his opponents are basing their understanding on this OT background. Even at a time when he is arguing that the community must "keep the word" of Jesus, the author states that "you know all" (2:20) and "[y]ou have no need for anyone to teach you." (2:27). There can be no doubt that the author is here attempting to articulate his view of "knowing" against the background of Jeremiah's prophecy about the end times. Thus it is easy to see that elements of the Gospel of John could be attractive to Gnostics who saw some similarity in them; but, in fact, in origin and nature they are radically different.

2. Jesus as Revealer

In Gnosticism redemption comes through revelation.[40] But Gnosticism has a variety of notions about the coming of revelation. In some systems, there is only a primeval revelation, once-and-for-all. In others, there is a continuing series of revelatory acts in different aeons, i.e. at different periods of time. But in all systems, as K. Rudolph states, "Man can only become aware of his calamitous situation because it has been made known to him by means of revelation. The Gnostic view of the world simply demands a revelation which comes from outside the cosmos and displays the possibility of deliverance."[41] This "redeemer" can also be called a "revealer or emissary or messenger, who at the command of the supreme God imparts the saving message of the redeeming knowledge."[42]

The Gospel of John, too, has an emphasis on "revelation." Yet, within the Johannine tradition, Jesus is, in Bultmann's much-discussed phrase, to a certain extent "a revealer without a revelation."[43] Jesus appears as a revealer who speaks primarily about himself. He does not reveal the hidden nature of the believer; he presents the believer with the possibility of receiving the Holy Spirit as a gift from the Father. In the Gospel, Jesus is essentially attempting to establish his credentials for announcing the offering the Spirit. Unless a person is willing to accept that Jesus is who he claims to be, the individual will not believe that Jesus is the herald of

---

[40] Pearson (*Ancient Gnosticism*, 12) comments: "In Gnosticism saving gnosis comes by revelation from a transcendent realm, mediated by a revealer who has come from that realm in order to awaken people to a knowledge of God and a knowledge of the true nature of the human self."

[41] Rudolph, *Gnosis*, 119.

[42] Ibid., 55, 66, 119.

[43] Rudolf Bultmann, *Theology of the New Testament*, vol. 2, trans. Kendrick Grobel (New York: Scribner, 1951–1955), 66.

the giving of the Spirit. In the second edition, Jesus explains that there are four witnesses to his identity (5:31–40): (1) John the Baptist witnesses to him; (2) his works witness to him; (3) the Father witnesses to him (through the word of Jesus which is the word of the Father); (4) and the scripture witnesses to him.

These four witnesses become the organizing principle for much of the second edition.[44] In the first four incidents of the public ministry, the second edition presents the disciples as responding (1) to the witness of John the baptizer (1:19–51); (2) to the works (signs) of Jesus exemplified in the first Cana miracle; (3) to the scripture (2:13–17, cf. 2:22); and (4) to the word of the Father given through Jesus (2:18–21, cf. 2:22). The second author also presents Jesus offering himself to "the Jews" in the major discourses of chapters 6–10 and showing once again how he is attested by (1) the witness of scripture in 6:30–50;[45] (2) the witness of his word in 8:12–59; and (3) the witness of his works in 10:22–39.

In all of this, there is no hint of Gnosticism but only the attestation of the credentials of Jesus to announce the giving of the Spirit—an attestation that is grounded in the OT scriptures, in miracles given to Jesus by the Father, and by the word of the Father proclaimed through Jesus. In all of this, Jesus himself is acting in response to the Spirit given to him by the Father.

3. *Jesus as a Heavenly Redeemer*

A prominent feature of Gnosticism is the descent of a heavenly Redeemer into the world of matter.[46] Although at one time it was thought that there was a single "redeemer myth" which underlay all Gnostic systems, scholars now know that this is not the case. While the purpose of the

---

[44] For a preliminary discussion of this feature of the Gospel, see my "The Witnesses to Jesus in 5:31–40 and Belief in the Fourth Gospel," *Catholic Biblical Quarterly* 43 (1981): 385–404.

[45] Although the word "witness" does not appear here, it is clear this is the purpose from the form-critical exposition of Scripture as applying to Jesus. The three discourses in chapters 6–10 have been extended by editing, but the foundational material comes from the second edition as is explained in the Commentary.

[46] See again Pearson, *Gnosticism*, 12: "As for the bearer of revelation, this differs from one Gnostic system to another. In Christian forms of Gnosticism, the revealer is Jesus Christ, but in other forms of Gnosticism other revealers are posited, often mythological beings (for example, Sophia, 'Wisdom,' in various manifestations), biblical characters (for example, Adam, Seth), or other noted figures from the past (for example, Zoroaster, Zostrianos)."

redeemer's advent is always the same, the forms and the nature of the revealer are manifold. At times, the redeemer is associated with Adam, Eve, the sons of Adam, Seth[47] and Enoch, Melchizedek,[48] Baruch and other anonymous figures. At other times, the redeemer is associated with abstract entities such as wisdom, spirit, insight, logos and "light-bearer."[49]

In one conception, the Redeemer himself is "redeemed." That is, the redeemer had fallen from heaven into the world at some time in the past. He was able to escape from this world only by leaving some parts of himself ("sparks of light") behind. He must then return to earth to gather to himself those "sparks." By doing so the redeemer redeems himself.[50] This redeemer is the supreme god's son sent to free the "self" from the material world by revealing the self's true identity and so enabling the self to return to its true home.[51]

In Christianized Gnosis, Jesus is understood to redeem through the imparting of knowledge (*gnosis*) rather than through an atoning death. This absence of an atoning death is also a feature of the second edition of the Johannine Gospel.[52] In that edition, Jesus is presented as the emissary of God who announces the eschatological outpouring of the Spirit. However, an analysis of the Gospel's literary genesis reveals that the actions of the Johannine Jesus are quite different from the actions of these figures and that the Johannine acts entirely in accord with the "orthodox" understanding of the Old Testament.

At the time of the second edition, Jesus was conceived of as "one sent by God" and as one who possessed the Spirit and so one who was "Son of God" and "anointed" (i.e. christos), but there is no indication that the community at the time of the second edition thought of Jesus as pre-existent or that his sonship was unique (Gk: *monogenēs*).[53] In the Gospel

---

[47] *Gospel of the Egyptians* 64, 1–2; *Zostrianos* 129–131.

[48] *Melchizedek* (NHC IX, 1:1, 1–27, 10). Melchizedek and the figure of Jesus are closely associated in this text.

[49] See Rudolph, *Gnosis*, 131.

[50] See, for example, *The Tripartite Tractate* (NHC I, 5.124–125); *The Gospel of Philip* (II 3.71); *The Odes of Solomon* 8.22.

[51] For example *Tripartite Tractate* NCH I, 5.125.1–10.

[52] Scholars note that both conceptions occur in the Gospel as a whole, yet the dominant conception is that the death of Jesus is a return to the Father rather than a sacrificial death. See, for example, G. Nicholson, *Death as Departure*, SBLDS 63 (Chico, Calif.: Scholars Press, 1983).

[53] Of course, it may well seem that to exclude preexistence and the uniqueness of Jesus' sonship from consideration is simply a kind of *deus ex machina* to support the view presented here. However, it goes beyond the bounds of this article to present the evidence for this view. The position is argued in detail in the Commentary.

of John, the new life brought by the Spirit and announced by Jesus is not in any sense a return to a state to which the individual is by nature associated. In the Gospel of John, the gift of the Spirit is just that—a gift—not something already possessed. This gift raises the believer to a new level of existence; it is not a return to a state that is already possessed and only in need of being brought to consciousness.

Yet, when the author of 1 John (and the author of the third edition of the Gospel after him) deepened the understanding of Jesus by articulating the belief in Jesus as preexistent, the picture of Jesus changed substantially. Yet, even here the picture of Jesus retains its full Jewishness. In John 5:19–29, the second author had portrayed Jesus as having received the power to give life and to judge. These were the activities unique to God in the OT. The third author built on that picture of Jesus and brought the image of Jesus even closer to that of the Father in that the Father was said to give to Jesus to have "life in himself," which is the very way in which the Father possess life. Consequently Jesus becomes all the more closely identified with the Father, but this is an identity with the Father of the OT.

4. *Dualism*

In at least some forms of Gnosticism there is a thorough-going dualism. There is a dualism within God, within humanity and within the world. Common to Gnosticism is a view in which, as Pearson says, "the transcendent God of the Bible [is split] into two: a super-transcendent supreme God who is utterly alien to the world, and a lower deity who is responsible for creating and governing the world in which we live."[54] In the Gospel of John, although there are two (three) "divinities," their relationship is entirely different than in Gnosticism. The creator god is not a lower god who is inferior to the supreme god and neither divinity is malevolent, as the inferior god sometimes is in Gnosticism. In the Gospel of John as in Judaism, the supreme God is the creator God. In the Gospel, the Son is not created and not inferior to the supreme God.[55]

---

[54] Pearson, *Ancient Gnosticism*, 12–13.

[55] The question whether the Son incarnate as Jesus was always considered divine and equal with the Father is a complicated one. It would appear that at the time of the second edition, Jesus, who had received the Spirit, had been given eternal life and so raised (?) to the status of Son of God through rebirth from that Spirit but in that edition it was possible for the Son to say "the Father is greater than I" (14:28). However, in the third edition and in 1 John, it is clear that Jesus was considered preexistent and able to identify himself with

In the Gnostic view of humanity there is also a dualism. "The human body and the lower emotive soul belong to this world, whereas the higher self (the mind or spirit) is consubstantial with the transcendent God from which it originated."[56]

Finally, "the spatio-temporal universe in which we live (the cosmos) is regarded by Gnostics as a prison in which the true human self is shackled. Created and governed by the lower creator and his minions, it is the realm of chaos and darkness in the view of most of the ancient Gnostics."[57]

The situation in the Gospel of John is complicated by the interweaving of three editions. In the material of the first edition, there is no evidence whatsoever of a dualism. In the second edition, there are a number of contrasts which are not truly dualistic, e.g. the contrast between spirit and flesh. These are contrasts but do not represent features of two opposed principles of good and evil as is characteristic of both modified and absolute dualism. That is, in the Gospel, the realm of the flesh is understood as the realm of naturally created humanity. The realm of the Spirit is another type of life, the life characteristic of God himself, eternal life, which is promised in the Scriptures as a freely given gift of God. It is not that spirit and flesh are related to one another as good to evil, as they are in Gnosticism where the material world is the work of the evil Demiurge. Rather they are related to one another as the original gift of life received at physical birth as contrasted to a higher, specially promised gift of God's own life (Spirit) beyond the natural. In the Gospel of John the contrast between Spirit and flesh is a stark one and one that is essential to comprehend and transcend if one is to have eternal life, but it is not dualism.[58]

Once this distinction is understood, it is easier to see that the same contrast (but not dualism) is implied in the distinction between "above" and "below" and between "earthly" and "heavenly." Even though these concepts may bear a superficial similarity to the thought of Gnosticism, they are radically different.

---

titles otherwise used only of God the Father (e.g. "I AM") and accepted such exalted titles from others (e.g. "My Lord and my God" in 20:28).

[56] Pearson, *Ancient Gnosticism*, 13.

[57] Ibid. Pearson goes on to say "However, it must be admitted that this radical dualism is somewhat mitigated in later Gnostic systems. Even so, the cosmos is regularly regarded as a product of creation, and not in any sense eternal."

[58] The clearest and most abrupt expression of this contrast in the Gospel of John is in John 6:63 ("The Spirit is what gives life; the flesh is useless").

However in the third edition, there is a true apocalyptic dualism. This dualism is often referred to as "modified" or "ethical" dualism. That is, this worldview is based on the conviction that there are two opposed personal beings: one is good (God) and the other is evil (Satan, Belial). However, these two beings are not thought of as equal. God is thought of as ultimately superior to the principle of evil. However, for a time and for reasons known only to him, God has allowed Satan to exercise his power within the universe. It is also part of the apocalyptic worldview that, in a time determined by him, God would reassert his kingly power and destroy the power of Satan. In this worldview, Jesus declares that "the ruler of this world" will be cast out at his death (12:31). In this worldview, God and Satan are truly opposed to one another. Both are personal beings and the images of "Light" and "Darkness" are just that—images used to symbolize these two opposed beings. The third edition speaks of some "who come to the light so that it can be seen that their deeds are done in God." Others remain in darkness because their works are evil (cf. 3:19–21). Near the end of his public ministry Jesus declares: "Yet a brief time the light is among you. Walk about while you have the light, lest the darkness overtake you. ... While you have the light, believe in the light, so that you may become sons of light." (12:35, 36).

Some individuals are said to be "of God"; some are said to be "of Satan." The same notion is conveyed by describing either God or Satan as one's "father" (cf. 8:41–49[59]). Dualistic allegiance is also expressed by the phrase "to do the works of" (e.g. 8:39, 41). This is clearly the dualism of opposed forces. Modified, apocalyptic dualism also employs other symbols to represent this opposition, for example, "truth" versus "falsehood" (cf. 8:38–49), and "Jesus" and "the believer" versus "the world" (cf. 8:23; 15:19; 17:6, 14–15).

Thus we see that the thought world of the Gospel is complicated by the interweaving of material (from the third edition) that describes true (modified) dualism together with other, earlier, material (from the sec-

---

[59] It is the failure to recognize the background of these verses that leads to the misunderstanding of 8:44 ("You are of your father the devil"), a verse that, because of misunderstanding, has been the cause of much prejudice and hatred throughout history. Once the apocalyptic background of the entire section is recognized, the statement can be understood and interpreted (correctly) within the framework of apocalyptic rather than (incorrectly) within the framework of twentieth and twenty-first century language and usage. On this, see, in more detail, my "'You Are of Your Father the Devil' in Its Context: Stereotyped Polemic in Jn 8:38–47," in *Anti-Judaism and the Fourth Gospel: Papers from the Leuven Colloquium, 2000*, ed. R. Bieringer, D. Pollefeyt, and F. Vandecasteele-Vanneuville (Assen: Royal Van Gorcum, 2001), 418–444.

ond edition) that describes contrasts rather than dualism. It is essential to distinguish these two types of expression in order to fully understand the Gospel. Undoubtedly it is the failure to properly distinguish these that has facilitated the (false) conclusion that the Gospel contains a notion of "spirit" and "flesh" parallel with the notion of "spirit" and "flesh" in Gnosticism (where the flesh is genuinely looked upon as evil).[60]

5. Attitude Toward the Material World

As we have seen, for the Gnostic, life in this world is an exile. The self is trapped within a material body within the material world and, when it becomes aware of its situation, longs to be freed from this situation in order to return to its true origin in heaven. For the one who is "spiritual" by nature, the material world is evil and the means by which the individual is entrapped.[61] As we have seen, such individuals who are spiritual by nature thought of themselves as saved entirely by the revelation of their true nature. For them, the notion of proper conduct within the "material" world was irrelevant because they were spiritual by nature and redeemed by "knowledge." For these persons, morality and their association with the material world in general was of no importance. Resurrection did not entail a corporeal dimension.[62]

However, as was mentioned above, in some Gnostic systems there were other types of individuals, the "psychics" who were able to attain an advanced status. For these, it was necessary to "achieve" salvation. For these persons, there were rituals such as baptism, anointing, sacred meals, the recitation of prayers and revealed incantations, and

---

[60] On "flesh" and the material world in general as evil, see note 8 above. It should be clear that the presence of modified dualism in the Gospel of John cannot be construed as evidence of Gnostic influence on the Gospel. Such modified dualism is found throughout the sectarian documents from Qumran as well as in other Jewish documents that have no relation to Gnosticism.

Pearson, *Ancient Gnosticism*, 18, comments: "... an important constituent of Gnosticism is a metaphysical dualism, somewhat akin to that of Platonism. Dualism is also a feature of apocalyptic Judaism, but in the latter the dualism is more of an ethical dualism involving contrasts between good and evil, light and darkness, and a divine struggle involving God and his angels on the one hand, and the Devil (under various names) and his angels on the other. Even so, it can clearly be seen that Gnosticism has borrowed some of these elements from Jewish apocalypses ...".

[61] Rudolph, *Gnosis*, 88.

[62] Pearson, *Ancient Gnosticism*, 175.

ceremonies connected with marriage and with death, all of which were
an aid to achieving proper "knowledge."[63]

In the Gospel of John, Jesus repeatedly disparages the flesh in favor of
the Spirit. When he speaks with Nicodemus about rebirth, Jesus reminds
him (3:6) that "That which is born of the flesh is flesh and that which
is born of the Spirit is Spirit." In response to the Samaritan woman's
question about the proper place for worship, Jesus declares that neither
place is correct because "… an hour is coming and is now here, when true
worshipers will worship the Father in Spirit and truth. … God is Spirit
and it is necessary that those who worship him do so in Spirit and truth."
In 6:63, we read "The Spirit is what gives life; the flesh is useless." Within
the context of the second edition, from which the above statements all
derive, Jesus declares that it is essential to have the Spirit in order to gain
eternal life. And because God is Spirit, those who worship him should do
so in the Spirit.

In the language of the second edition, the possession of the eschatological Spirit is possible for the believer in the present time. As a result, at
death, the material body dies but the person continues to live with God
forever in a spiritual state. The clearest statement of this belief appears in
5:24–25:

> Amen, Amen, I say to you, the one who hears my word and believes in
> the one who sent me has eternal life and does not come into judgment but
> has crossed over from death to life. Amen, Amen, I say to you, an hour is
> coming and is now present when the dead will hear the voice of the Son of
> God and those hearing it will live.

Here the second author is speaking of crossing over from *spiritual* death
to *spiritual* life and such a person will not come into judgment. This is
the view that most scholars would identify as the dominant paradigm of
the Gospel, "realized eschatology."[64]

---

[63] Rudolph, *Gnosis*, 172–173, 215–252.

[64] It is also clear that this conception of crossing over from death to life does not involve
any bodily existence after death (i.e., resurrection). This is most evident from 5:27–28,
which follow the above verses almost immediately:

> Do not marvel at this, that an hour is coming in which all those in the tombs will
> hear his voice and will come forth, those who have done good to a resurrection of
> life, those who have practiced evil to a resurrection of judgment.

This passage, which is from the third edition, presents a corrective view of that previous
to it. Here there is a clear belief in a bodily resurrection at the end of time and a
universal judgment. In spite of this passage, as was mentioned above, realized eschatology
is considered the dominant paradigm for the Gospel.

This view of "spiritual immortality" was regularly found in Jewish religious documents of the time and cannot be said to have derived from Gnosticism. Perhaps the most famous of the representatives of such spiritual immortality is the deuterocanonical Wisdom of Solomon. Such belief is echoed in statements such as 3:1 ("... the souls of the righteous are in the hand of God"), 3:4 ("... their hope is full of immortality"); 5:15 ("... the righteous live forever ..."); 6:18–19 ("... giving heed to her [Wisdom's] laws is assurance of immortality and immortality brings one near to God ...") (NRSV).

As a result we can see that Judaism at the time of Jesus had at least one current of thought that saw the material world as not being permanent and that the Spirit of God was the principle of eternal life in a spiritual (not material) existence with God.

At the same time, this notion of the material world is essentially different from that of the Gnostics. In spite of its *relative* lack of value, the material world of itself is never considered evil, as it is throughout Gnosticism. Although the attitude toward the material world in the second edition of the Gospel has several superficial similarities to Gnosticism, when the background of this view is understood in its context, it becomes clear that this has nothing to do with Gnosticism or beliefs stemming from Gnosticism.

6. Determinism

Among some gnostic schools, it was believed that, from its origin, the self was a spark of light entrapped in the material world and in need of awakening in order to be aware of its true source and destiny. This awakening occurs through the redeemer's revelation. For these Gnostics, one might speak of redemption being "determined."[65]

It is true that, in the Gospel of John, at the time of the second edition, there are statements that would seem to imply a predestination of the individual by God. At the same time, the Gospel contains other

---

[65] Valentinians held to a somewhat different view and understood this divine spark to be at times something freely given to the individual by God even if not possessed by nature. In such a case, it was necessary to conduct oneself properly in order to achieve the final redemption. At one part of the *Tripartite Tractate*, each person is said to contain elements of the pneumatic, psychic and hylic (104.4–108.12). But later, these terms are applied to three different kinds of persons (118.14–122.12). Perhaps the meaning here is that the reaction to the coming of the savior causes one or other element of the individual

statements that would seem to indicate a kind of determinism with regard to those who will receive the Spirit. In 6:37, Jesus says that only those whom the Father "gives" will come to Jesus (cf. 6:65; 17:2). In 10:26–30, Jesus explains that "the Jews" are not "of his sheep" and that no one is able to take anyone "from the hand of the Father" once that person has been "given." But this is simply the Gospel's way of affirming that an individual manifests by means of his / her belief or unbelief whether he / she has been given by God. The context of the second edition makes it clear that all are responsible for their acceptance or rejection of Jesus, but that at the same time even the rejection of Jesus does not take place outside the providence of God. For example, in John 6:44, Jesus says, "No one is able to come to me unless the Father who sent me draws the person." This could appear to express a kind of determinism. However, this expression is clarified by the context, where Jesus goes on to say (6:45): "It is written in the prophets 'And all will be taught by God.' Everyone listening to the Father and learning comes to me." Thus, while no one can come to the Father unless the Father draws the person, it is clear from the Scriptures that *all will be taught by God* and all that is needed is to listen to the teaching of God the Father.

Nowhere does the Gospel present a view of the believer as someone endowed by nature with a destiny. Rather the believer receives the Spirit as a gift from the Father. However, as we will see in the next section, for the community at the time of the second edition, once the Spirit had been received, there was no more effort needed to achieve eternal life, the person "does not come into judgment but has crossed over from death to life" (John 5:24). This conception of the believer bears some similarity to the "deterministic" type of Gnostic thought in that, *once the Spirit has been received*, the person has been reborn and one of the consequences of that rebirth is sinlessness.

7. Lack of Ethics

It is widely acknowledged that the Gospel of John, even in its present form, gives little attention to ethics. For example, R.E. Brown speaks of "the ethical silence of GJohn." He goes on to say: "No specific sins

---

to predominate. The concluding statement of *On the Origin of the World* (NHC II, 127.16) illustrates the relation of behavior to nature: "For each one by his deed and his knowledge will reveal his nature."

of behavior are mentioned in GJohn, only the great sin, which is to refuse to believe in Jesus (8:24; 9:41)."[66] D.M. Smith comments: "Only after he has withdrawn with his disciples, his own, does Jesus offer instruction regarding the conduct of life. Even then his instructions lack specificity."[67] W. Meeks states bluntly, "[The Gospel] offers no explicit moral instruction ... The maxims (gnomes) that are so characteristic of Jesus' sayings in the Q, Synoptic, and Thomas traditions ... are missing altogether from John."[68] In this respect, the Gospel shows considerable similarity to some of the strains of Gnosticism spoken about above. They differ, however, first with regard to the source of this "perfectionism" and also (at the time of the third edition) to its extent.

Gnostic systems had differing views of ethics and these were, to a certain extent, determined by the "type" of person the individual was.[69] Irenaeus says (*Adv. haer.* 1.6.4) that the "psychics" must practice morality to attain a higher state while the "spiritual" persons need not be concerned with such matters:

> On this account, they tell us that it is necessary for us whom they call animal men, and describe as being of the world, to practice continence and good works, that by this means we may attain at length to the intermediate habitation, but that to them who are called the spiritual and perfect such a course of conduct [i.e., avoiding evil] is not at all necessary. For it is not conduct of any kind which leads into the Pleroma, but the seed sent forth thence in a feeble, immature state, and here brought to perfection.

---

[66] Brown, *Epistles*, 80–81.

[67] D.M. Smith, "The Presentation of Jesus in the Fourth Gospel" in *Johannine Christianity* (Columbia: University of South Carolina, 1984), 175–189, quotation 178.

[68] W. Meeks, "The Ethics of the Fourth Evangelist" in *Exploring the Gospel of John*, ed. R.A. Culpepper and C.C. Black (Louisville: Westminster/John Knox, 1996), 317–326, quote 318.

[69] Rudolph, *Gnosis*, 252–263. For a view in which there was no system that advocated perfectionism among the pneumatics, see Perkins, *Gnosis*, 134–135, who refers to E. Pagels, "Conflicting Versions of Valentinian Eschatology: Irenaeus' Treatises vs. the Excerpts from Theodotus," *HTR* 67 (1974): 365–353.

However, I believe that Perkins misreads Pagels. In her book, *The Johannine Gospel in Gnostic Exegesis*, SBLMS 17 (Nashville: Abingdon, 1973), Pagels refers to her article and summarizes it. Pagels, *Johannine Gospel*, 96, observes that Irenaeus' statements in *Adv. haer.* 1.6, 8 [the text of *Adv. haer.* 1.6 is given below in the body of this article] agree with the statements of Theodotus and Heracleon and that it is only the statement in *Adv. haer.* 1.7.1 that is "polemically distorted." Speaking further of Heracleon's interpretation of John 4, Pagels, *Johannine Gospel*, 97, states "The psychic, as the 'called,' can never achieve in the present the certainty of his salvation. ... The pneumatic, as the "chosen," received even

But this is not the only determinant of the Gnostic's attitude toward ethics. Hans Jonas perceptively summarized the two attitudes:

> Generally speaking, pneumatic morality is determined by hostility toward the world and contempt for all mundane ties. From this principle, however, two contrary conclusions could be drawn, and both found their extreme representatives: the ascetic and the libertine. The former deduces from the possession of gnosis the obligation to avoid further contamination by the world and therefore to reduce contact with it to a minimum; the latter derives from the same possession the privilege of absolute freedom.[70]

At the same time, it is important to recognize that the Gnostic documents in the Nag Hammadi codices contain very little discussion of ethics but focus primarily on the "mythic" dimension of Gnostic thought.

The second edition of the Gospel of John also reflects a notion of "perfectionism." This inability to sin was understood to result from the reception of the Spirit, which constituted a rebirth to the (eternal) life of God as a child of God, a life that could not admit of any sin. While the second edition hints as such a perfectionism by the absence of any discussion of ethics, when we read 1 John, we become certain that the second edition spoke of such a perfectionism. In 1 John, there is an explicit discussion of perfectionism and the author, while admitting to a kind of perfectionism, rejects the *absolute* perfectionism of the opponents and modifies it in such a way that it is understood to be an *inchoative* perfectionism. That is, the believer has the roots of sinfulness but not a total inability to sin.[71]

Thus we see that both the second edition of the Gospel and some varieties of Gnostic thought held to theories of absolute perfectionism, nevertheless the origin of this perfectionism is radically different in each and the worldviews out of which those views came show no *intrinsic* similarities.

---

in this world an utterly "certain" and "imperishable" redemption. ... ... her "life" cannot be extinguished or lost."

Such would also seem to be the viewpoint of *Authoritative Teaching* (VI, 3), where the soul (in the image of a fish) is freed by knowledge and does not succumb to the lures of the world (in the image of a fisherman). The question is not whether instruction in ethics was superfluous for *all*, but whether it was superfluous for *some*.

[70] H. Jonas, *The Gnostic Religion*, 2nd ed. (Boston: Beacon Press, 1963), 46.
[71] See especially 1 John 3:3.

8. *Discourse Material*

We now come to a *literary* feature of the Gospel of John that is often said to be derived from Gnostic traditions: the frequency of long discourses in John. These are often thought to exhibit the same literary form as that of Gnostic revelation discourses.[72] Bultmann first suggested that these discourses were taken from what he called a "Gnostic discourse source." Over fifty years later, P. Perkins proposed that, while not directly Gnostic, the discourses of the Fourth Gospel suggested an origin in a similar milieu.[73]

However a look at the discourses reveals that, in several cases, the form of the Johannine discourses can be directly identified from Jewish rather than Gnostic parallels. For example, the discourses after the Last Supper (John 13:31–17:26) are in the format of a Jewish Farewell discourse. This is a form represented in the OT itself [e.g., Jacob (Gen 49); Moses (Deut)] but also in the collection of such farewell discourses in the Testaments of the Twelve Patriarchs.[74] Although the testamentary form was borrowed by the Apocalypse of Adam, the presence of a discourse in this form cannot of itself be considered a "Gnostic discourse."[75]

The discourse in John 6:30–58 can be identified form-critically as having the format of a Jewish synagogue-homily.[76]

But what of the other major discourses of the Gospel? Two observations can be made.

---

[72] Perkins, *Gnosticism*, 122, states: "The case for a connection between the Fourth Gospel's tradition and Gnostic origins does not rest solely on the parallels between its prologue and Gnostic texts. The style of revelation discourse in which Jesus speaks constitutes one of the most distinctive elements of the Fourth Gospel."

[73] Ibid., 241.

[74] It should also be noted that in Gnosticism the favorite period for imparting special revelation to the disciples is in the forty days between Jesus' resurrection and ascension. The discourses of John 13:31–17:26 fittingly occupy a position immediately before the death of Jesus, the appropriate time and place for a "farewell discourse."

[75] While it is true that Gnostic documents such as the Apocalypse of Adam take over apocalyptic and testamentary forms from Judaism, the origin of these literary genres is clearly Jewish. It would be wrong to conclude that because a document contains material in the form of a farewell discourse that therefore it is Gnostic. In addition, the Gnostic documents that most clearly reflect these genres are among the earliest of the Gnostic corpus.

[76] See P. Borgen, *Bread from Heaven. An Exegetical Study of the Conception of Manna in the Gospel of John and the Writings of Philo*, NovTSup 10 (Leiden: E.J. Brill, 1965).

First, apart from those considered above, the primary discourses are those of 5:19–47; 8:12–59 and 10:22–39.[77] Beginning in 5:19–30, Jesus presents and explains his claim to be able to give life and to judge because these powers were given to him by the Father. Within this discourse, Jesus makes it clear that his claims are directly related to the claims of God the Father as they are presented in the Old Testament.

Then in 5:31–40, Jesus lists four "witnesses" that testify to the validity of his claims: (1) the witness of John the Baptist (although his witness is not essential since he was a human); (2) the witness of the works of Jesus; (3) the witness of the word of the Father who speaks through Jesus; (4) the witness of scripture.

Then in the discourses of 6:30–50; 8:12–59; and 10:22–35, in conversation and debate with "the Jews," each of these witnesses is presented and rejected by "the Jews." In 6:30–50, Jesus interprets the scripture presented to him by the crowd in such a way that it testifies to his being the bread from heaven. In 8:12–59, Jesus presents and explains that his word is in reality the word of the Father and so can be a legitimate witness to him.[78] Finally, in 10:22–35, Jesus explains to "the Jews" that his works witness to him. Thus in spite of these witnesses to Jesus and the fact that "the Jews" had access to each of them, "the Jews" rejected them. This is hardly the form or content characteristic of Gnostic dialogues.[79]

Secondly, it is evident in all of these discourses that the purpose is not the relation of some heavenly doctrine but simply the establishment of Jesus' identity as the one who will reveal the Spirit.

But if these features of the discourses themselves indicate that they are not of Gnostic origin or purpose, what accounts for the distinctiveness of their form, so different from the words of Jesus in the Synoptics? The answer lies in the theology of Gospel itself. The authors and the community of which they were members had believed in Jesus and saw themselves as recipients of the Spirit of Truth. The Gospel was not only a recollection of the words of the historical Jesus but also the expression of

---

[77] Monologues such as that in 3:3–21 would have been understood as the result of the prophetic activity of the Paraclete but derive their length from the process of editing in which material from distinct editions was woven together.

[78] See the essence of the charge that Jesus witnesses to himself and his explanation in 8:14–17.

[79] It should also be pointed out that all of these discourses, in their present form, contain editing. The original length of the discourses and dialogues was shorter and, in that form, the fact that they are debates with "the Jews" is clearer.

their meaning, articulated through the power of the Paraclete. Thus the Gospel itself is a manifestation of what is proclaimed in Paraclete sayings:

> [T]he Paraclete, the Holy Spirit, whom the Father will send in my name, will teach you all things and will remind you of all things that I have told you (15:26). ... he will lead you in all truth. For he will not speak on his own but will speak whatever he hears and will proclaim to you what is to come. That one will glorify me because he will take from what is mine and will proclaim it to you. (16:13–14).

Unlike Gnosticism, this proclamation is not given to a select group of disciples after the resurrection. The message about Jesus is proclaimed to all: to the crowds, to the Samaritans, the Galileans, and the Jewish authorities. Moreover, there is no distinction between the message of Jesus before and after the resurrection, nor between the message given to the crowds and that given to the disciples. In fact, the author of 2 John specifically rejects the notion that there could be some revelation later that was not linked to the teaching of Jesus (2 John 9).[80]

9. "I am" Statements

Another literary form unique to the Gospel of John in the New Testament that is regularly said to derive from Gnosticism is the presence of "I am" statements with a predicate, e.g. "I am the shepherd," "I am the truth," etc.

There are three types of "I am" statements in the Gospel of John. The one that is most striking and that is unique to the Gospel of John in the New Testament is the so-called "absolute" "I am" statement. These have been shown conclusively to derive from the self-identification of Yahweh as expressed by "I AM" (*Ego Eimi*) of the Septuagint.[81]

The second type of statement is a secular use employed as self-identification. It is used to identify the speaker, presumably in cases where something in the context should enable the questioner to recognize the respondent. An obvious example of this is the ability to recognize the voice of the respondent even though the respondent does not mention

---

[80] It should be pointed out however that even the aberration of the opponents as described in the Johannine letters is not Gnostic but is simply a one-sided understanding of the role of the eschatological Spirit. The opponents believed that they had received the eschatological Spirit but they saw no intrinsic relation between what the Spirit taught and what Jesus taught. They may have been "heretical" but they derived the heresy from Judaism, not from Gnosticism.

[81] See the standard commentaries, e.g., R. Brown, *The Gospel According to John*, AB 29 (Garden City: Doubleday, 1966–1970), 533–538.

his own name. In English, the form of the statement would commonly be "It is I."

The third form of "I am" statement in the Gospel is the "I am" with a predicate (e.g. "I am the gate," "I am the good shepherd," "I am the way, the truth and the life").[82]

Several proposals have been made for the background of this last usage. Among them is the similarity to sayings of Isis in Egyptian religion and to statements in the Gnostic documents from Nag Hammadi. However a majority of scholars interpret them against the background of the OT. It is true that all or almost all of the predications are found in the OT but not in the same linguistic form (i.e. "I am the …"). R. Brown argued that in some of these latter statements the emphasis is as much on the "I" (indicating that only Jesus is the true embodiment of the quality discussed) as on the quality itself.[83] Thus "I am the gate" could be intended to emphasize that Jesus (and no other) is the gate as well as to emphasize that Jesus is in many ways like a "gate" to eternal life. Werner Kelber suggests that they are instances of prophetic speech intended to indicate the presence of Jesus in the midst of the community.[84] John Ashton also understands them to be instances of prophetic statements made within the community, which "express insights which can only have been reached through a profound reflection on the essence of Jesus' message."[85]

David Ball, in his study of the "I am" sayings, also finds the general background of the sayings in the OT. He comments that "The sayings occur in the context of discussions on Jewish subjects (Jn 4, 6, 8) involving the Jewish ancestors (Jacob, Jn 4; Moses, Jn 6; Abraham, Jn 8) and reflect Jewish expectations (Jn 6 and 11). Furthermore, Jesus explicitly tells the disciples that Jewish Scripture will be fulfilled in his betrayal and as a result they will believe that *ego eimi* (13:19)."[86]

I would count it as particularly significant that one instance appears as the topic sentence of the homiletic midrash of 6:30–50. The statement in 6:35 ("I am the bread of life.") constitutes the principal articulation of the theme of the discourse, that the bread given by the Father (which

---

[82] There are seven such predications. In addition to those listed in the text, there are four others: "I am the bread of life" (6:35, 51); "I am the light of the world" (8:12; 9:5); "I am the resurrection and the life" (11:25); "I am the vine" (15:1, 5).

[83] Brown, *Gospel According to John*, 533–538.

[84] W. Kelber, *Oral and Written Gospel* (Philadelphia: Fortress, 1983), 98–101.

[85] J. Ashton, *Understanding the Fourth Gospel* (Oxford: Clarendon, 1991), 187.

[86] D. Ball, *'I Am' in John's Gospel: Literary Function, Background and Theological Implications*, JSNTS 124 (Sheffield: Sheffield Academic, 1996), 257.

is superior to the bread given by Moses) is Jesus himself. Thus both the theme and the grammatical form of the statement are completely accounted for the (Jewish) context in which it appears.

Thus although the theme of the various "I am" statements is derived from the OT, the form in which they appear is very likely to be due to the prophetic prerogative the community understood itself to possess. There is no hint of a Gnostic background to the statements.[87]

10. *Humanity as Composed of Sparks of Light in a World of Darkness*

As we have seen above, in some Gnostic currents, dualism was conceived of as absolute. There is no evidence of this sort of dualism anywhere in the Johannine tradition. In other currents within Gnosticism, humanity was understood to be made up of three types of persons: the pneumatic, the psychic and the hylic. Those of the first type are best described as "sparks" of the heavenly light that have fallen from heaven and are imprisoned in a material body in this world, alienated from their true home and source.[88] Psychics are capable of enlightenment but such knowledge is not theirs by nature. Hylic individuals are not capable of enlightenment.

In the Gospel, there is no evidence of such a threefold division of humanity. This is another major difference between the Gospel and Gnosticism.

In the second edition of the Gospel there are no references to the dualism of light and darkness. The material that comes from the second edition of the Gospel and which is so clearly defined as associated with Jesus' offering of the eschatological Spirit and its prerogatives makes no use of the images of light and darkness.

There is *no* indication, in the second edition, that some are saved by nature or that some are by nature incapable of being saved.[89] Everyone is free and capable of coming to the light.

It is only in the third edition of the Gospel that we meet the images of light and darkness. Jesus describes himself as "the light of the world"

---

[87] Perkins, *Gnostic*, 134, also points out that in contrast to the "riddle" quality of Gnostic "I am" statements, those of the Gospel of John are quite straightforward and intelligible.

[88] See Rudolph, *Gnosis*, 113–115.

[89] It should be remembered that the discussion of determinism above showed that there was no sense of absolute determinism in either the second or third editions of the Gospel. Rather all individuals are capable of movement from one orientation to the other and the individual has both the freedom and the obligation to believe.

(3:19, 20, 21; 8:12; 9:5; 12:46; cf. 12:35–36). Believers are said to come
to the light (3:19, 21; cf. 11:9); unbelievers and those who do evil do not
come to the light (3:19–20). Individuals are urged to come to the light
so they might become "sons of light" (12:36). Throughout, this "light" is
opposed to "darkness."

However, this imagery of "light" and "darkness" is the modified, "ethical" dualism characteristic of apocalyptic. That is, it is possible for an
individual to move from darkness to light (3:19–21; 9:5; 11:9; 12:35–36).

While this bears some similarity to the "psychic" person described in
Gnostic systems, it would be rash to assume that this is the case since any
religious system holding to a belief in free will would qualify for such
similarity. When we search for the background of the dualism of light
and darkness in the third edition of the Gospel and in the letters, we find
its closest parallel in the apocalyptic worldview best exemplified in the
sectarian documents from Qumran and in the Testaments of the Twelve
Patriarchs.

For example, in the War Scroll, the opposition between the "sons of
light" and the "sons of darkness" appears at the beginning (cf. 1QM 1:1–
10) but also 13:6 "Truly they are the company of Darkness, but the company of God is one of [eternal] Light." 13:16 ("[For Thou hast appointed]
the day of battle from ancient times … [to come to the aid] of truth and
to destroy iniquity, to bring Darkness low and to magnify Light … to
stand for ever, and to destroy all the sons of Darkness").

In 1QS, the members of the community are urged "that they may
love all the sons of light … and hate all the sons of darkness …"
(1:10). Also: "All the children of righteousness are ruled by the Prince
of Light and walk in the ways of light, but all the children of injustice
are ruled by the Angel of Darkness and walk in the ways of darkness"
(3:21).

But, as was the case with the second edition of the Gospel, nowhere
is there the slightest evidence that persons were subject to an absolute
dualism or to any of the features typical of Gnosticism.

11. Mythopoeia

One of the most pronounced features of Gnosticism is, as Pearson proposes, "mythopoeia," that is "the construction of elaborate myths through
which revealed gnosis is transmitted." These myths dealt with the origin
of the universe, the nature of God, the varying spheres between the realm
of the transcendent almighty, the creator God, and the lower world. In

some cases this process reached remarkable extremes, with exotic names often taken from philosophy or other religions.

In the Gospel of John, there is none of this. The worldview of the second edition is simply the traditional view found in the OT. In the third edition, we encounter the worldview of Jewish apocalyptic. Consequently, in the most obvious of ways, there is a large gulf between the writings of the Gnostics and those of the Johannine community.

In addition to these features to which we have dedicated more attention, there are a number of other features that appear in Gnosticism that have some similarity to features in the Johannine Gospel but are less significant. For example, the Gnostics had an interest in secret revelations to special disciples, e.g. Mary Magdalene. This has been compared to the figure of the Beloved Disciple in the Gospel of John. At first sight, there could appear to be some similarity, especially since no figure such as the Beloved Disciple appears elsewhere in the New Testament. However, the Beloved Disciple is a title given to the individual who is the author of 1 John and who articulated the correct understanding of the tradition in the pages of 1 John. This person referred to himself simply as "the Elder" (2 John 1; 3 John 1). It was only the later community, at the time of the Gospel's third edition, after the disciple's death, that gave him the title of "the disciple whom Jesus loved."[90]

Moreover, the Beloved Disciple is not the recipient of special esoteric revelations but is the model of faithfulness and insight. At no time is he given special revelation not given to the others. In terms of the context of the Gospel, this is the "disciple whom Jesus loved" precisely because this disciple obeyed the commandments given by Jesus and so was loved by him (cf. John 15:10).

The term "living waters" appears frequently both in the Gospel of John and in both the *Trim. Prot.* and the *Apoc. Jn.* yet in very different senses. In the Gospel of John, the term "living water" (which appears only in the second edition) is a symbol for the Spirit. In the *Trim. Prot.* XIII 46, 16–19, the Logos pours forth "living water" *upon* the Spirit.

Gnostic writings were often put in the form of apocalypses. The Gnostics took over this genre from Judaism but gave it a content that was completely different. Very much as Christianity took over the genre but gave it its own unique content. But while the third edition of the Gospel of John

---

[90] The evidence for this view is presented in detail in Excurses on the Elder and the Beloved Disciple in my commentary.

is couched in an apocalyptic worldview, it is not an apocalypse and does not claim to present special revelations about the future. Rather it simply portrays the ministry of Jesus within the framework of apocalyptic's cosmic conflict between God and Satan, showing the ministry of Jesus as a victory over Satan.

Conclusions

My purpose in this study has been to examine features in the Johannine literature that have been said to bear some similarity to various elements of Gnosticism and to do so from the viewpoint proposed in my recently completed commentary. Although such a narrow inquiry may seem to be motivated simply by authorial narcissism, in fact, I believe the perspective provided in this commentary has something significant to contribute to the question of this relationship.

I would suggest that this proposal provides a perspective on the development of the Johannine tradition, that explains both the background of the editions as well as the way other features of each edition (especially of the second) relate to the root worldview and convictions of that edition. To use the image introduced at the beginning of this study, it provides both the "hub" as well as the "spokes" of the wheel.

When those features regularly identified as being "Gnostic" are examined from the perspective presented in this commentary, I believe that it becomes clear that these various "Gnostic-like" features are better explained as consistent with the ("traditional") Jewish outlook rather than by some relation to Gnosticism—and that their similarity to features in Gnosticism is only accidental.

In the past, attempts to describe the background and relationship of the Gospel to Gnosticism have been made more complicated by the interweaving of the two worldviews and the perspective of each. When these worldviews are distinguished and are able to be isolated from one another within the text of the Gospel, the task is simplified considerably.

In short, I believe that this perspective enables us to reject the possibility of *intrinsic* connections between the Johannine tradition and Gnosticism. However, the fact remains that there are a number of features that *are* similar, but this similarity is *extrinsic and accidental*.

Ultimately, it was not the Johannine community that had an interest in Gnosticism but rather Gnosticism that had an interest in the Johannine literature. The resemblance was accidental but the Gnostics found it appealing. The fact that the first extant commentary on the Gospel is from the Gnostic Heracleon is a clear testimony to this fact. The fact that the *Apocryphon of John* in its present state consists of a substratum of a non-Christianized Gnostic document that has been secondarily Christianized in clearly Johannine terms is also evidence of the fascination with the Johannine tradition on the part of Gnostics. But as scholars have regularly pointed out, Gnosticism regularly Christianized its own documents[91] but also interpreted Christian documents in such a way as to show that they were faulty and imperfect understandings of humanity and the true source of salvation.[92] The *Apocryphon of John* is an example of this first tendency; Heracleon's commentary on the Gospel is an example of the second.

At the beginning of this study, I called attention to the view of specialists in the study of Gnosticism that the origins of Gnosticism lay in the *re-interpretation of Jewish materials*. The perspective proposed in this current essay would seem to confirm this and to provide a clearer perspective on the Gospel and its relation to Gnosticism. We have seen that the thought of the second edition of the Gospel has derived in what might be called a "pure" and "simple" form from the traditional Jewish understanding of the eschatological outpouring of the Spirit and its prerogatives. There is no evidence that this Jewish perspective has in any way been modified in the direction of Gnosticism. Rather every aspect of its content derives from OT thought. Even in the third edition, where the worldview of apocalyptic Judaism is introduced, the *Tendenz* of the material is to correlate the thought of the Gospel with that of 1 John and with that of the Synoptic Gospels.

Perkins, in her discussion of Gnostic history, comments: "Writings from the Johannine school also attest the existence of Gnosticizing speculation in Asia Minor."[93] I cannot see evidence of this. Gnosticism made use of the Johannine writings, not the reverse!

Nevertheless it is true that, within the Prologue of the Gospel, there is evidence of a thought-world distinct from that of the remainder of the Gospel. Thomas Tobin, to whom this essay is dedicated, has argued persuasively that "the hymn in the Prologue, like [the works of] Philo of Alexandria, was part of the larger world of Hellenistic Jewish speculative

---

[91] A clear example of this is the *Apocryphon of John* although there are many others.
[92] An example of this is Heracleon's commentary.
[93] Perkins, *Gnosticism*, 43.

interpretations of biblical texts."[94] But Tobin does not argue that the background of the Prologue is in any way Gnostic. At the same time, just how the introduction of this worldview is to be accounted for and how it is to be correlated with that of the remainder of the Gospel remains an important question—one for another occasion.[95]

[94] Thomas H. Tobin, "The Prologue of John and Hellenistic Jewish Speculation," *CBQ* 52 (1990): 252–269, quotation 268.
[95] I am grateful to Professor Harold Attridge of Yale University who generously agreed to read the manuscript and made very helpful suggestions. The deficiencies, however, remain my own.

THE ACTS OF JOHN AND THE FOURTH GOSPEL

Harold W. Attridge

It is a pleasure to dedicate this essay to honor a colleague and friend, Thomas Tobin, S.J., who has made significant contributions to the study of Hellenistic Judaism and the interpretation of the New Testament. *Multos ad annos*!

The history of the interpretation of the Fourth Gospel in the early church has long been a subject of intense interest.[1] A particularly obscure period has been the second century. For some time the conventional wisdom has been that work was appreciated more by "heterodox" or "Gnostic"[2] folk in that century than by those Christians who would come to define the orthodox tradition. That position has been vigorously challenged by Charles Hill,[3] who argues both that the use of the Fourth Gospel was widespread among "proto-orthodox" Christians and that, contrary to the prevailing opinion, Christians with "Gnostic" proclivities were actually anti-Johannine. They were quite critical of the fundamental

---

[1] Important older works are Maurice F. Wiles, *The Spiritual Gospel: The Interpretation of the Fourth Gospel in the Early Church* (Cambridge: Cambridge University Press, 1960); T.E. Pollard, *Johannine Christology and the Early Church*, SNTSMS 13 (Cambridge: Cambridge University Press, 1970). More recently, see Titus Nagel, *Die Rezeption des Johannesevangeliums im 2. Jahrhundert: Studien zur vorirenäischen Aneignung und Auslegung des vierten Evangeliums in christlicher und christlich-gnostischer Literatur*, Arbeiten zur Bibel und ihrer Geschichte 2 (Leipzig: Evangelische Verlagsanstalt, 2000) and Kyle Keefer, *The Branches of the Gospel of John: The Reception of the Fourth Gospel in the Early Church*, Library of New Testament Studies 332 (London and New York: T. & T. Clark, 2006).

[2] The criticism of the categories "Gnostic" and "Gnosticism" is now familiar. See Michael A. Williams, *Rethinking "Gnosticism": An Argument for Dismantling a Dubious Category* (Princeton: Princeton University Press, 1996), and Karen L. King, *What is Gnosticism?* (Cambridge: Belknap Press of Harvard University Press, 2003). Nonetheless, I will continue to use the terms, referring not to all odd forms of second-century Christianity, but particularly to those pieces of literature and their authors who are associated with Sethian and Valentinian traditions. For a sensible overview of the phenomenon of Gnosticism, see Birger Pearson, *Ancient Gnosticism: Traditions and Literature* (Minneapolis: Fortress, 2007).

[3] Charles Hill, *The Johannine Corpus in the Early Church* (Oxford: Oxford University Press, 2004), 258–263.

positions adopted by the Gospel, positions which were characteristic of the mainstream of Christianity in the second century.

Much in Hill's impressive analysis of second century literature is quite persuasive and it is now quite impossible to attempt to trace a simple trajectory from the Fourth Gospel to the second century authors who have come to be grouped under the label of "Gnostic." Nonetheless, it may be that the characterization as "anti-Johannine" of believers who read the Gospel in ways that would come to be regarded as "heretical" may not do full justice to their reading of what would become a key canonical text.

To explore the phenomenon, I shall focus on the *Acts of John*,[4] a work of Christian fiction written sometime in the second century, perhaps as early as the second quarter of that century.[5]

The original Acts, known to Eusebius and the *Manichaean Psalm Book* of 340[6] and condemned by the Second Council of Nicaea in 787, has not come down to us directly from antiquity but has survived primarily through its incorporation in the later, quite orthodox, *Acts of John by (pseudo)-Prochorus*, and in partial form in other manuscripts. What

---

[4] For a general introduction, see Hans-Josef Klauck, *The Apocryphal Acts of the Apostles: An Introduction* (Waco, Tex.: Baylor University Press, 2008). A useful introduction to the work is also to be found in R. Alan Culpepper, *John, The Son of Zebedee: the Life of a Legend* (Columbia, S.C.: University of South Carolina Press, 1994; reprint, Minneapolis: Fortress, 2000), 187–205. Recent monographs include G. Sirker-Wicklaus, *Untersuchungen zu den Johannes-Akten* (Witterschlick and Bonn: Wohle, 1988); P.G. Schneider, *The Mystery of the Acts of John: An Interpretation of the Hymn and the Dance in the Light of the Acts' Theology* (San Francisco: Mellen Research University Press, 1991); Pieter J. Lalleman, *The Acts of John: A Two-Stage Initiation into Johannine Gnosticism*, Studies on Early Christian Apocrypha 4 (Leuven: Peeters, 1998). Translations are to be found in Kurt Schäferdiek, "Acts of John," in Wilhelm Schneemelcher, *New Testament Apocrypha*, 5th ed. (Louisville: Westminster / John Knox, 1992), 152–212, and J.K. Elliott, *The Apocryphal New Testament* (Oxford: Oxford University Press, 1993), 303–349. Translations in this essay are from Elliott.

[5] Eric Junod and Jean-Daniel Kaestli, *Acta Iohannis* (CChrSA 1–2; 2 vols.; Turnhout, Belgium: Brepols, 1983), 2:694–700, date the work to the second half of the second century, arguing that it was used by *Acts of Peter*, *Acts of Thomas* and *Acts of Paul*. Lalleman, *Acts of John*, 208–212, 268–270, dates the work to the second quarter of the century, arguing that it influenced the final form of the *Apocryphon of John* and *Apocalypse of Peter*, that its Christology, with its intense focus on Christ and its portrait of him as polymorphic and polyonymous, is attested for the first half of the second century, but not later, and that the kind of Gnosticism it attests is pre-Valentinian. Hill, *Johannine Corpus*, 259, dates the work to around 150.

[6] Eusebius, *Ecclesiastical History* 3.25.6. Clement of Alexandria, Fragments from Cassiodorus, "Comments on the First Epistle of John [1:1]," *ANF* 2:574, knows of Johannine traditions similar to those of the Acts, but there is no evidence that he knew the text itself. See Cullpepper, *John*, 187–188.

has been reconstructed, first by Maximillian Bonnet in the nineteenth century[7] and more recently by Eric Junod and Jean-Daniel Kaestli,[8] remains incomplete, comprising about 70 % of the 2,500 lines reported by the ninth-century Stichometry of Nicephorus to be the extent of the text. Yet that is enough material to reveal the character of the work.

Most scholars agree that what can be reconstructed is a composite work with strong affinities to some of the less "orthodox" varieties of second century Christianity. Exactly how the work was composed and what the precise affinities are has been a matter of continuing discussion. There is general recognition of the distinction between three large sections, traditionally numbered according to the chapters of Bonnet's edition. Section A, chapters 18–86, 106–108, and 110–115, tells tales of miracles, primarily resurrections, in Asia Minor and recounts the departure, or Metastasis, of the Apostle. Section B, chapters 87–93, 103–105, consists of reports by John about his relationship with Jesus, focusing on the initial call by Jesus and the transfiguration. Section C, chapters 94–102 and 109, the most distinctive part of the work, consists of an account of the events surrounding the passion of Jesus, including a liturgical hymn and dance at the last supper and an appearance to John at the time of the crucifixion in which Jesus explains to him the real nature of the event. Chapter 109, an account of a Eucharistic prayer, shows strong affinities with chapters 94–102.

Placement of the sections varies. Bonnet's placement of sections B and C, most of which (AJ 87–105) survives only in one manuscript,[9] has been challenged by Kurt Schäferdiek who situates the material after chapter 37.[10] Although followed by other scholars and recent translations, the location creates as many problems as it solves. Bonnet's placement of section C, after the episode of the raising of Drusiana, is more likely to be correct, as is argued by Lalleman.[11]

Scholars assess the relationship among the sections in slightly different ways, either as disparate compositions or, more likely, as redactional strata, with more or less tension between them. Section C in particular, with its distinctive and emphatic version of a "polymorphic" Christology also in evidence in section B (AJ 87–89), is probably, as Lalleman argues,

---

[7] Maximillian Bonnet, *Acta Apostolorum Apocrypha II, 1* (Leipzig: Mendelssohn, 1989; reprint, Hildesheim: Olms, 1972).

[8] See note 5.

[9] Vindobonensis 63, dated to 1319.

[10] See Schäferdiek, "Acts of John," 178–187.

[11] See Lalleman, *Acts of John*, 25–30.

the work of the final compiler of the whole text who shapes the whole work to culminate in this revelation.[12] Given its central place in the conceptual composition of the work, that section will be the focal point of our attention.

Most scholars find some version of Gnosticism at work in the text, although not uniformly in all parts of the text. Section A, for example, lacks any allusion to a cosmogonic myth or a vocabulary associated with Gnostic sources. In the story of the finally damned Fortunatus and the finally saved Callimachus (AJ 62–87), it may offer a narrative depiction of the anthropological division of humankind into three classes, typical of some forms of Gnosticism, although scholars unpack the logic in different ways. Junod and Kaestli find a version of Valentinian anthropology,[13] Schneider a "Sethian" anthropology later corrected by Valentinian perspectives.[14] The affinities with some form of Gnosticism in Section C are more pronounced. The technical terminology of speculative metaphysics, the Ogdoad and Duodecad, in the hymn at AJ 95, 23–25[15] recalls Valentinian terms for elements of the divine Pleroma, although the terms also appear in other, probably non-Valentinian texts.[16] Most intriguing perhaps is the description of the Cross as a symbolic divider of all things (διορισμὸς πάντων, AJ 98, 14), which resembles Valentinian speculation on the aeon, Horos.[17] Despite the tantalizing connections to Valentinian traditions, there is not enough to support a firm identification of the text with that tradition.[18]

The authors of the Acts certainly knew the Fourth Gospel, as did other Gnostic teachers of the second century,[19] but how did they use it?

---

[12] See Lalleman, Acts of John, 48–54. Schäferdiek, "Acts of John," 164, argues, against Junod and Kaestli, that the passage was part of the Acts of the John from the beginning.

[13] See Junod and Kaestli, Acta Johannis, 1:589–593, 612–614, 627–632.

[14] Schneider, Mystery, 79–143 205–206.

[15] Citation is by chapter and line number of the critical edition by Junod and Kaestli, Acta Johannis.

[16] See Gerard Luttikhuizen, "A Gnostic Reading of the Acts of John," in The Apocryphal Acts of John, ed. Jan N. Bremmer (Kampen: Kok Pharos, 1995), 119–152, here 148–149.

[17] See Einar Thomassen, The Spiritual Seed: the Church of the Valentinians, NHMS 60 (Leiden, Boston: Brill, 2006), 281, n. 30, agreeing with Lalleman, Acts of John, 186–190, that the notion is not limited to Valentinian sources.

[18] See Luttikhuizen, "Gnostic Reading," 145, and Lalleman, Acts of John, 188–189, 199–202.

[19] For two Valentinian readings of the Fourth Gospel, see Harold W. Attridge, "The Gospel of Truth as an Exoteric Text," in Nag Hammadi, Gnosticism, and Early Christianity, ed. Charles W. Hedrick and Robert Hodgson (Peabody: Hendrickson, 1986), 239–255, and idem, "Heracleon and John: Reassessment of an Early Christian Hermeneutical

Section B shows clear evidence of the Fourth Gospel, in, for instance, its reference (*AJ* 89, 11) to John reclining at the breast of Jesus, reminiscent of John 13:23.[20] At the same time it certainly does not give priority to the Fourth Gospel, relying on the Synoptics for its account of the call of the first disciples (*AJ* 88–89), and highlighting the transfiguration (*AJ* 90), an episode not recorded in the Fourth Gospel. The presence of the Fourth Gospel behind the material in section C is more clear, but the relationship to the text more problematic. The Acts knows of the tradition that John was present at the crucifixion, something recounted only in the Fourth Gospel. *AJ* 97, 3–5 however, has John flee the scene of the crucifixion and go to the Mount of Olives, where he receives his vision from the Lord instructing him about the true nature of suffering. The Acts seems to know but to retell radically the story of John's witness to the crucifixion.

At the heart of the vision that John sees on the Mount of Olives is a "cross of light" (σταυρὸν φωτός, *AJ* 98,1) and above the cross the Lord himself present only as a voice, "one sweet and kind … and one truly divine" (ἡδεῖαν καὶ χρηστὴν καὶ ἀληθῶς θεοῦ, *AJ* 98,5–6) The voice confirms the importance of John's witness: "It is necessary that one man should hear these things from me, O John, for I have need of someone who will hear" (*AJ* 98,7–8).

The Voice goes on to identify the Cross with various epithets,[21] most familiar from the Fourth Gospel (Word, Door, Way, Bread, Seed, Resurrection, Son, Father, Spirit, Life, Truth, Faith, Grace), but at least one, "Mind" (νοῦς, *AJ* 98, 9), not from the Fourth Evangelist's repertoire. The symbolic universe of the Fourth Gospel is present, but supplemented, or in the estimation of Lalleman, regarding both sections B and C, "replaced."[22]

The Voice goes on (*AJ* 101) to give a message about suffering, acknowledging but putting into perspective the elements of the account of the

---

Debate," in *Biblical Interpretation, History, Context, and Reality*, ed. Christine Helmer (Leiden and Boston: Brill, 2005), 57–72. On the *Gospel of Truth*, see also Hill, *Johannine Corpus*, 264–270.

[20] For a complete roster of evidence for use of the Fourth Gospel in Acts, see Lalleman, *Acts of John*, 110–123.

[21] This is part of what Lalleman, *Acts of John*, 174–184, labels the "polyonymy" characteristic of the text. See also his essay on the polymorphic Christology of the Acts, which he takes to be closely correlated with the notion of the Savior's polyonymy: "The Polymorphy of Christ," in Bremmer, *Apocryphal Acts*, 97–118.

[22] Lalleman, *Acts of John*, 115, noted favorably by Hill, *Johannine Corpus*, 261.

Passion, particularly that of the Fourth Gospel. The passage (*AJ* 101, 6–15) is worth extensive citation:

> You hear that I suffered, yet I suffered not; that I suffered not, yet I did suffer; that I was pierced, yet was I not wounded; hanged, and I was not hanged; that blood flowed from me, yet it did not flow; and, in a word, those things that they say of me I did not endure, and the things that they do not say those I suffered.

The allusions to the Fourth Gospel, especially the mention of the flowing blood, so important in the symbolism of the Gospel and in the defense of it by 1 John,[23] are clear as is the resistance by the Acts to the plain meaning of the text of the Gospel.

The accounts of the Beloved Disciple's witness and the character of the account of the passion certainly seem to warrant the claim that the Acts is involved in parody of the Gospel,[24] or that it is in some sense, as Hill argues, "anti-Johannine."

Yet this assessment does not quite do justice to the dynamics of the theology of Section C, and a fortiori, of the whole of the Acts. There are several elements of the account that evoke elements of the Gospel without quite the same resistance or quite the same sense of irony. The most important perhaps is the understanding of the crucifixion as a revelatory event, deriving its significance not primarily from the expiatory value of blood shed, but from what the (potential) believer "sees" when he or she really looks at the Cross.

The Fourth Gospel as a whole is, I have argued elsewhere, designed to focus the "vision" of the reader on the Cross and the one lifted up / exalted on it, to enable, through the refracted images of the rest of the text, to see the Cross in a new way, to have what a contemporary would call an "epoptic" experience.[25] The reader, that is, is set up to have the experience, foreshadowed in the references to the vision of the Son of Man as Jacob's ladder in John 1:51 and as a serpent 3:14–15, where what is seen brings amazement and healing.

---

[23] Cf. 1 John 5:6–8.

[24] For this judgment, see Richard I. Pervo, "Johannine Trajectories in the Acts of John," *Apocrypha* 3 (1992): 47–68.

[25] See especially Harold W. Attridge, "The Cubist Principle in Johannine Imagery: John and the Reading of Images in Contemporary Platonism," in *Imagery in the Gospel of John. Terms, Forms, Themes and Theology of Figurative Language*, ed. Jörg Frey, Jan G. van der Watt, and Ruben Zimmermann, with the collaboration of Gabi Kern, WUNT 200 (Tübingen: Mohr-Siebeck, 2006), 47–60.

There remains a problem for the reader of the Gospel. The dynamics of the epoptic experience are not explicitly specified. How exactly is "seeing" the event of the exaltation of the Son of Man on the cross to produce its salvific effect? An engaged reading of the Gospel produces answers to that question. The most satisfying way of doing so is to take a cue from the comments of Jesus in his last supper discourses, where he offers through injunction (John 13:31) and proverbial saying (John 15:13), the interpretation of the exaltation on the cross as a vision of unbounded, self-giving love, expressed in the reality of human flesh and memorialized in the ritual reminiscence of the crucifixion. The revelation that comes through the visionary experience is not the transmission of a doctrinal proposition, but an encounter with a gently compelling force that ultimately triumphs over death. Such was the reading of the significance of the death of Jesus on the cross offered by the author of the Johannine epistles, a prominent member of the Johannine community.

The reading of the Johannine epistolographer became the reading that dominated "orthodox" Christian tradition, but it is not the only reading possible of the dynamics of Gospel's potent image of the cross and the one exalted on it. That the author of the Acts (or at least of Section C) understood what was at stake is, I believe, clear. After Jesus leads his disciples in song and dance (an important part of the ritual correlate and appropriation of the vision), he tells them (*AJ* 96, 1–19):

> Now if you respond to my dancing, see yourself in me who speak; and when you have seen what I do, keep silence about my mysteries! You who dance, perceive what I do; for yours is this passion of mankind which I am to suffer! For you could not at all have comprehended what you suffer if I had not been sent to you as the Word by the Father. When you saw what I suffer, you have seen me as one suffering; and seeing that, you have not stood firm but were wholly moved. Moved to become wise, you have me for a support. Rest upon me!

> You shall know when I go away. What I am now seen to be, that I am not. You shall see[26] when you come. If you knew how to suffer, you would have had the power not to suffer. Learn suffering, and you shall have the power not to suffer. That which you do not know, I will teach you. I am your God, not that of the betrayer. I will that there be prepared holy souls for me. Know the word of wisdom!

"Seeing" the cross is a revelation, an encounter with the Divine Word, which produces understanding and ultimately wisdom. The content of

---

[26] Junod and Kaestli, *Acta Johannis*, 1:205, restore "What I am."

that vision consists in a doctrine about the meaning of suffering, cloaked here in paradoxes yet to be unpacked. Love is not the focal point of the revelation, suffering is. The reading of the significance of the cross is formally "Johannine" but materially distinct from the interpretive grid of the Gospel and the readers represented by the Johannine epistles.

The passage just cited also points to two other elements important for resolving the problem of how the "vision" is appropriated, and both are important motifs in the Fourth Gospel. The first is the intimate identification of beholder and the One who stands at the center of the vision. That identification is signaled in the opening of the passage, alluding back to the song and dance: "If you respond to my dancing, see yourself in me who speak" (*AJ* 96, 1).

The second Johannine element in this section is the suggestion that it is the absence of Jesus that makes possible the attainment of understanding. The claim that "You will know when I go away" (*AJ* 96, 11) stands in tension with the immediately preceding call to rest on Jesus. Neither the tension nor the basic claim is new in Johannine discourse, which delights in the juxtaposition of present and future throughout the Gospel and insists in the Last Supper discourses that Jesus must depart in order to fulfill his mission. In making these seemingly Johannine moves, the author of Acts again pours new wine into old wineskins. For the Gospel, the departure of Jesus is a necessary condition for the outpouring of the Spirit, who enables the disciples to proclaim and live a gospel of reconciliation (John 20:23). For the Acts, the departure of the physical Jesus makes abundantly clear the reality that he and his are spiritual beings for whom suffering is irrelevant.

Both the motif of the identification of seer and seen and the dependence of the identification on the absence of Jesus reappear later in the revealer's discourse. In explaining to John the vision of the Cross and the multitude gathered around it, Jesus describes the process of unification with him of at least a portion of humankind (*AJ* 100, 1–12):[27]

---

[27] This is one passage where the anthropological doctrines of Gnostic teachers of the second century become particularly relevant. Space precludes discussion of the various issues at stake and the modern efforts to sort through the patristic testimonies and the ancient sources. For a useful discussion of most of the sources, see Schneider, *Mystery*, 131–143. In general, I would argue that heresiological portrait of a rigid determinism, particularly among Valentinians, is a misreading of their attempts to develop a theological anthropology. The Acts of John, both in its narrative portions and in the revealer's discourse about the cross, is compatible with an understanding of the categories of humankind that represent the immediate, or delayed actualization or failure to actualize the potential to understand and hence to become divine. For discussion of the

Now the multitude about the cross which is the lower nature is not of one form; and those whom you see in the cross do not have one form. That is because every member of him who came down has not yet been gathered together. But when the nature of man shall be taken up, and the race which comes to me in obedience to my voice, then he who now hears me shall be united with it and shall no longer be what it now is, but shall be above them, as I am now. For as long as you do not call yourself mine, I am not that which I was. But if you hear and hearken to me, then you shall be as I am, and shall be what I was when I have you with myself. For from this you are. Therefore, ignore the many, and despise those who are outside the mystery! Know that I am wholly with the Father, and the Father with me.

The passage concludes with a strong reminiscence of the Johannine motif of the intimate relationship between Jesus and the Father, particularly prominent in the Last Supper discourses, which promises the extension of their relationship to the followers of Jesus (John 14:11, 20, 23). A further distinctive Johannine motif appears in this passage, the obedience to the "voice" of Jesus, which gathers up the new "race" of humankind.[28] The voice that elicits a responsive following evokes the Gospel's dramatic imagery of the encounter between Jesus and Mary Magdalene (John 20:16), which in turn echoes the identification of Jesus as the Good Shepherd who knows and calls his sheep by name (John 10:4, 14, 16).

The motif of the "voice" had already surfaced earlier in the revealer's discourse, at the start of the vision of the Cross of Light, in a passage already noted (*AJ* 98, 3–6): "And the Lord himself I beheld above the cross, not having a shape, but only a voice, and a voice not such as was familiar to us, but a sweet and kind voice and one truly divine."

Here, as in the other Johannine motifs that course through this revelatory discourse, old forms take on new meaning. The "voice" that in the Gospel had called out to the individual person to summon her to mission[29] now teaches about the cross as divider between above and below, between left and right (*AJ* 98, 14), separating out the "transient and inferior" (τὰ ἀπὸ γενέσεως καὶ κατωτέρω, *AJ* 99, 2). The content of the teaching is finally the claim that Jesus and those who respond to him

---

Valentinian position, see Harold W. Attridge and Elaine Pagels, "The Tripartite Tractate," *Nag Hammadi Codex I (The Jung Codex)*, NHS 22, 23 (Leiden: Brill, 1985), 1:159–337, 2:217–497.

[28] On language of "race" or "nation," see Denise Kimber Buell, *Why this new Race: Ethnic Reasoning in early Christianity* (New York: Columbia University Press, 2005).

[29] Cf. especially John 20:16, echoing John 10:3, 14. On the whole scene, see Harold W. Attridge, "Don't be Touching Me: Recent Feminist Scholarship on Mary Magdalene," in *A Feminist Companion to John*, ed. A.-J. Levine (Cleveland: Pilgrim, 2003), 2.140–166.

are spiritual. Whatever the Jesus story has to say about suffering is simply a symbol of the assault on the impassable Word (*AJ* 101, 12–14), "the slaying of the Logos, the piercing of the Logos, the blood of the Logos, the wounding of the Logos, the hanging of the Logos, the passion of the Logos, the nailing of the Logos, the death of the Logos." But knowing that the Logos cannot be pierced, shed blood, hung, nailed or die transforms the "mind," the one non-Johannine thing that the Cross symbolizes (*AJ* 98, 9). That mental transformation that results from the visionary experience enables the follower to laugh at those who persecute, just as John "laughed to scorn" the multitude fixated on the physical cross (*AJ* 102). With the appropriate "disposition of soul" (ψυχική διάθεσις, *AJ* 103, 4), at one with the Logos, the follower can face "bonds and dungeons … scourging, condemnations, conspiracies, plots, punishments" (*AJ* 103, 7–8). Paradoxically, the impassable one "suffers with us when we suffer" (*AJ* 103, 9) but such suffering is ultimately meaningless. What happens to the hearer of this voice is analogous to the kind of imperturbable detachment to which a Stoic might aspire,[30] a detachment exemplified in Section A by the figure of Drusiana and John's preaching to her husband.[31]

In the reflection on the Voice at the heart of the vision of the Cross, the author of the *Acts of John* exploits a fundamental conceptual element of the Gospel as it wrestles with an acute issue raised by the Gospel's account of the crucifixion of Jesus. For our author, what is necessary for a word to be heard was a voice, and that voice may be heard through the liturgy of song, dance and Eucharistic prayer (*AJ* 102–103, 109) that focuses not on the death of Jesus but on the eternal life of the Word. While the building sections are familiar, and the structure makes internal sense, it is certainly a different construal of Johannine elements than what we encounter in the Gospel, particularly as read through the eyes of the Johannine epistles.

---

[30] For a discussion of some potentially "Stoic" elements in the Fourth Gospel, see Harold W. Attridge, "An Emotional Jesus and Stoic Tradition," in forthcoming, ed. Troels Engberg-Pedersen. It will appear in *Stoicism in Early Christianity*, Tuomas Rasimus, Troels Engberg-Pedersen and Ismo Dunderberg, eds. (Peabody, Mass.: Hendrickson, 2010).

[31] See especially, *AJ* 63,9–11 for her commitment to continence and *AJ* 64,7–8 for her belief that one filled with (divine) words, will not fall to passion. Εἰ γὰρ ἦν τις ὑπὸ λόγων πεπληγώς, οὐκ ἂν εἰς τοσοῦτον ῥαθυμίας ἐληλύθει. ("If he were filled with God's word, he would not fall into such a passion," Elliott, 329, a little loosely). John's proclamation of dignified freedom from passion is detailed in *AJ* 68 and 69. On women in this work, see Jan N. Bremmer, "Women in the Apocryphal Acts of John," in *Apocryphal Acts of Thomas*, ed. idem (Leuven: Peeters, 2001), 37–56.

What then is the relationship between the Acts of John and the Fourth Gospel? Is the Acts "anti-Johannine"? Such a judgment does not do full justice to the appropriation of the key Johannine motifs in the Acts nor to the ways in which the Acts appears to wrestle with a fundamental Johannine affirmation, that the crucifixion of Jesus was a revelatory event that needed to be understood and internalized by believers. Whatever the date of the Acts, it seems plausible to construe them as a product of the impulse evident in the "opponents" of the Johannine epistles,[32] a strand of Johannine tradition that so emphasized the spiritual character of the Logos that the fleshly humanity of Jesus became irrelevant (1 John 4:2), a strand that celebrated the Christ event in word and song and Eucharistic prayer,[33] but could not, like the disgruntled disciples of John 6, accept the notion that the bread and wine of the eucharist was truly the body and blood of Jesus (John 6:53). The Christians who produced this account were not so much "anti-Johannine" as alternatively Johannine, or, perhaps to take a hint from the epilogue to the revealer's discourse (AJ 102), "symbolically Johannine."[34] The critical elements in the relation of the Acts to the Gospel are clear, but the foundation on which the Acts is built is also decidedly "Johannine" and the theology that it develops deals with a problem at the core of the Johannine formulation of the Gospel.

---

[32] The *Acts of John* are occasionally introduced in discussions of the Johannine epistles as something comparable to the position of the opponents criticized in those texts. See e.g., Georg Strecker, *The Johannine Letters*, Hermeneia (Minneapolis: Fortress, 1996), 74, but if an early second century date is correct for the Acts and their relationship to traditions of the Gospel are as significant as this essay suggests, they may be more valuable for reconstructing developments in the history of the Johannine circle than is often allowed.

[33] There has been debate about the relationship between the song and dance and the eucharist, especially the Eucharistic prayer of 109. J.D. Kaestli, "Le mystere de la croix de lumiere et le Johannisme: Acts de Jean ch. 94–102," *Foi et Vie* 86, 5 (Sept. 1987): 87, believes the dance and song replaces the eucharist, a position rejected by Schneider, *Mystery*, 208. On the character of the eucharist in the Acts, see Hans Roldanus, "Die Eucharistie in den Johannesakten," in Bremmer, *Apocryphal Acts*, 72–96.

[34] Despite his emphasis on the strong critique of the Gospel found in the Acts of John, Lalleman, *Acts of John*, 214, comes to a formally similar conclusion: "I would suggest that the present reading of the AJ affords us insight into the development of the spiritualizing form of the Johannine Christology and soteriology as it developed along a trajectory leading from the Fourth Gospel to Gnosis." See also Helmut Koester, *From Jesus to the Gospels: Interpreting the New Testament in its Context* (Minneapolis: Fortress, 2007), 180–181, who also understands the Acts of John to be rejecting how the Fourth Gospel has understood the Johannine tradition.

CHRIST, THE CHURCH, AND THE SHAPE OF SCRIPTURE: WHAT WE CAN LEARN FROM PATRISTIC EXEGESIS

BRIAN E. DALEY, S.J.

Every academic discipline has its growth points, even though it may not always be obvious to people practicing the discipline just what those growth points are. In the field of Patristic studies, one of those areas of new interest and development today is clearly early Christian exegesis: how the writers of the early Church, whose works have survived, interpreted and applied to their lives the Hebrew and Greek writings that came to be recognized, over the course of the first three centuries or so of the Church's life, as the Christian canon of Scripture. Although my friend and Jesuit colleague Thomas Tobin, SJ, as a scholar of both Philo and the New Testament, is clearly and exception, modern Christian students of the Bible, since the time of the Enlightenment, have tended to be dismissive, if not contemptuous, of the Fathers' attempts to find and express Scripture's meaning. In the 1880s, for instance, the socially conscious Evangelical Anglican scholar, Canon Frederic Farrar—who deeply admired the Church Fathers as examples of heroic Christian determination and faith[1]—waves away the early centuries of Biblical interpretation as "dominated with unproven theories, and overladen by untenable results."[2] In the mid-20th century, another Evangelical Anglican with a deep knowledge of Patristic theology, Bishop R.P.C. Hanson, in his early study of Origen's approach to Biblical interpretation, concludes that despite his sincere commitment to the Church's rule of faith,

---

[1] His two-volume collection of biographical sketches, *Lives of the Fathers* (Edinburgh: A. and C. Black, 1889), witnesses to this sympathetic interest in the Fathers of the Church as people.

[2] *History of Interpretation* (London: Macmillan, 1886), 8. In the introduction to his *Lives of the Fathers*, Farrar castigates the early second-century *Letter of Barnabas* for its "unsound opinions and artificial methods of interpreting the Old Testament" (2), and adds: "We are offended by its curious self-satisfaction in a most weak and untenable form of 'gnosis,' as exhibited in crude and almost grotesque allegorising of simple Scriptural passages by rabbinic and Philonian methods, both equally baseless" (4).

Origen was generally speaking not seriously restrained by the Bible; he knew very little about the intellectual discipline demanded for the faithful interpretation of biblical material in the Bible, though he was perfectly willing to accept the ideas of the Bible where they did not conflict with his presuppositions. He had in his hand a panacea for all biblical intransigence, allegory. Where the Bible did not obviously mean what he thought it ought to mean, he had only to turn the magic ring of allegory, and— Hey, Presto!—the desired meaning appeared. Allegory, in short, instead of ensuring that he would in his exegesis maintain close contact with biblical thought, rendered him deplorably independent of the Bible.[3]

For Hanson, Origen simply misses the importance of history, as the place where God's revelation of himself takes on the human form of words, persons and events. His favored use of allegorical interpretation, in Hanson's view, is "at best ... quaint and sometimes poetical; at worst it is a device for obscuring the meaning of the Bible from its readers."[4]

In the last ten or fifteen years, as we said above, tides of interest among students of early Christianity seem to be turning. Spurred on, perhaps, by the growing realization post-modern theorists have stimulated in the scholarly world, that the interpretation of any text is never wholly free from the cognitive and cultural "horizon" of the interpreter—that there can be no wholly "objective" approach to past events and personalities that puts us in touch with things "as they actually happened"—Biblical and Patristic scholars are beginning to realize that early Christian exegesis of the Bible is not simply an arbitrary, naïve way to read favorite doctrines into difficult Biblical passages; it rests, rather, on an understanding of the whole of Scripture that was almost universally shared, and that brought with it an interpretive logic different from what most modern readers assume, but coherent nonetheless.[5]

---

[3] *Allegory and Event* (London: SCM, 1959; reprint, Louisville: Westminster/John Knox, 2002), 371.

[4] Ibid., 367.

[5] For a clear and interesting attempt to work out the "logic" of early Christian Biblical interpretation, see John J. O'Keefe and R.R. Reno, *Sanctified Vision. An Introduction to Early Christian Interpretation of the Bible* (Baltimore, Md.: Johns Hopkins Press, 2005). For the history of Patristic exegesis, see especially Manlio Simonetti, *Biblical Interpretation in the Early Church: an Historical Introduction to Patristic Exegesis* (Edinburgh: T. and T. Clark, 1994); Paul Blowers, ed., *The Bible in Greek Christian Antiquity* (Notre Dame: Notre Dame Press, 1997); and Frances Young, *Biblical Exegesis and the Formation of Christian Culture* (Cambridge: Cambridge University Press, 1997).

I. *The Assumptions of Patristic Exegesis*

Although it is not our purpose here to offer an exhaustive survey of the assumptions behind early Christian Biblical interpretation, they would almost always include the following:[6]

1. God is the supreme, original reality, the ground of all other reality, and so that God is present in and to the history of creation. As a book about God's actions in the world, then, the Bible is recounting history in its most fundamental sense.

2. The narrative told by the books of the Biblical canon is a cohesive one, put together from different books, written at different times, to tell the one story of the creation and redemption of humanity through God's decisive action. For the Hebrew Bible, that redemption was centered on the election, formation, and eventual salvation of the people Israel, as the beginning of God's initiative to unify and save "the nations;" for the Christian Bible, it came to full realization in the person, work, death and resurrection of Jesus.

3. This Biblical narrative of salvation is summed up, for the Christian community, in the "Rule of Faith" acknowledged by the Churches that recognized each other, from the mid-second century on, as orthodox. For early Christian exegetes, the Rule of Faith (and its later, more formal expression in the more doctrinally developed creeds of the fourth and fifth centuries) was both derived from the Biblical narrative and provided the lens through which the Bible's correct interpretation could be assured. This Rule was, in bare outline, the confession that the whole world is the creation of a single God, whose Son has become one of us and has redeemed us from our alienation from God by his death and his entry into glory.

4. The teachings of Scripture, within this unifying framework, still remained diverse and could be legitimately interpreted in a wide variety of ways. Multiple meanings were not excluded by the narrative's central unity, and, in some cases, filled out that narrative with added richness.

5. The Bible, as the narrative of human salvation, includes *us*, its modern readers and hearers, within its scope. The application of Biblical events, warnings and prophecies to the life of the contemporary

---

[6] For a fuller reflection on these characteristics of Patristic exegesis, with examples, see my article, "Is Patristic Exegesis Still Usable? Reflections on Early Christian Interpretation of the Psalms," *Communio* 29 (2002): 185–216.

Church was not a secondary step, beyond ascertaining its "original" meaning. It *was* its meaning.

6. The meaning of any passage in Scripture, even of individual words, was wrapped by God, who had moved its human authors to write as they did, in the veil of mystery. This meaning was couched in the terms in which it now appears, partly to motivate and inspire the contemporary reader, partly to challenge him or her to deeper reflection and more ingenious mental activity. To penetrate into this mystery, however, was to open a chamber providentially built and sealed by God, so that the activity of interpretation must always be undertaken in a spirit of reverence, a sense that one was walking on holy ground.

For the exegetes of the early Church, many of these features were also present in secular works—in the prose narratives of history or even the poetic narratives of the epics, which were generally also meant "for us" as instruction. What was distinctive about the Bible, as it took shape in its Christian canonical form, was that its convoluted, yet more or less cohesive, narrative of creation, sinful alienation, and salvation by the God who is at the heart of all things finds its goal and its inner meaning in the person and story of Jesus of Nazareth, whom Christians believed to be God's own Son, "emptying himself" of divine glory to share, and ultimately to overcome, human weakness and mortality (see Phil 2:5–11). Although different Church Fathers expressed their sense of this Biblical history in different terms and categories, the heart of their reading of Scripture's message—from at least the second century on—was based on the prologue to John's Gospel: the news that the eternal Word, who was "with God" from "the beginning," divine in nature and active in the creation of "all things," and who, through Israel's long history, had called the descendants of Abraham to be his own people, his own children, eventually—in most recent times—"became flesh and dwelt among us," and "we," whose witness is written down in this document, "have seen his glory, glory as of the only Son from the Father, full of grace and truth" (John 1:14) To put the process in more theological terms, one might say that the development of Christian faith began in the recognition by the Jewish followers of Jesus that, although his preaching mission ended in bloody failure, Jesus was in fact—contrary to all expectations—the one promised by ancient Israel's Scriptures: that his person, his words, his death and resurrection, were thus the ultimate key to a faithful reading of Scripture's inner meaning; and that it was the Bible—Israel's

Bible—which provided the language and categories that alone allowed his disciples to understand him.

Just as the canon of Hebrew Scripture, formed in complex successive steps of redaction and re-contextualization, ultimately took its shape through a process in which later scribes received and re-read the narrative of the nation's long history from their own perspective, so the later Christian canon was determined in its shape—in what was included and excluded—by the conviction that the crucified and risen Jesus was to be acclaimed as Lord of history, his life and death understood as the fulfillment of the meaning of "the Law and the prophets." To unite the Torah, the histories and the prophetic books, the Psalms and the wisdom books and other "writings," in a single collection with the four Gospels, the letters of Paul and James and Peter and John, and the book of Revelation, all centered on the news that Jesus is Lord—to look on all these works as one book, one Bible—was itself an act of supreme theological importance: the Church's first and perhaps its most long-lasting work of interpreting history in Christological terms. As such, it laid the foundation for the whole later development of Christian theology. It was to say, in effect: although no one has realized it until now, the whole story of God's work, from the creation on, is a story that leads to Jesus, and all of it points to him as the one who will eventually bring human history to its climax. Jesus is the principle by which the Christian canon has been formed, as well as the principle of its authentic interpretation. The unity of the message and even the text of Scripture, for ancient and medieval exegesis, are rooted in the unity of salvation through and in the person of Christ.[7]

---

[7] John Behr, *The Way to Nicaea* (Crestwood, N.Y.: St. Vladimir's, 2001), 27–28, makes substantially this same point in his history of early Christian faith: "The proclamation of the death and resurrection of Christ is not straightforwardly derivable from Scripture. Rather, the death and resurrection of Christ acts as a catalyst. Because God has acted in Christ in a definitive, and unexpected, manner, making everything new, Scripture itself must be read anew. The 'word of the Cross,' the preaching of 'Christ crucified' may be a scandal for the Jews and folly for the Gentiles, but it alone is the 'power of God' making known 'the wisdom of God' (1 Cor 1:18–25) ... Read in the light of what God has wrought in Christ, the Scriptures provided the terms and images, the context, within which the apostles made sense of what happened, and with which they explained it and preached it, so justifying the claim that Christ died and rose 'according to the Scriptures.' It is important to note that it is Christ who is being explained through the medium of Scripture, not Scripture itself that is being exegeted; the object is not to understand the 'original meaning' of an ancient text, as in modern historical-critical scholarship, but to understand Christ, who, by being explained 'according to the Scriptures,' becomes the sole subject of Scripture throughout."

II. *Four Illustrations*

One might illustrate this reliance on Christ as the unifying center of Patristic Biblical interpretation by considering the preaching or Biblical commentaries of almost any of the Fathers as well as their treatment of Scripture in larger works of controversy.

Here it must suffice for us to give examples of this approach to the Bible—an approach that seems so strange to the modern reader, who looks instead to discover the "original intent" of the authors and redactors of each part of Scripture—by looking briefly at the exegetical styles of four influential and representative fathers, stretching from the late second to the early fifth centuries: Irenaeus of Lyons, Origen of Alexandria, Athanasius of Alexandria, and Augustine of Hippo. Although their ways of conceiving and applying this Christological hermeneutic vary considerably, they all agree in seeing in Scripture a single unified narrative, extending to all people, through Christ and his Church, the call and the promise originally made to Abraham and his children. Taking a brief look at their ways of conceiving the unity and meaning of the whole Bible may help us get a better sense of why Patristic exegesis tended to read its texts in such a distinctive way.

1. *Irenaeus*

As is well known, Irenaeus was mainly concerned, in his large, somewhat rambling treatise *Against the Heresies*, to expose what he saw as the seductive weaknesses of the "Gnostic" Christian sects of the mid- and late second century; even the title given to the work in the manuscripts, echoing 1 Tm 6:20, conveys this polemical purpose: "Five Books to Expose and Refute What is Spuriously Called Knowledge (*Gnosis*)." Against the promise of esoteric "insider knowledge" of the salvation brought to a struggling humanity by Jesus—a knowledge that normally resulted in undermining the value of the material world, the body, public institutions and responsible life in society by offering an alternative narrative of how the world came to be as it is—Irenaeus's work is really a sustained, if often circuitously argued, plea for the Christian relevance of ordinary things. To achieve this, Irenaeus emerges as an impassioned defender of unities: the unity of God, as creator and savior of humanity; the unity of Christ, as the eternal, unique divine Word of creation and revelation, incarnate in history as Jesus of Nazareth; the unity of the Church throughout the world, confessing its single tradition of faith in Jesus and his work in a symphony of languages; the unity of the Scripture then coming to use in the Churches, which largely corresponds to what we know as the Christian canon—a unity revealed in a single overarching narrative, with a harmonious array of moral and doctrinal messages; the unity of the human person in his or her material and spiritual dimensions. For Irenaeus, the fatal flaw of Gnostic forms of Christian preaching was their tendency to hint at a "real," alternative story behind or under the publicly proclaimed Gospel: a story that implied the salvation brought by Christ is essentially the release of humanity's "spiritual" core from the burdens of delusion and false responsibility imposed by our imprisonment in a material world, a world created by a God who was far inferior to the original fount of being whom Jesus called "Father."

To develop his own unitary view of the salvation brought by Jesus in and through the Church, Irenaeus realizes it is essential to place him, as the incarnate Word of God, in the center of the over-arching Biblical narrative. Irenaeus puts his viewpoint provocatively in Book IV of the work:

> If someone, then reads the Scriptures carefully, he will find in them language about Christ and the prefiguring of a new vocation. For he is "the treasure hidden in the field"—that is, in this world—"for the field is the world":[8] hidden, that is, in the Scriptures, because he was signified by types and parables, which could not be understood, insofar as lies in human power, before the fulfillment of the things prophesied had come—that is, before the coming of Christ.[9]

Irenaeus, like Justin and other second-century writers, takes very seriously John's designation of Christ as the eternal Logos or Word of God, made flesh in Jesus but operative as God's word of creation and revelation from the beginning of time. So, basing his argument on Jesus' claim in John 5:46 ("If you believed Moses, you would believe me, for he wrote of me"), Irenaeus asserts that "the writings of Moses are the words of Christ;"[10] Christ is the initiator of the Jewish law as well as what Paul calls its end; after all, he asks, "how is Christ the end of the law if he is not also its beginning?"[11] In fact, as the original word of creation, the Logos

---

[8] Irenaeus combines here phrases from two Matthaean parables: Mt 13:44 and Mt 13:38.

[9] *Adv. haer.* 4.26.1; see Irenaeus, *Adversus haereses*, ed. Adelin Rousseau, *Sources chrétiennes* 100 (Paris: Éditions du Cerf, 1965), 712.

[10] *Adv. haer.* 4.2.3 in SC 100, 400.

[11] *Adv. haer.* 4.12.4 in SC 100, 518. In *Adv. haer.* 4.20.9 in SC 100, 654, Irenaeus interprets Moses' request to see God on Mt. Sinai as the desire to see Christ in his human form,

is also the single channel of God's self-revelation, making an essentially invisible and unknowable God intelligible to human experience:

> For by means of creation itself, the Word reveals God the creator, and through the world, the Lord as maker of the world, and through the creature who has been formed the artisan who formed him, and through the Son that Father who generated the Son ... But through the law and the prophets the Word proclaimed at the same time both himself and his Father ... And through the Word himself, made visible and touchable, the Father was revealed; even though all did not believe him in the same way, all still saw the Father in the Son. For the Father is that which is invisible of the Son, but the Son is that which is visible of the Father.[12]

Just as the Logos spoke to Abraham and drew him to follow the command of the one God, so the Logos incarnate continues to speak to us, "drawing us away from a religion of stones and transferring us from a hard and unfruitful set of relationships, and establishing in us a faith like Abraham's."[13]

In the same way, Irenaeus sees the series of covenants, by which God has established a life-giving relationship with humanity, as a single process, leading gradually to full life and freedom for the human race, rather than as a succession of laws and institutions in tension with each other. So he writes of the Hebrew Scripture's ability to point to Jesus:

> Since the New Covenant was recognized and predicted by the prophets, and he who was to bring it into effect was predicted according to the good pleasure of the Father, he was revealed to the human race in the way God willed, so that they might always make progress in believing in him, and might grow mature through the covenants, until salvation became complete. For there is one salvation, and one God; but there are many commands that shape the human person, and not a few steps that bring him closer to God.[14]

---

something that was only granted to him in the event of Jesus' transfiguration reported in Matthew and Luke.

[12] *Adv. haer.* 4.6.6 in SC 100, 448–450. See also *Adv. haer.* 4.20.4 in SC 100, 634, where Irenaeus further suggests that God, the original creator, is unknown in his "greatness" (*magnitudo*), but has always been known in his "love" (*dilectio*) through the action of the Word and the Spirit: a distinction, it seems, between God's essential transcendence and his loving, self-disclosing involvement in history to draw creatures to himself.

[13] *Adv. haer.* 4.7.2 in SC 100, 458. Irenaeus sees here the fulfillment of John the Baptist's prophecy (Mt 3:9; Luke 3:8) that "God is able from these stones to raise up children to Abraham."

[14] *Adv. haer.* 4.9.3 in SC 100, 486. See also *Adv. haer.* 4.11.1 in SC 100, 496–498.

For Irenaeus, in fact, as for a significant majority of Patristic writers up to Augustine, the one who reveals God's will and God's presence to Old Testament figures—who speaks with Noah and Abraham, wreaks judgment on Sodom, accompanies Jacob on his journey, gives the law to Moses, and communicates with the prophets in dramatic signs—is always the Word, the Son, who himself became flesh in Jesus. So he remarks:

> If, however, an idea like this should take hold of you, to say: 'What new thing did the Lord bring in his coming?' you should know that he brought us every form of newness by bringing himself, just as he had been foretold. For this is what had been predicted, that something new was on the way that would give life to the human race ... He himself fulfilled all things by coming, and still brings to fulfillment, in the Church, the new Covenant that had been foretold in the law.[15]

The active presence of God's life-giving Word throughout history has become, for Christians, a human presence, promising full salvation to all who turn in faith to him.

2. Origen

The interpretive freedom criticized by Bishop Hanson in Origen's work, as an unhistorical way of reading Scripture that is at best quaint, at worst obscurantist and misleading, is founded on this same conviction: that the Word, who has become flesh as Jesus, is, precisely as God's Word, both speaker and content of all revelation, and is therefore the inner message of the whole Bible. This central assumption—which many modern readers of Origen miss or choose to disregard—could be illustrated by referring to many of his works, especially his Scriptural homilies and commentaries. Here, it will have to suffice for us to consider just a few significant passages revealing this side of his thought.

As probably the first professional Scripture scholar in the Church's history, Origen focused his rich gifts of intelligence, Hellenic learning, and ecclesial piety on the task of exposing the meaning of the Biblical text—a meaning he was convinced was often not obvious to all the Church's readers and hearers.[16] Like many of his late-second and early-third-century Gnostic contemporaries in Alexandria, Origen too thought that not every Christian believer was immediately capable of grasping the

---

[15] *Adv. haer.* 4.34.1–2 in SC 100, 846 and 850.
[16] See, for example, Origen, *On First Principles*, Preface 1–3 in SC 252, 76–80; 4.2.1–4 in SC 268, 292–316.

deepest meaning of many Biblical texts; unlike Gnostic teachers, however, he sided with Irenaeus in insisting that the God who has revealed
himself in both Testaments of the Bible is a single creator, judge and savior, and that his chief personal means of contact with humanity is his
dynamic, eternal Word, who has become flesh in Jesus of Nazareth.

At the beginning of his first homily on Leviticus, for example, Origen
makes what is for him a central hermeneutical point: that the Word of
God is always spoken to us in veiled human guise, whether that "veil" is
of a literary or a fleshly kind:

> Just as the Word of God, clothed in flesh from Mary, has come into this
> world 'in these last days' (Acts 2:17), and what was seen in him was one
> thing, what was understood in him another—for the visible form of flesh in
> him was obvious to everyone, but the recognition of divinity was granted
> only to a few chosen ones—so too when the Word of God is delivered
> to men and women through prophets and legislators, he is not delivered
> without appropriate clothing. For just as in the former case he is covered
> by the veil of flesh, so in the latter he is covered by the veil of the letter,
> so that the letter indeed appears as a kind of flesh, but the spiritual sense,
> hidden within it, is perceived like the divinity.[17]

And while the literal, external meaning of the Biblical text (especially,
it seems, its moral content) remains important for "the weak, who are
incapable of seeing the deeper mystery,"[18] the Church—while never fail-
ing to embody the Bible's moral concerns in its own way of life—"leaves
the letter to others and is built up in a more holy way by the Spirit."[19]

Origen develops this Christocentric understanding of the hidden
meaning of all Scripture in the first fifteen chapters of the first book of
his *Commentary on John*, a substantial work, written in the late 220s
and early 230s, largely to counteract the efforts made by Heracleon, a
Valentinian Gnostic of Alexandria, to interpret the Fourth Gospel. Origen begins this celebrated and ambitious overture to his own exposition
of the Gospel with a majestic tableau drawn from the seventh chapter of
the Book of Revelation, in which white-robed saints and martyrs stand
before the throne of the Lamb as the "first-fruits" of God's holy people.[20]
Similarly, the "priests and levites" of the new people of God, the Church,

---

[17] *On Leviticus*, Hom. 1.1; see Origen, *On Leviticus*, ed. Marcel Borret, SC 286 (Paris:
Éditions du Cerf, 1981), 66.

[18] Ibid. 4.2 in SC 286, 164.

[19] Ibid. in SC 286, 166.

[20] *Commentary on John* 1:1–2; see Origen, *Commentary on John*, ed. Cécile Blanc,
SC 120 (Paris: Éditions du Cerf, 1966), 56–60.

who dedicate their lives to his service not only by martyrdom but by study, offer as the first-fruits of discipleship their interpretation of the Gospel.[21]

This brings Origen to the key element of his introduction to the *Commentary on John*, which is to offer a definition of just what a "Gospel" is in the life of the Christian community. Origen begins with the position that within the whole of Scripture, "all the Old [Testament] is *not* Gospel, because it does not show the one who is coming but only announces him in advance, whereas all the New [Testament] *is* Gospel, ... because it contains various expressions of praise and teaching concerning the One through whom the Gospel is Gospel."[22] The term "Gospel," in other words, can be applied, in his view, to the letters of Paul or Peter, or to the Book of Revelation, as accurately as it can to the four Gospels. Among these four, however, which the mainstream Churches of his day apparently accepted for liturgical use, it is the Fourth Gospel which, in his opinion, claims first importance, because it tells of the origin and identity of Jesus in a much more profound and intimate way than the others.

> We may dare to say that the first-fruits of all the Scriptures are the Gospels, and that of the Gospels the first-fruit is that according to John, whose meaning no one can grasp who has not leaned on the breast of Jesus, or received from Jesus Mary, to become his own mother. It is necessary to become such a person if one is to be another John, so that it may be shown to him by Jesus—as it was to John—who Jesus is.[23]

To explain his meaning, Origen then goes on to define what he understands the word "Gospel" to mean: the good news of a promise fulfilled or nearing fulfillment. In the somewhat contorted phrasing of the commentary, he puts it this way:

> The Gospel is a writing that contains the announcement of things that give joy to the hearer, because of the likely benefits they bring once that which has been proclaimed is received ... Put another way, a Gospel is a writing holding out the presence of good for the one who believes it, or else a word proclaiming that the good thing that had been expected is actually present.[24]

---

[21] Ibid. 3–4 in SC 120, 62–64.

[22] Ibid. 5 in SC 120, 66. In this passage, it is not clear whether "the Old" and "the New," which both appear in the feminine form, should be taken to refer to "Scripture" (*graphe*) or "Testament" (*diatheke*).

[23] Ibid. 6 in SC 120, 70.

[24] Ibid. 7 in SC 120, 74.

In terms specifically applicable to the Christian body of Scripture, it is the announcement of the presence of Christ in the world now, as God's Word made flesh, which is the "Gospel" in the truest sense, since Jesus is the fulfillment of all the promises of God hinted at in earlier revelation.[25] So Jesus himself is the heart of the Gospel, and the texts of the Old Testament that are interpreted as pointing to him become, by that very identification, Gospel themselves. So, referring to his earlier definition of what a Gospel is, Origen adds:

> It might be said, in addition, that before the coming of Christ the Law and the Prophets did not contain the proclamation of what has been defined as 'Gospel,' since he had not yet come to make clear the Mysteries contained in them; but when the Savior dwelt among us and caused the Good News to be embodied, he brought it about through his Good News that everything becomes Good News.[26]

Anyone, then, with whom Christ "dwells"—because he shares the Church's faith, presumably, and has received the Holy Spirit—is enabled, in Origen's view, to worship God "in spirit and in truth," as Jesus himself promised the Samaritan woman (see John 4:24). This gift of divine knowledge enables the Christian reader of Scripture to see the whole collection of Biblical documents as Gospel, insofar as they are all seen as pointing to Christ:

> Before the Gospel, then, which came to be reality through the presence of Christ, nothing of the Old [Testament] was Gospel. But the Gospel, which is the New Covenant, by separating us from the oldness of the letter, made the newness of the Spirit, which never grows old—a newness proper to the New Covenant—to shine as a property of all the Scriptures, by the light of knowledge. Necessarily, then, the Gospel that lets Good News be recognized even in the Old Testament [i.e., the Fourth Gospel] is called 'Gospel' in the most outstanding sense.[27]

In Origen's scheme of understanding, then, the task of the Christian Scriptural interpreter is to enable those less enlightened or perceptive among their hearers and readers to discover the mysteries of Christ

---

[25] See Ibid. 10 in SC 120, 84: "Among those things understood as the Good News in the proclamation of blessings, the Apostles announced Jesus as Good News. For they are said to have announced the resurrection as a good thing, and that it is in some sense Jesus; for Jesus says, 'I am the resurrection' (John 11:25). But Jesus proclaims the things laid in store for the holy ones as Good News for the poor, inviting them to share in the divine promises." Jesus is, in other words, the clearest and most universal embodiment of what is proclaimed as a blessing for all who share in it.

[26] Ibid. 8 in SC 120, 78.

[27] Ibid. in SC 120, 78–80.

foreshadowed in the whole sweep of the Bible, and which, even in their New Testament form, still await clarification in the life of the Church, and presumably, in the age to come:

> We must recognize this, too: that as there is a Law which 'contains a shadow of the good things to come' (Heb 10:1), things that will be made clear by the law that will be proclaimed in truth, so the Gospel teaches a shadow of the mysteries of Christ, a Gospel which we assume will be understood by all who read it. And for those who know how to read everything contained there concerning the Son of God in a straightforward way—the mysteries presented by his words, and the things of which his actions were obscure images—it clearly presents what John calls the 'eternal Gospel' (Rv 14:6), which might properly be called the spiritual Gospel.[28]

The hard struggle facing the exegete, in this understanding of Scripture, is nothing less than "to translate the perceptible Gospel into a spiritual one: to try and penetrate to the depths of the Gospel's meaning, and to discover in it the bare truth of its figures."[29]

3. Athanasius

Athanasius of Alexandria, the implacable opponent of Arius and his followers in the fourth century and ultimately the impassioned defender of Nicaea's formula for expressing Jesus' divine status, was not primarily a Biblical interpreter, as we ordinarily conceive of that role—he left no commentaries or Biblical homilies, for instance. Yet his attempts to defend and promote the theological vision of the Council of Nicaea rested, in the end, on the interpretation of key passages from both the Old and the New Testament. To his opponents, these passages seemed to rule out the divinity of Jesus, the Son and Word of God, by suggesting he shared some of the principal qualities of creatures: a beginning in time, vulnerability and passibility, the need to make progress in his relationship to God, the recognition on his part that the one he called his "Father" was also his "God". For Athanasius, in contrast, the assumption that all Scripture forms a single book, with a single story, meant that the New Testament's affirmations of Jesus' divinity and primordial unity with God—passages like John 1:1–14 and Phil 2:5–11—provided a central pivot on which the meaning of all the rest of the canonical Scriptures turned; the interpretation of the whole canon, in other words, rested on

---

[28] Ibid. 9 in SC 120, 80–82.
[29] Ibid. 10 in SC 120, 84.

an affirmation of the reality of the Incarnation, of God the Son's "self-emptying," which was itself the center of history.

One could point to many examples in Athanasius's anti-Arian polemics of this approach to exegesis, but perhaps one will suffice. In his *Second Oration against the Arians*, written most likely in Rome during Athanasius's long second exile, in the early 340s, the bishop takes up—as one of these disputed passages—Proverbs 8:22, a text put in the mouth of heavenly Wisdom that had long been read in the Churches, in Philonic fashion, as referring to the divine Logos: in the Septuagint version, "The Lord created me as a beginning of his ways, for his works." For the Arians, and for a wider group of Greek-speaking theologians who wanted to maintain the traditional clear distinction between God, the ultimate source of all things, and the Logos who was formed to act as his intermediary in the work of creation and redemption, the implication was clear: although above the rest of creatures in status and before them all in his point of origin, the Word or Son of God who is speaking here had to be ranked on the side of those beings providentially produced by God—ranked among the creatures—rather than identified with God himself.

Athanasius, too, takes it for granted that this self-identification by Wisdom in Proverbs 8 is spoken by the Word who would be made flesh in Christ; but he insists that his phrase, "he created me," signifies "not the essence of his Godhead, nor his own everlasting and genuine generation from the Father, ... but his manhood and economy towards us."[30] In other words, the "creation" of which heavenly Wisdom speaks here is the creation of a human nature in which she would carry out the "works" for which God had eternally intended her: the restoration of life and order to a fallen world. Athanasius clarifies his position a few paragraphs later on:

> For the passage in the Proverbs, as I have said before, signifies, not the essence, but the humanity of the Word; for if he says that he was created 'for the works,' he shows his intention of signifying not his essence but the economy which took place 'for his works,' which comes second to being. For things which are in formation and creation are made specially that they may be and exist, and next they have to do whatever the Word bids them ... For before the works were made, the Son was ever, nor was there yet need that he should be created; but when the works were created and need

---

[30] Athanasius, *Oration II against the Arians* 45; see Athanasius, *Oration II against the Arians*, in PG 26.244A, *Nicene and Post-Nicene Fathers* II / 4, trans. John Henry Newman (Peabody, Mass.: Hendrickson, 1994), 372, translation slightly altered (alt.).

arose afterwards of the economy for their restoration, then it was that the Word took upon himself this condescension and assimilation to his works, which he has shown us by the word, 'he created.'[31]

The reasoning behind this insistence that "creation," when attributed to the Son, always refers to the human nature in which he was sent to share in the world's need and alienation, is clearly Christian and soteriological, rather than Jewish, sapiential or strictly exegetical. It is because he assumes that the Bible read in the Christian community has a single message, centered on the coming, death and resurrection of Jesus for the redemption of humanity, that Athanasius can read the fine details of passages from various levels of the earlier, Hebrew tradition in a new way, as part of the Christian Bible, seen in their normative Christian meaning as summarized in the Church's rule of faith. So Athanasius comments, a few paragraphs later:

> If the Son were a creature, the human person would have remained mortal as he was before, not being joined to God; for a creature would not have joined creatures to God, as itself seeking someone to join it [to him]; nor would a portion of the creation have been creation's salvation, as needing salvation itself. To provide against this, he sends his own Son, and he becomes Son of Man, by taking created flesh; that, since all were under sentence of death, he, being other than them all, might himself for all offer to death his own body; and that henceforth, as if all had died through him, the word of that sentence might be accomplished (for 'all died' in Christ: 2 Cor 5:14), and all through him might then become free from sin and from the curse which came upon it, and might truly abide forever, risen from the dead and clothed in immortality and incorruption.[32]

In a way that may surprise us at first glance, the story of the "economy," as understood in the Church—the Christian story of salvation through the Word made flesh—becomes here, for Athanasius, the guide to a correct reading of this controversial text from earlier Wisdom literature.

Another example of this approach of Athanasius to the Old Testament through the story of salvation in Christ is his way of interpreting the Psalms. In his fascinating *Letter to Marcellinus on the Interpretation of the Psalms*, Athanasius offers a correspondent named Marcellinus—perhaps one of the solitaries then populating the Egyptian desert—his view of the Psalter as a book capable of nourishing not only the Jewish worshipping community but the Christian person of prayer, in virtually every situation or need. The Psalms are like a mirror, he argues, reflecting to the one

---

[31] Ibid. 51 in NPNF, 376, alt.
[32] Ibid. 69 in NPNF, 386, alt.

who speaks or sings them a divinely provided glimpse of his or her own standing before God; this vision of the state of our own soul then helps us to steer and order ourselves more effectively towards God.[33] Such a modeling, in the Psalms, of both our present need and our ideal state, Athanasius seems to suggest, parallels the work of Christ, the incarnate Word in history:

> Each psalm is both spoken and composed by the Spirit so that in these same words, as we said earlier, the stirrings of our souls might be grasped, and all of them be said as concerning us ... Again, the same grace is from the Savior, for when he became human for us he offered his own body in dying for our sake, in order that he might set all free from death. And desiring to show us his own heavenly and well-pleasing life, he provided its type in himself, to the end that some might no more easily be deceived by the enemy, having a pledge for protection—namely, the victory he won over the devil for our sake ... For the same reason, even before his life among us, he made this resound from the lips of those who sing the Psalms. Just as he revealed the model of the earthly and the heavenly human being in himself, so also anyone who wishes can learn in the Psalms about the motions and conditions of soul, and can find in them the remedy and corrective measure for each of these motions.[34]

Understanding the effect of the Psalms on those who use them in his own Church leads Athanasius to an understanding of their intended meaning, in God's providence; and this intended meaning—which is to purify, order, and save the reader, to unite the one who uses them with the ever-active Word of God—only becomes clear when one has grasped the whole process of salvation in the life and death of Jesus, the Word made flesh. As Origen had suggested,[35] the Scriptural Word of God is in itself a kind of saving incarnation.

4. Augustine

A fourth theologian from the early Church whose work has left a lasting impression on later Christian Biblical interpretation and preaching is St. Augustine. Trained to a high professional level as a rhetorician in the 370s and 380s, deeply versed in the currents of antique philosophy, and constantly involved in the great theological and social debates of his day, Augustine was, for the last 35 years of his life, the bishop of Hippo Regius,

---

[33] *Letter to Marcellinus* 12; see PG 27.24.
[34] Ibid. 12–13 in PG 27.24–25; trans. Robert C. Gregg (New York: Paulist Press, 1980), 111–112, alt.
[35] See above, p. 10 and n. 17.

a medium-sized port city in North Africa; his pastoral duty there largely lay in preaching on passages of the Scriptures to ordinary congregations. Among the extensive works of Augustine we still have, there are almost 600 sermons on a variety of texts and subjects, as well as continuing series of expository homilies on the Gospel and the First Letter of John and on all 150 Psalms.[36]

One of the central themes in Augustine's approach to the Psalms, especially, is that of the *totus Christus*, the "whole Christ," whom he identifies as their constant speaker. Just as it is Christ who acts in the Church's sacraments, who makes himself present in the Eucharistic species and communicates life and renewal in baptism,[37] so Christ prays in the voice of the Church, his body, especially when it uses the Psalms given by God to be its common prayer. Sometimes passages in the Psalms need to be interpreted as the voice of Christ, the Church's head, speaking to his body; sometimes as the voice of Christ's body, speaking to its head; sometimes as the voice of the "whole" Christ, head and body, speaking to the Father or to the unbelieving world.[38] An example of this characteristic approach, chosen almost at random, is Augustine's comment on the first verse of Psalm 100 (101), "I will sing to you of your mercy and judgment, O Lord"—part of a homily he is thought to have delivered to his home congregation in 395, the year he became a bishop:

> Since the psalm sings to us of mercy and judgment, let us too act mercifully as in peace we await the judgment. Within Christ's body, let us sing of these things. Christ is singing about them to us. If the head were singing alone,

---

[36] For a helpful survey of the extent and character of Augustine's preaching, see the introduction by Daniel E. Doyle, O.S.A., to the volume of selected translations, *Saint Augustine: Essential Sermons* (Hyde Park, N.Y.: New City, 2007), 9–22.

[37] See, for instance, Augustine's arguments for Christ as being the real agent of baptism in some of his early works against the Donatists: *Contra literas Petiliani* 3.49.59, in CSEL 52, ed. M. Petschenig (Vienna / Leipzig: Tempsky / Freytag, 1909), 211–212; *Tractatus in Epistulam Joannis ad Parthos* 7.11, in SC 75, ed. P. Agaësse (Paris: Cerf, 1984), 334; *Tractatus in Joannis Evangelium* 5.18, in CCL 36, ed. R. Willems (Turnhout: Brepols, 1954), 51–52; 6.7–8 in CCL 36, 56–57. In Tractate 5.18 on John's Gospel, Augustine insists that whether Peter, Paul, or Judas is the minister of baptism, "he [Christ] is the one who baptizes"!

[38] For a full and very helpful discussion of this conception of the Church at prayer, precisely as a hermeneutical framework for interpreting the Psalms, see Michael Fiedrowicz, *Psalmus Vox Totius Christi: Studien zu Augustins 'Enarrationes in Psalmos'* (Freiburg: Herder, 1997), as well as Fiedrowicz's summary of his book, which appears as the introduction to the English translation of these sermons: *Saint Augustine: Expositions of the Psalms* 1 (Hyde Park, N.Y.: New City, 1999), 13–66.

the song would be about the Lord but would not belong to us; but if Christ is a whole, head and body (*si autem totus Christus, id est caput et corpus eius*), you must be among his members and cleave to him by faith and hope and charity. Then you are singing in him, and rejoicing in him, just as he labors in you, and thirsts in you, and hungers in you, and endures tribulations in you … We have spoken to you assiduously about Christ, and I know that these truths are familiar to you. Christ the Lord is the Word of God, through whom all things were made. In order to redeem us this Word was made flesh and dwelt among us; he who is God above all things, the Son of God who is equal to the Father, became human, so that as God-man he might be the mediator between humankind and God. He became human to reconcile to God those who were far off, to unite those who were divided, to recall the estranged and to bring back those sojourning away from home. He became the head of the Church, and so he has a body and limbs. Look for his limbs. At present they are groaning throughout the whole world, and at the end they will be full of joy over that crown of righteousness of which Paul says, 'The Lord, as a just judge, will award it to me on that day.' (2 Tm 4:8) Let us then sing in hope, all of us, gathered into one. Having put on Christ we, with our head, are Christ, for we are Abraham's posterity. The apostle tells us so. I have just said, 'We are Christ.' Let me explain that. The apostle teaches, 'You are the seed of Abraham, his heirs, according to the promise' (Gal 3:29). So we are Abraham's posterity … It is quite clear from this that we are part of Christ; and since we are his limbs and his members, we form one single person with our head.[39]

As the words of Christ present in his body, the Church, this Psalm becomes for Augustine an instrument by which Christ continues to work in the community of faith, calling it to share his saving concern for the poor and the alienated.

In his influential treatise (also from the late 390s) on Scriptural interpretation, *De Doctrina Christiana* (*On Christian Erudition*, or as an influential contemporary version translates it, *Teaching Christianity*), before launching on an elaborate exposition of how the Christian exegete and preacher might draw on the accumulated intellectual wealth of antiquity's grammatical and rhetorical arts to unfold and communicate the Bible's message, Augustine devotes a first book to summarizing the content of the Church's faith: the reality of God, as Father, Son and Holy Spirit; the saving Wisdom of God, active in the world; the Christian narrative of the incarnation of this Wisdom, and of the hope implied for the Church in

---

[39] *Enarratio in Psalmum* 100.3 in CCL 39, ed. E. Dekkers and J. Fraipont (Turnhout: Brepols, 1956), 1408; for English translation, see Augustine, *Saint Augustine: Expositions of the Psalms* 5, trans. Maria Boulding (Hyde Park, N.Y.: New City Press, 2003), 32–33. This homily, it has been suggested, may come from the Easter season of 395.

Jesus' death and resurrection; the central command of Jesus, taken from
Hebrew Scripture, to love God above all things and our neighbor as ourselves. Towards the end of the book, Augustine summarizes:

> So if it seems to you that you have understood the divine scriptures, or any
> part of them, in such a way that by this understanding you do not build
> up this twin love of God and neighbor, then you have not yet understood
> them. If on the other hand you have made judgments about them that
> are helpful for building up this love, but for all that have not said what
> the author you have been reading actually meant in that place, then your
> mistake is not pernicious ...[40]

Like a person who wanders off the road and reaches his intended des-
tination by crossing the fields, he continues, this sort of interpreter may
be mistaken, but at least has arrived at the desired end of all exegesis: "to
build up charity."[41]

Perhaps five or six years later, Augustine wrote another tract on Christian instruction in which he makes much the same point, and connects
it with the Gospel of Christ, in still more moving terms: his treatise *On
Catechizing the Uninstructed* (*De catechizandis rudibus*), addressed to the
Carthaginian deacon, Deogratias. Observing here that the purpose of the
whole Biblical narrative, from Genesis to the Book of Revelation, is to
show us the full extent and implications of the love of God, a love that
goes before any love of ours but that constantly summons our love forth
in return, Augustine comments:

> If, then, Christ came mainly for this reason, that the human race might
> know how much God loves us, and might know this in order to glow
> with love for him by whom we have first been loved, and might love our
> neighbor according to the command and the example of him who became
> our neighbor by loving one who was not his neighbor, but a distant alien;
> and if all of holy Scripture, written before him, was written to foretell the
> coming of the Lord, and whatever has later been committed to writing and
> sealed with God's authority tells of Christ and persuades us to love; then
> it is obvious, not simply that "all of the Law and the Prophets depends on
> those commandments to love God and our neighbor" (Mt 22:40)—the Law
> and Prophets that formed all of holy Scripture at the time the Lord said
> this—but also that whatever was written later, for our benefit, whatever
> books of divine writings have been given us to remember, teach us the
> same thing ...[42]

---

[40] *De Doctrina Christiana* 1.36.40; see Augustine, *De Doctrina Christiana*, in CCL
32.29, trans. Edmund Hill, O.P. (Hyde Park, N.Y.: New City, 1996), 123.

[41] Ibid.

[42] *De catechizandis rudibus* 4.8 in CCL 46, 128.

God's love for us, God's call to us to love him for his own sake and each other in his name, is what all of Scripture primarily is meant to tell us; and Christ is the one who makes this meaning clear.

At the beginning of his second homily on the First Letter of John, Augustine makes this same point more simply. Alluding to Jesus' instruction of the two disciples on the road to Emmaus on the first Easter afternoon, he remarks: "He touched on the whole scriptural text of the Old Testament. Whatever is in those Scriptures echoes Christ!"[43]

III. *Conclusions*

As we listen to these passages from early Christian Biblical interpreters, chosen almost randomly from the abundant literature of the Patristic age, it is easy enough to recognize why so many modern scholars, especially those committed to interpreting the Bible faithfully for the Church, find early Christian exegesis puzzling and arbitrary. The reason is simply that Biblical interpretation, since the time of the Enlightenment, has increasingly seen its task to be different from what these ancient Biblical scholars saw to be theirs. It is not that Patristic interpreters—the best of them, at least—lacked linguistic skills or perceptiveness in reading earlier texts; nor is it that they lacked a sense of the importance of literary or historical context for determining a text's meaning. It is simply that they saw their role, and indeed the significance and context of the Bible itself, differently from the way modern exegetes do.

For the modern interpreter of the Bible, the first task of the exegete or preacher is to identify, as far as one can, what the original author of a passage probably said and what he or she meant by it. For those intentionally aware also of the importance of the canonical assimilation of texts into larger literary wholes, it is important to ask in addition what concerns may have motivated the work of redaction and arrangement, the juxtapositions and eliminations that have formed traditional texts into holy books for study and liturgical celebration, ultimately into normative collections. But the methodological assumption behind most modern attempts at such interpretation is that this original meaning of these texts is to be found simply through the careful, objective study of linguis-

---

[43] *In Epistulam Joannis ad Parthos Tractatus* 2.1 in SC 75, 152: "Omnem veterem textum Scripturarum circumplexus est [Christus]. Quidquid illarum Scripturarum est, Christum sonat."

tic and historical and archaeological evidence—a process that, in principle at least, can be carried out just as well by the unbeliever as the believer, by the person who sees in these texts a norm to live by, and by the one who does not.

Ancient exegetes, clearly, had a somewhat different sense of history and of what is historical. Many of them—Origen and Augustine, for example, and those influenced by them—were deeply concerned to identify the original author's intentions behind a text as a primary goal of exegesis. They understood the research on texts and events of the past, however, not so much as an empirical process of discovering and evaluating evidence, of testing hypotheses and reconstructing a past reality independent of ourselves, in the way historians since the eighteenth century have done, but rather as laying out pieces of a narrative that holds central lessons for our lives—much as Thucydides or Plutarch saw the process of telling the stories of the past ages and leading figures of their own societies, or as Ignatius of Loyola invites those making the *Spiritual Exercises* to enter personally into the Scriptural narratives, to receive direction and light. For them, their faith that God was the central figure in human history and that God's actions through the ages led directly to the graced situation in which their own worshipping community stood, was the starting and ending point of the Scriptural narrative, not a private conviction to be bracketed out for the sake of methodological integrity.

In this context, explaining a text that their community regarded as holy Scripture—as normative and revelatory, in other words—required that one interpret it in the context of what they took to be God's longer plan: the "economy" or management of history that summed up their understanding of their own place in the process. Otherwise it would not be *Scripture* at all, but simply a catena of assorted religious fragments, a museum rather than a living voice. For the Hebrew people of the Persian period, that "place" of the community was post-exilic Jerusalem: inspired by its memories of election and rescue, exile and return, struggling with its new role as a small province in a large Empire, peering into the significance that stories of God's previous actions held for them now. For the early Church, four centuries later and more, the "place" was a scattered community of Jews and Gentiles living throughout the world, unified by their conviction that they had been reconciled to God by the coming of Jesus, his Son, and that they lived in hope of Jesus' final coming. For both Jews and Christians, the rearranged traditions of Scripture, formed into new books and a developing canon, were not just history, but a word of life.

Exegesis, then, for ancient Jews and Christians, was marked not so much by a distinctive "method" of opening up the meaning of texts, as by its distinctive theological assumptions; reading the Bible *as* Bible, after all, is an expression of faith. The object of exegetical study was a collection of earlier texts, Jewish and Christian, that had come to be regarded as a single book, precisely because it conveyed—circuitously, in bafflingly complex ways—a single message. For the Christian community, the heart of that message was Christ: his person, his work, his continuing presence in the community through the gift of his Spirit; and the person of Christ, especially in the view of the Fathers who defended the faith of Nicaea, was the person of the Word of God, present as a human being in history. The process by which the Christian Scriptural canon was formed, by which "Scriptures" came to be understood as a single collection including an Old and a New Testament, took place not by accident, but within the community of the Church, as part of its interpretation of its own past and its growing awareness of its own identity. Liturgical use, authoritative structures, and the growing practice of exegesis and preaching were inseparable from the formation of the canon itself: for Christians, there is no Bible without a worshipping Church, in other words, and no Church without a Bible.

For us, as modern and post-modern readers, the question remains: how much is early Christian exegesis, with all its theological presuppositions, usable today? How far is it possible, culturally or intellectually, for modern interpreters to read Biblical texts from a theological and ecclesial as well as a secular, historical perspective? This is a question each practicing exegete, and every religious community, must confront for oneself. However we read it, it seems to me, the important thing is that we take early Christian Biblical interpretation seriously, in its own terms, as witnessing to a view of history, and to a faith in the Lord of history, that is both coherent in its own right and challenging to many of our modern assumptions about reality and truth. To say, with Augustine, that "the whole of the Scriptures echoes Christ" is to confess not so much a skewed view of what the Bible says, as the ability—for him, the God-given ability—to read it with the eyes of faith.

BIBLIOGRAPHY

Adam, A.K.M. "Twisting to Destruction: A Memorandum on the Ethics of Interpretation." *Perspectives in Religious Studies* 23 (2002).

Alcinous. *Enseignement des doctrines de Platon.* Edited by John Whittaker. Translated by Pierre Louis. 2d ed. Paris: Belles Lettres, 2002.

Alcinous: The Handbook of Platonism. Translated with introduction and commentary by John M. Dillon. Oxford: Clarendon, 1993.

Allison, Dale C. *Jesus of Nazareth: Millenarian Prophet.* Minneapolis: Fortress Press, 1998.

Alter, Robert. "How Important are the Dead Sea Scrolls?" *Commentary* 93 (1992).

Amir, Yehoshua. "The Transference of Greek Allegories to Biblical Motifs in Philo." In *Nourished with Peace: Studies in Hellenistic Judaism in Memory of Samuel Sandmel.* Edited by Frederick E. Greenspahn, Earle Hilgert, and Burton L. Mack. Chico, Calif.: Scholars Press, 1984.

Apollodorus. *The Library.* Translated by J.G. Frazer. LCL. London: W. Heinemann and New York: G.P. Putnam, 1921.

Aristeas to Philocrates: Letter of Aristeas. Edited and translated by Moses Hadas. New York: Harper, 1951. Reprint, Eugene, Oreg.: Wipf & Stock, 2007.

Aristotle. *Art of Rhetoric.* Translated by J.H. Freese. Loeb Classical Library. Cambridge: Harvard University Press, 1926.

———. *The Nicomachean Ethics.* In *Aristotle in Twenty-three Volumes.* Vol. 9. Translated by H. Rackham. Cambridge, Mass.: Harvard University Press and London: William Heinemann, 1982.

Arterbury, Andrew. *Entertaining Angels: Early Christian Hospitality in its Mediterranean Setting.* Sheffield, U.K.: University of Sheffield, 2005.

Ashton, J. *Understanding the Fourth Gospel,* 1st ed. Oxford: Clarendon, 1991.

Athanasius. *Letter to Marcellinus.* In PG 27.24. Translated by Robert C. Gregg. New York: Paulist Press, 1980.

———. *Oration II against the Arians.* In PG 26.244A. *Nicene and Post-Nicene Fathers* II / 4. Translated by John Henry Newman. Peabody, Mass.: Hendrickson, 1994.

Athanassakis, Apostolos N. *The Homeric Hymns.* Baltimore / London: Johns Hopkins University Press, 1984.

Attridge, Harold W. "The Cubist Principle in Johannine Imagery: John and the Reading of Images in Contemporary Platonism." In *Imagery in the Gospel of John. Terms, Forms, Themes and Theology of Figurative Language.* Edited by Jörg Frey, Jan G. van der Watt, Ruben Zimmermann, with the collaboration of Gabi Kern. WUNT 200; Tübingen: Mohr-Siebeck, 2006.

———. "Don't be Touching Me: Recent Feminist Scholarship on Mary Magdalene." In A.-J. Levine, ed., *A Feminist Companion to John.* Cleveland: Pilgrim, 2003.

———. "An Emotional Jesus and Stoic Tradition." In forthcoming. Edited by Troels Engberg-Pedersen.

———. "The Gospel of Truth as an Exoteric Text." In *Nag Hammadi, Gnosticism, and Early Christianity*. Edited by Charles W. Hedrick and Robert Hodgson. Peabody: Hendrickson, 1986.

———. "Heracleon and John: Reassessment of an Early Christian Hermeneutical Debate." In *Biblical Interpretation, History, Context, and Reality*. Edited by Christine Helmer. Leiden, Boston: Brill, 2005.

Attridge, Harold W. and Elaine Pagels. "The Tripartite Tractate." *Nag Hammadi Codex I (The Jung Codex)*. NHS 22, 23; Leiden: Brill, 1985.

———. "The Tripartite Tractate (I, 5)." *The Nag Hammadi Library in English*. Edited by James M. Robinson. 3rd ed. San Francisco: Harper & Row, 1988.

Aune, David E. *ABD*. s.v. "Eschatology (Early Christian)."

Augustine. *City of God*. Translated by William M. Green. Loeb Classical Library 412. Cambridge, Mass.: Harvard University Press, 1963.

———. *Contra literas Petiliani*. In CSEL 52. Edited by M. Petschenig. Vienna / Leipzig: Tempsky / Freytag, 1909.

———. *De Doctrina Christiana*. In CCL 32.29. Translated by Edmund Hill, O.P. Hyde Park, N.Y.: New City, 1996.

———. *Enarratio in Psalmum*. In CCL 39. Edited by E. Dekkers and J. Fraipont. Turnhout: Brepols, 1956.

———. *Saint Augustine: Expositions of the Psalms 5*. Translated by Maria Boulding. Hyde Park, N.Y.: New City Press, 2003.

———. *Sermons (341–400) on Various Subjects*. Pt. 3, vol. 10. *The Works of Saint Augustine: A Translation for the 21st Century*. Edited by John Rotelle. Translated by Edmund Hill. Hyde Park, N.Y.: New City, 1995.

———. *Tractatus in Epistulam Joannis ad Parthos*. Sources chrétiennes 75. Edited by P. Agaësse. Paris: Éditions du Cerf, 1984.

———. *Tractatus in Joannis Evangelium*. Edited by R. Willems. CCL 36. Turnhout: Brepols, 1954.

Austin, J.L. *How to Do Things with Words*. 2nd ed. Edited by. J.O. Urmson and Marina Sbisa. Cambridge, MA: Harvard University Press, 1962.

Bailey, Kenneth E. *Poet and Peasant: A Literary-Cultural Approach to the Parables in Luke*. Grand Rapids: Eerdmans, 1976.

Ball, D. *'I Am' in John's Gospel: Literary Function, Background and Theological Implications*. JSNTS 124. Sheffield: Sheffield Academic, 1996.

Barclay, John M.G. "'By the Grace of God I Am What I Am': Grace and Agency in Philo and Paul." In *Divine and Human Agency in Paul and His Cultural Environment*. Edited by John M.G. Barclay and Simon J. Gathercole. London and New York: T&T Clark, 2006.

———. *Colossians and Philemon*. Sheffield, U.K.: Sheffield, 1996.

———. *Jews in the Mediterranean Diaspora: From Alexander to Trajan (323 BCE – 117 CE)*. Edinburgh: T & T Clark, 1996.

———. "Paul, Philemon and the Dilemma of Christian Slave-Ownership." *New Testament Studies* 37 (1991): 170–175.

Barrera, Julio Trebolle and Luis Vegas Montaner, eds. *The Madrid Qumran Congress: Proceedings of the International Congress on the Dead Sea Scrolls, Madrid 18–21 March 1991*. 2 vols. Leiden: E.J. Brill, 1992.

Bartchy, Scott S. *MALLON CHRESAI*: First Century Slavery and 1 Corinthians 7:21. SBLDS 11. Missoula, Mont.: Society of Biblical Literature, 1973.

Barth, Markus and Helmut Blanke. *The Letter to Philemon: a New Translation with Notes and Commentary*. Grand Rapids, Mich.: Eerdmans, 2000.

Barthélemy, D. and J.T. Milik. *Qumran Cave I*. Discoveries in the Judaean Desert I. Oxford: Clarendon Press, 1955.

Bassler, Jouette M. *Divine Impartiality: Paul and a Theological Axiom*. Chico: Scholars Press, 1981.

Baumgarten, Joseph. Review of *Reclaiming the Dead Sea Scrolls: The History of Judaism, the Background of Christianity, the Lost Library of Qumran*. By Lawrence Schiffman, in *Jewish Action* (fall 5756 / 1995): 92–93, 96.

Beavis, Mary Ann. "Ancient Slavery as an Interpretive Context for the New Testament Servant Parables with Special Reference to the Unjust Steward (Luke 16:1–8)." *JBL* 111 (1992): 37–54.

Bednarz, T. "Lukan Humor and the Parable of the Dishonest Household Manager (Luke 16:1–17)." Paper presented at the annual meeting of the SBL, New Orleans, La., November 22, 2009.

Behr, John. *The Way to Nicaea*. Crestwood, N.Y.: St. Vladimir's, 2001.

Benoit, Pierre. "Rapports littéraires entre les épîtres aux Colossiens et aux Ephésiens." *Neutestamentliche Aufsätze*. Regensberg: Pustet, 1963.

Benoit, Pierre and Jerome Murphy O'Connor, eds. *Paul and Qumran: Studies in New Testament* Exegesis. London: G. Chapman, 1968.

Berthelot, Katell. "L'interprétation symbolique des lois alimentaires dans la Lettre d'Aristée: une influence pythagoricienne." *Journal of Jewish Studies* 52 (2001): 253–268.

Betz, Hans Dieter. *Galatians*. Hermeneia. Philadelphia: Fortress, 1979.

Betz, Otto and Martin Hangel and Peter Schmidt, eds. *Abraham Unser Vater. Juden und Christen im Gespräch über die Bibel. Festschrift für Otto Michel*. Leiden: Brill, 1963.

Birnbaum, Ellen. *The Place of Judaism in Philo's Thought: Israel, Jews, and Proselytes*. Atlanta: Scholars Press, 1996.

Blomberg, Craig. *The Parables of Jesus*. Downers Grove, Ill.: InterVarsity, 1990.

Blowers, Paul, ed. *The Bible in Greek Christian Antiquity*. Notre Dame: Notre Dame Press, 1997.

Bock, Darrell. *Luke*. 2 vols. BECNT 3. Grand Rapids: Baker, 1994–1996.

Bonaventure. *Commentary on the Gospel of Luke*. 3 vols. Translated by Robert J. Karris. St. Bonaventure, N.Y.: Franciscan Institute Publications, 2001–2004.

Bonnet, Maximillian. *Acta Apostolorum Apocrypha II,1*. Leipzig: Mendelssohn, 1989. Reprint, Hildesheim: Olms, 1972.

Booth, Wayne. *The Company We Keep: An Ethics of Fiction*. Berkeley: University of California Press, 1988.

Borg, Marcus J. *Jesus, A New Vision: Spirit, Culture and The Life of Discipleship*. New York: HarperCollins, 1987.

———. *Meeting Jesus Again for the First Time: The Historical Jesus and the Heart of Contemporary Faith*. New York: HarperCollins, 1994.

Borgen, P. *Bread from Heaven. An Exegetical Study of the Conception of Manna in the Gospel of John and the Writings of Philo*. NovTSup 10 Leiden: E.J. Brill, 1965.

Boulogne, Jacques. "L'intempérence verbale: L'imaginaire de Plutarche dans la thérapie des maladies de l'âme." In *Les passions antiques et médiévales*. Edited by Bernard Besnier, Pierre-François Moreau, and Laurence Renault. Paris: Presses universitaires de France, 2003.

Boyancé, Pierre. "Écho des exégèses de la mythologie grecque chez Philon." In *Philon d'Alexandrie*. Paris: Éditions Centre National de la Recherché Scientifique, 1967.

Boyce, Richard Nelson. *The Cry to God in the Old Testament*. Atlanta, Ga.: Scholars Press, 1988.

Bradley, Keith R. *Slaves and Masters in the Roman Empire: A Study in Social Control*. New York: Oxford University Press, 1984.

Bremmer, Jan N., ed. *The Apocryphal Acts of John*. Kampen: Kok Pharos, 1995.

———. "Women in the Apocryphal Acts of John." In *Apocryphal Acts of John*. Edited by idem. Kampen: Kok Pharos, 1995.

———. "Women in the Apocryphal Acts of John." In *Apocryphal Acts of Thomas*. Edited by idem. Leuven: Peeters, 2001.

Bretscher, Paul G. "Brief Studies: The Parable of the Unjust Steward—A New Approach to Luke 16:1–9." *CTM* 22 (1951): 756–762.

Brown, Colin. "The Unjust Steward: A New Twist?" In *Worship, Theology, and Ministry in the Early Church: Essays in Honor of Ralph P. Martin*. Edited by Michael J. Wilkins and Terence Paige. JSNTSup 87. Sheffield: Sheffield Academic Press, 1992.

Brown-Driver-Briggs Hebrew and English Lexicon. Edited by F. Brown and S. Driver and C. Briggs. Peabody, Mass.: Hendrickson, 1996.

Brown, Judith Anne. *John Marco Allegro: The Maverick of the Dead Sea Scrolls*. Grand Rapids, Mich.: Eerdmans, 2005.

Brown, R.E. *The Epistles of John*. Anchor Bible 30. Garden City, N.J.: Doubleday, 1982.

———. *The Gospel According to John*. Anchor Bible 29, 29A. Garden City: Doubleday, 1966–1970.

Brown, William P. *Character in Crisis: A Fresh Approach to the Wisdom Literature of the Old* Testament. Grand Rapids: Mich.: Eerdmans, 1996.

Bruce, F.F. *The Epistle to the Colossians, to Philemon and to the Ephesians*. Grand Rapids, Mich.: Eerdmans, 1984.

Buckley, Jorunn Jacobsen. *Female Fault and Fulfillment in Gnosticism*. Chapel Hill: University of North Carolina Press, 1986.

Buell, Denise Kimber. *Why this new Race: Ethnic Reasoning in early Christianity*. New York: Columbia University Press, 2005.

Bultmann, Rudolf K. "Die Bedeutung der neuerschlossenen mandäischen und manichäischen Quellen für das Verstädis des Johannesevangeliums." *ZNW* 24 (1925): 100–146.

———. *The Gospel of John*. ET; Philadelphia: Westminster, 1971.

———. *History of the Synoptic Tradition*. Translated by John Marsh. Rev. ed. Oxford: Blackwell, 1972.

———. *Primitive Christianity in Its Contemporary Setting*. New York: Meridian Books, 1956.

——. *Theology of the New Testament*. 2 vols. Translated by Kendrick Grobel. New York: Scribner, 1951–1955.

Burkett, D. "Make Friends with Unrighteous Mammon (Luke 16:9): A Form of Early Christian Fundraising." Paper presented at the Annual Meeting of the SBL, New Orleans, La., November 22, 2009.

Burrows, Millar. *Palestine is Our Business*. Philadelphia: Westminster Press, 1949.

Byron, John. *Recent Research on Paul and Slavery*. Sheffield, U.K.: Sheffield University Press, 2008.

Callaghan, Allen Dwight. *Embassy of Onesimus: The Letter of Paul to Philemon*. Valley Forge, Pa.: Trinity Press International, 1997.

Calvin, John. *Commentary on Harmony of the Gospels*. Vol. 17. Calvin's Commentaries. Grand Rapids: Baker Book House, 2005.

Carroll, Noël. "Interpretation and Intention: The Debate Between Hypothetical and Actual Intentionalism." In *The Philosophy of Interpretation*. Edited by Joseph Margolis and Tom Rockmore. Oxford, U.K.: Blackwell, 1999.

Carroll, Scott T. "Aristobulus 3." In *ABD*, edited by David Noel Freedman. Vol. 1. New Haven, Conn.: Yale University Press, 1992.

——. "Janneus." In *ABD*, edited by David Noel Freedman. Vol. 3. New Haven, Conn.: Yale University Press, 1992.

Catchpole, David. "Paul, James and the Apostolic Decree." *New Testament Studies* 23 (1977): 428–444.

Clement of Alexandria, Fragments from Cassiodorus, "Comments on the First Epistle of John [1:1]." In *Fathers of the Second Century: Hermas, Tatian, Athenagoras, Theophilus, and Clement of Alexandria (Entire): The Writings of the Fathers Down to AD 325*. Edited by Alexander Roberts and James Donaldson and A. Cleveland Coxe. ANF. Vol. 2. N.p.: Hendrikson, 1994.

Clifford, Richard J. "The Roots of Apocalypticism in Near Eastern Myth." In *The Encyclopedia of Apocalypticism*, edited by Bernard McGinn, John J. Collins, and Stephen J. Stein. 3 vols. New York: Continuum, 1998.

Cohen, Shaye. *The Beginnings of Jewishness: Boundaries, Varieties, Uncertainties*. Berkeley, Calif.: University of California, 1999.

Collins, Adela Yarbro. "Christian Messianism and the First Jewish War with Rome." In *Biblical Traditions in Transmission: Essays in Honour of Michael A. Knibb*, edited by Charlotte Hempel and Judith M. Lieu. Supplements to the Journal for the Study of Judaism 111. Leiden: Brill, 2006.

——. "The Dream of a New Jerusalem at Qumran." In *The Bible and the Dead Sea Scrolls*, edited by James H. Charlesworth. 3 vols. Waco, Tex.: Baylor University Press, 2006.

——. "Jesus' Action in Herod's Temple." In *Antiquity and Humanity: Essays on Ancient Religion and Philosophy Presented to Hans Dieter Betz on His 70th Birthday*. Edited by eadem and Margaret M. Mitchell. Tübingen: Mohr Siebeck, 2001.

——. *Mark*. Hermeneia. Minneapolis, Minn.: Fortress, 2007.

——. "Pergamon in Early Christian Literature." In *Pergamon, Citadel of the Gods: Archaeological Record, Literary Description, and Religious Development*, edited by Helmut Koester. Harvard Theological Studies 46. Harrisburg, Penn.: Trinity Press International, 1998.

Collins, John J., trans. "Artapanus." In *The Old Testament Pseudepigrapha*, edited by James H. Charlesworth. Vol. 2. New York: Doubleday, 1985.

———. *Between Athens and Jerusalem*. 2nd ed. Grand Rapids, Mich.: Eerdmans, 2000.

———. *Daniel*. Hermeneia. Minneapolis, Minn.: Fortress, 1993.

———. "Forms of Community in the Dead Sea Scrolls." In *Emanuel: Studies in Hebrew Bible, Septuagint, and Dead Sea Scrolls in Honor of Emanuel Tov*, edited by Shalom M. Paul, Robert A. Kraft, Lawrence H. Schiffman, and Weston W. Fields. Supplements to Vetus Testamentum 94. Leiden and Boston: Brill, 2003.

Collins, Raymond F. *Letters Paul Did Not Write: The Letter to the Hebrews and the Pauline Pseudepigrapha*. Wilmington, Del.: Wipf & Stock Publishers, 1988.

———. *The Power of Images in Paul*. Collegeville, Minn.: Michael Glazier, 2008.

Commentaries on Early Jewish Literature. Edited by L. Stuckenbruck, P.W. van der Horst, H. Lichtenberger, D. Mendels, and J. Mueller. 58 vols. Berlin: Walter de Gruyter Press, 2002-forthcoming.

Cooper, John M. "Posidonius on Emotions." In *Reason and Emotion: Essays on Ancient Moral Psychology and Ethical Theory*. Princeton: Princeton University Press, 1999. First published in *The Emotions in Hellenistic Philosophy*. Edited by Juha Sihvola and Troels Engberg-Pedersen. New Synthese Historical Library 46. Dordrecht: Kluwer Academic Publishers, 1998.

Cotter, Wendy. "Women's Authority Roles in Paul's Churches: Countercultural or Conventional." *NovT* 36 (1994).

Crook, John. *Law and Life in* Rome. Ithaca: N.Y.: Cornell University Press, 1967.

Crossan, J. Dominic. *The Essential Jesus: Original Sayings and Earliest Images*. New York: HarperCollins, 1994.

———. *The Historical Jesus: The Life of a Mediterranean Jewish Peasant*. New York: HarperCollins, 1991.

———. *Jesus: A Revolutionary Biography*. New York: HarperCollins, 1994.

———. *In Parables: The Challenge of the Historical Jesus*. 2nd ed. Sonoma: Polebridge Press, 1992.

Cross, Frank Moore. *The Ancient Library of Qumran and Modern Biblical Studies*. Garden City, N.Y.: Doubleday, 1958.

Culpepper, R. Alan. *John, The Son of Zebedee: the Life of a Legend*. Columbia, S.C.: University of South Carolina Press, 1994. Reprint, Minneapolis: Fortress, 2000.

Curtis, John. "On Job's Response to YHWH." *JBL* 98,4 (1979): 497–511.

Cyril of Alexandria. *Commentary on the Gospel of Saint Luke*. Translated by R. Payne Smith. Astoria, N.Y.: Studion, 1983.

Daley, Brian E. "Is Patristic Exegesis Still Usable? Reflections on Early Christian Interpretation of the Psalms." *Communio* 29 (2002): 185–216.

D'Angelo, Mary Rose. "Gender Refusers in the Early Christian Mission; Gal 2:28 as an Interpretation of Gen 1:27b." In *Reading in Christian Communities*, edited by Charles A. Bobertz and David Brakke. Notre Dame: University of Notre Dame Press, 2002.

Derrett, J. Duncan M. "Fresh Light on St. Luke 16." *NTS* 7 (1961): 198–219.

——. "'Take thy Bond … and Write Fifty' (Luke xvi.6): The Nature of the Bond." *JTS* 23 (1972): 438–440.

Dillon, John. "Ganymede as the Logos: Traces of a Forgotten Allegorization in Philo." *Studia Philonica* 6 (1979–1980): 37–40.

——. *The Middle Platonists, 80 BC to AD 220.* Rev. ed. Ithaca, N.Y.: Cornell University Press, 1996.

Dio Cassius. *Roman History.* Translated by E. Carey and H.B. Foster. LCL. 9 vols. Cambridge, Mass.: Harvard University Press, 1955–1961.

DiPaolo, Jr., Lawrence. *Hymn Fragments Embedded in the New Testament: Hellenistic Jewish and Greco-Roman Parallels.* New York: Edwin Mellen Press, 2008.

Dodd, C.H. *The Parables of the Kingdom.* Rev. ed. New York: Charles Scribner's Sons, 1961.

Donahue, John R. *The Gospel in Parable.* Philadelphia: Fortress, 1988.

Doyle, Daniel E. *Saint Augustine: Essential Sermons.* Hyde Park, N.Y.: New City, 2007.

Dunn, J.D.G. *The Epistles to Colossians and Philemon.* Grand Rapids, Mich.: Eerdmans, 1996.

——. *Romans 9–16.* Word Biblical Commentary 38b. Dallas, Tex.: Word Books, 1988.

——. *Unity and Diversity in the New Testament.* 2nd ed. Philadelphia, Pa.: Trinity, 1990.

Ehrman, Bart D. *Jesus: Apocalyptic Prophet of the New Millennium.* Oxford: Oxford University Press, 1999.

Eisenbaum, Pamela M. "Is Paul the Father of Misogyny and Antisemitism?" *Cross Currents* 50 (2000–2001): 506–524.

Elliott, J.K. *The Apocryphal New Testament.* Oxford: Oxford University Press, 1993.

Engberg-Pedersen, Troels. *Paul and the Stoics.* Edinburgh: T. & T. Clark, 2000.

Epp, Eldon Jay. *Junia: The First Woman Apostle.* Minneapolis: Fortress, 2005.

Euripides. Translated by D. Kovacs and A.S. Way. LCL. 8 vols. Cambridge, Mass.: Harvard University Press, 1912–2002.

——. *Bacchae.* Edited by E.R. Dodds. Oxford: Oxford University Press, 1960.

——. *Bacchae.* Edited by Richard Seaford. Warminster, U.K.: Aris and Phillips, 1996.

Evanston, Edward. *The Dissonance of the Four Generally Received Evangelists and the Evidence of Their Respective Authenticity Examined.* 2nd ed. Ipswich: G. Jermym, 1805.

Ewald, Heinrich. *Die Sendschriften des Apostels-Paulus.* Göttingen, 1857.

Farrar, Frederic. *History of Interpretation.* London: Macmillan, 1886.

——. *Lives of the Fathers.* Edinburgh: A. and C. Black, 1889.

Fee, Gordon. *The First Epistle to the Corinthians.* The New International Commentary on the New Testament. Grand Rapids, Mich.: Eerdmans, 1987.

Feldmeier, Reinhard. "Weise hinter 'eisernen Mauer': Tora und jüdisches Selbstverständnis zwischen Akkulturation und Absonderung im Aristeasbrief." In *Die Septuaginta zwischen Judentum und Christentum.* Edited by Martin Hengel and Anna Maria Schwemer. WUNT 72. Tübingen: Mohr, 1994.

Février, James Germain. *La date, la composition et les sources de la Lettre d'Aristée à Philocrate.* Bibliotheque de l'Ecole des Hautes Etudes 242. Paris: Édouard Champion, 1925.

Fiedrowicz, Michael. "Introduction." In *Saint Augustine: Expositions of the Psalms* 1. Hyde Park, N.Y.: New City, 1999.

———. *Psalmus Vox Totius Christi: Studien zu Augustines 'Enarrationes in Psalmos.'* Freiburg: Herder, 1997.

Fields, Weston W. *The Dead Sea Scrolls: A Full History.* Leiden-Boston: Brill, 2009.

Finley, Moses I. *Ancient Slavery and Modern Ideology.* New York: The Viking Press, 1980.

Fiorenza, Elisabeth Schüssler. *Jesus and the Politics of Interpretation.* London: Continuum, 1997.

———. *In Memory of Her: A Feminist Theological Reconstruction of Christian Origins.* New York: Crossroad, 1983.

———. *Rhetoric and Ethic: The Politics of Biblical Studies.* Minneapolis, Minn.: Fortress, 1999.

Fitzmyer, Joseph A. *The Acts of the Apostles: A New Translation and Commentary.* Anchor Bible 18C. New York: Doubleday, 1998.

———. *The Letter to Philemon.* Anchor Bible 34C. New York: Doubleday, 2000), 17–18, 20–23.

———. *Romans: A New Translation and Commentary.* Anchor Bible 33. New York: Doubleday, 1993.

———. "The Story of the Dishonest Manager (Luke 16:1–13)." *TS* 25 (1964): 23–42.

Fletcher, Donald R. "The Riddle of the Unjust Steward: Is Irony the Key?" *JBL* 92 (1963): 15–30.

Flint, Peter F. and James C. Vanderkam, eds. *The Dead Sea Scrolls after Fifty Years: A Comprehensive Assessment.* 2 vols. Brill: Leiden, 1998.

Fowl, Stephen E. *Engaging Scripture: A Model for Theological Interpretation,* Challenges in Contemporary Theology. Malden, Mass. and Oxford, U.K.: Blackwell, 1998.

Freeman, Kathleen, trans. *Ancilla to the Pre-Socratic Philosophers: A Complete Translation of the Fragments in Diels.* Fragmente der Vorsokratiker. Cambridge, Mass.: Harvard University Press, 1978.

Frey, Jörg and Jens Herzer and Martina Janssen and Clare K. Rithschild, eds. *Pseudepigraphie und Verfasserfiktion in frühchristlichen Briefen.* WUNT 236. Tübingen: Mohr Siebeck, 2009.

Fung, Ronald Y.K. "Ministry in the New Testament." In *The Church and the Bible and the World.* Edited by D.A. Carson. Grand Rapids: Baker, 1987.

Funk, Robert. *The Five Gospels: The Search for the Authentic Words of Jesus.* New York: Polebridge, 1993.

García Martínez, Florentino and and Eibert J.C. Tigchelaar, trans. and eds. *The Dead Sea Scrolls Study Edition,* 2 vols. Leiden: Brill, 1997–1998.

Garnsey, Peter. *Ideas of Slavery from Aristotle to Augustine.* Cambridge, U.K.: Cambridge University Press, 1996.

Gätcher, Paul. "The Parable of the Dishonest Steward after Oriental Conceptions." *CBQ* 12 (1950): 121–131.

Gillihan, Yonder. "Civic Ideology among the Covenanters of the Dead Sea Scrolls and Other Greco-Roman Voluntary Associations." Ph.D. diss., University of Chicago, 2007.

Glucker, John. *Antiochus and the Late Academy*. Hypomnemata 56. Göttingen: Vandenhoeck & Ruprecht, 1978.

Goulet, Richard. *La philosophie de Moïse: Essai de reconstitution d'un commentaire philosophique préphilonien du Pentateuque*. Paris: Librairie Philosophique J. Vrin, 1987.

Gracia, Jorge J.E. "Relativism and the Interpretation of Texts." In *The Philosophy of Interpretation*. Edited by Joseph Margolis and Tom Rockmore. Oxford, U.K.: Blackwell Publishers, 1999.

Green, Joel B. *The Gospel of Luke*. NICNT. Grand Rapids: Eerdmans, 1998.

Groothuis, Rebecca Merrill. *Good News for Women: A Biblical Picture of Gender Equality*. Grand Rapids: Eerdmans, 1997.

Grossmann, M.L. and C.M. Murphy, eds. "The Dead Sea Scrolls in the Popular Imagination." *Dead Sea Discoveries* 12 / 1 (2005).

Gruen, Erich. *Heritage and Hellenism*. Berkeley, Calif.: University of California Press, 1998.

Guthrie, W.K.C. *The Sophists*. Cambridge, U.K.: Cambridge University Press, 1971.

Hadas, Moses, ed. and trans. *Aristeas to Philocrates: Letter of Aristeas*. New York: Harper, 1951. Reprint, Eugene, Ore.: Wipf & Stock, 2007.

Hadot, Pierre. "Spiritual Exercises." In *Philosophy as a Way of Life: Spiritual Exercises from Socrates to Foucault*. Edited by Arnold Davidson. Translated by Michael Chase. Oxford: Blackwell, 1995.

Haenchen, E. *John 1*. Hermeneia. Philadelphia: Fortress, 1984.

Hanson, R.P.C. *Allegory and Event*. London: SCM, 1959. Reprint, Louisville: Westminster / John Knox, 2002.

Harnack, Adolf von. *What is Christianity? Lectures delivered in the University of Berlin during the Winter-Term 1899–1900*. Translated by T.B. Saunders. 2nd ed. rev. New York: G.P. Putnam's Sons; London: Williams and Norgate, 1908.

Harrill, J. Albert. *Slaves in the New Testament*. Minneapolis: Fortress, 2006.

Hartman, Lars. *Prophecy Interpreted: The Formation of Some Jewish Apocalyptic Texts and of the Eschatological Discourse Mark 13 Par*. CBNTS 1. Lund: Gleerup, 1966.

Hay, David M. "Philo's References to Other Allegorists." *Studia Philonica* 6 (1979–1980): 41–75.

Hecht, Richard D., "Patterns of Exegesis in Philo's Interpretation of Leviticus." *Studia Philonica* 6 (1979–1980): 77–155.

Heine, S. "Diakoninnen—Frauen und Ämter in den ersten christlichen Jahrhunderten." *Internationale Kirchliche Zeitschrift* 78 (1988): 213–227.

Heinemann, Isaak. *Philons griechische und jüdische Bildung: Kulturvergleichende Untersuchungen zu Philons Darstellung der jüdischen Gesetze*. Breslau: Marcus, 1932. Reprint, Darmstadt: Wissenschaftliche Buchgesellchaft, 1962.

Herodotus. Translated by A.D. Godley. LCL. 4 vols. Cambridge, Mass.: Harvard University Press and London: W. Heinemann, 1920–1925.

Herzog II, William R. *Parables as Subversive Speech*. Louisville: Westminster / John Knox, 1994.

Hesiod. *The Homeric Hymns and Homerica*. Translated by Hugh G. Evelyn-White. LCL 57. Cambridge, Mass.: Harvard University Press, 1977.

Hill, Charles. *The Johannine Corpus in the Early Church*. Oxford: Oxford University Press, 2004.

Holland, Glenn S. *The Tradition that You Received from Us: 2 Thessalonians in the Pauline Tradition*. Hermeneutische Untersuchungen zur Theologie 24. Tübingen: Mohr Siebeck, 1988.

Holmberg, Bengt. *Paul and Power: The Structure of Authority in the Primitive Church as Reflected in the Pauline Epistles*. Philadelphia: Fortress, 1978.

Homer. *The Iliad*. Translated by A.T. Murray. 2 vols. LCL 170, 171. 1924. Reprint, Cambridge, Mass.: Harvard University Press, 1999.

———. *The Odyssey*. Translated by A.T. Murray. 2 vols. LCL 104, 105. Cambridge, Mass.: Harvard University Press, 1925; London: Macmillan and New York: St. Martin's Press, 1965; Cambridge, Mass.: Harvard University Press, 1984.

The Homeric Hymns. Edited by Helene P. Foley. Princeton: Princeton University Press, 1994.

Hopkins, Keith. *Conquerors and Slaves*. Cambridge: Cambridge University Press, 1978.

Horsley, Richard A. *Jesus and the Spiral of Violence: Popular Jewish Resistance in Roman Palestine*. San Francisco: Harper & Row, 1987.

———. "Paul and Slavery: A Critical Alternative to Recent Readings." In *Semeia 83/84: Slavery in Text and* Interpretation. Edited by Allen Dwight Callaghan, Richard A. Horsley, and Abraham Smith. Atlanta: Scholars Press, 1998.

Horst, P.W. van der. 'Thou Shalt Not Revile the Gods:' The LXX Translation of Ex. 22:28 (27), its background and influence." In *Hellenism, Judaism, Christianity: Essays on their Interaction*. Edited by idem. Kampen: Kok Pharos, 1994.

Houlden, J.H. *Paul's Letters from Prison*. London: SCM, 1970.

Hove, Richard W. *Equality in Christ? Galatians 3:28 and the Gender Dispute*. Wheaton: Crossway Books, 1999.

Hölbl, Günther. *A History of the Ptolemaic Empire*. London: Routledge, 2001.

Hultgren, Arland. *The Parables of Jesus: A Commentary*. Grand Rapids: Eerdmans, 2000.

Hunt, Alice. *Missing Priests: The Zadokites in Tradition and History*. Library of Hebrew Bible / Old Testament Studies 452. New York and London: T & T Clark, 2006.

Ingenkamp, Heinz Gerd. *Plutarchs Schriften über die Heilung der Seele*. Hypomnemata: Untersuchungen zur Antike und zu ihrem Nachleben 34. Göttingen: Vandernhoeck & Ruprecht, 1971.

Ireland, Dennis J. "A History of Recent Interpretation of the Parable of the Unjust Steward (Luke 16:1–13)." *WTJ* (1989): 293–318.

Irenaeus. *Adversus haereses*. Edited by Adelin Rousseau. *Sources chrétiennes* 10. Paris: Éditions du Cerf, 1965.

Jackson-McCabe, Matt, ed. *Jewish Christianity Reconsidered: Rethinking Ancient Groups and Texts*. Minneapolis: Fortress Press, 2007.

Jacobson, Howard. "Artapanus Judaeus." *JJS* 57 (2006): 210–221.

Jarrett, Charles E. "Philosophy of Language in the Service of Religious Studies." *Semeia* 41 (1988).

Jeremias, Joachim. *The Parables of Jesus*. Translated by S.H. Hooke. Rev. ed. New York: Charles Scribner's Son, 1963.

Jewett, Robert. *Romans: A Commentary*. Hermeneia. Minneapolis: Fortress, 2007.

Johnson Luke Timothy and William S. Kurz. *The Future of Catholic Biblical Scholarship: A Constructive Conversation*. Grand Rapids, Mich.: William B. Eerdmans, 2002.

Jonas, H. *The Gnostic Religion*. 2nd ed. Boston: Beacon Press, 1963.

Jones, C.P. "The Teacher of Plutarch." *Harvard Studies in Classical Philology* 71 (1967): 205–213.

Josephus, *Josephus: The Jewish Antiquities, Part VI, Books IX–XI*. Translated by Ralph Marcus. LCL. Cambridge, Mass.: Harvard University Press/London: Heinemann, 1937.

Junod, Eric and Jean-Daniel Kaestli. *Acta Iohannis*. CChrSA 1–2. 2 vols. Turnhout: Brepols, 1983.

Just, Arthur A. *Luke*. ACCS 3. Downers Grove, Ill.: InterVarsity, 2003.

Kaestli, J.D. "Le mystere de la croix de lumiere et le Johannisme: Acts de Jean ch. 94–102." *Foi et Vie* 86,5 (Sept. 1987).

Kahl, Brigitte. "No Longer Male: Masculinity Struggles behind Galatians 3.28?" *Journal for the Study of the New Testament* 79 (2000): 37–49.

Kamlah, Ehrhard. "Die Parabel vom ungerechten Verwalter (Luk. 16:1 ff.) im Rahmen der Knechtsgleichnisse." In *Abraham unser Vater*. Edited by O. Betz, M. Hengel, and P. Schmidt. Leiden: Brill, 1963.

Kearsley, R.A. "Women in public life in the Roman east: Iunia Theodora, Claudia Metrodora and Phoebe, benefactress of Paul." *Tyndale Bulletin* 50 (1999): 189–211.

Keefer, Kyle. *The Branches of the Gospel of John: The Reception of the Fourth Gospel in the Early Church*. Library of New Testament Studies 332. London and New York: T. & T. Clark, 2006.

Kelber, W. *Oral and Written Gospel*. Philadelphia: Fortress Press, 1983.

Kerferd, G.B. *The Sophistic Movement*. Cambridge, U.K.: Cambridge University Press, 1981.

Kessler, Edward and Neil Wenborn, eds. *A Dictionary of Jewish-Christian Relations*. Cambridge: Cambridge University Press, 2005.

Kiley, Mark. *Colossians as Pseudepigraphy*. JSOT. Sheffield, U.K.: Sheffield Press, 1986.

King, Karen L. *What is Gnosticism?* Cambridge, Mass.: Belknap Press of Harvard University Press, 2003.

Kister, M., ed. *The Qumran Scrolls and their World*. 2 vols. Jerusalem: Yad Ben-Zvi Institute, 2009.

Klauck, Hans-Josef. *The Apocryphal Acts of the Apostles: An Introduction*. Waco, Tex.: Baylor University Press, 2008.

Kloppenborg, John S. "The Dishonoured Master (Luke 16:1–8a)." *Bib* 70 (1989): 474–475.

Klöpper, Albert. *Der Brief an die Colosser, kritsch untersucht und in seinem Verhältnisse zum paulinischen Lehrbegriff exegetisch und biblisch-theologisch erortet.* Berlin: G. Reimer, 1882.

Knapp, Steven and Walter Benn Michaels. "Against Theory." In *Against Theory: Literary Studies and the New Pragmatism.* Edited by W.J.T. Mitchell. Chicago / London: University of Chicago Press, 1985.

——. "Against Theory 2: Hermeneutics and Deconstruction." *Critical Inquiry* 14 (Autumn 1987).

——. "Reply to George Wilson." *Critical Inquiry* 19 (Autumn 1992).

——. "A Reply to Richard Rorty: What is Pragmatism?" *Critical Inquiry* 11 (March 1985).

Koester, Helmut. *From Jesus to the Gospels: Interpreting the New Testament in its Context.* Minneapolis: Fortress, 2007.

Kugel, James L. *Traditions of the Bible: A Guide to the Bible As It Was at the Start of the Common Era.* Cambridge, Mass. and London: Harvard University Press, 1998.

——. "What the Dead Sea Scrolls Do Not Tell." *Commentary* 99 (1998): 49–52.

Kugler, Robert. "Hearing the Story of Moses in Ptolemaic Egypt: Artapanus Accommodates the Tradition." In *The Wisdom of Egypt: Jewish, Early Christian, and Gnostic Essays in Honour of Gerard P. Luttikhuizen.* Edited by Anthony Hilhorst and George H. van Kooten. Leiden: Brill, 2005.

Kugler, Robert A. and Eileen M. Schuller, eds. *The Dead Sea Scrolls at Fifty: Proceedings of the 1997 Society of Biblical Literature Qumran Section Meetings.* Atlanta: Scholars Press, 1999.

Kümmel, W.G. *Introduction to the New Testament.* Translated by Howard Kee. Rev. ed. Nashville: Abingdon, 1975.

LaCocque, André and Paul Ricoeur. *Thinking Biblically: Exegetical and Hermeneutical Studies.* Translated by David Pellauer. Chicago: University of Chicago Press, 1998.

Lalleman, Pieter J. *The Acts of John: A Two-Stage Initiation into Johannine Gnosticism.* Studies on Early Christian Apocrypha 4. Leuven: Peeters, 1998.

Lamarque, Peter. "Objects of Interpretation." In *The Philosophy of Interpretation.* Edited by Joseph Margolis and Tom Rockmore. Oxford, U.K.: Blackwell, 1999.

Lamberton, Robert. *Homer the Theologian: Neoplatonist Allegorical Reading and the Growth of the Epic Tradition.* Transformation of the Classical Heritage 9. Berkeley: University of California Press, 1986.

Landry, David T. and Ben May, "Honor Restored: New Light on the Parable of the Prudent Steward (Luke 16:1–8a)." *JBL* 119 (2000): 287–309.

Lanser, Susan S. "(Feminist) Criticism in the Garden: Inferring Genesis 2–3." *Semeia* 41 (1988).

Le Boulluec, Alain. "La place des concepts philosophiques dans la réflexion de Philon sur le plaisir." In *Philon d'Alexandrie et le langage de la philosophie: actes du colloque international organisé par le Centre d'études sur la philosophie hellénistique et romaine de l'Université de Paris XII-Val de Marne, Créteil, Fontenay, Paris, 26–28 octobre 1995.* Edited by Carlos Lévy. Turnhout: Brepolis, 1998.

Levine, Amy-Jill. "Feminist Criticism." In *The Blackwell Companion to the New Testament*. Oxford: Wiley-Blackwell, 2010.

———. "A Jewish Reading of the Document." *The Bible Today*. May / June 2003.

———. "Roland Murphy, The Pontifical Biblical Commission, Jews and the Bible." *Biblical Theology Bulletin* 33 (2003): 104–113.

Levine, Lee I. "Herod the Great." In *ABD*, edited by David Noel Freedman. Vol. 3. New Haven, Conn.: Yale University Press, 1992.

Levison, John R. "Paul's Letter to Philemon." In *The Blackwell Companion to the New Testament*. Edited by David E. Aune. Oxford: Wiley-Blackwell, 2010.

Licht, Jacob. *Megilat ha-hahodayot mimegilot midbar yehuda*. Jerusalem: Mosad Bialik, 1957.

———. *Megilat ha-serakhim: mimegilot midbar yehuda*. Jerusalem: Mosad Bialik, 1965.

Liddell, Henry George and Robert Scott, *A Greek-English Lexicon*, 9th ed. Revised. Supplement edited by P.G.W. Glare. Oxford: Clarendon Press, 1996.

Lidzbarski, M. *Ginza: Der Schatz oder das Große Buch der Mandäer*. Göttingen: Vandenhoeck & Ruprecht; Leipzig: J.C. Hinrichs, 1925.

Lightfoot, J.B. *St. Paul's Epistle to the Colossians and to Philemon*. London: Macmillan, 1895.

Loader, William R.G. "Jesus and the Rogue in Luke 16,1–8a: The Parable of the Unjust Steward." *RB* 96 (1989): 518–532.

Lohse, Eduard. *Colossians and Philemon*. Hermeneia. Philadelphia, Pa.: Fortress, 1971.

Lunt, Ronald G. "Expounding the Parables: III. The Parable of the Unjust Steward (Luke xvi.1–15)." *ExpTim* 77, 5 (1965–1966): 132–136.

Lupieri, E. " 'Businessmen and Merchants Will Not Enter the Places of My Father' (Gos. Thom. 64 [NHC II, 2; 44:34 f.]): Early Christianity and Market Mentality." In *The Standardized Monetarization of the Market and the Impact on Religion, Politics, Law and Ethics*. Edited by M. Welker and J. von Hagen. Forthcoming.

———. *A Commentary on the Apocalypse of John*. Grand Rapids: Eerdmans, 2006.

Luther, Martin. *Sermons of Martin Luther*. 8 vols. Edited by John Nicholas Lenker. Translated by John Nicholas Lenker, et. al. Minneapolis: Lutherans in All Lands, 1904. Reprint, Grand Rapids: Baker, 1983.

Luttikhuizen, Gerard. "A Gnostic Reading of the Acts of John." In *The Apocryphal Acts of John*, edited by Jan N. Bremmer. Kampen: Kok Pharos, 1995.

Lyre, John G. "Of What Charges? (Luke 16:1–2)." *BTB* 32 (2002): 21–28.

MacDonald, Margaret Y. "Rereading Real Women Through the Undisputed Letters of Paul." In *Women & Christian Origins*. Edited by Ross Shepard Kraemer and Mary Rose D'Angelo. New York: Oxford: Oxford Press, 1999.

Mack, Burton L. "Exegetical Traditions in Alexandrian Judaism: A Program for the Analysis of the Philonic Corpus." *Studia Philonica* 3 (1974–1975): 71–112.

———. *Logos und Sophia: Untersuchungen zur Weisheitstheologie im hellenistischen Judentum*. Göttingen: Vandenhoeck & Ruprecht, 1973.

———. "Philo Judaeus and Exegetical Traditions in Alexandria." *ANRW*. 22.1; *Principat*, 22.1. Edited by H. Temporini and W. Haase. New York: de Gruyter, 1984.

———. "Weisheit und Allegorie bei Philo von Alexandrien: Untersuchungen zum Traktat *De Congressu eruditionis*." *Studia Philonica* 5 (1978): 57–105.

Mackenzie, John L. "Letter to the Colossians." *Dictionary of the Bible*. New York: Bruce and London: Collier-Macmillan, 1965.

MacLachlan, Bonnie. *The Age of Grace*: Charis *in Early Greek Poetry*. Princeton: Princeton University Press, 1993.

Malherbe, A.J. *The Cynic Epistles: A Study Edition*. Missoula, Mont.: Scholars Press, 1977.

Malina, Bruce J. "Understanding New Testament Persons." In *The Social Sciences and New Testament Interpretation*, edited by Richard Rohrbaugh. Peabody: Hendrickson, 1996.

Malina, Bruce J. and Jerome H. Neyrey. *Portraits of Paul: An Archeology of Ancient Personality*. Louisville: Westminster John Knox, 1996.

———. "First-Century Personality: Dyadic Not Individual." In *The Social World of Luke-Acts: Models for Interpretation*, edited by Jerome H. Neyrey. Peabody: Hendrickson, 1991.

Marshall, I. Howard. *The Gospel of Luke: A Commentary on the Greek Text*. NIGTC. Grand Rapids: Eerdmans, 1978.

Martin, Dale B. *The Corinthian Body*. New Haven: Yale University Press, 1995.

Martin, Troy. "The Covenant of Circumcision (Genesis 17:9–14) and the Situational Antithesis in Galatians 3:28." *Journal of Biblical Literature* 122 (2003): 111–125.

Martyn, J. Louis. *Galatians: A New Translation with Introduction and Commentary*. Anchor Bible 33A. New York: Doubleday, 1997.

Mann, C.S. "Unjust Steward or Prudent Manager?" *ExpTim* 102, 8 (1990–1991): 234–235.

Martens, John W. *One God, One Law: Philo of Alexandria on the Mosaic and Greco-Roman Law*. Boston and Leiden: Brill Academic Publishers, 2003.

Mason, Steve. "Jews, Judaeans, Judaizing, Judaism: Problems of Categorization in Ancient History." *JJS* 38 (2007): 457–512.

Mathewson, Dave L.T. "The Parable of the Unjust Steward (Luke 16:1–13): A Reexamination of the Traditional View in Light of Recent Challenges." *JETS* 38 (1995): 29–39.

Mayerhoff, Ernst. *Der Brief an der Colosser, mit vernehmlicher Beruchsichtigung der Drei Pastoralbriefe kritisch geprüft*. Berlin: Mayerhoff, 1838.

Meier, John P. *A Marginal Jew: Rethinking the Historical Jesus*. 4 vols. Anchor Bible Reference Library. New York: Doubleday, 1991–2009.

Mendelson, Alan. *Secular Education in Philo of Alexandria*. Cincinnati: Hebrew Union College Press, 1982.

Menken, Maarten J.J. *2 Thessalonians: Facing the End with Sobriety*. New Testament Readings. London and New York: Routledge, 1994.

Merklein, Helmut. "Paulische Theologie in der Rezeption der Kolosser- und Epheserbriefes." In *Paulus in den neutestamentliche Spätschriften: Zur Paulusrezeption im Neuen Testament*. QD 89. Freiburg: Herder, 1981.

Michaels, Walter Benn. "The Shape of the Signifier." *Critical Inquiry* 27 (Winter 2001).

———. *The Shape of the Signifier: 1967 to the End of History*. Princeton: Princeton University Press, 2006.

Milik, Josef T. *Ten Years of Discovery in the Wilderness of Judea*. Translated by J. Strugnell. London: SCM Press, 1959.

Miller, Patrick. *They Cried to the Lord: The Form and Theology of Biblical Prayer*. Minneapolis, Minn.: Fortress Press, 1994.

Mimouni, Simon Claude. *Le Judéo-Christianisme Ancien: Essais Historiques*. Paris: Éditions du Cerf, 1998.

Morgan, Robert and John Barton. *Biblical Interpretation*. Oxford Bible Series. Oxford, U.K.: Oxford University Press, 1988.

Mosès, André. *De specialibus legibus III et IV: Introduction, traduction at notes*. Edited by R. Arnaldez, J. Pouilloux, and C. Mondésert. Les œuvres de Philon D'Alexandrie 25. Paris: Cerf, 1970.

Moss, Jessica. "Pleasure and Illusion in Plato." *Philosophy and Phenomenological Research* 72 (2006): 503–535.

Nagel, Titus. *Die Rezeption des Johannesevangeliums im 2. Jahrhundert: Studien zur vorirenäischen Aneignung und Auslegung des vierten Evangeliums in christlicher und christlich-gnostischer Literatur*. Arbeiten zur Bibel und ihrer Geschichte 2. Leipzig: Evangelische Verlagsanstalt, 2000.

Najman, Hindy. "The Law of Nature and the Authority of Mosaic Law." *The Studia Philonica Annual* 11 (1999): 55–73.

———. "A Written Copy of the Law of Nature: An Unthinkable Paradox?" *The Studia Philonica Annual* 15 (2003): 54–63.

Newsom, Carol. "Response to George Nickelsburg: 'Currents in Qumran Scholarship.'" In *The Dead Sea Scrolls at Fifty: Proceedings of the 1997 Society of Biblical Literature Qumran Section Meetings*. Edited by Robert A. Kugler and Eileen M. Schuller. Early Judaism and Its Literature. Atlanta, Ga.: Scholars Press, 1999.

Nicholson, G. *Death as Departure*. SBLDS 63. Chico, Calif.: Scholars Press, 1983.

Nickelsburg, George W.E. *1 Enoch 1: A Commentary on the Book of 1 Enoch Chapters 1–36, 81–108*. Hermeneia. Minneapolis, Minn.: Fortress, 2001.

Nojeim, Michael J. *Gandhi and King: The Power of Nonviolent Resistance*. Westport: Praeger, 2004.

Nongbri, Brent. "Greek Authors on Jews and Judaism." In *The Dictionary of Early Judaism*, edited by John J. Collins and Daniel C. Harlow. Grand Rapids, Mich.: Eerdmans, 2010.

Nordling, John G. "*Onesimus Fugitivus*: A Defense of the Runaway Slave Hypothesis in Philemon." *Journal for the Study of the New Testament* 41 (1991): 97–119.

———. *Philemon*. St. Louis, Mo.: Concordia University Press, 2004.

Novitz, David. "Interpretation and Justification." In *The Philosophy of Interpretation*. Edited by Joseph Margolis and Tom Rockmore. Oxford, U.K.: Blackwell, 1999.

O'Keefe, John J. and R.R. Reno. *Sanctified Vision: An Introduction to Early Christian Interpretation of the Bible*. Baltimore, Md.: Johns Hopkins Press, 2005.

Oliver, James H. *Demokratia, the Gods, and the Free World*. Baltimore: Johns Hopkins Press, 1960.

Origen. *On First Principles. Sources chrétiennes* 252. Edited by Henri Krouzel and
     Manlio Simonetti. Paris: Éditions du Cerf, 1978.
———. *On First Principles. Sources chrétiennes* 268. Edited by Henri Krouzel and
     Manlio Simonetti. Paris: Éditions du Cerf, 1980.
———. *On Leviticus.* Edited by Marcel Borret. *Sources chrétiennes* 286. Paris:
     Éditions du Cerf, 1981.
———. *Commentary on John.* Edited by Cécile Blanc. *Sources chrétiennes* 120.
     Paris: Éditions du Cerf, 1966.
Osiek, Carolyn. *Philippians; Philemon.* ANTC. Nashville, Tenn.: Abingdon,
     Press, 2000.
Ovid. *Metamorphoses.* Translated by F.J. Miller. LCL. Cambridge, Mass.: Harvard
     University Press and London: W. Heinemann, 1984.
The Oxford Classical Dictionary, 3rd ed. Revised. Edited by Simon Hornblower
     and Antony Spawforth. Oxford: Oxford University Press, 2003.
Pagels, E. "Conflicting Versions of Valentinian Eschatology: Irenaeus' Treatises
     vs. the Excerpts from Theodotus." *HTR* 67 (1974): 365–353.
———. *The Gnostic Gospels.* New York: Random House, 1979.
———. *The Johannine Gospel in Gnostic Exegesis.* SBLMS 17. Nashville: Abingdon,
     1973.
Parente, Fausto. "La Lettera di Aristea come fonte per la storia del giudaismo
     alessandrino durante la prima metà del I secolo a.C." *Annali della Scuola
     Normale Superiore di Pisa* 3.2.1–2 (1972): 177–237, 517–567.
Parrott, Douglas M. "The Dishonest Steward: Luke 16:1–8a and Luke's Special
     Parable Collection." *NTS* 37 (1991): 499–515.
Paterson, Orlando. *Slavery and Social Death: A Comparative Study.* Cambridge,
     Mass.: Harvard University Press, 1982.
Patte, Daniel. "Speech Act Theory and Biblical Exegesis." *Semeia* 41 (1988).
Pausanias. *Description of Greece.* Translated by W.H.S. Jones and H.A. Omerod.
     LCL. 5 vols. Cambridge, Mass.: Harvard University Press, 1918–1935.
Pearce, Sarah J.K. *The Land of the Body: Studies in Philo's Representation of Egypt.*
     Tübingen: Mohr Siebeck, 2007.
Pearson, B.A. "1 Thessalonians 2:13–16: A Deutero-Pauline Interpolation." *HTR*
     69 (1971): 79–94.
———. *Ancient Gnosticism: Traditions and Literature.* Minneapolis, Minn.: For-
     tress, 2007.
Pearson, Brook W.R. *Corresponding Sense: Paul, Dialectic & Gadamer.* Leiden:
     Brill, 2001.
Perkins, P. "Gnostic Revelation and Johannine Sectarianism: Reading 1 John
     from the Perspective of Nag Hammadi." In *Theology and Christology in the
     Fourth Gospel: Essays by the Members of the SNTS Johannine Writings Semi-
     nar.* BETL 184. Leuven: Peeters, 2005.
———. *Gnosticism and the New Testament.* Minneapolis: Fortress, 1993.
Perrin, Norman. *Rediscovering the Teaching of Jesus.* New York: Harper & Row,
     1967.
Pervo, Richard I. "Johannine Trajectories in the Acts of John." *Apocrypha* 3
     (1992): 47–68.
Philo. *Philo in Ten Volumes (and Two Supplementary Volumes).* Translated by

F.H. Colson, G.H. Whitaker, and Ralph Marcus. LCL. Cambridge, Mass.: Harvard University Press, 1929–1962.

Plato. Translated by Paul Shorey. LCL. Vols. 6–10. Cambridge, Mass.: Harvard University Press. 1935.

———. *Meno*. In *Plato in Twelve Volumes*. Vol. 2. Translated by W.R.M. Lamb. London: William Heinemann and Cambridge, Mass.: Harvard University Press, 1967.

Pleiss, I.J. du. "Philanthropy or Sarcasm? Another Look at the Parable of the Dishonest Manager (Luke 16:1–13)." *Neot* 24 (1990): 1–20.

Plisch, Uwe-Karsten. *The Gospel of Thomas: Original Text with Commentary*. Stuttgart: Deutsche Bibelgesellschat, 2008.

Plutarch. *Lives*. Translated by B. Perrin. LCL. 9 Vols. Cambridge, Mass.: Harvard University Press. 1968–1988.

Plutarch, *Moralia*. Translated by F.C. Babbitt et al. 16 vols. Loeb Classical Library. Cambridge: Harvard University Press, 1927–1976.

Pollard, T.E. *Johannine Christology and the Early Church*. SNTSMS 13. Cambridge: Cambridge University Press, 1970.

Pontifical Biblical Commission, *The Jewish People and Their Sacred Scriptures in the Christian Bible*. Vatican City: Vatican Press, 2002.

Porter, Stanly E. "The Parable of the Unjust Steward (Luke 16:1–13): Irony as the Key." In *The Bible in Three Dimensions: Essays in Celebration of Forty Years of Biblical Studies in the University of Sheffield*. Edited by David J.A. Clines, et al. JSOTSup 87. Sheffield: JSOT Press, 1990.

Pseudo-Andronicus de Rhodes *"ΠΕΡΙ ΠΑΘΩΝ"*: *Édition critique du texte grec et de la traduction latine médiévale*. Edited by A. Gilbert-Thirry. Corpus latinum commentariorum in Aristotelem graecorum. Supp. 2. Leiden: Brill, 1977.

Puech, Emile. *Qumrân Grotte 4: XXVII, Textes Araméens Deuxième Partie 4Q550–4Q575a, 4Q580–4Q587*. Discoveries in the Judaean Desert XXXVII. Oxford: Clarendon Press, 2009.

Rabbow, Paul. *Seelenfürung: Methodik der Exerzitien in der Antike*. München: Kösel, 1954.

Reed, Annette Yoshiko and Adam H. Becker, eds., "Introduction: Traditional Models and new Directions." In *The Ways that Never Parted: Jews and Christians in Late Antiquity and the Early Middle Ages*. Tubingen: Mohr Siebeck, 2003.

Rhodes, James N. "Diet and Desire: The Logic of the Dietary Laws According to Philo." *Ephemerides Theologicae Lovanienses* 79 (2003): 122–133.

Ricoeur, Paul. *Interpretation Theory: Discourse and the Surplus of Meaning*. Fort Worth: Texas Christian University Press, 1976.

Roldanus, Hans. "Die Eucharistie in den Johannesakten." In *Apocryphal Acts*, ed. Jan S. Bremmer.

Roetzel, Calvin J. "Theodidaktoi and Handwork in Philo and I Thessalonians." In *L'âpotre Paul: Personnalité, style et conception du ministère*. Edited by A. Vanhoye. Leuven: Leuven University Press, 1986.

Roitman, Aldofo. "Exhibiting the Dead Sea Scrolls: Some Historical and Theoretical Considerations." In *Archaeology and Society in the 21st Century: The*

Dead Sea Scrolls and Other Case Studies. Edited by N.A. Silberman and
E.S. Frerichs. Jerusalem: Israel Exploration Society, the Dorot Foundation,
2001.

Roitman, Adolfo, Lawrence H. Schiffman, and Shani Tzoref, eds. *The Dead Sea
Scrolls and Contemporary Culture: Proceedings of the International Conference
held at the Israel Museum (July 6–8, 2008)*. Leiden: Brill, forthcoming.

Romaniuk, K. "Was Phoebe in Rom 16,1 a Deaconness?" *Zeitschrift für die
Neutestamentliche Wissenschaft* 81 (1990): 132–134.

Rudolph, K. *Gnosis*. ET; Edinburgh: T&T Clark, 1983.

Rynne, Terrence J. *Gandhi and Jesus: The Saving Power of Nonvolence*. Maryknoll:
Orbis Books, 2008.

Samuel, Mar Athanasius Y. *The Treasure of Qumran, My Story of the Dead Sea
Scrolls*. Philadelphia: Westminster Press, 1966.

Sandbach, F.H. *The Stoics*. London: Chatto & Windus, 1975.

Sanders, E.P. *The Historical Figure of* Jesus. London: Penguin Books, 1993.

———. *Jesus and Judaism*. Philadelphia: Fortress Press, 1985.

Sandmel, Samuel. *The First Christian Century in Judaism and Christianity: Certainties and Uncertainties*. New York: Oxford University Press, 1969.

Satran, David. "Qumran and Christian Origins." In *The Scrolls of the Judaean
Desert, Forty Years of Research*. Edited by M. Broshi, S. Japhet, D. Schwartz
and Sh. Talmon. Jerusalem: Bialik Institute and The Israel Exploration Society,
1992.

Schatz, L. *Der Glaubende und die Feindliche Welt. Beobachtungen zum Gnostichen Dualismus und seiner Bedeutung für Paulus und das Joahnnesevangelium*. WMANT 37. Neukirchen-Vluyn: Neukirchener Verlag, 1970.

Schäferdiek, Kurt. "Acts of John." In Wilhelm Schneemelcher, *New Testament
Apocrypha*. 5th ed. Louisville: Westminster / John Knox, 1992.

Schellenberg, Ryan S. "Which Master? Whose Steward? Metalepsis and Lordship
in the Parable of the Prudent Steward (Lk 16.1–13)." *JSNT* 30 (2008): 263–
288.

Schifferdecker, Kathryn. *Out of the Whirlwood: Creation Theology in the Book of
Job*. Harvard Theological Studies 61. Cambridge, Mass.: Harvard University
Press, 2008.

Schiffman, Lawrence H. "Confessionalism and the Study of the Dead Sea
Scrolls." *Forum of the World Union of Jewish Studies* 31 (1991) 3–14.

———. "Judaism and Early Christianity in Light of the Dead Sea Scrolls." In
*Jewish-Christian Encounters over the Centuries: Symbiosis, Prejudice, Holo-
caust, Dialogue*. Edited by M. Perry and F.M. Schweitzer. New York: Peter
Lang, 1994.

———. "The Scrolls and the Search for the Secret Gospel." *Jewish World* (April 16–
23, 1993), 18–19.

———. *Reclaiming the Dead Sea Scrolls: The History of Judaism, the Background
of Christianity, the Lost Library of Qumran*. New York: Doubleday, 1994.

Schiffman, Lawrence H., Emanuel Tov, and James C. Vanderkam, eds., *The Dead
Sea Scrolls: Fifty Years After their Discovery: Proceedings of the Jerusalem
Congress, July 20–25, 1997*. Jerusalem: Israel Exploration Society and the
Shrine of the Book, Israel Museum, 2000.

Schiffman, Lawrence H. and James C. VanderKam. *Encyclopedia of the Dead Sea Scrolls*. London: Oxford University Press, 2000.

Schneider, P.G. *The Mystery of the Acts of John: An Interpretation of the Hymn and the Dance in the Light of the Acts' Theology*. San Francisco, 1991.

Schnelle, Udo. *Theology of the New Testament*. Translated by M.E. Boring. Grand Rapids: Baker Academic, 2009.

Schoeps, Hans-Joachim. *Jewish Christianity: Factional Disputes in the Early Church*. Translated by Douglas R.A. Hare. Philadelphia: Fortress Press, 1969.

——. *Paul: The Theology of the Apostle in the Light of Jewish Religious History*. Philadelphia: Westminster Press, 1959.

Schrage, Wolfgang. *The Ethics of the New Testament*. Translated by David E. Green. Philadelphia: Fortress Press, 1988.

Schuller, Eileen and Moshe Bernstein, trans. and ed. "371–373. 4QNarrative and Poetic Composition (a-c): Introduction." In *Qumran Cave 4.XXVIII, Miscellanea, Part 2*. DJD 28. Oxford: Clarendon Press, 2001.

Schwartz, Shalom H. "Individualism-Collectivism: Critique and Proposed Refinements." *Journal of Cross-Cultural Psychology* 21 (1990).

Schweitzer, Eduard. "The Letter to the Colossians Neither Pauline nor Postpauline?" *Pluralisme et oecumenisme en recherches* théologiques. Edited by R.E. Hoeckman. BETL 43. Louvain: Peeters, 1976.

Scott, Brandon Bernard. "A Master's Praise: Luke 16:1–8a." *Bib* 64 (1983): 173–188.

Scott, Dominic. *Plato's Meno*. Cambridge, U.K.: Cambridge University Press, 2006.

Scott, F.F. *The Epistles to the Colossians, to Philemon and to the Ephesians*. 1930. Reprint, London: Hodder and Stoughton, 1958.

Scott, James C. *Domination and the Arts of Resistance: Hidden Transcripts*. New Haven and London: Yale University Press, 1990.

Searle, J.R. "Literary Theory and Its Discontents." *New Literary History* 25 (1994): 643–648.

——. "What is a Speech Act?" In *The Philosophy of Language*. Edited by idem. Oxford, U.K.: Oxford University Press, 1971.

Seneca. *On Benefits*. In *Seneca in Ten Volumes*. Vol. 3. Translated by John W. Basore. Cambridge, Mass and London: Harvard University Press, 1989.

Sherwin-White, A.N. *The Letters of Pliny: A Historical and Social Commentary*. Oxford: Clarendon Press, 1966.

Shorey, Paul. "*Physis, Meletē, Epistēmē.*" *Transactions and Proceedings of the American Philological Association* 40 (1909): 185–201.

Siegert, Folker. "Early Jewish Interpretation in a Hellenistic Style." In *Hebrew Bible / Old Testament: The History of Its Interpretation*. Vol. 1. Edited by Magne Sæbø. Göttingen: Vandenhoeck & Ruprecht, 1996.

Simon, Marcel. *Versus Israel: A Study of the Relationship between Jews and Christians in the Roman Empire, 135–425*. Littman Library of Jewish Civilization. Oxford: Oxford University Press, 1986.

Simonetti, Manlio. *Biblical Interpretation in the Early Church: an Historical Introduction to Patristic Exegesis*. Edinburgh: T. and T. Clark, 1994.

Sirker-Wicklaus, G. *Untersuchungen zu den Johannes-Akten.* Witterschlick and Bonn: Wohle, 1988.

Skarsaune, Oskar and Reidar Hvalvik, eds. *Jewish Believers in Jesus: The Early Centuries.* Peabody: Hendrickson Publishers, 2007.

Smith, Barbara Herrnstein. *Contingencies of Value: Alternative Perspectives for Critical Theory.* Cambridge, Mass.: Harvard University Press, 1988.

Smith, D.M. *The Composition and Order of the Fourth Gospel: Bultmann's Literary Theory.* New Haven: Yale University Press, 1965.

Smith, Wilfred Cantwell. *The Meaning and End of Religion.* New York: Macmillan, 1962; Minneapolis: Fortress Press, 1991.

———. *What is Scripture? A Comparative Approach.* Minneapolis: Fortress Press, 1993.

Snodgrass, Klyne. *Stories with Intent: A Comprehensive Guide to the Parables of Jesus.* Grand Rapids: Eerdmans, 2008.

Spinoza, Benedict de. *A Theologico-Political Treatise.* Translated by R.H.M. Elwes. New York: Dover Publications, 1951.

Stanford, W.B. *The Odyssey of Homer.* London: Macmillan & Co., New York: St. Martin's Press, 1965.

Stegemann, Hartmut with Eileen Schuller. *Qumran Cave I.III: 1QHodayot^a with Incorporation of 1QHodayot^b and 4QHodayot^{a-f}.* Discoveries in the Judaean Desert XL. Oxford: Clarendon Press, 2009.

Stendahl, Krister. *The Bible and the Role of Women.* Philadelphia: Fortress, 1966.

———. "Qumran and Supersessionism—And the Road Not Taken." *Princeton Seminary Bulletin* 19 (1998): 134–142.

———. ed. *The Scrolls and the New* Testament. New York: Harper, 1957.

Sterling, Gregory E. " 'The School of Sacred Laws': The Social Setting of Philo's Treatises." *Vigiliae Christianae* 53 (1999): 148–164.

Ste. Croix, G.E.M. de. *The Class Struggle in the Ancient Greek World from the Archaic Age to the Arab Conquest.* Ithaca: Cornell University Press, 1981.

Stern, Menahem, trans. and ed. *Greek and Latin Authors on Jews and Judaism.* Vol. I: From Herodotus to Plutarch. Jerusalem: Publications of the Israel Academy of Sciences and Humanities, 1976.

Sternberg, Meir. *The Poetics of Biblical Narrative: Ideological Literature and the Drama of Reading.* Bloomington, Ind.: Indiana University Press, 1987.

Stone, Michael Edward. *Fourth Ezra.* Hermeneia. Minneapolis, Minn.: Fortress, 1990.

Strecker, Georg. *The Johannine Letters.* Hermeneia. Minneapolis: Fortress, 1996.

Suetonius. *The Lives of the Caesars.* Translated by M. Ihm and J.C. Rolfe. LCL. 2 vols. Cambridge, Mass.: Harvard University Press and London: W. Heinemann, 1964–1965.

Sukenik, Eleazar L. *The Dead Sea Scrolls of the Hebrew University.* Jerusalem: Magnes Press, 1955.

Svebakken, Hans. "Philo of Alexandria's Exposition of the Tenth Commandment." Ph.D. diss., Loyola University Chicago, 2009.

Sweeney, Marvin. *Reading the Hebrew Bible After the Shoah: Engaging Holocaust Theology.* Minneapolis: Fortress Press, 2008.

Tcherikover, Victor. "The Ideology of the Letter of Aristeas." *Harvard Theological Review* 51 (1958): 59–85.

Termini, Cristina. "Taxonomy of Biblical Laws and ΦΙΛΟΤΕΧΝΙΑ in Philo of Alexandria: A Comparison with Josephus and Cicero." *Studia Philonica Annual* 16 (2004): 1–29.

Theological Dictionary of the Old Testament. 15 vols. Grand Rapids, Mich.: Eerdmans, 1977–2006.

Thoma, Clemens. *Lexikon der Jüdisch-Christlichen Begegnung.* Freiburg: Herder, 1989.

Thomassen, Einar. *The Spiritual Seed, the Church of the Valentinians.* Nag Hammadi and Manichaean Studies 60. Leiden: Brill, 2006.

Thompson, Marianne Meye. *Colossians & Philemon.* Grand Rapids, Mich.: Eerdmans, 2005.

Tiller, Patrick A. *A Commentary on the Animal Apocalypse of 1 Enoch.* Early Judaism and Its Literature 4. Atlanta, Ga.: SBL Scholars Press, 1993.

Tisserant, Cardinal. "A Word of Thanks." In *The Bridge: A Yearbook of Judaeo-Christian* Studies. Edited by J.M. Oesterreicher. Vol. 2. New York: Pantheon Books, 1955.

Tobin, Thomas H. *The Creation of Man: Philo and the History of Interpretation.* Washington, D.C.: The Catholic Biblical Association of America, 1984.

———. *Paul's Rhetoric in its Contexts: The Argument of Romans.* Peabody, Mass.: Hendrickson, 2004.

———. "The Prologue of John and Hellenistic Jewish Speculation." *CBQ* 52 (1990): 252–269.

Topel, L. John. "On the Injustice of the Unjust Steward: Lk 16:1–13." *CBQ* 37 (1975): 216–227.

Tov, Emanuel. "Israeli Scholarship on the Texts from the Judaean Desert." In *The Dead Sea Scrolls at Fifty: Proceedings of the 1997 Society of Biblical Literature Qumran Section Meetings.* Edited by Robert A. Kugler and Eileen M. Schuller. Early Judaism and Its Literature. Atlanta, Ga.: Scholars Press, 1999.

Tramontano, Raffaele. *La Lettera di Aristea a Filocrate: Introduzione, testa, versione e commento.* Napoli: Ufficio succursale della civiltà cattolica, 1931.

Trever, John. *The Untold Story of Qumran.* Westwood, N.J.: F.H. Revell, 1965. Reprinted, *The Dead Sea Scrolls: A Personal Account.* Grand Rapids, Mich.: Eerdmans, 1977.

Triandis, H.C. and R. Bontempo and M.J. Villareal and M. Asai and N. Lucca. "Individualism and Collectivism: Cross-Cultural Perspectives on Self-Ingroup Relationships." *Journal of Personality and Social Psychology* 54 (1988): 323–338.

Turner, J. "Sethian Gnosticism and Johannine Christianity." In *Theology and Christology in the Fourth Gospel: Essays by the Members of the SNTS Johannine Writings Seminar.* BETL 184. Leuven: Peeters, 2005.

Turner, Max. "Historical Criticism and Theological Hermeneutics of the New Testament." In *Between Two Horizons: Spanning New Testament and Systematic Theology.* Edited by Joel B. Green and Max Turner. Grand Rapids, Mich./Cambridge, U.K.: William B. Eerdmans, 2000.

Udoh, Fabian E. *To Caesar What Is Caesar's: Tribute, Taxes, and Imperial Admin-istration in Early Roman Palestine (63 BCE – 70 CE)*. Brown Judaic Studies 343. Providence, R.I.: Brown Judaic Studies, 2005.

VanderKam, James C. *The Dead Sea Scrolls Today*. Grand Rapids, Mich.: Eerd-mans, 1994.

———. *From Joshua to Caiaphas: High Priests after the Exile*. Minneapolis, Minn.: Augsburg Fortress / Assen, the Netherlands: Royal van Gorcum, 2004.

Vanderlip, Vera F. *The Hymns of Isidorus*. Toronto: A.M. Hakkert, 1972.

Vanhoozer, Kevin J. "Discourse on Matter: Hermeneutics and the 'Miracle' of Understanding." In *Hermeneutics at the Crossroads*. Edited by Kevin J. Van-hoozer, James K.A. Smith, and Bruce Ellis Benson. Bloomington / Indiana-polis: Indiana University Press, 2006.

Vermes, Géza. *The Complete Dead Sea Scrolls in English*. Rev. ed. London: Penguin Books, 2004.

———. *Discovery in the Judaean Desert*. New York: Desclee Co., 1956.

———. "The Impact of the Dead Sea Scrolls on Jewish Studies in the Last Twenty-Five Years." *Journal of Jewish Studies* 26 (1975): 1–14.

Vermes, Géza and Martin D. Goodman, eds. *The Essenes according to the Classi-cal Sources*. Sheffield, U.K.: JSOT Press for the Oxford Centre for Postgraduate Hebrew Studies, 1989.

Via, Dan O. *The Parables: Their Literary and Existential Dimensions*. Philadel-phia: Fortress, 1967.

Vian, Giovanni Maria. "Purità e culto nell'esegesi giudaico-ellenistica." *Annali di storia dell'esegesi* 13 (1996): 67–84.

Virgil. Translated by H.R. Fairclough. LCL. 2 vols. London: W. Heinemann. 1965.

Wahlde, Urban C. von. *A Commentary on the Gospel and Letters of John*. 3 vols. Eerdmans Critical Commentary. Grand Rapids: Eerdmans, 2010.

———. *The Earliest Version of John's Gospel*. Wilmington, Del.: M. Glazier, 1989.

———. *The Johannine Commandments: 1 John and the Struggle for the Johannine Tradition*. Mahwah, N.J.: Paulist, 1990.

———. "The Witnesses to Jesus in 5:31–40 and Belief in the Fourth Gospel." *Catholic Biblical Quarterly* 43 (July 1981): 385–404.

———. "'You Are of Your Father the Devil' in Its Context: Stereotyped Polemic in Jn 8:38–47." In *Anti-Judaism and the Fourth Gospel: Papers from the Leuven Colloquium, 2000*. Edited by R. Bieringer, D. Pollefeyt, and F. Vandecasteele-Vanneuville. Assen: Royal Van Gorcum, 2001.

Walsh, Jerome T. *1 Kings*. Berit Olam: Studies in Hebrew Narrative and Poetry. Collegeville, Minn.: Liturgical Press, 1996.

Weed, Michael. *The Letters of Paul to the Ephesians, the Colossians and Philemon*. Austin, Tex.: R.B. Sweet, 1971.

Wenham, David. *The Parables of Jesus*. Downers Grove, Ill.: InterVarsity, 1989.

Westerman, W.L. *The Slave Systems of Greek and Roman Antiquity*. Philadelphia: The American Philosophical Society, 1955.

White, Hugh C. "Introduction: Speech Act Theory and Literary Criticism." *Semeia* 41 (1988).

———. ed. *Speech Act Theory and Biblical Criticism*. Semeia: An Experimental Journal for Biblical Criticism. Decatur, Ga.: Scholars Press, 1988.

Wiedemann, Thomas. *Greek and Roman Slavery*. Baltimore: Johns Hopkins University Press, 1981.

Wiles, Maurice F. *The Spiritual Gospel: The Interpretation of the Fourth Gospel in the Early Church*. Cambridge: Cambridge University Press, 1960.

Wiley, Tatha. *Paul and Gentile Women: Reframing Galatians*. New York: Continuum, 2005.

Williams, Francis E. "Is Almsgiving the Point of the 'Unjust Steward'?" *JBL* 83 (1964): 293–297.

Williams, M. *Rethinking "Gnosticism": An Argument for Dismantling a Dubious Category*. Princeton: Princeton University Press, 1996.

Wilson, R. McL. *Colossians and Philemon: A Critical and Exegetical Commentary*. New York: T & T. Clark, 2005.

Wimsatt, W.K. and Monroe C. Beardsley. "The Intentional Fallacy." In Wimsatt, W.K. *The Verbal Icon: Studies in the Meaning of Poetry*. Lexington, Ky: University of Kentucky Press, 1954.

Winter, S.C. "Paul's Letter to Philemon." *NTS* 33 (1987): 1–15.

Wintermute, Orville. "Jubilees." In *The Old Testament Pseudepigrapha*. Edited by James H. Charlesworth. 2 vols. Garden City, New York: Doubleday and Company, 1985.

Wise, Michael O. "*4QFlorilegium* and the Temple of Adam." *RevQ* 15 (1991): 105–106.

Witherington III, Ben. *Letters to Philemon, the Colossians, and the Ephesians: A Socio-Rhetorical Commentary on the Captivity Epistles*. Grand Rapids, Mich.: William Eerdmans, 2007.

Wright, N.T. *Colossians and Philemon*. Tyndale New Testament Commentaries 12. Nottingham, U.K.: InterVarsity Press, 1986.

Yadin, Yigael. *The Message of the Scrolls*. New York: Simon and Schuster, 1957.

———. *The Temple Scroll*. Jerusalem: Israel Exploration Society, 1983.

Young, Frances. *Biblical Exegesis and the Formation of Christian Culture*. Cambridge: Cambridge University Press, 1997.

Zellentin, Holger. "The End of Jewish Egypt: Artapanus and the Second Exodus." In *Antiquity in Antiquity*, edited by Kevin Osterloh and Greg Gardner. Tübingen: Mohr Siebeck, 2008.

Zeller, Dieter. *Charis bei Philon und Paulus*. Stuttgart: Verlag Katholisches Bibelwerk, 1990.

INDEX OF MODERN AUTHORS AND SUBJECTS

INDEX OF ANCIENT SOURCES

Deutero-canon

New Testament

EXTRA-BIBLICAL SOURCES (in alphabetical order)

Somn.

1	57n43
1.52–60	80n27
1.59–60	81n29
1.68	84n36
1.115	71n6, 88
1.129	87, 87n43
1.159–170	82
1.167–168	70n4
1.168	76n19, 88
1.173	84n36, 86n40
1.182	71n6
1.194	84n36
1.208	88
1.46	88
2.10	84
2.10–11	84n34
2.179	104n41
255	87n43

Spec. (leg.)

1.162	98n17
1.173	105n45
1.223	100n29
1.53	66n26
3.85	106n47
4.79	105n43
4.79–94	111
4.79–131	97n14, 105
4.84	111n62
4.95–131	111
4.97	105n43
4.99	105n43, 111n63
4.100	105nn44, 45
4.100–118	97, 106n50
4.101	105nn43, 45, 46
4.103	101n30, 107n51
4.103–104	97, 101nn30, 31; 103, 106n50, 108, 108n54, 110
4.103–105	106n50
4.103–109	98, 100, 109
4.104	100nn28, 29, 106nn48, 49
4.106–109	97n14
4.110–112	109, 109n55
4.113–115	109

4.114–115	99n18, 108, 108n55, 109n55
4.116	99nn22, 24; 100nn28, 29; 110n58
4.116–117	97, 109
4.116–118	98
4.117	100n26
4.118	109n57
4.124	105n43

Plato 61, 65, 74–75
  Meno
    70a 75
  The Republic
    377d 208n3
  Timaeus 112

Pliny the Younger 176n81, 186n2, 187
  Epistulae (Ep.)
    9.21 187n6
    10.96.1 155n8
    10.96.8 176n81

Plutarch 104n40, 110, 111, 111n61, 112, 208, 214–215, 287
  Alexander
    3.4–6 215n21
  Cohib. ira.
    460 A–C 104n40
    460 C 106n47
  Garr. 110n61
  Virt. mor. 105n42

Pseudo-Andronicus
  231.81 105n43

Pseudo-Crates
  Ep.
    34 171n57

Quintilian
  Institutio Oratoria
    1.26–27 75n16

SUPPLEMENTS TO NOVUM TESTAMENTUM

ISSN 0167-9732

Recent volumes in the series

93. Bauckham, R. *The Fate of Dead.* Studies on the Jewish and Christian Apocalypses. 1998. ISBN 90 04 11203 0
94. Standhartinger, A. *Studien zur Entstehungsgeschichte und Intention des Kolosserbriefs.* 1998. ISBN 90 04 11286 3
95. Oegema, G.S. *Für Israel und die Völker.* Studien zum alttestamentlich-jüdischen Hintergrund der paulinischen Theologie. 1999. ISBN 90 04 11297 9
96. Albl, M.C. *"And Scripture Cannot Be Broken".* The Form and Function of the Early Christian *Testimonia* Collections. 1999. ISBN 90 04 11417 3
97. Ellis, E.E. *Christ and the Future in New Testament History.* 1999. ISBN 90 04 11533 1
98. Chilton, B. & C.A. Evans, (eds.) *James the Just and Christian Origins.* 1999. ISBN 90 04 11550 1
99. Horrell, D.G. & C.M. Tuckett (eds.) *Christology, Controversy and Community.* New Testament Essays in Honour of David R. Catchpole. 2000. ISBN 90 04 11679 6
100. Jackson-McCabe, M.A. *Logos and Law in the Letter of James.* The Law of Nature, the Law of Moses and the Law of Freedom. 2001. ISBN 90 04 11994 9
101. Wagner, J.R. *Heralds of the Good News.* Isaiah and Paul "In Concert" in the Letter to the Romans. 2002. ISBN 90 04 11691 5
102. Cousland, J.R.C. *The Crowds in the Gospel of Matthew.* 2002. ISBN 90 04 12177 3
103. Dunderberg, I., C. Tuckett and K. Syreeni. *Fair Play: Diversity and Conflicts in Early Christianity.* Essays in Honour of Heikki Räisänen. 2002. ISBN 90 04 12359 8
104. Mount, C. *Pauline Christianity.* Luke-Acts and the Legacy of Paul. 2002. ISBN 90 04 12472 1
105. Matthews, C.R. *Philip: Apostle and Evangelist.* Configurations of a Tradition. 2002. ISBN 90 04 12054 8
106. Aune, D.E., T. Seland, J.H. Ulrichsen (eds.) *Neotestamentica et Philonica.* Studies in Honor of Peder Borgen. 2002. ISBN 90 04 126104
107. Talbert, C.H. *Reading Luke-Acts in its Mediterranean Milieu.* 2003. ISBN 90 04 12964 2
108. Klijn, A.F.J. *The Acts of Thomas.* Introduction, Text, and Commentary. Second Revised Edition. 2003. ISBN 90 04 12937 5
109. Burke, T.J. & J.K. Elliott (eds.) *Paul and the Corinthians.* Studies on a Community in Conflict. Essays in Honour of Margaret Thrall. 2003. ISBN 90 04 12920 0
110. Fitzgerald, J.T., T.H. Olbricht & L.M. White (eds.) *Early Christianity and Classical Culture.* Comparative Studies in Honor of Abraham J. Malherbe. 2003. ISBN 90 04 13022 5
111. Fitzgerald, J.T., D. Obbink & G.S. Holland (eds.) *Philodemus and the New Testament World.* 2004. ISBN 90 04 11460 2
112. Lührmann, D. *Die Apokryph gewordenen Evangelien.* Studien zu neuen Texten und zu neuen Fragen. 2004. ISBN 90 04 12867 0
113. Elliott, J.K. (ed.) *The Collected Biblical Writings of T.C. Skeat.* 2004. ISBN 90 04 13920 6

114. Roskam, H.N. *The Purpose of the Gospel of Mark in its Historical and Social Context*. 2004. ISBN 90 04 14052 2

115. Chilton, B.D. & C.A. Evans (eds.) *The Missions of James, Peter, and Paul*. Tensions in Early Christianity. 2005. ISBN 90 04 14161 8

116. Epp, E.J. *Perspectives on New Testament Textual Criticism*. Collected Essays, 19622004. 2005. ISBN 90 04 14246 0

117. Parsenios, G.L. *Departure and Consolation*. The Johannine Farewell Discourses in Light of Greco-Roman Literature. 2005. ISBN 90 04 14278 9

118. Hakola, R. *Identity Matters*. John, the Jews and Jewishness. 2005. ISBN 90 04 14224 6

119. Fuglseth, K.S. *Johannine Sectarianism in Perspective*. A Sociological, Historical, and Comparative Analysis of Temple and Social Relationships in the Gospel of John, Philo, and Qumran. 2005. ISBN 90 04 14411 0 (in preparation)

120. Ware, J. *The Mission of the Church*. in Paul's Letter to the Philippians in the Context of Ancient Judaism. 2005. ISBN 90 04 14641 5

121. Watt, J.G. van der (ed.) *Salvation in the New Testament*. Perspectives on Soteriology. 2005. ISBN-13: 978 90 04 14297 8, ISBN-10: 90 04 14297 5

122. Fotopoulos, J. (ed.) *The New Testament and Early Christian Literature in Greco-Roman Context*. Studies in Honor of David E. Aune. 2006. ISBN-13: 978 90 04 14304 3, ISBN-10: 90 04 14304 1

123. Lehtipuu, O. *The Afterlife Imagery in Luke's Story of the Rich Man and Lazarus*. 2006. ISBN 978 90 04 15301 1

124. Breytenbach, C., J.C. Thom and J. Punt (eds.) *The New Testament Interpreted*. Essays in Honour of Bernard C. Lategan. 2006. ISBN 13: 978 90 04 15304 2; ISBN 10: 90 04 15304 7

125. Aune, D.E. & R. Darling Young (eds.) *Reading Religions in the Ancient World*. Essays Presented to Robert McQueen Grant on his 90th Birthday. 2007. ISBN 978 90 04 16196 2

126. Pennington, J.T. *Heaven and Earth in the Gospel of Matthew*. 2007. ISBN 978 90 04 16205 1

127. Petersen, S. *Brot, Licht und Weinstock*. Intertextuelle Analysen johanneischer Ichbin-Worte. 2008. ISBN 978 90 04 16599 1

128. Hultin, J.F. *The Ethics of Obscene Speech in Early Christianity and Its Environment*. 2008. ISBN 978 90 04 16803 9

129. Gray, P. and G.R. O'Day (eds.) *Scripture and Traditions*. Essays on Early Judaism and Christianity *in Honor of Carl R. Holladay*. 2008. ISBN 978 90 04 16747 6

130. Buitenwerf, R., H.W. Hollander and J. Tromp (eds.) *Jesus, Paul, and Early Christianity*. Studies in Honour of Henk Jan de Jonge. 2008. ISBN 978 90 04 17033 9

131. Huizenga, L.A. *The New Isaac*. Tradition and Intertextuality in the Gospel of Matthew. 2009. ISBN 978 90 04 17569 3

132. Rasimus, T. (ed.) *The Legacy of John*. Second-Century Reception of the Fourth Gospel. 2010. ISBN 978 90 04 17633 1

133. Lau, T.-L., *The Politics of Peace*. Ephesians, Dio Chrysostom, and the Confucian Four Books. 2010. ISBN 978 90 04 18053 6

134. Friesen, S., D. Schowalter and J. Walters (eds.) *Corinth in Context*. Comparative Studies on Religion and Society. 2010. ISBN 978 90 04 18197 7

135. Breytenbach, C. *Grace, Reconciliation, Concord*. The Death of Christ in Greco-Roman Metaphors. 2010. ISBN 978 90 04 18608 8

136. Walters, P. (ed.) *From Judaism to Christianity: Tradition and Transition*. A Festschrift for Thomas H. Tobin, S.J., on the Occasion of His Sixty-fifth Birthday. 2010. ISBN 978 90 04 18769 6